Children and Adolescents

The Author

THERON ALEXANDER (Ph.D., University of Chicago) is Professor of Human Development in the Division of Educational Psychology at Temple University. In addition, he is director of the University's Child Development Research Center, which is supported by the Federal Government's Head Start program.

Dr. Alexander has been Professor of Psychology in Pediatrics at the University of Miami School of Medicine and director of child development programs in the Miami area for the Office of Economic Opportunity; Associate Professor of Psychology in Pediatrics at the University of Iowa College of Medicine, and Assistant Professor of Psychology at Florida State University. His publications include *Psychotherapy in Our Society* and many professional journal articles.

CHILDREN *and* ADOLESCENTS

A Biocultural Approach to Psychological Development

Theron Alexander

TEMPLE UNIVERSITY

ATHERTON PRESS · NEW YORK · 1969

Acknowledgments

I am grateful for the help given me by many people at various stages in the writing of this book. The influence of colleagues is an important part of the background. Those who read all or parts of the manuscript were of much help, and my association with colleagues in research, teaching, and clinical work has been of special value. Students with their questions and interest have been of much support.

I owe a debt of gratitude to the many librarians who assisted me in countless significant and essential ways. I also owe much to a number of people who worked diligently to prepare the manuscript.

Because this book is about the knowledge amassed by many research workers, I have made every effort to indicate the sources of the information and ideas used. This is so large a task, however, that the possibility of error is indeed great; I hope, therefore, for tolerance of inadvertent omissions or inadequacies.

The book includes material describing events in the lives of real people, but circumstances and names have been disguised. I am most grateful to these people for allowing me to be a part of their lives, and I hope that a description of their struggles and courage will be a source of help to others.

I owe much to my wife Marie; her help has been invaluable at every stage. My son Tom and my daughter Mary appear in several places; being part of their growing up has influenced me in many ways.

The publisher and those associated with him deserve much credit. Charles D. Lieber advised in the development and revision of the manuscript; Professor Jerome L. Singer provided many kindly suggestions in the process of revision; and Marlene Mandel showed skill and extraordinary patience in bringing the manuscript into print.

I also wish to thank the publishers and authors from whose works I have drawn material, especially those who allowed me to quote directly.

Theron Alexander

Contents

Chapter 14 / **Methods and Theories Contributing to Child and Adolescent Psychology** *324*

Children and Adolescents

[*one*]

Biological and Cultural Influences on Development

$\mathbf{A}$n individual's understanding of himself must begin with an understanding of his origin. Thus, the concern of modern man to understand his behavior has led to an investigation of the forces that influence human development. Investigation encompasses many academic subjects: genetics, biology, medicine, physiology, anatomy, biochemistry, sociology, anthropology, history, and psychology. However, each of these subjects falls into one or both of two broad categories—the biological and the cultural. In short, all human behavior is determined by both the biological characteristics and the environmental characteristics of the culture into which an individual is born.

Although the effects of the biological influences and the cultural influences overlap, each should be examined separately before a full understanding of their combined influence can be attained.

BIOLOGICAL INFLUENCES

Life consists of biological processes of change. Even within a single cell—the smallest structural unit of a living thing—continuing change takes place. The whole organism is in a process of continuing change; but the process of the whole is infinitely more complex than the process within a cell. It is primarily the central nervous system, comprised of the brain and spinal cord, that makes possible the holistic functioning of the organism. And it is through the functioning of the brain that an infinite number of cell lives, carrying on complicated processes in organs and systems, are brought together into a meaningful whole. These coordinated processes culminate in man's control of himself and his attainment of satisfaction from the world about him.

The brain's functioning, of course, is modified by experience. Through learning, for example, the individual can differentiate among stimulations having closely related meanings. And individual receptor stimulations become more than just stimulations when the brain relates present stimuli to responses learned in the past. As a result of both the integrative function and the utilization of experience, the vastly complex activities of human beings take place. There is still much to be learned about the conditions that influence the individual's capacity for successful response to the environment. Obviously, knowledge about the brain and its functions has considerable relevance for the study of human behavior (see Chapter 3).

Much of an individual's behavior is directed toward his environment. Internal conditions necessitate such an interchange not only to sustain life, but also to provide a minimum of irritation. Apparently, some predilection toward certain types of behavioral responses exists to facilitate this interchange. In the past, this predilection was called *instinct.* Now, most theorists prefer the term *drive,* which better describes the complex use of energy as well as man's more sensitive response to many types of influences. A drive is defined as an intraorganic condition which acts as a stimulus for behavior but which usually, or perhaps always, is influenced by the environment.[1] An example of this principle of interaction would be as follows: A native of the South Seas experiencing the chemical stimulation of hunger will get into his dugout canoe and begin to fish, while his counterpart 10,000 miles away will go into a restaurant and order food. Internal activity and needs within an organism are constantly changing, and so are perceptions and reactions to the environment. And so, both the South Sea native and his civilized counterpart will change their behavior after hunger is satisfied.

Drives serve to bring about stable internal conditions. Regulatory processes in the body maintain the stability of temperature, amount of water, supply of oxygen, the acid-base balance of the blood, amount of blood

---

[1] Drives have been given an important place in psychology and will be discussed in detail in Chapter 5.

sugar, and the like. The individual will engage in behavior to maintain these balances and is actually driven by the body's needs to obtain food or water. Behavior of the individual to fulfill acquired needs is considered to be based on learned drives; an example of this would be the drive to fulfill the need for social approval.

The concepts of drive and motivation are basic to understanding behavior, and their importance is readily seen in the process of learning or in the solving of problems (White, 1952). Unless an individual has a drive strong enough to cause him to channel his effort in order to achieve certain responses, he will not be able to solve problems effectively. Since man's capacity for response permits much complexity and sensitivity in behavior, elaborate systems develop in response to both internal stimuli associated with a drive and external stimuli from the environment.

The Origins of Biological Influences

The relationship of behavior to genetic bases is being increasingly unraveled with advancements in the science of genetics. It is not always possible to make a distinction between inherited and environmental influences. However, some characteristics that are now deemed hereditary include type of body build, shape of facial features, color of hair and eyes, sex, and blood type (Fuller and Thompson, 1960).

It is important to understand that a person's biological characteristics are essentially determined at conception and, from that point on, development is influenced by the environment. At conception, when the male's sperm combines with the female's ovum, all hereditary characteristics of the individual are determined. Within the nucleus of each of the male and female reproductive cells are threadlike parts called chromosomes.[2] Different species have different numbers of chromosomes, but in man it is known that there are 46. (Until the last ten years or so, there were thought to be 48 chromosomes.)

In the process of maturation of a sex cell, a division of each chromosome pair occurs. In this division (meiosis), each of the 23 pairs of chromosomes splits so that each new cell has only 23 chromosomes, or one of each pair. In the female germ cell before division, all of the 23 pairs of chromosomes are X chromosomes, including the sex chromosome, and thus after division each chromosome must be an X. In the male germ cell before maturation and division, 22 pairs are X; but the pair of sex chromosomes are different in that one of the pair is X and one is Y.

---

[2] So named because they will absorb dye coloring, making them visible under a high-powered microscope.

Thus, after division, there will be two types of sperm, one bearing an X and one bearing a Y.

The male germ cells, containing either an X or Y chromosome, occur in equal numbers; hence, the probability of fertilization of the ovum with either an X or Y is even. If the ovum (always X) is fertilized by a sperm cell containing a Y, the individual will be a male; if the ovum is fertilized by a sperm cell containing an X, the individual will be a female. It should be remembered that each sperm and ovum contains 23 chromosomes, and thus when a sperm cell unites with an ovum, the zygote, the fertilized ovum, will have 46 chromosomes, 23 from each parent.

With the inherited characteristics from his parents, the child's life begins at conception, and to some extent many of his life directions are then established. On each chromosome there are ultramicroscopic particles called genes, which occupy specific places. Through their chemical activity, these particles, or genes, are the modifiers of development. Each chromosome is thought to contain approximately 3,000 genes (Scheinfeld, 1965). Therefore, the wide variation in physical characteristics among siblings may be due mainly to the extremely large number of possible combinations of the genes.

Geneticists usually speak of the "influence of the genes." Characteristics are not inherited directly, but the genes cause certain physical characteristics to come into being. The influence of the genes is quite complicated and at the present time much has yet to be learned about them. Some genes apparently are more significant in their influence than others, and the traits carried by these genes are more likely to appear; these genes are called the dominant genes. Other genes seem to be less powerful, and their effect is suppressed; these are called recessive genes. The dominant genes tend to disguise the effects of the recessive genes, although there is a definite ratio between the expression of dominant and recessive combinations.

Each child inherits a wide number of variations in genes and, from the time of conception onward, his development is influenced by the interaction of the genes and the factors surrounding the united germ cells. Since so many possibilities exist for combinations of genes from parents, it is impossible to predict specific characteristics of a child. Some expectations can be expressed in probabilities, however, as in the case of some anomalies occurring in families. At present, the only known way to prevent the inheritance of anomalies is to avoid the marriage of two people carrying the defect. It seems that defective genes are neutralized by pairing them with normal ones. The defective gene, however, may still be carried in the chromosomes and eventually may be expressed if an individual carrying it mates with a person who has a similar gene. Other factors which may bring about abnormalities are conditions within the cell, hormonal levels, or possible infection (Watson and Lowrey, 1962).

In the process from conception to the development of an adult human being, an important question is: How can the single cell develop into billions of differentiated cells comprising a complex human body? Scientists have traced the responsibility for this development to substances called DNA and RNA. Biochemists designate both DNA and RNA as nucleic acids, so called because they were first discovered in the nucleus, or the central part, of a body cell. The chemical label of *NA* stands for nucleic acid and *R* stands for ribose, a sugar in the substance. In DNA, the ribose, or sugar, contains one less oxygen atom and so the prefix *deoxy* is used to mean one less oxygen atom; thus, "deoxyribonucleic" acid—DNA.

DNA is the substance that determines the physical characteristics of the developing individual, and it is found in the nucleus of every cell in the body. In the fertilized human egg, half of the DNA is supplied by the sperm and the other half by the ovum. The DNA molecule is able to duplicate itself by splitting in two, so that each new cell will have its full set of genetic instructions for further growth.

DNA does not leave the nucleus of a cell, but it influences cell activities through the RNA. (DNA actually makes two kinds of RNA—one kind of RNA is called "messenger RNA" and another kind is called "transfer RNA.") For example, one of the important activities of DNA is to make proteins out of chemicals called amino acids. The actual manufacturing of protein is carried on in the main body of the cell with the help of RNA. The "messenger RNA" carries the directions from DNA in the nucleus of the cell. The "transfer RNA" brings into the process the needed kinds of amino acids. Through the discovery of DNA and the nature of the processes going on within a cell, scientists may be able to prevent inherited defects and, in fact, to determine the physiological characteristics an individual will have.

Biological Influences during the Prenatal Period

Although life begins simply with the fertilized egg, ensuing development is complex and far from understood. It is now recognized that the environment is important, since from the very beginning the fertilized cell is dependent on certain environmental conditions for food, oxygen, water, and the proper temperature.

The period from conception until birth, called the prenatal period, is usually divided into three developmental divisions: the germinal period, the embryonic period, and the fetal period. Generally speaking, in human beings the germinal period is said to consist of the period comprising the first or second week after fertilization. From this beginning, the individual grows from one cell to about 200 billion cells at the time of birth. Many divisions and redivisions of cells take place as the fertilized egg—now called the zygote—moves down the Fallopian tube toward the mother's uterus. The progress down the tube requires about three days. After approximately a week, the zygote attaches to the inner uterine wall and the end of the germinal period is reached. Even in this short time, growth has been extensive, and the individual is as much as one-fifth of an inch in diameter. From now on, the developing embryo receives its nourishment from the mother until the time of birth.

During the second, or embryonic, period, structural changes occur so that adequate nourishment and protection can be achieved. The placenta develops in the tissues of the uterus and is joined to the embryo by the umbilical cord. The placenta grows until it ultimately becomes part of the inner wall of the uterus. It absorbs oxygen, water, and nutritive substances from the mother and passes them through the cord to the developing embryo. Waste products of the developing child are returned through the cord to the placenta and from there to the mother's bloodstream. The mother's blood does not circulate through the developing child and the blood systems are separate, with the placenta acting as a filter. Surrounding the embryo is an amniotic sac filled with fluid which protects the embryo from outside injury. Both of these significant structures—the placenta and the amniotic sac—are in existence only during prenatal life; the amniotic sac breaks just before birth, and the placenta and cord are discarded as the afterbirth.

During the first few weeks of life, cell division of the embryo results in the development of the *mesoderm,* the basis for development of connective tissues, blood vessels, heart, muscles, and skeleton; the *endoderm,* or innermost layer, the basis for liver, pancreas, lungs, stomach, and intestines; and the *ectoderm,* the basis for brain, spinal cord, nervous system, and skin. By the end of the third week of life, the heart begins to function and at about this time the development of the nervous system begins with a fold in the ectodermal tissue. Although provision exists for nourishment and safety of the developing embryo, many problems can develop during the prenatal period to cause abnormality. These difficulties will be discussed in detail in Chapter 13.

During the third period of development, the fetal period, independent behavior of the organism occurs: Movement begins and the fetus is able to respond to external stimulation. Growth occurs at an extremely rapid rate; at the beginning of the fetal period, or the third month, the fetus grows about 1½ millimeters per day. The increase in weight from the time of fertilization to birth is approximately 6 billion times. Viability becomes possible by the time the fetus reaches the age of seven months.

Toward the end of the fetal period, the developing individual shifts position until the head is within the pelvic basin. Imminent birth is signaled by contractions of the uterus, usually at first of mild intensity and some fifteen or twenty minutes apart but gradually increasing in frequency, duration, and intensity. The origin of the initiation of labor is unknown, but it is assumed to be a chemical interaction between mother and fetus. As the contractions of the uterus increase, they are aided by the abdominal musculature. The first part of labor, usually about fourteen hours, consists of the dilation of the cervix; the second part consists of the passage of the fetus in the birth canal, which may require an hour or less but which is usually longer for the firstborn child; and labor ends with the delivery of the placenta and amniotic sac—some twenty or thirty minutes after the delivery of the child.

Biological Influences during the Neonatal Period

The newborn infant begins a lifelong interchange with his surroundings—he breathes, exchanging air in his lungs for fresh supply; he takes in nutrients from the outside; and he adjusts to a great many external stimuli. Thus, in the neonatal period (the first two weeks after birth) the infant moves toward independent existence and depends on his own processes of respiration, digestion, and temperature control. A few hours after birth, the oxygen level in his blood reaches a sufficient amount, blood pressure continues to adjust for several days until it reaches appropriate levels, and the digestive system utilizes simple foods with the exception of starches. Infants are not fed for several hours after birth, and in the beginning, fluids are frequently regurgitated with some weight loss occurring. Urination and defecation usually begin in the neonatal period, but they may take place before birth. Respiration, however, is a new activity for the neonate and he may encounter difficulties. At first, the infant's breathing is often shallow and irregular, for the lungs may be somewhat congested with mucus and amniotic fluid. Adapting to a different temperature and being dependent upon his own temperature-controlling mechanism can also be difficult for the infant and he will chill easily.

At first the infant's needs and responses are simple. He sleeps a great deal of the time and only gradually does he begin to spend more time awake. Reactions in general to stimuli are diffuse. The discomfort of hunger is made known by crying in conjunction with a squirming movement of arms and legs. The mouth moves and hands clutch anything within reach. However, the infant must develop many new motor abilities before he can become independently mobile, for in the weeks following birth he is even unable to raise his head or roll over.

Although in the first few weeks of life the infant's needs are mainly biological, with the passage of time his need for personal relationships with other human beings assumes greater significance.

CULTURAL INFLUENCES

The second area of significant influence on the development and behavior of the individual comes from the culture. Culture is defined as a way of life of a people, and includes techniques and tools for making a living, social relationships, beliefs in the nature of things as related to supernatural beings, and how these are all organized into a system that influences individuals within it throughout life. Culture, accordingly, consists of the customs, traditions, and ways of thinking and acting that have been handed down from parent to child through the ages. From the earliest history of man to the present day, culture has provided definitions and meanings of the world, as well as a guide to appropriate responses to situations encountered in daily life. Long ago primitive man developed thoughts and actions associated with food, shelter, reproduction, family life, and child care; he also developed modes of self-expression through painting, expressive dances, and other arts. These ways of behaving were taught to children by example and by approval. In fact, many customs and mores arose because of man's need for security, approval, food, shelter, and emotional exchange.

Culture is a process and an activity. It is not an entity, but it operates within humankind and constantly affects behavior (Frank, 1953). Culture includes all the learned behavior patterns brought together into a diverse system, varying in different parts of a particular culture according to various sets of parents but still comprising a system to be transmitted to children. Culture, of course, is an abstraction that is applied to a composite of meanings. Mead (1953a) emphasizes that culture is not only a system of external influences upon the individual, but also an internalized part of each person. Internalization results in a particular type of functioning of the physiological structure and causes biological response patterns to differ from culture to culture. In addition, because of the variations of heredity, perceptions, and emotional reactions, each person, although conforming in the main to demanded cultural patterns, still develops an individuality peculiar to him alone.

The Enculturation Process

Enculturation is a broad term referring to the process in which the child gives up some autonomy and accepts culturally appropriate behavioral patterns.[3] These behavioral patterns are associated with the broad areas that make up a culture—techniques and tools for coping with the environment, relationships to and beliefs in spiritual entities, customs of social relationships, and the like. Widely diverse patterns of behavior, Margaret Mead (1953b) asserts, can be transmitted with equal success. The principal cultural agent is usually the mother, for it is she who leads, cajoles, and forces the child into culturally derived patterns of behavior.

Increasingly, other important and significant cultural forces impinge upon the child and bring about lasting patterns of behavior. These patterns of behavior become firmly fixed.[4] As Benedict (1934) described, the child has become "a creature of his culture," with its opportunities, restrictions, and impossibilities laid out before him. In the first five years of life, then, a plethora of cultural forces are brought to bear, which bend the child this way and that until he sees no other way than that provided by the cultural agents. His responses have become so firmly established and so much a part of him that although he has lived only a fraction of his life, they are part of his very being and their influence never entirely passes from him.

The psychological significance of the methods used in the enculturation process, aside from the successful patterning of behavior in the various areas just described, is of much importance to the child. Cultural learnings

[3] Socialization, similar in meaning to enculturation, is discussed in Chapter 9. The term *socialization* refers to specific teachings about food, excretory processes, cleanliness, and the like, as well as to specific teaching methods for training the child to fit into a social order. Enculturation, on the other hand, is used in a broader sense and refers to broad cultural teaching.

[4] In Western culture, by the time the child is ready for school and begins to move away from the domination of the parents into the significant influence of another cultural agent—the educational system, personified by the teacher in kindergarten or first grade—he is already enculturated to a considerable degree.

are not easily accomplished. There are frustrations and negative emotions for both the child and the cultural agent, which is, in most societies, the parent. The child struggles to retain physiological autonomy and to fulfill body needs as he himself desires. Gradually, however, he accepts the behavior that the parent demands because of strong affectional bonds. These bonds are incompletely understood and to some degree defy scientific analysis and measurement; however, they are nonetheless real and significant. Child and parent become a part of each other's life with an increasing interdependence for emotional satisfaction—the child conforms to his parent's wishes as he seeks to avoid disapproval or displeasure. This desire for approval under normal conditions develops simultaneously with the desire for autonomy. Hence, much of the time in the early years the child tries to conform to the parent's expectations of behavior and inner controls. In the process of development, the child comes to accept parental values and learns to behave in accordance with cultural standards even when the parent is not present to enforce them. For example, although the parent may be out of the room, the child will not play with the cherished vase or take forbidden food. Thus, the teachings of the parent are slowly internalized, thereby channeling or limiting responses to the environment. Some parents believe that fear of punishment accomplishes this internalization; but it is much more complex, since the close emotional bond with the parent and the opportunity for affectional closeness causes the child to desire to behave in approved ways. These principles will be discussed in Chapter 9.

Intercultural Variations

Because cultures vary greatly in their influence on developing members, some behavioral scientists, especially anthropologists, emphasize the importance of the study of simple societies, believing that through such study new and generalized understandings may be reached about human behavior. For example, Margaret Mead (1939) developed her "storm and stress" thesis about adolescence from her study of Samoan children. She found that Samoan children do not have a "stormy" adolescence; thus, she concluded, such behavior results from factors in American culture rather than from factors associated with biological change. Similar findings about human development might be uncovered through the study of simple societies. For example, the acquisition of specific developmental skills according to a certain chronology (that is, placing the attainment of specific behavior patterns on a chronological continuum) may be the result of our own cultural conditioning. Perhaps the very nature of our expectations brings about the acquisition of developmental skills. For example, in our culture five-year-olds are considered to be negativistic, but it is likely that this negativisim is caused by cultural expectations imposed upon the child at about this age and that the behavior does not come from biological or maturational factors alone. And, certainly, the experience of many five-year-old children in our culture is far different from the experience of five-year-old children in primitive cultures. In American culture, many children move away from home and into complex group experiences in school whereas in primitive cultures such is not the case. If cultural comparisons are to be made, it is important to begin such undertakings soon, before the isolated and primitive societies become influenced by the outside world. Many of the practices of these primitive peoples are interrelated (Barnett, 1959), and a seemingly minor change introduced into their culture often results in unexpected changes of a significant nature in other customs. Some of the few primitive cultures left in the world today are in New Guinea (Archbold, 1941; Held, 1957; Hildebrand, 1927; Hogbin, 1951; Maher, 1961; Mead, 1939; and Whiting, 1941). Sorenson and Gajdusek (1966) collected on film and tape specimens and observations in several of the New Guinea tribes so that information about these primitive people will not be lost. These investigators were particularly interested in the health and development of the children in the tribes.

It is of value at this point to examine a primitive culture in one part of New Guinea and then compare the customs of these peoples with comparable customs in our own culture.

The Papuans living in the southern part of New Guinea are indeed a part of a very primitive culture. They locate their villages near waterways and seashore and live in rectangular, irregularly arranged, coconut-palm—thatched houses erected on high poles from 3 to 5 feet above the ground or water. Logs from the beach to the doorway give access to the house, and other logs placed across the doorway keep the children inside. Usually the houses have a single room with a wall running across the middle, with each half occupied by a separate family. Palm-leaf mats serve as furniture and bedding. In some villages, a type of building is set aside for informal meetings, and the villagers go there to talk and chew betelnut, the fruit of an areca palm that is believed to have a narcotic effect. This meeting house has two stories: The lower part consists of a platform and the upper part is thatched and used for sleeping. The tribes having such special meeting houses do not allow women in them. The women must bring food and firewood to the meeting house that the husbands frequent. These "clubs," or groups, form a working unit for house building, canoe construction, and certain types of communal fishing. They also serve other functions: For example, in some tribes a young person wishing to marry must secure the approval of the elders of his group. Such groupings have some similarity to fraternal organizations in more complex societies.

About the age of fifteen, young boys are initiated into the "club" with feasts and ritualistic ceremonies. Each boy must be sponsored by a man who is already a member. The ordeals begin when the men seek out the boys and have them climb on their backs in order that they may take them into the jungle. Other men stand along the path with firebrands, sticks, and nettles, and as each boy passes he is beaten or burned; the sponsors do not escape either. The ritual begins several months of trials, with the boys being told that, depending upon their conduct, they might avoid being fed to monsters. If they are worthy, everything will be all right. If a boy does not conduct himself appropriately, he may at this time be killed; but once this rite is passed, a feast of celebration is prepared.

In this society, girls' entry into womanhood is also a period of initiation, although the initiation is not as elaborate. At the beginning of puberty, girls are secluded for several months. Usually they are forced to live in a small compartment of the house, but they do not have to undergo any ordeals except that they cannot wash or drink water. They also must observe the taboos of a special diet. After a period of time, a girl's father provides food for a feast and arrangements are made for a celebration. In the morning, companions take the girl to a stream for a ritual bath. Some elementary sex instruction is given at this time and then the girl is carried to the village, where the girls and the people accompanying them are beaten lightly with plant stalks. A feast is held and the girls are painted and decorated with family ornaments. If a girl is to be married at this time, she is taken ceremoniously to the new home by her kinfolk, where all are entertained by the bridegroom's relatives. Later the man's kinsmen will return the visit and take with them the dowry for the bride, which usually consists of pigs, taro, sago, and dogs' teeth.

The religion of the people living near the Huon Gulf is animistic. According to Hogbin (1951), they believe in several types of spirits—spirits of the land and sky, spirits of the dead, lonely female spirits, and monsters. The sky spirits have human form and carry torches—the two brightest torches are carried by the spirits of the sun and the moon. These sky gods are responsible for the seasonal cycles of weather, distribution of resources, language, and marriage rules. Spirits of the land frequent a special location: Sometimes, they are found in a cave near a waterfall where there is much cold spray or by a lonely, deep pool of water. Surrounding areas belonging to the natives are held in cooperation with the spirits for mutual protection of property. These land spirits are invisible, but they can sometimes take the forms of snakes or lizards. Storms and heavy rains are attributed to land spirits, who are also believed to cause the deaths of children. If a person is visited by the wrath of these spirits, he must make a sacrifice. Usually, however, sacrifices are carried out only after some unfortunate event, such as an illness, occurs. Then, the individual must retrace his past actions to discover where he has offended the land spirits. Upon discovering the offense, he offers several wild boars' tusks or a string of dogs' teeth to the spirits. The individual in disapproval appoints a delegate, who takes the gifts to the sacred place near the waterfall and hangs them on a tree.

Outside influences are increasingly changing the customs and culture of these people, and as with primitive people elsewhere, an amalgamation of their culture with ideas and customs from the outside world is under way. The importance of careful study of primitive cultures lies in the necessity for understanding aspects of our own culture that may have been accepted previously without question. Study of primitive cultures also can give better understanding of the possible modifications of human behavior and how these modifications are passed from generation to generation.

Although one is tempted to turn away from primitive beliefs and customs, which at first glance seem to have little relevance for our own lives, it should be remembered that much of our child rearing today is still based on folklore. Many parents are guided by hearsay and by information from their own parents. Although in primitive societies cruel and ritualistic ordeals must be passed by young people approaching adulthood, such rituals have the advantage of specifying how to attain status as an adult. Having passed these ordeals, young people are then clearly accepted and accorded the rights and privileges of adults. In American culture, no well-defined route exists, and young people are not certain when they are accepted as adults. In Western culture, some similarity to the New Guinea rites is found in the religious rites of confirmation and bar mitzvah; yet, these transitional rites do not in reality bring adult status or adult opportunity, but are merely steps *toward* adulthood. Therefore, although an individual may reach physical maturity at the age of twelve and legal marriage as well as military service may be possible at eighteen, he usually cannot vote until twenty-one. Accordingly, it is possible for an individual to be a parent, taxpayer, wage earner, or a soldier and still not have reached legal adulthood!

Perhaps some of the problems encountered in adolescence in American society grow in part from the confusion of both the adolescents and adults about *how* children move from childhood to adulthood. Some adolescents may be confused and hostile if they are not accepted as adults when they think they should be. On the other hand, adults may see the adolescent's behavior as unacceptable for adult status. By making cultural comparisons, problems within cultures may be delineated and possibly rectified.

Long ago man found that fulfillment of physical needs and the need for self-expression was better achieved in collective endeavor. As cooperation developed, a societal structure grew so that desirable ways of behaving for groups could be maintained and enforced. Thus society, or a social order, supports cultural practices and beliefs. It enforces, interprets, objectifies, and applies the cultural heritage through organizations of individuals, institutions, and specifications for social roles. Enforcement can vary—it will sometimes be quite subtle and it will sometimes be openly punitive. But the goal that society creates for an individual is conformity without force and the internalization of cultural expectations. Conformity is a basis for conflict, however; although society demands conformity, it sometimes rewards the nonconformist. Furthermore, in a changing society, a demand for internalization of a certain role may exist; but once this internalization is accomplished, another demand may then be made for the internalization of a different role. It is not important here, however, to deal extensively with the problem of societal conflicts; it has been necessary only to point to their existence and significance for the individual.[5]

A crucial point for consideration is the degree of flexibility that a society will allow for deviation. Society, as has been pointed out earlier, exists for the purpose of avoiding deviation. Extreme cultural deviation from expectations necessarily brings disapproval; it may even bring some kind of punishment (Martindale, 1962). Many societies view homicide, threats to the security of the group, and misappropriation of property as severe deviations, and formal and severe punitive action is often taken. Failure to find an acceptable social role usually results in various forms of disapproval. Degrees of tolerance for deviation vary within a society and from society to society. But deviation as a concept must depend upon a framework of expected behavior, otherwise no deviation can be said to exist. Probably in every society there are some individuals who cannot conform and some individuals who can only meet the demands of their own society but not of another.

Although culture is something to which individuals must to some extent conform, in the last analysis individuals modify, maintain, and perpetuate the culture (Whiting and Child, 1953). Thus, as time passes, a society may

[5] Further discussion of conformity and nonconformity may be found in Chapter 8 and in Chapter 11.

change under the pressure of deviations within and influences without. Drastic and rapid changes in the culture are seldom brought about in a beneficent way, and they usually involve some traumatic effects for the individuals within it. An example of a rapid change from without would be the conquest of the American Indians and the change forced upon their cultures. An example of a relatively slower change within the American culture would be the gradual removal of ordinances prohibiting commercial activity on Sunday.

Cultures are complex and not easily described, and the culture of the United States, for example, has many differing groups within it. Some people have come from other countries and live in close-knit groups in order to preserve the way of life followed in their native country. Other groups maintain little contact with other parts of the society because of geographical barriers or isolation and thereby develop some variance from that of the whole country. Culture and its complexities, as well as its multifaceted influences on individual development, are only briefly dealt with here. They will be discussed, however, at varying points in following chapters.

INTEGRATION OF BIOLOGICAL AND CULTURAL INFLUENCES

It is important to recognize the significance of biological events and influences throughout the life span. Although some students of human behavior tend to place little emphasis on constitutional factors because these factors are to a large extent not easily changed, biological characteristics, nevertheless, provide the foundation from which an individual's behavior is fashioned. The physical characteristics at any point in time hold potentialities as well as limits for the attainment of individual satisfaction. Biological factors in part determine the capacity for learning, reaction time, expenditure of energy, and tolerance of deprivation of essential life elements. They are the basis for biological rhythms or circadian systems relating to fatigue, activity, emotion, and the like. And they are the basis for certain constitutional characteristics, such as stature, strength, and culturally acceptable physical features which influence man's fulfillment of needs and his success in meeting the expectations of his world.

Constitutional factors, however, must be seen in a realistic perspective, even though they limit, surround, or constrain the individual in varying degrees. Although the human being must be seen first as a biological being, he also must be seen as a product of his culture. In reality, none of the biological processes remains free of cultural influence. Thus, a separation of those units of behavior seemingly biological or dependent upon nature from those units of behavior culturally induced is a vain quest.

A POINT OF VIEW

Once environmental stimuli have impinged upon receptors, the whole experience becomes organic and within the person. Stimuli in the environment can have no effect on an individual until a receptor is activated, but after that they become internal stimuli and part of an idiosyncratic and wholly organic process. Another way of looking at this complexity, then, is to say that all behavior is biological in actuality. Thus, differentiation among stimuli, in reality, is possible only on the basis of the point of origin; that is, a biological event inside the organism may be a stimulus, and also a stimulus may come from the outside to activate a receptor; but once activated, the behavior is a physiological process. The essential point to be noted is that the environment is made over into the individual's own image of it because its influence must be conveyed over internal pathways that are to some extent unique and different from those of all other individuals.

A second essential fact in relating the two types of influences is the dependence of organic functioning upon stimuli from the environment for favorable development. This point will be dealt with frequently in subsequent chapters; however, it is important to point out here that deprivation of environmental stimuli may actually alter the course of organic development and this alteration may, in fact, be irreversible. While such a view reflects pessimism in regard to alleviation of some human problems, it also can be seen as hopeful, in that, by intervening early in the development of human beings, many difficulties can be prevented.

REFERENCES

Archbold, R., 1941. "Unknown New Guinea," *National Geographic Magazine,* **79,** 315–344.
Barnett, H. G., 1959. "Peace and Progress in New Guinea," *American Anthropologist,* **61,** 1013–1019.
Benedict, R., 1934. *Patterns of Culture.* Boston: Houghton Mifflin.
Frank, L. K., 1953. "Cultural Control and Physiological Autonomy," in *Personality in Nature, Society, and Culture,* 2d ed., edited by C. Kluckhohn and H. A. Murray, pp. 119–122. New York: Knopf.
Fuller, J. L., and W. R. Thompson, 1960. *Behavior Genetics.* New York: Wiley.

Held, G. J., 1957. *The Papuans of Waropen*. The Hague: Martinus Nijhoff.

Hildebrand, J. R., 1927. "The Columbus of the Pacific," *National Geographic Magazine*, **51**, 85–132.

Hogbin, H. I., 1951. *Transformation Scene: The Changing Culture of a New Guinea Village*. London: Routledge.

Maher, R. F., 1961. *New Men of Papua*. Madison, Wis.: The University of Wisconsin Press.

Martindale, D., 1962. *Social Life and Cultural Change*. Princeton, N.J.: Van Nostrand.

Mead, M., 1939. *From the South Seas*. New York: Morrow.

Mead, M., 1953a. "The Concept of Culture and the Psychosomatic Approach," in *Contributions Toward Medical Psychology*, edited by A. Weider, pp. 368–397. New York: Ronald.

Mead, M., 1953b. "Social Change and Cultural Surrogates," in *Personality in Nature, Society, and Culture*, 2d ed., edited by C. Kluckhohn and H. A. Murray, pp. 651–662. New York: Knopf.

Scheinfeld, A., 1965. *Your Heredity and Environment*. Philadelphia: Lippincott.

Sorenson, E. R., and D. C. Gajdusek, 1966. "The Study of Child Behavior and Development in Primitive Cultures," *Pediatrics* (Supplement), **37**, 149–176.

Watson, E. H., and G. H. Lowrey, 1962. *Growth and Development of Children*. Chicago: The Year Book Medical Publishers.

White, R. W., 1952. *Lives in Progress*. New York: The Dryden Press.

Whiting, J. W. M., 1941. *Becoming a Kwoma*. New Haven, Conn.: Yale University Press.

Whiting, J. W. M., and I. L. Child, 1953. *Child Training and Personality: A Cross-Cultural Study*. New Haven, Conn.: Yale University Press.

[*two*]

Development in Infancy

In the first few months of life, behavior consists of activity primarily related to biological processes, involving nourishment, excretion, breathing, and body movements. As maturation progresses and as the child becomes more responsive to external stimuli, his behavioral patterns become more complex. Experience is organized in increasingly complex relationships, random responses come to be purposeful ones made in association with external events, and discriminative abilities improve so that stimuli become more and more meaningful.

BIOLOGICAL PROCESSES AND BEHAVIORAL DEVELOPMENT

At birth, the infant establishes a certain amount of physiological autonomy: He takes over oxygenation of his own blood; he relies on his own temperature-controlling mechanisms and on his own excretory processes; and he takes over digestion of food. All of these processes, of course, are necessary for survival and are the basic areas of activity and behavior on which his life rests. The period just following birth is called the perinatal period and lasts for the first fifteen to thirty minutes of life. The neonatal period comprises the two weeks following the perinatal period, although some scientists consider it to last for four weeks.

Respiration

At birth, the part of the brain that controls respiration is activated by sensory and chemical stimuli (Donald, 1962). The interruption of oxygen flow through the umbilical cord results in anoxia, which causes chemical changes in the blood (accumulation of acid metabolites). This accumulation then affects the respiratory center of the brain.

The moist surface of the lungs tends to be cohesive and the first few breaths are difficult. Most of the alveoli, the air cells of the lungs, are yet to open; those already open are filled with fluid. After the first few inspirations, the alveoli enlarge and continue to enlarge with growth. The respiration of infants is achieved primarily through diaphragmatic action, and dependency on this type of respiration continues throughout early childhood. The rate as well as the depth of respiration is quite variable, and a period of time is required before the child establishes a normal rhythm.

Soon after birth the infant must be able to maintain a constant supply of oxygen in his blood. In the transfer to independence, although he is resistant to oxygen deprivation, the infant's life depends upon the circulation of blood, which in turn depends upon the adequacy of cardiac glycogen. Damage to the brain is likely when prolonged lack of oxygen occurs and although the exact length of time is unclear for the toleration of respiration delay, a period longer than fifteen minutes endangers survival.

Temperature Regulation

The maintenance of temperature equilibrium is important, because variations adversely affect essential chemical processes in the body (Brobeck, 1960). The activities of enzymes (substances, usually protein, produced by cells to accelerate metabolism) are limited by temperature variation as is the functioning of the central nervous system. Also, cardiovascular and respiratory systems must work much harder as the result of increased metabolic rate at high temperatures.

Regulation of temperature is difficult for the newborn infant (Farquhar, 1962) and his temperature falls immediately after birth, even though efforts are made to keep him warm and even though the nursery temperature is maintained at 80° to 85°F. Usually a drop of approximately three degrees in the infant's temperature occurs in the first hour. His temperature gradually rises as metabolism increases, and this rise is aided by crying. The infant's greater surface area, poorly developed sweating and shivering mechanisms, and limited amount of subcutaneous fat to act as insulation are all conducive to temperature instability.

The regulatory centers, one for heat and one for cold, are in the hypothalamus, a region at the lower part of the brain. Neural impulses come to the hypothalamus from cutaneous thermoreceptors activated by stimulation of the skin as well as by stimulation of other parts of the body. The thalamus (a mass of gray matter in the lower part of the brain) and the cortical area of the brain also deal with temperature sensations. In the older child, these areas initiate activity to bring about a more favorable environment (Patton, 1960). The thyroid and adrenal glands also have an important function in the regulation of temperature (Hardy, 1961).

Human beings have diurnal and nocturnal temperature changes—higher in the day and lower at night. Usually the infant attains normal patterns by the end of the first year. However, fluctuations of temperature throughout the childhood period are greater than in adulthood.

Immune Reactions

At birth, most infants have a natural immunity to certain viral and bacterial infections resulting from the transfer of antibodies from mother to fetus through the placenta. This passive immunity, which lasts for a short time after birth, gives protection during the time when the child is poorly equipped to produce specific antibodies against such diseases as measles, diphtheria, smallpox, and poliomyelitis.

Antibacterial bodies in the blood of the infant last for a shorter time than do the antitoxic and antiviral substances. The titer (measurement of the amount of serum required to react immunologically) decreases after birth, so that by the second month antibodies for bacteria become insignificant (Watson and Lowrey, 1962). Human colostrum (the first milk of the mother's breasts) and the serum of the mother's blood have similar antibodies. These antibodies, however, do not seem to significantly influence or increase antibodies in the infant. Gradually, as the child grows older, the titer of the usual antibodies increases. Such increase is thought to be associated with various infectious agents.

Nutrition

Food intake is of major consequence in the first years of life and continues to be, of course, of much significance throughout life. The infant's well-being is directly related to the amount and nutritional quality of his food, and recent years have seen a great deal of effort put into the preparation of infant food and the prevention of bacteriological hazards in its processing. This care has led to significant reduction of the mortality rates of infants.

Important scientific advances affecting the health and growth of infants are exemplified by the pasteurization of milk in order to reduce bacteria; the recognition of the value of vitamin A in milk fat and fish-liver oil; the discovery of the importance of vitamin D in skeletal development, as well as the feasibility of its addition to milk; the discovery of vitamin C and its importance in preventing scurvy; and the development of the homogenization process to make milk digestion easier.

It is important that the infant be given vitamin D, an essential substance for bone growth and metabolism, because neither human nor cow's milk contains sufficient amounts. Physicians usually prescribe some preparation containing vitamin D from fish-liver oil, such as cod. It is also important that the level of vitamin C (abscorbic acid) be maintained in the blood level, since soon after birth the amount of vitamin C in the blood begins to lessen. Sometimes human milk is deficient in this vitamin, and it is necessary to give supplementary amounts of vitamin C. In general, the other vitamins are likely to be ingested in adequate amounts in infancy.

Nutritional goals for children should not be based solely on growth rate and body size (Fomon and Owen, 1964). Efficient body functioning and a delay of the aging process should be the important considerations in nutrition studies. It seems reasonable to expect that nutrition is a significant factor in the rate of the aging process and that nutrition in infancy and early life may affect physiological well-being as well as the onset of pathological processes. Experimental work with animals has shown that certain factors do affect longevity. For example, rats fed on a restricted diet lived longer than rats allowed to eat whenever they wanted food. Longevity of the rats was also affected by the composition and quantity of food ingested. Frequency of eating also seems to affect body composition, at least in experimental tests on rats. Animals fed at regular mealtimes, in contrast to animals fed frequent small amounts of food, were found to have more body fat (Cohn et al., 1962). As more information is gained about the significance of body fat for later life, changes in feeding of infants and children may be desirable. Fomon and Owen (1964) believe that more studies need to be undertaken to determine optimal human nutrition and to relate acquired information to life goals, health, and longevity.

Feeding

During the first few hours of life the infant is not fed; instead, he usually is given sterile water. The water requirement is greater for infants than adults because of a higher rate of metabolism, greater excretion, and because of proportionately larger skin surface. Hansen and Bennett (1964) report that the infant's requirement of water is usually 10 to 15 per cent of his body weight, while the adult's requirement is only 2 to 4 per cent. In warmer temperatures, the infant needs an additional amount of water because of greater evaporation from the skin.

After about twenty-four hours, milk or some type of derivative of milk is provided. Because colostrum contains less fat and more protein than milk, it is better adapted to the immature digestive system of the newborn infant than milk. Most nutritionists and pediatricians, however, see no reason to consider cow's milk unsuitable for the human infant. Investigations continue in the area of infant nutrition and more information is becoming available about the effect of pasteurization, usefulness of prepared formulae, differences in the effect of human and cow's milk, and the effect of various diets on concentration of cholesterol in the blood of infants (Fomon et al., 1959; Fomon and Bartels, 1960).

The normal infant continues to grow and develop satisfactorily on a diet of milk until about the age of three months. At this time, because of development and need for more energy, additional foods are usually introduced. There is no specific age when solid foods should be introduced, because the growth of infants varies; but introduction often is related to the infant's weight. Solid foods usually consist of cereals, meat, fruits, and vegetables, but commercial preparation of infant foods now allows almost any food to be introduced. Consequently, pediatricians usually follow the infant's order of preference. In a study of 65 children, Beal (1957) found that the earlier solid foods were offered, the greater the number of children who refused them. The average age of acceptance of cereal was between 2½ and 3½ months; for vegetables from 4 to 4½ months; for meat and soups, 5½ to 6 months; and for fruit, 2½ to 3 months. Over the period of this study, which lasted about ten years, the age of transition from prepared baby foods to the diet of the family decreased from two years to about thirteen months. As a child grows older, not only does his diet change, but also he needs to eat less frequently. Usually by the time he is five months old, it is possible for him to go for as long as four to five hours without food.

Some infants develop difficulties in feeding due to food allergies associated with certain types of milk substitutes. Meyer (1960) believes that true milk allergies are rare, but in such cases consideration should be given to the possibility of allergy to food protein, particularly in infants who have symptoms of colic. The exact nature of colic is unknown; however, infants with colic seem to be in pain. They also appear to be hungry and vigorously suck fingers or pacifiers. The sucking effort often results in an excessive amount of swallowed air, which in turn tends to cause regurgitation. Despite these difficulties, colic is not usually a serious problem, and infants with it usually develop normally.

Learning and training become significant in the area of feeding, for it is here that conflict situations often arise in the social interaction between parent and child. The socialization processes limiting the autonomy of the child begin by the imposition of routine, demand for the child's acceptance of specific food types, and a patterning of social interchange accompanying provision of food. Parental expressions of approval and enjoyment or disapproval and impatience tend to have much consequence, for they may affect not only food preferences and hence nutrition, but also social learning and perception of parental training methods. Parental anxiety, inflexibility in training methods, or harsh punishment provide foundations for later difficulty, and the infant may be conditioned in such a way that behavioral consequences extend beyond food to other areas of behavior and social interaction.

Interaction between parent and child at feeding times can bring satisfaction and pleasure or it can be the basis for conflict. Quite early, the infant is capable of enjoying interpersonal activities surrounding his feedings and by the time he has reached the age of eight or nine months, he expects opportunities for social interaction. Excessively rigid demands by parents, however, may lay the foundations for emotional difficulties about food that may later lead to psychopathology and even physical aberrations.

Excretory Processes

The ingestion of food requires that waste products be eliminated. Some waste is eliminated through the skin and lungs. However, the major waste-removal activity is through the intestines and kidneys. Excretory processes remove the waste from body fluids and transport these wastes to the lungs, bladder, and gastrointestinal system where they are expelled. The cells of the body are largely responsible for the excretory processes, and they carry on their activities through osmosis, filtration, diffusion, and electrical force, although these processes are only a part of the cells' total activities (Carlson et al., 1961).

By the time the infant is born, his kidneys are able to function, although there may be some delay in developing mature efficiency (Watson and Lowrey, 1962). Urine is composed of materials extracted from the blood, and a study of the urine reveals much about body functioning. The volume of extracellular fluid in the infant is nearly double that in the adult, and not only is this volume greater than in the adult, but also the rate at which fluids are exchanged is greater. The result of this rapid water exchange accounts for the quick dehydration of infants in illness.

In the first twelve hours after birth, the infant normally passes a material called meconium from the intestine. The first bowel actions containing meconium are usually without bacteria, but soon the intestines contain ingested bacteria. Subsequently, the number of bowel actions usually range from two to four a day. When solid foods are introduced, fecal material is formed and becomes dark in appearance. It is not until about the first year when the child has moved out of infancy that control of defecation is begun.

Sleep Patterns

During the first six months of life, most infants sleep between sixteen and twenty hours a day. At about the age of six months, infants begin to sleep from six to eight hours through the night and waking periods are longer during the day as is shown in Table 1. The amount of sleep needed tends to remain constant through the first year, although there are shifts in patterns from more sleeping at night to less sleep during the day (Kleitman and Englemann, 1953; Kleitman, 1963). As the child gradually increases his time of wakefulness, he becomes more aware of his surroundings and the lessening needs for sleep indicate increasing maturity.

Alternation between active and quiet sleep occurs in approximately one-hour intervals in infancy and the period increases to about 1½ hours in adulthood. The quiet phase of the cycle changes little, but the active phase of sleep increases (Aserinsky and Kleitman, 1955). During sleep, metabolism, respiration, heart action, body movements, and other processes are generally reduced, but in active sleep these processes and movements increase, while in quiet sleep they decrease.

The routine care in infancy helps to establish sleep patterns: Feeding times, bathing, interpersonal interaction, and play all influence the rhythm of the sleeping patterns. Gradually, the infant becomes accustomed to family routines and conforms to the family's patterns of living.

Sensory Capacities and Perceptual Development

Learning and interaction with the environment depend upon the capacities of the infant to become aware of the various aspects of his environment. To interact with the environment, an individual must be able to see, hear, taste, and smell it. Although much has yet to be learned about the infant's sensory capacities, some definitive information is presently available.

Hearing is quite well developed at birth, and even in the first few days after birth, infants have considerable hearing acuity. Stimuli of low intensity, however, do not usually elicit an overt response from the neonate. Experiments by Steinschneider et al. (1966) using the response of the heart to auditory stimuli indicated that the neonate's heart is responsive to an auditory stimulus and that the cardiac response is influenced by changes in the intensity of stimulation.

Experiments have indicated that infants respond with more activity to tones of higher pitch. Responses seem to increase with an increase in stimulus duration. Intense or abrupt auditory stimuli are more effective than low-pitched and moderately intense stimuli in effecting a response. Moderately intense stimuli tend to bring about less activity, as in the quieting effect of a mother's lullaby.

Although the gustatory, or taste, sense is not highly developed in the neonate, experiments indicate that the neonate can differentiate between sweet and sour and reflects this discrimination in his facial expressions. Grimaces in response to sour solutions increase in frequency with increase in age. Evidence supports the view that responses of infants to food substances differ from the responses of adults.

Research involving olfactory, or smelling, sensitivity in neonates is difficult to conduct. Most studies depend upon observance of changes in the neonate's behavior, such as body movement and crying. Engen et al. (1963) found that infants less than fifty hours old could respond to olfactory stimulation, but these investigators were unable to establish whether or not their subjects could distinguish between pleasant and unpleasant olfactory stimuli. Accordingly, available evidence indicates that the olfactory sense is not very well developed in the newborn and that it does not influence behavior as do the sense capacities of vision and hearing.

The neonate has some capacity to respond to changes of his position in space. If the infant is held upside down, he makes some body movements toward adjusting to an upright position. Rotation of the child causes movements of his head and eyes.

Observation of neonatal behavior indicates that sensitivity to pain or noxious stimuli, while present, is less in the infant than in the adult. After the first few days of life, however, sensitivity increases markedly. In the first few hours of life, response to pinpricks is minimal, but within a few days minimal stimulation brings response. Some evidence suggests that a sex difference exists in pain tolerance. More response to pain is seen in female infants than in male infants.

Visual and neuromuscular structures function inadequately at birth, but they improve rapidly. Apparently, shortly after birth the infant's ability to respond to light depends to a great extent upon the intensity and duration of the light stimulus. A light of a high degree of intensity and lasting a short time typically causes a closing or movement of the eyelids. In the neonate, strabismus (crossing of eyes) and nystagmus (oscillation of the eyes) are frequently observed. Progress in eye convergence and the coordination necessary for fixation and depth perception is made within a few weeks. The following visual abilities develop in the order listed: fixation, horizontal following, vertical following, and circular following.

Compared with an adult's, the visual perception of an infant is not well organized. Nevertheless, within the first six months of life the infant has some perception of depth and demonstrates some capacity for perceiving a figure as separate from ground and can differentiate between simple and complex patterns. Gradually, perceptual ability improves and as the result of learning, organization and integration of aspects of the environment take place. Much more needs to be known about perceptual development, and at the present time the processes of development involved in organization and integration of sensation are little understood.

Piaget (1954) believes that infants have difficulty in distinguishing themselves from objects about them. It is only with experience and the extension of sense impressions from the environment through seeing and touching that the child can distinguish between objects and himself. Werner (1948) has emphasized that the gradual development of perception in the child is characterized by movement away from "a diffuse perceptual organization dependent upon qualities of the whole." The infant at first depends upon a global quality of perceptions and only gradually is able to distinguish essential characteristics. Thus, very young children recognize the picture of an animal in a book but are unable to point out the animal's separate characteristics, such as the head or tail. In addition, Werner believes that the quality of a "whole" is extended. For example, an infant associates his bib with feeding; thus, the quality of the whole perception is diffused and extended so that the whole perception is contained in the bib.

It has been demonstrated that infants are capable of form perception and respond to differences in the shapes of objects. Subjects as young as six months learned to select a saccharine-coated block in specific geometrical form. Berlyne (1958) found that infants aged three to nine months preferred patterns with more context.

In a study of patterns of fixation in three-month-old infants, Lewis et al. (1966) found a sex difference in fixation time. They used a filmstrip projector to throw pictures on a screen 1½ feet from the infant. The film contained the following units: a photograph of a male face, a photograph of a female face, a line drawing of a male face, a bull's-eye, a checkerboard, and a nursing bottle. They also used a series of blinking lights, which were arranged in patterns. The infants' fixations on the stimuli were recorded by an observer with a key-operated recorder. The infants tended to show one long fixation for "interesting stimuli." For boys, a total-fixation measure indicated there were no significant differences among the stimuli. The girls, however, looked at faces much more than at the other stimuli. In a study by Kagan et al. (1966), it was found that infants aged four months responded much more frequently with smiles to a "regular face" than to a "scrambled face" (stimuli were sculptured faces painted a flesh color). Such findings seem to indicate that infants of this age can distinguish between stimuli patterns that resemble human facial characteristics.

Ability to differentiate and perceive parts from wholes comes somewhat slowly. At first, the infant seems unable to differentiate characteristics of parents. For example, an infant will not recognize his parents if they wear unusual clothing.

When infants are only a few days old, they are able to distinguish between objects on the basis of brightness and hue. A very young infant also will follow brightly colored objects. A child of six months can distinguish between colored bottles containing bitter and sweet substances (Mussen, 1963). Such information points to the fact that learning has an important part in such perception. Information about color vision in infancy is incomplete, but the evidence is that the use of color discrimination in interaction with the environment follows that of form and improves only gradually with experience.

Perceptual constancies, or the perceived stability of physical characteristics of objects under varying conditions, is of interest to those studying perceptual development. Despite the fact that there is inconsistency between the structural constancy of individual objects and the way they stimulate the sense organs, it is possible to perceive the necessary identifying characteristics. When an object is close, it stimulates a larger area of the retina of the eye than it does at a greater distance. Consequently, although there is a change in the area of stimulation of the retina, a dog running away, for example, still seems to be the same size. In one experiment of perceptual efficiency, it was arranged for a farther object (by being magnified) to throw an image of the same dimensions on the retina as a nearer object. Under such conditions an infant six months of age chose the nearer object when the two were presented. Constancies of perception develop gradually until considerable ability is gained in differential perception in reference to size, form, brightness, and hue, so that regardless of distance or the angle from which an object is perceived, its characteristics are determined with relative success.

This biological and developmental change in perceptual efficiency is seen by Schachtel (1959) to be characterized by a shift from an undifferentiated dependence on all of the senses in early infancy, primarily on the basis of comfort and discomfort (autocentricity), to predominance of the higher senses of sight and hearing in reference to qualities of objects (allocentricity). Accordingly, Schachtel believes in a hierarchy of the senses. Piaget (1954) believes that the understanding of objects must be related to some understanding of space. As the infant begins to separate himself from other objects or to see objects as separate parts of a field of experience, he then moves to a concept of space. Spatial concepts and ideas of separateness or distance, however, gradually develop, and although realistic perceptions begin in the first year of life, perceptual realism and the child's awareness of himself as an object in a complex environment are closely associated with physical development and opportunities to explore the environment.

Activity

Activity is an important part of the life processes of all higher organisms. The activity of the human newborn is related at times to internal stimuli since activity tends to increase before feeding, whereas after feeding a decrease in activity occurs. Infants, however, increasingly respond with activity to auditory and visual stimuli.

At birth, the infant has a number of reflex responses that include coughing, sneezing, eye closing, and grasping. The latter reflex can be seen upon stimulation of the infant's palm with a finger. He will grip the finger tightly. This reflex gradually lessens and disappears by about the fourth month (Pratt, 1954). The sucking reflex is sufficiently developed so that fluids can be ingested. The tonic neck reflex is observed when the infant's head is turned from the preferred side to the opposite direction and the infant simultaneously extends arm and leg in the direction in which the head is turned. He also flexes the opposite extremities. This reflex tends to disappear by the time the infant is six months old.

Another reflex, the Moro reflex, is in evidence when the infant is startled or when his position is changed suddenly. This reflex is characterized by the spreading of arms and legs with muscles tensed. After spreading his arms and legs apart, the infant brings them together in an "embracing action" (Breckenridge and Murphy, 1963; McKay and Smith, 1964; Watson and Lowrey, 1962). It is difficult to obtain this reflex movement after two months, and it has usually disappeared by three months.

The Babinski reflex can be obtained by stimulating the lateral area of the sole of the foot so that the infant will extend his toes. This reflex changes to the plantar reflex, or contraction of the toes, under the same type of stimulation as early as four months in some children and by eighteen months in most children.

The development of the body is cephalocaudal and moves from the center of the body outward. By the time an infant is between four and six months old, he can hold up his head and usually can roll from stomach to back. By about six months of age, the infant can sit up with a little support; around the ninth month, he becomes mobile and begins to crawl. At about the same time he learns to stand with support.

MODIFICATION OF THE EARLY BIOLOGICAL AND BEHAVIORAL PROCESSES

By the end of the first year, some of the basic physiological processes are modified. Food ingestion is changed in character and timing, excretory processes become controlled, and sleep patterns become more similar to those of adults.

Changes in Nutrition

Protein is the chief constituent of the child's body and is an important nutrient in the formation of cell protoplasm. It is an important constituent of the muscular and nervous systems, the visceral and glandular tissues, and many body fluids and secretions. Between four and six months, the infant acquires protein from a variety of sources: lentils, cereals, meat, fish, eggs, milk, cheese, peas, and beans.

The bulk of the child's diet comes from carbohydrates in milk, cereals, fruits, vegetables, and sucrose (Hansen and Bennett, 1964). In digestion, foods are broken down into simpler structures and most of the absorbed sugar is converted to glycogen and stored in the liver. Glycogen is also stored in the muscles. Carbohydrates that are not oxydized or stored are converted to fats. Fat is necessary for normal growth and development. If the diet is too low in fat content, the deficiency causes too much intake of carbohydrates and will result in frequent hunger and fatigue.

Infants vary in energy needs. Energy is dependent upon heat accompanying metabolic processes. The unit of heat in metabolism is a calorie, which is the amount of heat necessary to raise the temperature of 1 kilogram of water from 15° to 16° centigrade. The amount of heat resulting from metabolism varies according to foods.

Changes in Excretory Processes

As the child leaves infancy, he is forced to learn to control bladder and bowel action in a relatively short time. A child's inability to learn such control often arouses anxiety in parents, particularly if the child has not learned control by the time he is expected to go to nursery school or kindergarten. On the other hand, children who are expected to learn this control before sufficient maturation has taken place may be in such conflict with parents that favorable learning experiences are impaired.

Changes in Sleep Patterns

At about the age of two, the child is sleeping between twelve and fourteen hours a day and gradually the need for sleep decreases. Most children seem to benefit from a nap in the afternoon or rest periods up through kindergarten or even in first grade.

As with problems of feeding, sleep difficulty sometimes comes with the physiological changes of maturation. As the needs for sleep lessen, parents must change their own living patterns. The child's needs change quickly, and parents who insist that their child follow earlier sleeping schedules encounter resistance. Those parents who have found a time after the evening meal to be together in quiet relaxation, soon discover that the child who heretofore quietly and willingly went to bed now wishes to take part in this time and begins to demand bedtime stories or numerous drinks of water. Parental responses of resentment may lay the foundation for conflict between them and the child and as the result of this conflict, the child may find it increasingly difficult to go to sleep or to leave his parents for a solitary time in his own room. Furthermore, telling the child that it is "time for sleep" and that his health is in danger if he does not get sufficient sleep usually has little effect, as the parents of Ken Wilson in the following story discovered.

> Ken's parents encountered difficulty with their son when he moved out of the early period of infancy and his sleep needs lessened. They demanded that he abide by a scheduled time for sleep. As Ken grew older he rebelled against their demands and found satisfaction in thwarting his parents' requests that he go to bed. He became quite clever in finding excuses to stay up. His parents resented his infringement on their privacy and re-

TABLE 1

The Sleep of Children

Age	Total hours sleep	Character of sleep
Newborn	22	Irregular
3 months	18–20	Long night sleep
6–11 months	14–16	Morning and afternoon naps
12–23 months	13–14	One nap daily, usually afternoon, 2 hours
2–5 years	12–13	One nap daily, usually afternoon, 1 hour
6–13 years	11 decreasing to 9	No nap

From H. Bakwin and R. M. Bakwin, *Clinical Management of Behavior Disorders in Children*. Philadelphia: W. B. Saunders Company, 1960, p. 44. (Used by permission.)

laxation time, so they resorted to various forms of punishment. These methods were not successful and Ken continued to lie awake and periodically call out to his parents. By the time he was five, he would not go to sleep until his parents were in bed, often quite late at night. Now quite distressed at Ken's behavior, the parents asked their physician for drugs that might help. They also thought that Ken must have some abnormality because of this peculiar behavior. Needless to say, Ken was not ill and no physical reason existed for his remaining awake. A cyclic aspect of the problem had been set in motion: The more his parents resented his staying awake, the more uneasy Ken became about his relationship to them. As the conflict increased, Ken's need to be with his parents and to be a part of their lives also increased. The parents' subsequent rejection and response to his actions with increased scoldings and admonitions only served to upset him further. Ken's parents, however, did at last understand that it was necessary to allow Ken to be a part of their activities in the evening and to share some of their time with him. After experiencing the change in his parents' attitudes and feelings so that his relationship with them was one of comfort and security in the evening, Ken then could go to bed and go to sleep.

Occasionally a child will have "nightmares" and "night terrors." He may wake up in the night calling out in great fear. Sometimes it is difficult for him to orient himself to his surroundings or to realize that his parents are with him and comforting him. Most children now and then will have terrifying dreams. However, if these become excessive, the life of the child should be examined and the source of his insecurity and anxiety should be sought. General betterment of the child's relationship in the family or at school is often helpful in dealing with sleep disturbances.

If parents are aware of the child's changing pattern of sleep needs and will teach him to conform to patterns of family life, difficulties will be less likely to arise. During childhood at varying times, it is not unusual for sleep to be affected to some extent by emotional upsets, illness, and frightening experiences. Excessive sleep disturbances, however, are often symptomatic of difficulties in the child's life.

Growth: Changes in Height and Weight

Growth refers to an increase in the size of the body or its parts. It should be emphasized that growth is similar in all children, but each child has an individual growth pattern, and growth chart averages, while providing a basis for judgment of adequacy, nevertheless must be cited with caution.

Infancy is one of two periods of very rapid growth; the other is adolescence. In the first year of life, weight increases around 200 per cent and height around 50 per cent. During the first three months of life, the infant usually gains an ounce each day; by six months he usually has doubled his birth weight; and by one year he has tripled it. It is important to realize that as the child grows and develops, his rapid gains normally lessen. At birth, most infants range from about 18 to 21 inches in length. By the time the average infant is three months old, he has increased his length by 20 per cent, and by one year he has increased it by about 50 per cent. Accordingly, at the beginning of the second year of life, the average child is between 31 and 34 inches in height and weighs approximately 25 pounds. At the age of three, boys and girls are about 38 inches in height and some 33 pounds in weight (Watson and Lowrey, 1962).

Increases in height continue to drop in extent in early childhood, and the increase is only about 8 per cent between the ages from three to four and around 5 per cent between the ages of five and six. Increases in weight drop to about 12 per cent between the ages of three and six years. During early childhood, a child grows relatively evenly, with the average increase in height being about 3 inches and the increase in weight about 3 to 5 pounds each year. The sex differences in height and weight are not pronounced during this period of early childhood. By the time a child comes to the end of this period, both boys and girls are within the range of 40 to 55 pounds and between 44 and 48 inches tall.

During this period, body proportions change and the trunk becomes twice as long and wide as it was at birth. Of course, arms and legs have lengthened and hands and feet have grown larger. The bones harden throughout childhood and the muscles become larger and stronger.

Changes in Physiological Processes

Macy and Kelly (1957) point to the importance of the chemical and physiological growth of the child and emphasize that this type of growth is the "invisible growth" involving sequences of biochemical and physiological adjustment. These adjustments include the transformation of foodstuff into new tissues and changes in the chemical or metabolic functions, as well as the enlargement of organs and tissues making up body structure and composition. The body is increasingly better able to convert complex foodstuff into simpler molecules, to select required nutrients and to synthesize them into complex chemical units. These chemical changes can be assessed through the metabolic-balance method, or the determination of the difference between the food consumed and the outgo in body excretions and growth by oxygen consumption and heat production. Body composition is studied by the determination of body water and total body fat. Accordingly, Macy and Kelley (1957) emphasize that as the body increases in visible size, the increase is accompanied by vast chemical changes and enlargement of tissues and organs.

From the very first, as has been indicated, many physical characteristics come to have psychological and learned components through interaction with the environment. Hence, understanding of behavior requires much knowledge of structure and function of an individual's biological attributes.

A POINT OF VIEW

There is evidence to suggest that even in infancy certain patterns of behavior may develop and certain processes may occur which will determine to some extent an individual's destiny throughout the life span. It seems particularly tragic that certain kinds of deprivation of "stimulus input" in this period might possibly interfere with the capacity to establish satisfying emotional relationships during an individual's entire life. This period, however, is no longer viewed as one in which the infant needs only biological care and a safe environment—the quality of experiences of both an affective and cognitive nature now is seen to be significant.

REFERENCES

Aserinsky, E., and N. Kleitman, 1955. "A Motility Cycle in Sleeping Infants as Manifested by Ocular and Gross Bodily Activity," *Journal of Applied Physiology,* **8**, 11–18.

Bakwin, H., and R. M. Bakwin, 1960. *Clinical Management of Behavior Disorders in Children.* Philadelphia: Saunders.

Beal, V. A., 1957. "On Acceptance of Solid Foods, and Other Food Patterns, of Infants and Children," *Pediatrics,* **20**, 448–457.

Berlyne, D. E., 1958. "The Influence of the Albedo and Complexity of Stimuli on Visual Fixation in the Human Infant," *British Journal of Psychology,* **49**, 315–318.

Breckenridge, M. E., and M. N. Murphy, 1963. *Growth and Development of the Young Child.* Philadelphia: Saunders.

Brobeck, J. R., 1960. "Regulation of Energy Exchange," in *Medical Physiology and Biophysics,* edited by T. C. Ruch and J. F. Fulton, pp. 984–1008. Philadelphia: Saunders.

Carlson, A. J., V. Johnson, and H. M. Cavert, 1961. *The Machinery of the Body.* Chicago: The University of Chicago Press.

Cohn, C., D. Joseph, and M. D. Allweiss, 1962. "Nutritional Effects of Feeding Frequency," *American Journal of Clinical Nutrition,* **11**, 356–361.

Donald, I., 1962. "Prenatal Development," in *Child Health and Development,* edited by R. W. B. Ellis, pp. 29–57. London: Churchill.

Engen, T., L. P. Lipsitt, and H. Kaye, 1963. "Olfactory Responses and Adaptation in the Human Neonate," *Journal of Comparative and Physiological Psychology,* **56**, 73–77.

Farquhar, J. W., 1962. "The Newborn," in *Child Health and Development,* edited by R. W. B. Ellis, pp. 58–79. London: Churchill.

Fomon, S. J., and D. J. Bartels, 1960. "Concentrations of Cholesterol in Serum of Infants in Relation to Diet," *American Medical Association Journal of Diseases of Children,* **99**, 27–30.

Fomon, S. J., and G. M. Owen, 1964. "Influence of Age, Sex and Diet on Rate of Growth and Body Composition during Early Infancy," *Proceedings of the Sixth International Congress of Nutrition,* pp. 66–74.

Fomon, S. J., D. M. Harris, and R. L. Jensen, 1959. "Acidification of the Urine by Infants Fed Human Milk and Whole Cow's Milk," *Pediatrics,* **23**, 113–120.

Hansen, A. E., and M. J. Bennett, 1964. "Nutritional Requirements," in *Textbook of Pediatrics,* 8th ed., edited by W. E. Nelson, pp. 108–125. Philadelphia: Saunders.

Hardy, J. D., 1961. "Physiology of Temperature Regulation," *Physiological Reviews,* **41**, 521–606.

Kagan, J., B. A. Henker, A. Hen-Tov, J. Levine, and M. Lewis, 1966. "Infants' Differential Reactions to Familiar and Distorted Faces," *Child Development,* **37**, 519–532.

Kleitman, N., 1963. *Sleep and Wakefulness*. Chicago: The University of Chicago Press.

Kleitman, N., and T. G. Englemann, 1953. "Sleep Characteristics of Infants," *Journal of Applied Physiology*, 6, 269–282.

Lewis, M., J. Kagan, and J. Kalafat, 1966. "Patterns of Fixation in the Young Infant," *Child Development*, 37, 331–341.

McKay, R. J., and C. A. Smith, 1964. "Physical Examination of the Newborn Infant," in *Textbook of Pediatrics*, 8th ed., edited by W. E. Nelson, pp. 339–344. Philadelphia: Saunders.

Macy, I. G., and H. J. Kelly, 1957. *Chemical Anthropology: A New Approach to Growth in Children*. Chicago: The University of Chicago Press.

Meyer, H. F., 1960. *Infant Foods and Feeding Practice*. Springfield, Ill.: Charles C Thomas.

Mussen, P. H., 1963. *The Psychological Development of the Child*. Englewood Cliffs, N.J.: Prentice-Hall.

Patton, N. D., 1960. "Higher Control of Autonomic Outflows: The Hypothalamus," in *Medical Physiology and Biophysics*, edited by T. C. Ruch and J. F. Fulton, pp. 234–248. Philadelphia: Saunders.

Piaget, J., 1954. *The Construction of Reality in the Child*, translated by M. Cook. New York: Basic Books.

Pratt, K. C., 1954. "The Neonate," in *Manual of Child Psychology*, 2d ed., edited by L. Carmichael, pp. 215–291. New York: Wiley.

Schachtel, E. G., 1959. *Metamorphosis: On the Development of Affect, Perception, Attention, and Memory*. New York: Basic Books.

Steinschneider, A., E. L. Lipton, and J. B. Richmond, 1966. "Auditory Sensitivity in the Infant: Effect of Intensity on Cardiac and Motor Responsivity," *Child Development*, 37, 233–252.

Watson, E. H., and G. H. Lowrcy, 1962. *Growth and Development of Children*. Chicago: The Year Book Medical Publishers.

Werner, H., 1948. *Comparative Psychology of Mental Development*, rev. ed. Chicago: Follett.

[*three*]

Physiological Foundations of Behavior

During development, the organs of the body change by increasing in size and, in some instances, by changing their physiological functioning. A great deal more is known about changes in the external characteristics of the body, particularly height and weight, than is known about changes in internal characteristics. In fact, very little is known about the growth patterns of the internal organs of the body. However, with the development of transistorized instruments, longitudinal studies in the future will be able to yield more information than currently is available. Heretofore, investigators have depended upon roentgenographic and autopsy methods, although both have considerable limitations. On the other hand, great advances have been made in recent years in the field of biochemistry, and much more information is now available about physiological functioning of the organ systems.

Some of the organ, or body systems are directly related to psychological functioning, while others are only indirectly related. Probably all systems, however, can be affected by the emotions and, through malfunction, all can have some adverse influence on the emotional, intellectual, or perceptual processes. Therefore, it is important to relate basic morphological and physiological information about organ systems to psychological functioning.

This chapter will give an over-all survey of the organ systems that are of significance in understanding human behavior. It is the main purpose of this chapter to provide a basis for understanding behavior and development. The importance of integration of biological and cultural information and concepts in approaches to the study of human behavior is illustrated particularly well by certain research studies done in reference to mental abilities. While there is much present-day emphasis on the influence of cultural factors on levels of mental functioning and differences in mental capacities of various groups, some investigators are seeking information about the importance of biological conditions. Broverman et al. (1968), for example, hypothesized that sex differences in mental abilities should not be attributed to cultural influences but instead to biological influences. They took the position that differences in mental abilities between the sexes result from hormonal processes. Although influence of such processes is complex, these investigators suggest that sex differences result from relationships between adrenergic activation and cholinergic inhibition of neural processes, which are responsive to the sex hormones—androgen and estrogen. Sex differences in mental abilities include (1) the superiority of females over males in perceptual-motor tasks, as exemplified in tasks of fine manual dexterity, and (2) the superiority of males over females in locating a simple pattern imbedded in a complex pattern, in assembling objects, and in completing mazes. Broverman and his associates conclude that the understanding of cognitive processes will be enhanced by attending to differences in abilities, which vary according to bodily conditions and processes. Such evidence is illustrative of the importance of understanding biological factors even in the performance of simple learning tasks. Investigators or students unaware of the influence of physiological factors may make erroneous conclusions on the basis of incomplete information.

BODY SYSTEMS DIRECTLY RELATED TO BEHAVIOR

The endocrine gland system and the nervous system are directly involved in psychological functioning in complex ways. For example, the activity of the sex glands directly influences such functions as perception and choice of activities. Also, the functioning of the adrenal glands directly influences emotional behavior. Similarly, the nervous system, particularly the central nervous system, is primarily involved in the intellectual processes—in cognition, conceptualization, and the like. As knowledge of the body systems increases, understanding and investigation of human behavior will also increase and will be dependent upon a background and understanding of the essential facts about the body's organic systems.

The Endocrine Gland System

The endocrine glands, or ductless glands, are located throughout the body (see Figure 3-1). These glands absorb certain elements from the

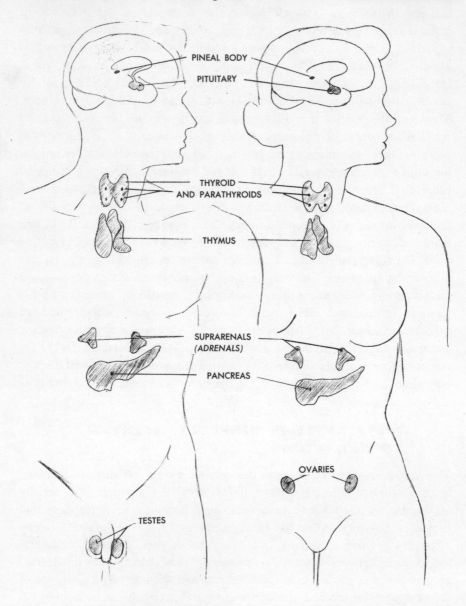

Figure 3.1. The endocrine glands.

blood and change them into the glands' characteristic secretions, which in turn are passed directly into and through the blood stream to various tissues throughout the body and are used to control the activities of these tissues. The secretions from the endocrine glands are called "internal secretions," or hormones,[1] in order to distinguish them from the secretions, like bile, that are distributed through ducts (Winton and Bayliss, 1962). The hormones not only exert a powerful influence on other glands in the system, but also influence *all* physiological processes (D'Amour, 1961; Grollman, 1964; Kahn, 1965). It now seems, however, that the pituitary gland, the thyroid gland, the sex glands, the adrenal glands, and the pancreas are more directly related to behavior than are the pineal gland, the thymus gland, and the parathyroid glands.

The Pituitary Gland. The pituitary gland, also called the "hypophysis," has a profound effect on physical development in adolescence (Harris and Donovan, 1961; McArthur, 1960; Migeon, 1960; Turner, 1960). This small organ, attached by a stalk to the floor of the brain, is one of the most inaccessible and best protected of the body organs (see Figure 3-5). Its functioning is closely related to the hypothalamus and the central nervous system, as well as all of the other endocrine glands. Knowledge of its many functions and its influence on many vital processes has led some scientists to refer to it as the "master gland." Despite much knowledge about the pituitary gland, some of its effect and the nature of its inter-relationships with other body systems still remain a mystery. Enough is known at the present time to determine that complex body functioning and behavior depend upon its hormones. For example, ability to respond to stimuli in the environment seems to be dependent upon this gland, but the exact nature of its influence is yet to be discovered.

The pituitary gland has two lobes, each of which secretes different hormones. Some of these hormones influence the functioning of all of the body and some stimulate other glands in the endocrine system (see Figure 3-2).[2] The front, or anterior, lobe of the pituitary (adenohypophysis)

---

[1] The word *hormone* is derived from a Greek word meaning "I arouse to activity." New scientific findings are continually being made about hormonal activity. For example, it is now known that adrenalin from the adrenal medulla is supplemented by the adrenalin from certain nerve endings. Even the brain produces small amounts of a hormone-like substance called serotonin, which is believed to be useful in aiding neural activity. Serotonin is mainly produced in intestinal mucosa and moves into the blood, where it acts to lower blood pressure and prevent hemorrhage (Morgan, 1965). Woolley (1967) believes that varying amounts of serotonin in the brain bring about changes in emotions and intellectual functioning. However, much important knowledge is yet to be obtained about the interrelationship of the nervous and endocrine gland systems in the body.

[2] The pituitary hormones that affect other glands were named according to the glands influenced, followed by the suffix *tropic,* from a Greek word meaning "to

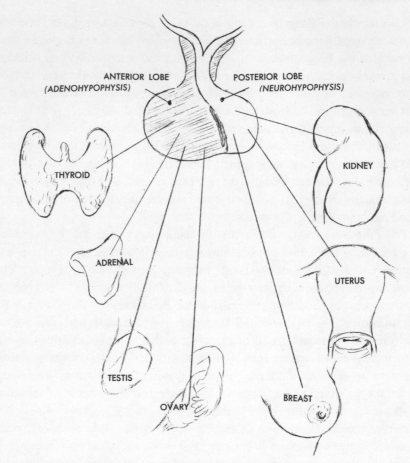

Figure 3.2. The pituitary (hypophysis), a control center in the function of other glands or organs.

secretes seven known hormones. Among these hormones of the anterior lobe are the thyrotrophic hormone (thyroid-stimulating hormone, TSH), which affects the thyroid; the adrenocorticotrophic hormone (ACTH), which acts upon the adrenal glands; and the gonadotrophic hormones, which affect the gonads, or sex glands (discussed in a later section of this chapter, The Reproductive System). Another hormone of the anterior part of the pituitary gland is the growth hormone, or somatotrophin. This hormone stimulates body growth (Morgan, 1965).

turn." Endocrinologists now think it is more appropriate to change the suffix to *trophic,* meaning "to nourish" (Miller and Goode, 1960).

The secretion of the posterior lobe of the pituitary (neurohypophysis) is pituitrin. It has three known effects on the body: it raises blood pressure by constricting blood vessels, it affects the functioning of smooth muscles, and it has an antidiuretic effect. Recently, two hormones have been isolated from pituitrin: vasopressin and oxytocin. Vasopressin regulates water in the body and aids in reabsorption of water. Because the body's normal reabsorption of water into the blood maintains normal urine volume, the agent, vasopressin, is termed the "antidiuretic hormone," or ADH. Impairment of the pituitary's secretion of vasopressin results in *diabetes insipidus,* a condition causing the person to lose excessive quantities of water in dilute urine (polyuria) and to drink large quantities of water (polydipsia) to relieve the resulting thirst.

Oxytocin stimulates the functioning of the smooth muscles. In females it is believed to stimulate contractions of the uterus and aid in the expulsion of the fetus at birth. After childbirth certain tactile and other external stimuli cause increased secretion of oxytocin and the operation of a neurohormonal reflex culminating in increased lactation. Another function of oxytocin in the female is to aid in conception. Some physiologists believe that spermatozoa reach the Fallopian tubes too quickly in terms of their own movement alone and that oxytocin must account for the rapid ascent.

The Thyroid Gland. The growth of the adolescent is particularly affected by the activity of the thyroid gland. This gland, located in the throat, has two lobes, one on each side of the larynx, which are joined by an isthmus. The thyroid releases its hormone (thyroxin) directly into the bloodstream when stimulated by the pituitary's thyrotrophic hormone, TSH. Growth is dependent upon thyroxin's action in bringing about conversion of food into tissue cells and energy (fuel burning). As oxygen is necessary for this process, the conversion activity (metabolism), or the proper utilization of food, can be measured by the consumption of oxygen. Thyroxin is also essential in skeletal growth, sexual growth, and normal brain development (Gardner, 1960; Houssay, 1955).

An essential and important part of thyroxin is iodine. Since the ocean contains much of this element, those who live near the ocean or salt waterways and use sea food have no difficulty in obtaining a sufficient amount. People who live far from the sea and where natural sources of iodine do not exist may develop an enlargement of the thyroid gland that is called a goiter. Continued deficit of iodine causes the pituitary to secrete more TSH, which in turn brings gland enlargement by increasing the size of the cells (hypertrophy) and the number of cells (hyperplasia). As a result of the discovery of the importance of iodine to the thyroid gland, iodine salt (potassium iodide) has been added to most commercial table salts.

Perinetti et al. (1961) tell in the following story about the dramatic effect of the use of iodized salt.

> The province of Mendoza, lying at the feet of the great Andes range in the interior of Argentina, cultivated most of its land by the use of irrigation. Problems of goiter had been widespread throughout its entire history of settlement. Children, adults, and the aged were all victims. Even the dogs in the area were affected. Investigations in 1952 revealed that there was very little iodine in the drinking water or the irrigation water. The following year, the government passed a law that all salt used in the province had to be iodized. Generally, the people acquiesced, but some dealers labeled their salt as "iodized" when it was not, and some bakers thought iodized salt would change the taste of their bread. Eventually, however, the inhabitants of Mendoza all used iodized salt. In studying the population a few years later, the investigators found that the problem of goiter had disappeared.

Extreme deficiency in the functioning of the thyroid gland, or hypothyroidism, results in a condition known as *cretinism,* which is usually produced by an embryonic defect in the thyroid gland. It occasionally happens that the deficient functioning of the gland is not treated, resulting in severely limited growth. Symptoms include retardation of skeletal maturation, dry skin, coarse hair, and lethargic behavior. Upon diagnosis of the deficiency of the gland, thyroxin is given and, if administered in time, the condition of cretinism can be avoided. It is frequently observed that a child discovered to have hypothyroidism is initially conforming and well behaved, but on receiving thyroid medication begins to cause trouble in school. However, because of his improved health and well-being, he later conforms and his school work is at a higher level of performance than it was originally.

Hyperthyroidism, or overactivity of the thyroid gland, is more common in adolescence than it is in childhood. However, knowledge about the incidence and etiology of the problem is insufficient. One of the most common types of hyperthyroidism is called "exophthalmic goiter." Symptoms are weight loss, protruding eyeballs, nervousness, and increased pulse. The history of the treatment of hyperthyroidism illustrates the application of advancement in scientific knowledge (D'Amour, 1961). At first there was the discovery of the significance of the functioning of the thyroid gland.

This was soon followed by the idea of surgical removal of the entire thyroid gland to correct extreme cases of hyperthyroidism. Surgery only partly solved the problem, for if part of the gland were allowed to remain, hypertrophy was the result and the problem would recur. In addition, surgery was quite difficult. By chance, a much better solution to the problem was discovered. In experimenting with sulfa drugs and sulfur compounds, it was found that a particular compound called "thio-urea" caused rabbits to develop goiters. It was realized that the drug inhibited the action of the thyroid gland and that therefore it would be of value to people who had hyperthyroidism. Since this discovery, other drugs have been found effective in the treatment of this condition (McClintock and Gassner, 1961).

The Adrenal Glands. The adrenal glands, one on each kidney, differ in structure from all of the other endocrine glands: Each adrenal gland is really two glands—one within another. The inner gland, the *medulla,* differs both in structure and in function from the outer gland, the *cortex.*

The medulla is sometimes referred to as the "emergency gland," since it plays an important role in readying the body to meet stressful situations by secreting the hormone adrenalin (the proper name is *epinephrine*).[3] When stress is encountered, this hormone is released, causing a number of important changes in body functioning. The heart beats faster, thus increasing the circulation of the blood; blood pressure is raised, making more blood available to the muscles and to the brain; the liver releases extra glucose, thereby increasing muscle efficiency by providing fuel for the muscles; the pupils of the eyes are dilated, so that more light can enter them; and the blood clots more quickly. Most of these reactions are valuable in times of threat, when fighting or fleeing is necessary.

The cortex of the adrenal gland apparently has no neural connections and can only be stimulated by the pituitary gland through the particular hormone called the adrenocorticotrophic hormone, or ACTH. The cortex seems to be more like the sex glands in cellular origin than the medulla. The hormones, too, are similar in chemical structure to the sex hormones. The hormones of the cortex are divided into three types: (1) the glucocorticoids, (2) the mineralocorticoids, and (3) sex hormones. The first, the *glucocorticoids,* are active in the metabolism of food. Cortisone, one of the glucocorticoids, has been found to be helpful in treatment of in-

---

[3] The medulla also secretes *norepinephrine,* a hormone similar to epinephrine in its effect. For example, blood pressure is raised by both, but epinephrine does it by increasing heart rate while norepinephrine accomplishes the same action by general vasoconstriction.

flammations of body organs and areas as well as connective tissues. It has become well known through its use in the treatment of arthritis and rheumatic disease. The second, the *mineralocorticoids,* are important in normal kidney functioning. One of the most important of these hormones is aldosterone, which is necessary for the regulation of sodium and potassium in the body. The third type of hormone produced by the adrenal cortex is that of the *sex hormones,* both androgen and estrogen, but predominantly androgen. In the past, "maleness" and "femaleness" were thought to be determined by ratios of androgen to estrogen, but it seems that such dif-ferentiation is not plausible, since to some extent both boys and girls have similar hormonal influences. Sometimes tumors occur in the adrenal cortex and cause an increase in the male sex hormones. If a tumor occurs in a boy, it may cause early secondary sexual development (perhaps as young as five years old). If it occurs in a girl, it has a masculinizing effect.

The Pancreas. The pancreas is an elongated organ, larger at one end than the other, lying among the organs of digestion with the stomach and duodenum around it. Most of this endocrine gland is devoted to the production of pancreatic juice, which is important in the splitting of starches and fats and in the digestion of proteins. An interesting characteristic of this part of the organ is that it can respond to external stimuli—for example, simply the odor or taste of food causes the pancreas to pour its secretion into the duodenum.

The pancreas has another important function: insulin production. Island-like clusters of a different type of cell are scattered through the ordinary cells of the pancreas. These clusters are called Islets of Langerhans in honor of Paul Langerhans, a German scientist who first discovered them. These cells release insulin into the bloodstream as a result of stimulation by an insulinotrophic hormone from the pituitary gland. Insulin is an essential hormone in the regulation of sugar in the blood. It assists in storage of sugar compounds in the muscles and liver, inhibits the liver's production of sugar when the body is not in need, and helps in the burning of carbohydrates. In addition to insulin, the pancreas secretes glucagon, a hormone that has an effect opposite to that of insulin, since it increases blood sugar.[4]

Malfunctioning of the pancreas has a number of significant effects on the individual. The most common problem is the chronic disease of diabetes.

---

[4] The time of glucagon's effect is short and an injection of both insulin and glucagon, while resulting in a temporary increase in blood sugar, actually causes blood sugar to be lowered over longer periods of time. Glucagon causes liver glycogen to be converted to glucose.

Although diabetes is more common in middle adult life, it can occur in adolescence. Sometimes the disease begins with warnings not clearly recognized, as in the case of Phyllis Johnson in the following story.

> Phyllis, a junior high school student, not only maintained a high average in all her studies, but also took part in many activities in the school, including music and sports. She particularly liked basketball and she also enjoyed playing baseball with boys. Toward the end of the school year, Phyllis found that her activities encroached on her time for study at school and at home, so she began to study early in the morning before school. As examination time approached, she increased the time devoted to her studies, while also maintaining her other activities.

> Eventually, Phyllis felt so fatigued that she was unable to go to school. She told her mother that she was very tired and that she felt thirsty much of the time; in fact, she said, she felt so thirsty that her "throat burned." Early one Saturday morning, Phyllis sank into unconsciousness and was rushed to a large medical center. There her parents were told that she was in a diabetic coma. After several weeks under a specialist's care, Phyllis was well enough to leave the hospital. However, she had to learn to deal with the disease of diabetes.

The pancreas of the normal person produces sufficient insulin to deal with sugar eaten. In diabetes, however, the insulin supply is inadequate and the body cannot use or store all of the sugar accumulated. Thus, the sugar content in the bloodstream rises to unusually high levels (hyperglycemia). Important symptoms of diabetes, as was the case with Phyllis, are excessive thirst (polydipsia), excessive urination (polyuria), and an increase in appetite (polyphagia). Sometimes, in addition, the person experiences fatigue or nervousness and tingling of fingers and toes (Ford, 1960).

The isolation of insulin by Banting and Best in 1922, and its later use by Collip is considered to be one of the great achievements of modern medicine. Thirteen years later, in 1935, Hagedorn in Denmark mixed protamine, a very simple protein obtained from the sperm of certain fish, with insulin. He found that this mixture was utilized more slowly by the body and that the effect lasted much longer than when insulin was used by itself. Soon thereafter, others found that by adding zinc to the mixture, a still longer effect could be obtained (Bell et al., 1965). It is an advantage for insulin to be slow-acting in order to lengthen the time between injections.

Ordinarily, an adolescent is expected to manage the disease by himself with the aid of his physician. This care entails the injection of insulin, the testing of urine to see if it contains excessive sugar, the adjustment of the quantity of insulin, an adherence to a diet, and considerable care of general health. The adolescent who has diabetes needs special psychological consideration, since the disease requires that certain specific behavior patterns be followed. These tasks cannot be neglected or carelessly performed. An adolescent often is particularly concerned about body functioning and development; therefore, the diagnosis of a chronic disease can be especially devastating at this period.

> Janet Lindsey was found to have diabetes at the age of sixteen. She was a particularly attractive girl and her beauty had been recognized by her classmates. Shortly before the diagnosis was made, she had been elected beauty queen of her high school. Upon hearing from her physician that she had diabetes, she believed her life was no longer worth living and she became very depressed. She had placed much emphasis upon the value of the attractive characteristics of her body and now to find that in reality it was not nearly as acceptable as she earlier had thought was more than she could face. Fortunately, it was possible to help her to see that by meeting certain requirements she could live in a normal way and continue her enjoyment of life and success in school.

Another problem of pancreas malfunctioning that can occur in adolescence is pancreatitis. The precise cause of this inflammatory condition is not known with certainty, but it sometimes follows the mumps, injury to the abdomen in athletics, and extreme dietary changes. For example, boys who try to make a particular weight class in boxing or wrestling often will undertake a strict diet almost to the point of starvation and then, after weighing in, eat large quantities of food. The sudden additional strain on the digestive system can cause the acute illness of pancreatitis. The primary symptoms are abdominal pain and nausea. Pancreatitis also can result from some obstruction of the pancreatic ducts or a slight anatomical malformation that becomes a problem under the stimulation of the pancreas to increased activity (Bluemstock et al., 1957; Gallagher, 1960).

The Gonads.   The gonads—the ovaries in females and the testes in males—are influenced in their maturing process by hormones from the pituitary gland (gonadotrophic hormones), which stimulate the gonads and assist in bringing about sexual maturity. The secretion of the pituitary hormones have an increasingly important effect on the gonads as these organs become more sensitive to hormonal influences during their development. In the male, a pituitary hormone controls the multiplication and maturation of the cells in the testes into spermatozoa. Another pituitary hormone stimulates other specialized cells in the testes to produce male sex hormones known as androgens. The development of the reproductive organs of girls is also influenced by the gonadotrophic hormones from the pituitary. One hormone influences the growth of the ovaries and the maturation of the ovarian follicle and its germinal cell. Another pituitary hormone functions as does the first but in addition it brings about ovulation and secretion of estrogen and progesterone. Still another pituitary hormone, prolactin, affects the development of the mammary glands.

At puberty, the dissimilarity of the appearance of boys and girls increases, primarily through the development of the secondary sex characteristics. These characteristics are brought about by the influence of the sex hormones and accompany the development of the sex organs. Secondary sex characteristics in the male are developed through the action of one of the androgens, testosterone. Early effects are first observed as a temporary swelling of the male mammary glands. Pubic hair, another secondary characteristic, appears at about the same time as the increase in size of the primary sex organs. Soon thereafter, axillary and facial hair appear and become darker and coarser as the male matures. Also occurring in the male approximately in midadolescence is the voice change, characterized by huskiness, "breaking," and finally a drop of about an octave in pitch. The deepening of the voice is caused by an increase in the ventrodorsal diameter of the larynx.

Secondary sex characteristics in the female are influenced by the hormones known as estrogens. The first characteristic to occur is an increase in the transverse diameter of the pelvis (Johnston, 1960). Soon thereafter, the breasts begin their enlargement, which continues for about two to four years until the girl reaches maturity. About a year preceding menarche, pubic hair appears—fine, straight, and unpigmented initially; with maturation it becomes pigmented, coarse, and curled. The growth of axillary hair begins about the time of menarche. The voice changes from high-pitched to lower tones, but this change is much less pronounced than in the male.

This age period holds some particular problems for the development and functioning of the sex organs. Boys sometimes have a condition (cryptorchism) in which a testis has not descended properly from the inguinal canal into the scrotum. Usually this condition is treated before the boy reaches adolescence, but some physicians believe that waiting until puberty is best, since at that time a testis will sometimes descend normally without surgery or medical intervention. Orchiopexy, or surgery to bring the testis into the scrotum, is often advised if the condition persists until puberty because of the possibility of neoplastic disease. If both testes are undescended, then fertility is quite unlikely anyway and surgery is by far the best course. Surgeons believe that surgery should be delayed until at least the age of ten because of the fragility of the tissues involved and the possibility of limiting the blood supply. Some evidence is available to indicate that if the testis is not brought down surgically before late adolescence, its capacity to produce spermatozoa is impaired (Gallagher, 1960; Grollman, 1964). Psychological complications are greatly lessened if the operation is performed before adolescence, but after the age of eight or nine.

For the girl, a delicate physiological and psychological balance in relation to the menstrual cycle must be attained. Because of the difficulty of attainment of this delicate balance, it is several years before the cycle is established with regularity and the girl achieves psychological equanimity about it. Various types of problems can develop, some of which seem to be only an extension of what the adolescent girl normally experiences, thus making difficult the differentiation between that which is normal and abnormal.

Boys on the other hand do not have to adjust to a cycle, but their psychological problems associated with their heightened sex drive can be a source of difficulty. Anxiety frequently develops about sexual development and concepts of normality.

The adolescent girl's premenstrual tension is usually in association with psychological upset. The extent of tension and the discomfort accompanying menstruation seem to be related to the teaching and emotional conditioning associated with the reproductive processes. Little evidence is available at present to indicate that the physiological aspects of the menstrual cycle alone should produce psychological upset. "Premenstrual tension" is usually described as consisting of excessive water retention in the tissues and some mental depression, both preceding menstrual flow by a few days. Other symptoms are headache, frequent urination, irritability, tenderness of the breasts, and a feeling of weight in the lower abdomen. These symptoms subside once menstruation has set in. Unfortunately, however, studies of the incidence of difficulties in adolescence surrounding menstruation are lacking.

Irregularity in the menstrual cycle usually includes irregularity of ovulation, and for the first few years after the menarche, ovulation may occur irregularly or at times not at all. For most girls, the menstrual cycle is within a range of twenty-two and thirty-four days. Shorter or longer intervals, however, have been considered within normality. The menstrual period ordinarily lasts from three to seven days. Individuality in the maturation process and in the parent's teaching about physiological processes causes each adolescent's problem to be different. Individuals who reach menarche at a later age tend to become regular more quickly than those whose menarche occurs at an earlier age.

Dysmenorrhea (painful menstruation) usually does not occur until several years following the menarche and the onset of ovulation. It is possible for the condition to result from some anatomical or physiological abnormality. Although dysmenorrhea can be accounted for on the basis of such abnormality, psychological factors in association with the processes need to be considered (Harris and Donovan, 1961; Menzer, 1953). Emotional trauma affecting the adolescent during her first experience with menstruation is frequently a part of the difficulty. The psychological problems of adolescents are of sufficient nature in themselves so that they easily can be extended to the menstrual cycle.

Amenorrhea, the absence of menstruation, indicates that normal functioning is in some way disturbed. Since the menstrual cycle is dependent upon complicated interrelationships among the ovaries, pituitary gland, adrenal glands, and hypothalamus, any disturbance in these relationships can result in an interruption of the cycle. Ovarian difficulty causing amenorrhea sometimes is a sequel to tumors and other diseases. Deficiencies in vitamin B, minerals, or protein can cause malfunctioning. Individuals who gain excessive weight may also encounter interruption. While adolescents often become concerned about missing a menstrual period, usually three periods must pass before concern is warranted. Amenorrhea is relatively common in adolescence and is frequently related to psychological stress.

Sometimes excessive bleeding (menorrhagia) occurs during the menstrual cycle. The problem should be considered significant when bleeding persists for more than a week, since by this time the blood hemoglobin is reduced and dizziness and weakness will occur. In adolescent girls, the most common type of difficulty results from some uterine irritation. Systemic problems associated with excessive bleeding may come, however, from a vitamin deficiency and blood disorders or from a chronic illness, such as rheumatic fever. Here, too, maturational factors are often important.

The Reproductive System

In the female, the internal reproductive organs are the vagina, uterus, Fallopian tubes, and ovaries (see Figure 3-3). The two ovaries lie deep in the pelvic cavity, with one on each side of the uterus. At birth, it is

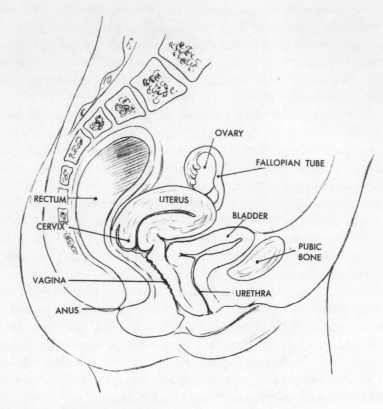

Figure 3.3. Female genital organs.

estimated that each ovary contains about 400,000 immature, or "primary," follicles (a follicle is a saclike structure containing an ovum). The follicle, when it matures at puberty, is called a "Graafian follicle" and contains a mature ovum. About midway in the menstrual cycle, the wall of the ovary ruptures, and the ovum and the follicular fluid of its sac are released into the abdominal cavity and within the peritoneum (the membrane lining the abdominal cavity). The fimbriated end of the Fallopian tube catches the ovum and moves it along within the lumen, or interior of the tube.

The ovum requires about seventy-two hours to reach the uterus. If fertilization takes place, it usually occurs at the upper end of the Fallopian tube. If the egg is fertilized, it subdivides as it floats into the uterus, which has been prepared for the egg by the hormone progesterone, which escaped from the follicle when the ovum was released. The multiplying cells of the ovum develop a network of blood vessels, or "roots," and the ovum implants itself in the mucous membrane of the uterus. If fertilization has not taken place, the ovum atrophies, and the thickened membrane in the uterus disintegrates and passes out of the body with the menstrual fluid.

Interaction between the pituitary and the ovaries begins when the girl is between twelve and fifteen years. The pituitary's hormone FSH (follicle-stimulating hormone) is then produced and is carried to the ovaries by the bloodstream. This hormone influences the development of the follicle and causes it to mature and secrete estrogen. Progesterone and estrogen will temporarily prevent the maturation of the ovum and therefore ovulation. This kind of action occurs naturally during pregnancy. Taken orally in the form of pills, the two hormones are now widely used to prevent pregnancy.

The male generative organs include the penis, the prostate, the seminal vesicles, the seminal duct, and the testes (see Figure 3-4). The testes

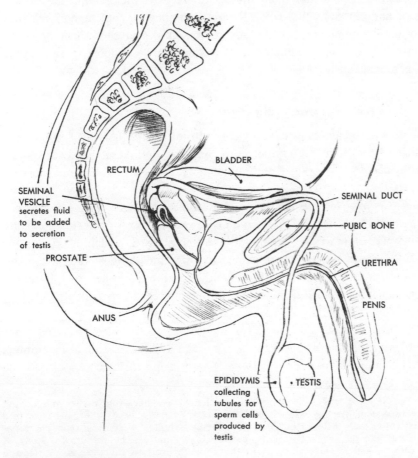

Figure 3.4. Male genital organs.

become suspended outside the body in a sac (the scrotum) during the seventh to ninth month of prenatal life. Each testis contains about a thousand tubes coiled inside to form a plexus or mass of canals (the epididymis) on the upper part of each testis. The cells of the linings of the tubes become sperm cells, which are stored in the epididymis.

Sperm travel in the spermatic canal through the prostate gland, then to the urethra, and then through the urethra to the penis. The prostate gland and the seminal vesicles produce secretions as a carrier for the sperm cells. In addition to producing spermatozoa, the testes also produce the sex hormone, testosterone, which is responsible for the function of the other sex organs and genitalia, as well as secondary sex characteristics. In addition to androgen, the testes secrete an estrogenic hormone (Grollman, 1964; Kahn, 1965).

Both the female and male hormones have so much influence on behavior and emotions that some theoreticians believe that human behavior is primarily dominated by the sex drive. At the present time, however, human behavior is so complex that it is difficult to support or reject such a theoretical construct.

The Nervous System

The nervous system is usually divided into the central nervous system, consisting of the brain and spinal cord, and the peripheral nervous system, which includes the cranial and spinal nerves and the autonomic nervous system.

The Central Nervous System. The central nervous system is composed of a great many neurons, or nerve cells, and it is well protected by membranes and bones. The brain and the spinal cord, which make up the central nervous system, are protected by three membranes: the dura mater (hard outer cover), the arachnoid (middle membrane), and the pia mater (inner membrane). Both the brain and spinal cord are also protected by bone.

A canal running the length of the spinal cord widens out into four ventricles in the brain. Between the pia mater and the arachnoid membrane, a fluid, known as the *cerebrospinal fluid,*[5] helps to lessen shocks to the

---

[5] This fluid is useful in diagnostic studies of conditions involving the central nervous system. At the base of the cord, away from the brain, the cord ends in a bundle of nerves enclosed in a sac. By placing a hollow needle between the vertebrae and into the sac, some of the cerebrospinal fluid can be withdrawn. Study of its composition provides clues as to the cause of various illnesses. Also, removal of some of it relieves pressure on the brain which builds up in certain diseased conditions.

brain. Part of the cord's function is carried on through fibers known as *afferent* and *efferent* fibers. Afferent fibers carry impulses from the lower parts of the cord to the upper part and to the brain; and the efferent fibers, with their cell bodies in the brain, conduct impulses downward.

The main mass of the brain is composed of the cortex and the cerebellum (see Figure 3-5). The cortex is divided into right and left halves, or

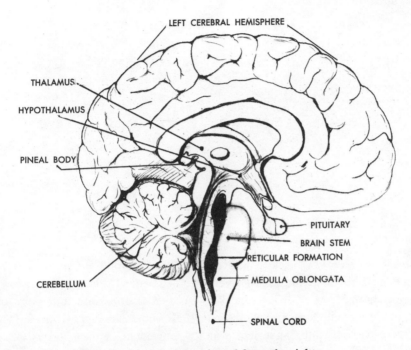

Figure 3.5. Left cerebral hemisphere viewed from the right.

hemispheres, by a longitudinal fissure. These parts of the brain are believed to be recently acquired in evolutionary development and sometimes are called the "new brain" in contrast to the "old brain," the extension of the spinal cord called the brain stem.

A cross section of the cortex reveals gray and white matter: The gray matter consists mainly of nerve-cell bodies composing the convoluted surface of the cortex; and the white matter, lying beneath the cortex, is composed of nerve fibers leading to the lower centers of the brain and spinal cord. These fibers also connect the various parts of the cortex with each other. Deeper in the cerebral hemispheres, more gray matter, composed of nerve-cell bodies, acts as a relay station to the cortex. The convolutions of the cortex are believed to be brought about by the rapid growth of the surface. While animals higher in the phylogenetic scale have more folds

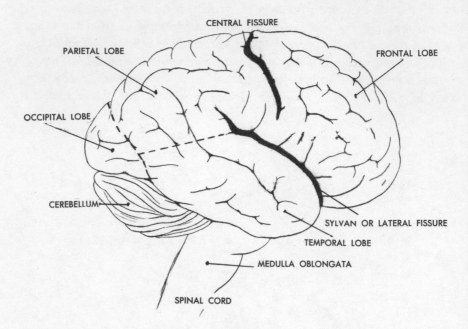

Figure 3.6. Brain, right view.

than those lower in the scale, differences in the convolutions from man to man cannot be substantiated in reference to behavior (Carlson et al., 1961). The cerebral cortex is divided by deep folds or fissures into four pairs of lobes: the frontal, the parietal, the occipital, and the temporal lobes (see Figure 3-6). The internal structure and arrangement of the neurons differ from each other in these four parts and even within each of the four areas some differences in structure are encountered.

The belief in localization of parts of the brain according to function is very old, but it is only with experimentation and observation of recent years that scientific backing for localization has been obtained. Information has come from experimental destruction of various areas in animals, stimulation of specific areas in animals, and observations of human beings who have had areas of the brain destroyed through accident or disease. Also, information has been obtained under certain conditions in surgery performed on human beings. It has been possible in some procedures to stimulate both motor and sensory areas and to observe the responses. Another important method of experimentation is to observe changes in the electrical potentials of the brain. For example, stimulation (tactile or visual) causes electrical changes in the pathways of the brain, and the ultimate destination of these electrical changes can be observed. Much of the present-day information about areas of the brain which initiate body movements and sensory activities has thus been obtained. Body, or muscular, movements originate in the frontal lobe, just in front of the central fissure, or sulcus, which separates the frontal from the parietal lobes (motor area; see Figure 3-7). Brain control is exercised over groups of muscles rather than over a single muscle. Movement complexity seems to require the use of more cortical area; and therefore, hand movements require a larger brain area than do leg movements. Some sensation mechanisms are in the motor area with the motor neurons and, accordingly, awareness of muscle tension and position of the arms and legs is possible. The area in front of the motor area is called the "premotor" area, and stimulation of this area causes group muscular response; for example, the movement of all of the leg.

Just behind the motor area and in the front part of the parietal lobe lies the sensory area, which is associated with the sensations of temperature change, touch, and pressure. This area controls recognition of and response to sensations coming from stimulation of the receptors in the skin.

The brain itself is insensitive to pain. The membranes covering the brain do have nerves, which bring a pain response, and surgeons must desensitize these; but otherwise they can work in the brain itself without pain to the individual.

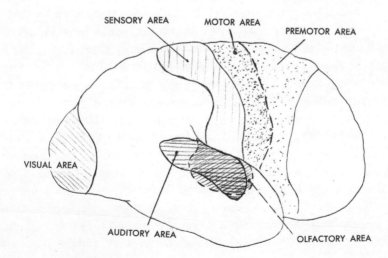

Figure 3.7. Localization of function of the cerebral cortex.

Hearing and auditory sensations are dealt with by a large part of the temporal lobe. Sensations from the cochlea of the ear are brought to this area by the auditory nerve.

Visual sensations are dealt with in the pair of occipital lobes at the back of the cerebral hemispheres. Neural pathways from the optic nerve lead to this area. If the area is experimentally stimulated, sensations of light are experienced.

Sensations of taste and smell involve a part of the cortex on the under part of the brain near the temporal lobe. Sensations from the viscera, such as hunger and thirst, are not concerned with the cortical area, but instead involve the lower parts of the brain.

Most of the cerebral cortex is not concerned with specific functions. The areas not previously mentioned of the frontal and parietal lobes and much of the occipital and temporal lobes are called the "association areas." The association areas are often referred to as the areas involving complex behavioral processes, since they have to do with imagination, learning, reasoning, and memory. These processes are incompletely understood at present, at least in regard to the brain's functioning.

Integrative activities depend mainly on the association areas. The association process, however, is not entirely clear and specific functioning of the association areas cannot be described. For example, identification of a bird as a robin would involve the following processes, some of which are not yet completely understood: Stimulation of the eye initiates impulses traveling over neural pathways, bringing information about shape and color to the visual cortex of the occipital lobe. If the bird sings, stimulation of the internal ear would start impulses over the auditory nerve and to the hearing part of the temporal lobe. The sensory data need to be fitted together into the whole and such a fitting together is done by the association areas.

Destruction of a specific area, Broca's speech area, will result in a condition called motor aphasia, or an inability to speak. This area, located in the left frontal lobe, if destroyed will leave a right-handed person without speech (Bell et al., 1965). There is other evidence of the effect of destruction of certain areas of the brain; for example, impairment of the visual area of the brain prevents vision, although the eye and the neural pathways of the brain still remain intact. This principle applies to all of the sensory systems—the sense organs themselves can be intact and capable of response, yet the individual behaves as if these organs were lacking.

Apparently, afferent neural action does not end in the sensory areas of the cortex or in the association areas; rather, efferent systems are also involved and in an automatic fashion. If the visual area of the brain is stimulated by the sight of food, digestive juices may increase in supply without conscious effort, indicating that efferent nerve fibers also have been involved.

Reflexes involving the cortex are complex; nevertheless, training can modify them. As a result of training, the responses can become automatic and predictable from individual to individual. These automatic responses make interaction with the environment easier and more efficient. Once the complicated skills and tasks are learned and become virtually automatic, the brain and its energy can be utilized in even more complex tasks and processes. It should be noted, too, that the brain can be involved in activity without afferent stimulation; that is, it can carry on activity that seems to be initiated within itself and without outside stimulation. An example of this is reverie.

Just where consciousness is determined is unclear. It may be in the cortex alone or it may depend upon the functioning of the whole brain, including the thalamus and other parts of the brain stem. Some years ago, Penfield and Jasper (1954) sought to explain the significance of the "reticular formation," a mass of gray matter coming from the medulla and into many parts of the brain, by describing its function in consciousness as maintaining an emanation of impulses outward. If this outflow is impaired or inhibited by a particular inflow of impulses into the reticular formation, the individual becomes unconscious. Some explanation about the functioning of the reticular formation is as follows: If a person is asleep and a noise is made, nerve impulses from the auditory nerve are carried to the reticular formation as well as to the cortex. Impulses then travel from the reticular formation to the cortex and the person awakens. Because the reticular formation has to do with sleep, wakefulness, and arousal, it is also called the "reticular activating system" (RAS) (D'Amour, 1961; Morgan, 1965).

The *cerebellum* grows out of the hindbrain and nerve-fiber tracts connect it to the brain stem. The two hemispheres and the midportion (vermis) have a gray surface with white fibers underneath. Some localization of function is found, since each hemisphere controls muscles of the arm and leg on the same side and the midportion of the cerebellum controls the muscles of trunk, neck, and head. Cerebellar impairment results in poorly controlled muscle movements. The cerebellum's main function seems to be to aid in the smoothness of muscle action and to enhance muscle tone.

The *brain stem* is considered to be an extension of the spinal cord.

Generally, the brain stem is divided into three parts called the hindbrain, the midbrain, and forebrain (see Figure 3–5). The hindbrain contains the medulla oblongata, which deals with respiration, cardiac activity, and circulation. The midbrain is concerned with certain hearing and vision reflexes. The forebrain contains the thalamus, a large mass of gray matter that is important in dealing with sensory impulses from the receptors on the way to the cortex. Below the thalamus is the hypothalamus, which influences body temperature, water balance, blood sugar, metabolism, blood pressure, and sleep (Carlson et al., 1961).

Much of the energy of the brain comes from carbohydrates (sugars and starches), but its ability to store these substances is very limited. Thus, a deficiency in the supply to the brain of the necessary sugar carried by the blood causes mental upset. For example, an overdose of insulin will reduce available blood sugar, and mental confusion or unconsciousness will result. The oxidation of carbohydrates is dependent upon vitamin B_1 and, therefore, this vitamin is particularly important to the brain's processes.

The brain requires from 40 to 50 milliliters of oxygen each minute. Interruption of the availability of oxygen, even for the matter of seconds, brings unconsciousness; and irreparable damage results after four minutes of deprivation.

The brain has a high concentration of glutamic acid, an amino acid. Presumably, availability of this acid would affect functioning of the brain. Some children with mental impairment have been given this substance in the belief that it would increase mental performance, but studies to support this contention are unconvincing (Morgan, 1965).

The Autonomic Nervous System. The body's organs and visceral muscles are influenced by a part of the nervous system called the *autonomic nervous system.* This system includes efferent nerve fibers innervating the alimentary canal, uterus, urinary bladder, glands, heart, and lungs. Conscious and voluntary control of the action of these structures is minimal or nonexistent. Most of the autonomic nervous system consists of efferent fibers, but it also has afferent fibers, for example, in the stimulation of the lungs in respiration. Innervation of the visceral organs usually consists of two types of efferent fibers: One type stimulates the organ to activity and the other inhibits activity. The functioning of the autonomic nervous system is of particular significance in the body systems discussed in the following section. Further descriptions of the functions of the autonomic nervous system can be found in Morgan (1965).

BODY SYSTEMS INDIRECTLY RELATED TO BEHAVIOR

Much of the justification given for the study of the endocrine and nervous systems can be given also for the understanding of other body systems indirectly related to psychological functions. For example, investigators have established that an empty stomach or hunger will influence perception and that intense anxiety and fear will affect digestive processes, heart action, and kidney function. But the physiological-psychological interrelationship is even more complicated. Malfunctioning or disease in the systems can affect emotions, which in turn can increase malfunctioning. Of course, much is yet to be learned about such interrelationships; and since new information is so rapidly being acquired in the biological sciences, those studying human behavior must continually extend their knowledge of biological information as it pertains to psychological functioning.

The Urinary System

The two kidneys are organs about 4 inches in length, lying in the lumbar region, one on each side of the vertebral column (see Figure 3–8). They are composed of about 2 million minute tubes called "uriniferous tubules," or nephrons. From each kidney, a tube called the ureter extends to the bladder. Another tube, the urethra, carries urine from the bladder to the outside of the body. The kidneys are important in maintaining osmotic pressure, temperature, volume of blood and lymph, acid-base balance, and removal of harmful materials from the blood. When a substance in the blood rises above the normal level, the kidneys excrete the excess. The quantity of urine excreted varies according to the amount of water taken into the body and the amount of water eliminated by the lungs or skin. The average amount excreted is probably from 1 to 1½ liters each day. The total amount of solids excreted each day is probably from 50 to 70 grams in an adult, but solids and water content vary, as does the urine's specific gravity.

The functioning of the urinary system as related to behavior is particularly apparent in the problem of enuresis, a child's wetting his bed at night (technically, nocturnal enuresis); however, enuresis may refer also to wetting of clothing during the day (diurnal enuresis). The cause of this problem is often unclear; the difficulty can result from disease and malfunctioning of the urinary system, but usually, the cause lies in the child's relationships within the family.

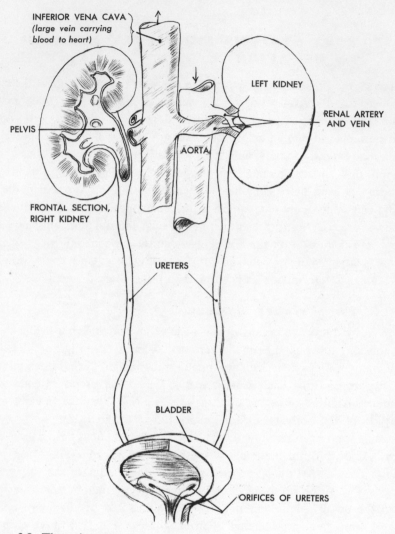

Figure 3.8. The urinary system.

Infections in the upper part of the urinary passages are common in early life and in adolescence. In adolescence, they sometimes become chronic. Urinary infections are most frequent in girls and are usually caused by colon bacilli. In chronic cases, the infections are frequently caused by several types of organisms. These organisms usually invade the system through the blood or by passage upward through the urinary tract. Although antibiotics are effective as treatment, reinfection is common (Lattimer et al., 1959; Rubin, 1964).

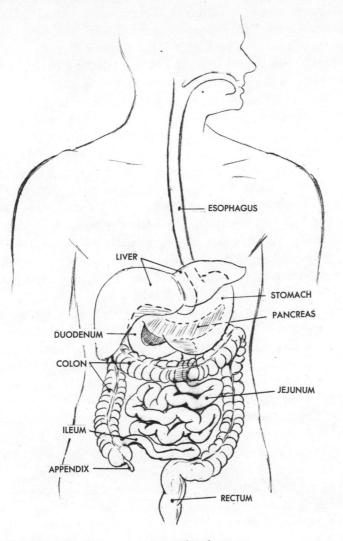

Figure 3.9. The digestive tract and associated organs.

The Gastrointestinal System

The gastrointestinal tract is a tube extending in coils throughout the length of the trunk and is divided into mouth and pharynx, esophagus, stomach, small intestine, and large intestine (see Figure 3-9). The stomach is the enlarged part of this otherwise narrow tube, and it varies in shape and position from individual to individual. The primary function of the stomach is to initiate digestion. In an adult, it can usually hold from 3 to

5 pints. Glandular digestive secretions, composed of water, mucin, salts, hydrochloric acid, and the enzymes—pepsin, rennin, and gastric lipase—come from the walls of the stomach.

The stomach wall is protected against the injurious effects of pepsin and hydrochloric acid by a supply of blood and mucus; but in certain situations, the mucous membrane is eroded and a sore, or ulcer, develops. Sometimes, if the ulcer increases in size, perforation of the stomach wall takes place. Investigators are not in complete agreement about the cause of ulcers. Some believe that excessive acidity produced in response to stress is the underlying cause, since persons having ulcers have an excessive secretion of gastric juices. At night especially, a much higher acidity is found in the person with ulcers than is found in a normal person. Excessive gastric secretion is associated with the body's response to stress, and it seems that ulcers are commonly contingent upon emotional upset. However, other investigators believe that hyperacidity and external stress factors are only part of the problem and that ulcers are often associated with accidents or irritation by particular foods.

Duodenal ulcers, usually found on the posterior part of the duodenum, occur more frequently than stomach ulcers. Individuals with ulcers will complain about abdominal pain and discomfort but are unable to cite a specific location of the pain. Adolescents who are found to have ulcers are believed by many physicians to have the difficulty in association with psychological problems.

Ulcerative colitis, although not a common disease, occurs more frequently in adolescence than at any other time during the developmental years. The incidence of this disorder is not easy to determine nor is its etiology. The ordinary problems of adolescent development apparently influence the course of the disease, but physicians believe that some predisposition, perhaps of a biochemical nature, causes certain individuals to be highly susceptible to stress and to respond to this stress in the form of either physical illness or psychological disturbance. Ulcerative colitis, which refers to ulcers in the intestine, usually begins with ulcers in the lower part of the intestinal tract; these lesions gradually spread, until most of the large bowel is involved. Anemia, a reduction of the red blood cells, which are the oxygen carriers in the body, often accompanies colitis. Symptoms of this condition include diarrhea, cramps, and fever, but sometimes the disease may be quite advanced, despite minimal symptoms (Kirsner et al., 1955; Texter, 1957).

Treatment of ulcerative colitis is difficult and prolonged, and the course of this disease is usually one of remission and exacerbation. Treatment must be individualized and in acute states involves the use of antibiotics and cortisone (Gallagher, 1960). The administration of cortisone is done with extreme care because of possible side effects. In severe cases of ulceration, surgery sometimes is undertaken (Sawyer et al., 1960).

Psychological factors as a cause of ulcerative colitis are given varying degrees of importance by different physicians. Psychological characteristics of adolescents with the disease consist of generalized resentment, withdrawal, passive-aggressive tendencies, refusal to participate in social activities, and refusal to go to school or to carry out ordinary life activities. In a study of children aged eleven to fourteen years, Alexander (1965) found a predominance of negative responses over positive responses when subjects were asked to describe feelings and social interactions of figures depicted on five stimulus cards. The positive and negative emotional reactions in the responses were counted. The study indicated that there were many more negative responses of a threatening, hostile, or depressing nature in the responses of the children with ulcerative colitis than in those of normal children. As an example of the serious effects of psychological stress in a case of ulcerative colitis, the life story of Anna is particularly pertinent.

> Anna's parents were highly educated, her father was a successful attorney and her mother an interior decorator. By the time Anna was twelve, the family had a large house and the advantages of wealth. When Anna was in junior high school, she became ill with "Asian flu" and a severe gastrointestinal upset. Although she recovered, Anna had frequent recurrences of diarrhea and was unable to continue her pattern of regular school attendance and achievement. Medical study showed that Anna had ulcers in her colon, indicating the threat of serious illness.

> In addition to medical treatment, Anna and her parents were studied psychologically, and two important factors were discovered in the pattern of family life. Although Anna had achieved quite well in elementary school, her ability was only average and her success in school was gained at the cost of great effort. Her parents, both gifted individuals, had excelled in their intellectual careers, and now they exerted subtle pressure on her to achieve as well as they had. As she entered junior high school, the work became increasingly difficult and Anna's anxiety increased. She could never quite meet her parents' expectations for achievement and she could never feel secure unless she worked much more than her classmates. In the face of greater competition in junior high school, she became resentful,

morose, and at times expressed her feelings in aggressive tantrums or by withdrawal to her room with complaints of illness.

In talking with Anna's parents, another factor in the pattern of family behavior was revealed. The individual careers and the demands of their occupations had gradually separated husband and wife, so that with the onset of Anna's illness each felt resentful toward the other. As Anna's parents drew apart, a closer relationship developed between Anna and her father. This emotional interchange between father and daughter alienated husband and wife even further. Anna's mother resented the father-and-daughter outings and the emotional liaison between them. As Anna's mother felt annoyance and resentment toward Anna, she also developed feelings of guilt and disappointment about herself. Perhaps she saw that her career had taken her away from her husband and that part of the situation resulted from her own choice of a life pattern. In any event, the family situation brought to all three people much anxiety, guilt, insecurity, and compulsive strivings for an elusive security. Caught up in these crosscurrents of emotional turmoil, Anna's disturbance increased and she became emotionally unstable, vacillating between outbursts of temper and withdrawal, negativism, and surrender to illness.

In addition to medical treatment, psychotherapy was undertaken with Anna, but her parents were willing to be only partially involved. While some progress was made and Anna was able to continue in school, although missing much of it, insufficient progress was made in changing the fundamental pattern of living of the family. The characteristic aspect of the disease continued —several months free of symptoms followed by periods when Anna would not be able to go to school or carry on normal activities. Sometimes it was necessary to return to the hospital for intensive medical treatment. The return of symptoms was a problem because it heightened the anxiety of the family members and made school more difficult for Anna when she returned. In addition, each recurrence of the symptoms frightened Anna about the eventual outcome of her disease. As a result of the care she received, Anna was at least able to continue her school work; although not overcoming the disease, Anna did not regress to a point where her life was immediately threatened.

The Respiratory System

The life processes of the body depend upon a constant supply of oxygen and the elimination of carbon dioxide (CO_2), the waste product of cell metabolism. Although the body is able to store certain necessary materials, such as carbohydrates and fats, it is unable to store oxygen. Nor can it tolerate for any length of time the unfavorable effects of carbon dioxide. Consequently, an exchange of gases between the body and the environment, called respiration, is necessary for life. The word *respiration* actually refers to three distinct processes: (1) the intake and expulsion of air, pulmonary ventilation; (2) gas exchange among the lungs, blood, and cells; and (3) utilization of oxygen by the cells (an essential part of the utilization of oxygen by the body is the transportation of oxygen to the cells by the blood).

Ordinarily, the lungs inflate and deflate about 20 times in each minute. This contraction and expansion is done primarily through the work of a muscle, the diaphragm, which forms the floor of the chest. (See Figure 3-10.) The diaphragm contracts and moves downward, enlarging the chest

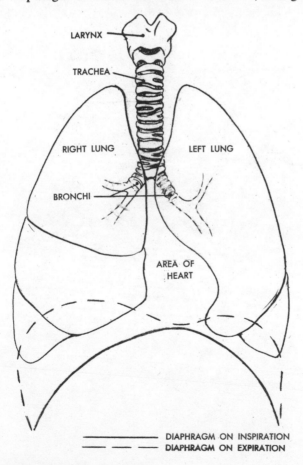

LARYNX

TRACHEA

RIGHT LUNG   LEFT LUNG

BRONCHI

AREA OF HEART

———————— DIAPHRAGM ON INSPIRATION
— — — — DIAPHRAGM ON EXPIRATION

Figure 3.10. The respiratory system.

cavity, while the ribs are moved upward and outward by the intercostal muscles (muscles between the ribs). As the entire chest expands, the lungs stretch and the air rushes in (Cook and Ferris, 1964). Air is taken in through the nose and passes through the corridors of the larynx, the trachea (or windpipe), and into the bronchial tubes of the lungs, the bronchi. These bronchial tubes branch into smaller ones called "bronchioles" and become smaller and smaller. Blood is circulated around the lungs in a vast network—perhaps as much as a thousand square feet—of small blood vessels (Miller and Goode, 1960). The blood at this point is at the depth of only one cell. This film of blood is separated by an extremely thin membrane from the air in the tiny air sacs (alveoli) in the lungs (see Figure 3–11). Carbon dioxide molecules move from red cells through the porous membrane into the air sac, while oxygen molecules cross from the air to the red blood cells. The hemoglobin of the red blood cells has a special ability to take on oxygen.

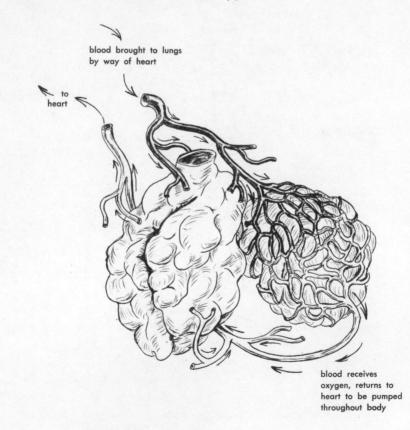

blood brought to lungs
by way of heart

to
heart

blood receives
oxygen, returns to
heart to be pumped
throughout body

Figure 3.11. Terminal sacculations in lung, where blood is oxygenated.

The lungs are quite exposed. They take in whatever is in the surrounding atmosphere—gases or particles that may be floating in the air. Despite their exposure, the lungs have a number of protective devices. Air much below body temperature can be inhaled because it is warmed in the nasal passages by the blood supply there, and very dry air can be breathed without difficulty because it is moistened in the mucous lining. To some extent particles and bacteria are in every breath that is taken, but the body filters out much of this matter with cilia (threadlike structures lining the passageway of the bronchial tubes). The cilia catch all types of particles and, by moving them outward, they push the matter into the naso-pharynx. Particles too large to be so moved are brought out by the reflexive responses of sneezing or coughing.

Respiration changes at adolescence. At adolescence, the respiratory volume increases in boys, but very little if at all in girls (Cook and Ferris, 1964). In both boys and girls, the percentage of oxygen decreases and that of carbon dioxide increases in expired air. During adolescence, boys enter upon strenuous physical activity or begin careers as athletes. In athletic activities, the respiratory rate is increased to at least 50 times each minute. In a track meet or a 100-yard dash, the body cannot supply sufficient oxygen in the brief time of the event and lactic acid accumulates as a waste product of muscle metabolism. At this point the body is hardly better off than if the athlete had held his breath during the entire dash. After the race, the athlete's body must resume the normal metabolic cycle. In longer races athletes are able to attain a "second wind." The breathing in a longer race becomes deep and rapid and the heart beats faster; the blood pressure also rises. These responses increase and facilitate the transfer of oxygen and carbon dioxide. The "second wind" consists of an adjustment by the body through its respiratory and circulatory activities, so that the actual quantity of oxygenated blood is larger.

The Cardiovascular System

Concern about the functioning of the heart in our society is prevalent, and physicians are frequently consulted about physical activities appropriate for adolescents in relation to their heart functioning and the possibility of abnormal heart conditions. The heart increases in diameter during the adolescent growth spurt, and probably the increase in size is in cell volume rather than in the number of cells. Boys' hearts increase in size over girls' and possibly the size increase is related to the more strenuous activity of boys (Tanner, 1962).

The heart is a muscle, but it differs somewhat from other body muscles, such as the striped muscles, which move the bones of the skeleton, or the short-fibered and smooth muscles of the digestive tract and blood vessels. The heart muscle is something of a combination of the striped and smooth muscles. It has the power and ability to contract rapidly, as do the skeletal muscles, and it also has the rhythmic capability of the smooth muscles.

A small area of the heart is developed into a particular kind of tissue in the right auricle. This area seems to be responsible for the rhythmic contraction, or heartbeat, by providing electrical stimulation. The stimulation moves to both sides so that there is synchronization of the entire organ.

The heart can be described as having four parts. The two upper chambers, or auricles, are the "receiving" chambers (see Figure 3–12). Blood

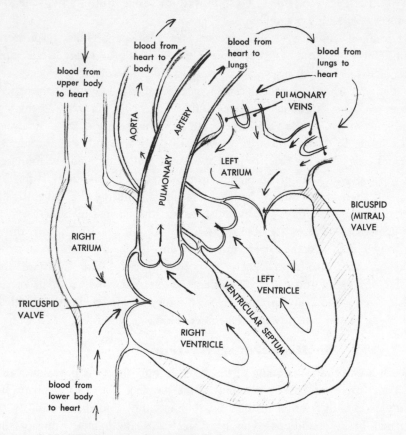

Figure 3.12. The heart, major vessels and valves.

can leave each auricle in only one direction—*downward* into the ventricle on its own side. The ventricles are the parts of the heart that provide the force to push the blood through the body. The auricles have thin walls and exert a mild contraction, only strong enough to push the blood into the ventricles. The ventricles send the blood out into the lungs and body. The ventricular systole, or contraction, takes much longer than the auricular one. Both ventricles have thick muscular walls, but the left ventricle, which must force the blood through the body's entire circulatory system, is more muscular than the right. The right ventricle pumps the blood to the lungs, and the blood entering it from the upper (right) auricle is termed "venous blood," since it has been returned to the heart by the veins of the body. Venous blood, which is somewhat blue in color, has given up much of its oxygen to cells throughout the body, and it is necessary for this blood now to take up new oxygen in the lungs. The right ventricle forces the venous blood into the pulmonary artery and sends it through the lungs' blood vessels. In the lungs the blood receives its full load of oxygen and becomes bright red. It is then returned to the left side of the heart and into the left auricle. From there it is forced into the left ventricle. When this ventricle contracts, the blood is sent under great pressure through the entire body and carries, in addition to oxygen, nutrients provided by the digestive system, chemical products of the endocrine glands, salts, water, body wastes, and other substances.

The blood can flow through the body only in one direction because of valves. These valves respond to changes of pressure of fluid on one side or the other and can open in only one direction. Two valves operate within the heart—one opening from auricle to ventricle on each side. The valve on the left side of the heart is the *mitral valve*. Its name comes from two cusps, or bits of tissue thought to resemble a bishop's miter. On the right side of the heart is the *tricuspid valve* with three cusps, or bits of tissue. Both valves function in the same way. When the pressure becomes greater in the auricle than in the ventricle, the valve opens downward and the blood passes into the ventricle. With each systole, or contraction, the blood can go only in one direction and that is outward from the heart into the arteries—to the pulmonary artery on the right, which leads to the lungs, and to the body's great artery—the aorta—on the left. Also, at these points, where the arteries are attached to the ventricles, valves exist so that the pressure after the valves close prevents a return flow during the diastole, or relaxed part of the heart's cycle (Tuttle and Schottelius, 1961).

During adolescence, concern sometimes develops about heart sounds. Sounds of the heart come from different locations and occur in different phases of the heart's cycle. Two major sounds are heard. The first sound comes with ventricular systole as the open mitral and tricuspid valves close with a snap. The second sound is derived from the vibration produced by the closing of the pulmonary and aortic valves.

Heart "murmurs" are common and usually normal, but the interpretation of these sounds and their diagnostic significance may be difficult. The most common murmur is the "functional murmur," which is heard in a heart without structural abnormality and is caused by turbulence in the flow of blood. Problems occasionally arise from abnormal structural changes in the heart, such as narrowing or leaking of the valves or a constriction of the main artery leading away from the heart.

In hypertension (abnormally high blood pressure) two main classifications are made: (1) variable hypertension due to stress or emotional upset, and (2) hypertension due to disease. Under stress, some individuals' blood pressure rises higher than the pressure in normal individuals under the same types of conditions. Ordinarily, when the stressful conditions are removed, the blood pressure then will return to normal. Hypertension may also be caused by a number of diseases, particularly kidney infections, anatomical abnormalities of the kidney, or constriction of the aorta (Chase, 1957).

Physical activity causes an increase in systolic blood pressure as well as heart rate. Three types of blood pressure related to physical activity are noted. In the first type, under exercise the blood pressure rises above the heart rate as measured in beats per minute; in the second type, the blood pressure remains about the same as the heart rate; and in the third type, the blood pressure remains at a much lower level than the heart rate. Some people in excellent physical condition, even under strenuous exercise, find that their systolic blood pressure will be greater than the heart rate.

The examination of adolescents to determine their capacity to withstand physical stress and to participate in athletics is a frequent task of physicians. If no abnormally high blood pressure is found and if the heart functioning after mild exercise, such as hopping on one foot 50 times, reveals no problems, further observations are not usually carried out. Adolescents contemplating severe physical strain and activity probably should have studies made under more severe physical stress, so that the conditions of study can be more closely related to the physical strain planned.

INTEGRATION OF PHYSIOLOGICAL PROCESSES AND ENVIRONMENTAL INFLUENCES

While this chapter has outlined the functions of the various organ systems and illustrated relationships to behavior, no one organ system functions in isolation to influence behavior. Thus, a totality and integration of physiological functioning of the whole organism exists. Complementary and even compensatory processes exist, so that a unity of function characterizes the ebb and flow of individual system activity. This flexible unity makes possible the variations in organismic behavior that are necessary for environmental interaction.

Biological Clocks and Behavior

Research investigations are being carried on to discover more information about the significance of a common characteristic found throughout nature —that of biological periodicities superimposed upon the functioning of the various organ systems and the activity of the whole individual. These cyclic changes have been variously termed: rhythms, cycles, or circadian systems. Cycles of organismic activity, although biologically based in origin, may be influenced by internal or external conditions. The change from sleep to wakefulness is an example of a cycle that is influenced by many factors (Kleitman, 1963). Increasing research suggests that infants begin to sleep through the night not only because of environmental factors associated with parental training and activity, but also because of maturational changes in the central nervous system. It is not possible to say at the present time whether or not man requires a long period of sleep once in every twenty-four hours or whether sleep actually could be broken into shorter periods.

The alternation between sleep and activity seems to be closely related to "biological clocks" in the cells and organs. Each body cell contains hundreds of chronons, or timers, which work with RNA to process proteins on a twenty-four-hour cycle. These controls within the cells and organs are related to environmental periodicity. For example, the earth's revolution around the sun brings changes in functional processes and the activity of most living things. Thus, much of the behavior of living organisms varies in concert with revolutions of the earth and the moon (Luce and Segal, 1966). Many examples of the relationship of man's activity and sleep to these two natural influences can be found. Even agricultural activity has been tied not only to the seasons, but also to the phases of the moon. Life in the sea is particularly related to phases of the moon and its pull on the oceans affecting biological clocks that place organisms in harmony with these natural episodic conditions.

In man there is a rhythm called a "circadian rhythm," [6] the origin of which seems to be internal. It is exemplified by variation in body temperature during a twenty-four-hour period. Individual differences in reference to body temperature and activity cycle have been established. Studies re-

[6] From the Latin *circa dies,* meaning "about a day."

ported by Kleitman (1963) show a rhythm between low points in the morning and late at night with the maximum being in the middle of the day. People feel and perform best when their temperature is highest during the cycle.

Many processes within the endocrine glands, the digestive organs, and the various parts of the nervous system are affected by cyclic changes. If activity or the wakefulness-sleep pattern is changed from the usual cycle characteristic of the individual, some of the body processes adjust to the change and others do not. Increased understanding of the importance of individual patterns in relation to health and well-being, particularly during the developmental years, is important. Evidence suggests that concern about the cycle's influence on learning programs is justified.

Differences in study patterns of college students are easily apparent. Some individuals study best late in the day or at night, while others find that a short period of work in the early morning hours is much more beneficial than several hours of work at night.

Motivation and Arousal

Motivation and arousal are probably related to internal states and are influenced by cyclic change. A motive, for example, makes the organism alert by affecting the various organ systems and musculature. This internal preparation for behavior is called "arousal" (Oswald et al., 1960). The preparation is believed to be brought about by the reticular activating system (RAS). It is important to see that overt behavior by an individual is triggered by an environmental stimulus, although an arousal state had preceded the activity. Response, however, to the stimulus may vary according to internal or cyclic states. Furthermore, certain types of deprivation of body needs will affect internal states. For example, sleep deprivation interferes with a state of arousal and slows down organismic processes, thus influencing overt behavior (Murray, 1965).

Interaction of influences between environmental stimuli and internal states thus constitute the complex nature of human behavior. If environmental conditions interfere with the readiness or appropriate internal cyclic conditions, an individual's efficiency in learning or in coping with his environment is reduced. On the other hand, when environmental conditions are in harmony with internal states, the individual's efficiency is at its maximum. One practical application of such a principle might be achieved in helping children to deal with complex learning tasks. Such tasks might be arranged so that the teaching would not have to overcome natural biological obstacles which frustrate both the child and the teacher.

A POINT OF VIEW

The physiological foundations of behavior sometimes are neglected in the study of such complex processes as learning or in the use of such a theoretical abstraction as motivation. For example, the significance of the proper functioning of the thyroid gland or of the pituitary may not be easily apparent in motivation to achieve. Nevertheless, even within small ranges of functional differences, there is likely to be important influence. Consequently, such knowledge of the functioning of the body is necessary if a beginning is to be made toward the understanding of human behavior.

As increased understanding of physiological processes is gained, however, it is likely that the interaction of cultural influences in such processes will be seen as having even more complexity and closer bonds than is now realized. Hence, a goal in the search of understanding should not be separation but the understanding of relationships.

REFERENCES

Alexander, T., 1965. "An Objective Study of Psychological Factors in Ulcerative Colitis in Children," *The Journal-Lancet,* **85**, 22–24.
Bell, G., J. Davidson, and H. Scarborough, 1965. *Textbook of Physiology and Biochemistry*. Baltimore: Williams & Wilkins.
Bluemstock, D. A., J. Mithoefer, and T. V. Santulli, 1957. "Acute Pancreatitis in Children," *Pediatrics,* **19**, 1002–1010.
Broverman, D. M., E. L. Klaiber, Y. Kobayashi, and W. Vogel, 1968. "Roles of Activation and Inhibition in Sex Differences in Cognitive Abilities," *Psychological Review,* **75**, 23–50.
Carlson, A. J., V. Johnson, and H. M. Cavert, 1961. *The Machinery of the Body*. Chicago: The University of Chicago Press.
Chase, P. P., 1957. *Your Wonderful Body*. Englewood Cliffs, N.J.: Prentice-Hall.
Cook, C. D., and Ferris, B. G., 1964. "Respiratory Physiology and Its Applications to Pulmonary Disease," in *Textbook of Pediatrics,* 8th ed., edited by W. E. Nelson, pp. 787–800. Philadelphia: Saunders.
D'Amour, F. E., 1961. *Basic Physiology*. Chicago: The University of Chicago Press.
Ford, F. R., 1960. *Diseases of the Nervous System,* 4th ed. Springfield, Ill.: Charles C Thomas.
Gallagher, J. R., 1960. *Medical Care of the Adolescent*. New York: Appleton-Century-Crofts.
Gardner, L. I., 1960. "Biochemical Events at Adolescence," Pediatric Clinics

of North America. *Symposium on Adolescence,* Vol. 7, No. 4, edited by L. T. Meiks and M. Green, pp. 15–31. Philadelphia: Saunders.

Grollman, S., 1964. *The Human Body.* New York: Macmillan.

Harris, G. W., and B. T. Donovan, 1961, "The Pituitary Glands or Hypophysis Cerebri," in *The Physiological Basis of Medical Practice,* edited by C. H. Best and N. B. Taylor, pp. 957–996. Baltimore, Md.: Williams & Wilkins.

Houssay, B. A., J. T. Lewis, O. Orias, E. Braun-Menendez, E. Hug, V. G. Foglia and L. F. Leloir, 1955. *Human Physiology,* translated by J. T. Lewis and O. T. Lewis. New York: McGraw-Hill.

Johnston, J. A., 1960. "Metabolic and Nutritional Considerations in Adolescence," Pediatric Clinics of North America. *Symposium on Adolescence,* Vol. 7, No. 4, edited by L. T. Meiks and M. Green, pp. 33–42. Philadelphia: Saunders.

Kahn, F., 1965. *The Human Body.* New York: Random House.

Kirsner, J. B., H. F. Raskin, and W. L. Palmer, 1955. "Ulcerative Colitis in Children," *American Medical Association Journal of Diseases of Children,* **90**, 141–152.

Kleitman, N., 1963. *Sleep and Wakefulness.* Chicago: The University of Chicago Press.

Lattimer, J. K., H. Seneca, H. H. Zinsser, and O. Troc, 1959. "Increasing Seriousness of Resistant Urinary Infections with Aerobacter Aerogenes," *Journal of the American Medical Association,* **170**, 938–941.

Luce, G. G., and J. Segal, 1966. *Sleep.* New York: Coward-McCann.

McArthur, J. W., 1960. "Pituitary Gonadotropins," in *Hormones in Human Plasma,* edited by H. N. Antoniades, pp. 191–199. Boston: Little, Brown.

McClintock, J. D., and F. X. Gassner, 1961. "Antithyroid Drugs in the Treatment of Hyperthyroidism," in *Advances in Thyroid Research,* edited by R. Pitt-Rivers, pp. 39–41. New York: Pergamon Press.

Menzer, D., 1953. "Importance of Psychologic Factor in Gynecology," *New England Journal of Medicine,* **249**, 519–522.

Migeon, C. J., 1960. "Androgens in Human Plasma," in *Hormones in Human Plasma,* edited by H. N. Antoniades, pp. 297–332. Boston: Little, Brown.

Miller, B. F., and R. Goode, 1960. *Man and His Body.* New York: Simon and Schuster.

Morgan, C. T., 1965. *Physiological Psychology.* New York: McGraw-Hill.

Murray, E. J., 1965. *Sleep, Dreams, and Arousal.* New York: Appleton-Century-Crofts.

Oswald, I., A. M. Taylor, and M. Treisman, 1960. "Cortical Function During Human Sleep," in *The Nature of Sleep,* edited by G. E. W. Wolstenholme and M. O'Connor, pp. 343–348. Boston: Little, Brown.

Penfield, W., and H. Jasper, 1954. *Epilepsy and the Functional Anatomy of the Human Brain.* Boston: Little, Brown.

Perinetti, H., M. Giner, A. Barbeito, R. J. Cangiani, I. M. Parish, E. O. Paturzo, and H. Martino, 1961. "The Use of Iodized Salt in a Region Suffering Goiter Due to the Lack of Iodine," in *Advances in Thyroid Research,* edited by R. Pitt-Rivers, pp. 283–288. New York: Pergamon Press.

Rubin, M. I., 1964. "Infections of the Urinary Tract," in *Textbook of Pediatrics,* 8th ed., edited by W. E. Nelson, pp. 1107–1113. Philadelphia: Saunders.

Sawyer, K. C., R. B. Sawyer, and R. E. McCurdy, 1960. "Surgical Treatment of Ulcerative Colitis in Children," *Journal of the American Medical Association,* **174,** 1574–1578.

Tanner, J. M., 1962. *Growth at Adolescence.* Oxford: Blackwell Scientific Publications.

Texter, E. C., 1957. "The Natural History of Ulcerative Colitis," *Journal of Chronic Diseases,* **5,** 347–369.

Turner, C. D., 1960. *General Endocrinology.* Philadelphia: Saunders.

Tuttle, W. W., and B. A. Schottelius, 1961. *Textbook of Physiology.* St. Louis: Mosby.

Winton, F. R., and L. E. Bayliss, 1962. *Human Physiology.* Boston: Little, Brown.

Woolley, D. W., 1967. "Involvement of the Hormone Serotonin in Emotion and Mind," in *Neurophysiology and Emotion,* edited by D. C. Glass, pp. 108–116. New York: The Rockefeller University Press.

[*four*]

Behavioral Development in Early Childhood

Early childhood usually refers to the period covering the ages from two to five. In this period there is great accomplishment in growth, development of many types of skills, and the acquisition of information. In this period a significant transition is made from the highly dependent, often reflexive, and minimally communicative behavior of infancy to the independently mobile, purposive, and conversational behavior of childhood. In the study of this transition it is necessary to consider certain foundations of behavior established at the beginning of life and during the period of infancy.

PERCEPTUAL-COGNITIVE DEVELOPMENT

At first, the responses of the infant are generalized, encompassing a totality of experience rather than a specific part. Thus, perceptual-cognitive development proceeds from generalized experience toward specific organization, which in turn is dependent upon similarities, differences, and continuity of stimulus characteristics. Eventually, this organization of perception leads to the development of capacity to see units and to complete incomplete units (Vinacke, 1951; Werner, 1948).

The Organizing and Conditioning of Percepts

As the child's experiences expand, percepts (names and meanings of stimuli in the environment) tend to be merged into wholes, then wholes into patterns, and, finally, patterns into concepts. Basic to this development are percepts of form, color, and space. Also basic to perceptual development is the development of sensitivities of the individual dependent upon the functioning of the sense organs and the acquisition of the capacity to respond to qualities of stimulation. This type of development is basically linked to thinking and learning. It is obvious that there is a similarity between the perceptual situation and the conditioning situation. For example, after only a few months, the infant learns to recognize his bottle and begins sucking movements even before the nipple reaches his mouth. His increased activity at the sight of the bottle shows he has learned to perceive it as a source of satisfaction. In this instance, association occurs between two essential stimuli—the bottle and the remembered sensation of its contents in his mouth; one set of stimuli becomes symbolic for the other. Hence, it can be seen that the basic mechanisms of behavior that operate in the development of conditioned responses in infancy also operate in the increasingly complex perceptual learning characteristic of the early-childhood period. These abilities lead to the development of tendencies to see units and to complete incomplete units.

The Importance of "Set"

It is also important to consider the "set," or expectancy, of the individual. For example, in the above illustration, the infant is *set* for the food (Solley and Murphy, 1960). Similarly, emotions and emotional states influence perception and contribute to the idiosyncratic character of perceptual experience. Thus, no two persons have the same perceptual experience because of the variation in their backgrounds and their emotions associated with previous experience.

That feelings of satisfaction and reward influence perceptual experience is demonstrated in the study by Tajfel and Winter (1963). They found that when four-year-old children were given a task in which they were to match the size of tokens before and after a reward, the children consistently overestimated the size of the tokens after reward. Apparently, the rewards made the tokens appear larger or perhaps of greater value.

Exploration and Learning

As learning proceeds, increased awareness of environmental experience brings further development in perceptual capacity, with the processes of learning and perception contributing to each other. Observation of infant behavior reveals that an infant explores certain objects visually and at the same time listens to sounds that have come to his attention. When he is given an object, such as a rattle or toy, he waves it about and listens to its noise; he puts it in his mouth, tasting it and feeling it; he takes it out and waves it about for further noise; then he returns it to his mouth for further exploration. Such elementary learning in reference to the qualities of objects gradually leads in the second or third years to formation of perceptual units of form, size, and color. Thus, as objects begin to have meaning, the foundation is laid for the child's understanding about his relationships to these objects and their use.

Exploration and learning include concepts of *perceptual curiosity* and *arousal* (Berlyne, 1960; Berlyne and Frommer, 1966). According to Berlyne, when a stimulus is associated with the occurrence of a certain response, the response can be said to be "aroused." The term *perceptual curiosity* is used in connection with states of "high arousal" or "epistemic curiosity" induced by "conceptual conflict." Conceptual conflict occurs when the stimulus situation contains elements of novelty, complexity, and surprise, and thereby, conflict with earlier concepts. The child is able to reduce such arousal states by engaging in exploratory behavior.

Concepts of Reality

From exploration and utilization of sensory experience, the child develops concepts about reality. Often these beginning concepts are inaccurate. In early experience, according to Piaget, thought processes are limited by the words and names that the child knows. As the child's experience expands, he becomes less centered in his own perception of the world and comes to see reality not simply by information that is immediately given, but also by information from meanings and learnings of the past (Piaget 1930a; 1930b).

Freud saw the *ego* developing in the child because the child's needs require him to deal with reality, or the objective world. The ego must help the individual distinguish between his subjective reality and the reality of the environment. The ego develops a plan for the satisfaction of need and proceeds to test this plan. And, according to Freud, the ego comes to control all of the cognitive and intellectual functions in order to help the individual to determine reality.

For the child in early life, experience is still lacking, so that his ability to evaluate information given to him by peers is limited. It is important, however, for a child during the preschool years to have an opportunity to learn to deal with reality principles. For example, Donald, aged five, was walking one day with his father in his backyard, which bordered on an expanse of dense woods. As they walked in the yard, the following conversation took place.

> *Donald:* Daddy, there is a wolf in those woods down there.
> *Father:* A wolf lives in those woods.
> *Donald:* Yes, there is a wolf down there because Glen told me there was.
> *Father:* I don't think that a wolf lives in there. There are very few wolves left in the whole country.
> *Donald:* There *is* a wolf in there! Glen told me there is and I *know* there is one there.
> *Father:* Since Glen told you that there is a wolf in there, you *think* there is.
> *Donald:* Yes, *there is!*

> Donald and his father continued their walk in the yard and after some time had passed, Donald again brought up the subject of the wolf: "Daddy, you know, I don't really think there is a wolf in those woods. I think that Glen just told me that."

Although Donald's father did not agree with him about the wolf, he did not insist that Donald accept his point of view. He did provide contrary evidence as well as a reflection of Donald's assertions so that Donald could deal with the information himself. By allowing Donald to weigh the evidence as to the likelihood that a wolf lived in the woods, his father helped Donald to make his own determination of reality. Had the father insisted on his point of view, he would have failed to provide Donald with an opportunity to examine the evidence and relate it to his father's information.

A quantitative aspect is present in the child's relationship to reality, since his understanding of the world about him is greatly limited by the absence of much factual knowledge available to the adult. This limited knowledge and experience causes the child to be troubled because of the necessity for understanding himself and for relating himself to the environment (Wolff, 1946). Some of the child's difficulty with reality also exists because he gives all experiences relatively the same weight—fairy tales or fictional experiences on television cannot be distinguished from actual experiences. Wolff holds that the child's entire perceptual experience is different from the adult's. As an example, Wolff points to the child's small size, which necessitates the perception of objects from the bottom up. In addition, the child perceives his own ability to control objects as being limited and confusing. The child knows he can manipulate many objects, but distinguishing between those over which he has power and those over which he does not, is difficult.

Lack of information is a contributing factor in the development of concepts of the realities of sexuality and birth. Hartup and Zook (1960) found that children as young as three years old are aware of sex difference in interest and sex appropriateness of objects. Studying four- and five-year-olds, Kreitler and Kreitler (1966) obtained data about many misconceptions that children have. In the area of sex concepts, these investigators take issue with certain aspects of the theories of both Freud and Piaget. They maintain that their study refutes two of Freud's theoretical concepts—the "universality of the penis" and "birth through the anus," as well as Piaget's belief that children consider the baby to have existed fully alive before it comes into relation to its parents (the "preartificialist" concept). Perhaps modern children are better informed or have fewer sexual taboos than those of Freud's day, for Kreitler and Kreitler found that the majority of the children in their study were able to give accurate information about the sexual organs of the other sex. They found that the boys had more exact information about the structure of the sex organs of girls than girls had about sex organs of boys. Girls, however, in a study by Goodenough (1957), made fewer errors than boys in distinguishing between pictures of nude adult males and females.

DEVELOPMENTAL ACCOMPLISHMENTS

The child's progress in mastering control of his body and in developing skills leading to his own independence has been of great interest to psychologists. Some workers have devised scales to measure behavioral development or to objectify judgments about the attainment of developmental accomplishment (Doll, 1953; Gesell and Amatruda, 1947). Many items on these scales must, of necessity, concern motor behavior. Because of their dependence on motor-behavior tasks, such scales are used cautiously by clinicians in the study of an individual child, since individual differences in child behavior and motor development are to be expected. Despite the limitations of these scales, however, attainment of over-all normative data is possible and general behavioral expectations can be obtained. Meeting certain expectations provides some basis for prediction that a child will continue to develop within the ranges established for his age. Rosenblith (1966) believes that it is possible to make controlled observations and measures of newborn behavior that will adequately predict later development. She believes that such measures will help to identify children who will have difficulty in the future.

Body Movement and Control

Some body movement and control are present at birth, but adequate control awaits maturation. At birth, an infant is unable to turn his body; yet by the time he is two months old, he can turn from side to side. Progressively, the infant gains more control over his body until he can turn over completely at about six months of age. By the time he reaches the age of nine or ten months, the infant usually can sit unsupported. Between seven and nine months he begins to crawl, and by about twelve months he can stand without support. As maturation progresses, more well-coordinated movements are possible. A one-year-old child has learned to pull himself up to a standing position, perhaps to walk with support, or he may even have learned to walk alone. Usually some attempt at walking has been made in the first quarter of the second year.

Learning Related to Physical Needs and Development

By the latter part of their first year, children usually have been introduced to solid foods, indoor and outdoor clothing, cleanliness, and feeding routines. They have had some toilet training, have established definite patterns for food intake and for sleep, have learned to recognize family members, and have developed emotional response patterns accompanying gratification or the lack of gratification of physical needs. By this time, almost all children have been given some training in behavior concerning objects; for example, the use of utensils in relation to the correct management of food.

By the age of fifteen months, a child usually has learned to use a spoon in conjunction with a dish and has become proficient in removing socks, shoes, caps, and mittens. Before his second birthday, the child has begun to dress himself. At two years, neurological maturation and musculature development has increased to the point that children of this age like to run, jump, and climb.

The Acquisition of Skills

By 3½ years of age, a child has acquired a large number of new skills. If he goes to nursery school, he has learned to use scissors; to work with crayons, pencils, and paint; to draw a man; and perhaps to print or write.

By four, the child has learned to wark downstairs without help, to skip, to march, and to enjoy rhythmic activities. He has learned to find pleasure in group activites and in those involving fantasy. He has made a beginning toward responsible behavior by carrying out assigned tasks and has made some progress in care of his possessions. He also has learned to enjoy caring for pets, especially if the care is in association with his parents or older siblings.

By the latter part of the early-child period, the child has learned to use one side of his body more than the other. Some specialists believe that specific encouragement to use the right hand more than the left should be carried on in this period. Children of this age also take great delight in climbing and enjoy going up and down ladders. Some go on to learn other more advanced motor skills, such as roller skating, ice skating, swimming, and the like.

Emulation of adult roles is common among five-year-olds, who enjoy pretending in play to be cowboys, spacemen, or other heroes. Their understanding of reality is usually uninhibited—they may draw a house only to quickly change it into an airplane. This is an age of vigorous physical activity, such as performing tricks on the climbing frame, running up and down stairs, and riding with great speed on tricycles. In contrast, however, they have learned to sit quietly for periods of time in imaginative play with building blocks, dolls, trucks, and small toys.

In summary, in five years most children have matured enough physically to use their large muscles in vigorous play and their finer muscles in the activities of drawing, writing, and skills involving finger dexterity. They have matured enough emotionally and socially to engage in group play, to comply with parental expectations as to time and place of play, to avoid hazards, and to attend school.

THE ONTOGENESIS OF EMOTIONS

The significance of emotional experience for behavioral development is believed to be of much consequence, although definitive research studies to support such a view are few. Consideration of theoretical approaches now available and knowledge of major research trends in the study of emotions are of importance to those who seek an understanding of influential factors in human development and behavior.

Theoretical Approaches to the Understanding of Emotional Development

A number of theoretical approaches are currently in favor in reference to emotions. Theoretical and experimental approaches to emotions are hampered to some extent, however, in much the same way that the study of personality or intelligence is hampered—a precise definition is lacking. Peters (1963) asserts that five sources of confusion exist in reference to emotions. One source of confusion exists because of meaning at three levels: (1) the term *emotion* may refer to the "felt" emotion, which is "private" to the individual; (2) *emotion* may refer to visceral response, the action of smooth muscles or the action of the autonomic nervous system; and (3) *emotion* may refer to the action of the skeletal muscles as those used in "fighting." Other sources of confusion relate to definitions which ignore "cognitive-perceptual" meanings; to terms that involve a multiplicity of meanings to be applied to emotions; to the effort to tie emotions to the term *instinct,* and to the "reification" concepts with which some investigators seek to make "nature" correspond to a word used for emotion. But the term *emotion* refers to a whole system of behavior and, thus, unity in meaning is yet to be achieved.

In considering the basic emotions, a list is also difficult to obtain. Some psychologists believe it is only appropriate to speak of two types of emotion in infants: the pleasant, or integrative, type and the unpleasant, or disintegrative, type. Hebb (1949) described the pleasant and integrative sensations as being a tendency to augment or supplement the original stimulation and the unpleasant emotions as being a tendency to decrease the stimulation. Plutchik (1962), on the other hand, believes that eight primary emotions exist: fear, anger, disgust, sorrow, joy, acceptance, startle, and expectation. He sees these emotions as identified with certain prototypes of behavior; for example, the association of anger with destructive behavior. He believes also that the emotions have an "intensive" dimension, as in annoyance and rage, which are both associated with a destructive pattern.

Plutchik maintains that learning influences emotion to only a limited extent and that the prototype patterns of behavior associated with the primary emotions are not learned. He does believe, however, that learning may modify "external expressive signs of emotions" and may determine which emotion will be most predominantly in evidence.

Wenger et al. (1956) also have taken the stand that eight primary emotions are to be found. They see the following correlates between infantile patterns and the emotions of adults: startle/surprise; struggle/anger; tonic quiescence-tumescence/initial sexual excitement; exaggerated flexion/pain; general activity/excitement; poststimulation quiescence/relief; spitting-mouth aversion/distaste; and, exhaustion/grief. Tomkins (1962) holds that there are six "innate affective responses" or desires: to remain alive, to have sexual experience, to experience novelty, to communicate, to be in contact with others, and to resist shame.

Because adults tend to label infant emotions according to visible or known stimuli, basic or primary emotions are difficult to determine with certainty. The response of crying, for example, occurs when an infant is exposed to stimuli with varying characteristics: variability of the origin of noxiousness (i.e., internal or external); degree of noxiousness (i.e., from simple restriction of arms or legs to actual pain); and duration of noxiousness (i.e., length of time the stimulus persists). According to Young (1967), the solution for the problem of the determination of primary emotions may come by describing affective processes in only physiological terms. Young takes this point of view because present research trends point to the bodily nature of emotions and even a locus for them.

Experimentation in Reference to Emotional Behavior

It is important to relate theoretical approaches to investigations of brain function and morphology. Nerve impulses from receptors must pass through the thalamus before they reach the upper parts of the brain. The hypothalamus consists of a group of nerve centers with which there are interconnections with the reticular formation and the septum (see Chapter 3). It has been found that the hypothalamus can be experimentally damaged in animals, thus causing a loss of emotional response. One theoretical explanation is that when stimuli cause emotions, the hypothalamus relays impulses to the cerebral cortex and thus feelings are aroused. At the same time, the hypothalamus sends impulses to the viscera and skeletal muscles for "actions" of emotion.

Support for giving the hypothalamus a prominent place in emotions is obtained by electrical-stimulation studies of the brain. Some investigators, for example, Delgado et al. (1956), have shown that stimulation of a specific part of the hypothalamus of monkeys brings about "avoidance learning," suggesting the existence of a "pain center." It has been found also that stimulation of the septal region adjacent to the hypothalamus will produce responses in rats that suggest the presence of a "pleasure center" (Olds and Milner, 1954). Gellhorn (1957) found that electrical stimulation of a part of the hypothalamus will bring an aggressive reaction of biting in cats. It is now known that the cerebral cortex is also greatly significant in emotional behavior, particularly in the persistence of emotions. For example, behavior resulting from a fear-producing stimulus may be quite complex, thereby indicating behavior based upon cortical activity.

Such experimentation indicates research trends that provide widening bases for the understanding of emotions and clarification about locations within the brain. Much of the information currently available, however, comes from animals. Consequently, much more work is yet to be done before the understanding of emotional experience in man is complete.

Types of Emotional Behavior

Differentiation of emotional behavior apparently becomes less difficult as the child moves into the latter part of the early-childhood period. For example, if a five-year-old child strikes, kicks, and pounds with his fists, observers will usually agree on the label of "anger." Emotions are labeled as "pleasant" when they are observed in interpersonal experiences in which an individual receives affection, comfort, and food.

That emotions influence choosing behavior in young children is demonstrated in the "color-mood" association. Lawler and Lawler (1965) found that children after hearing a "happy" story tended to choose yellow in preference to brown and after hearing a "sad" story tended to choose brown in preference to yellow.

Less research and attention have been given to the positive emotional experiences of children than the negative ones. This lack is possibly explained on the basis that the pleasant emotions provide no problems for parents and ordinarily no concern is given to their presence. On the other hand, the negative emotions affect parents and siblings adversely, and parents thus seek understanding of those characteristics that interfere with the training of their children.

Affection is difficult to define or measure scientifically. Some behavioral scientists hold that the need for affection is an innate characteristic of the human organism and that infants will not thrive—indeed, may even die—if it is not provided (Rheingold, 1956; Ribble, 1965; and Spitz, 1949). Available evidence seems to indicate that most children thrive much better when they have an affectionate relationship with their parents. Certainly, affectionate behavior observed later in childhood is conditioned by previous experiences with parents (Banham, 1950). The child's behavior becomes increasingly generalized, and the affectionate behavior learned from parents is shown in relationship to siblings and peers. Consequently, if affection is received from parents, the child too will be affectionate. Parents who maintain that their child has never been affectionate very likely have had some difficulty themselves in expressing affection.

The quality of the maternal relationship is more important than the quantity of affection in establishing "basic trust," according to Erikson (1950). Trust comes about through the "sensitive care" of the child and the "personal trustworthiness" of the parent. These factors in maternal behavior lead to "identity formation," which contributes to a sense of well-being in the child as well as to his freedom to be what he wants to be. Taking a somewhat similar view, Spitz (1949) has emphasized the importance of an affectional relationship with a maternal figure in the attainment of normal developmental accomplishments. Spitz has observed that the smiling response in recognition of a smiling familiar face comes earlier than other forms of recognition. It was found that children in an orphanage, where affectional relationships are not established with one person, learn to speak, walk, and feed themselves at later dates than children who have affectional relationships.

Anger and aggression are expressed in childhood in diverse and subtle patterns of behavior that sometimes continue into adulthood. Aggressive behavior may actually interfere, however, with goal attainment and may bring disintegrative results. Although an aggressive individual becomes aware of the results of his behavior, he often continues to engage in it. In anger or aggressive behavior, a child frequently is not aware of the possible deleterious effects of his behavior on others and often deliberately sets out to injure or deprive his peers. As Sears and his coinvestigators (1953) point out, the manner of expressing anger and aggression is greatly influenced by parents and teachers. Lövaas (1961) found that after reinforcement of aggressive verbal behavior, children tended to engage more in aggressive nonverbal behavior. Inselberg (1958) found that as children move toward the latter part of the early-childhood period, they tend to display emotional behavior more often with physical activity than with vocal activity. That there is a sex difference in the expression of aggression is supported by a study by McCandless et al. (1961), in which teacher judgments and free-play observations indicated that girls seemed to begin fewer conflicts in play in nursery school than boys, which suggests that expectations in training of girls may differ from that of boys.

Generally, as children increase in age, more overt physical aggression is observed. Some children have been trained to direct their aggression toward objects, and in fantasy the child uses objects as an outlet for hostile feelings. Such children scold or kick at an inanimate object nearby whenever another child has frustrated or hurt them. However, this type of expression is only a dubious and temporary solution, for in later childhood or adolescence such behavior will be disapproved. Furthermore, this type of outlet for hostility does not lay a foundation for a realistic means of dealing with negative feelings.

Aggression of children has been investigated by play with dolls (Ammons and Ammons, 1949; Despert, 1940; Hollenberg and Sperry, 1951; Levin and Sears, 1956; Levy, 1943; Muste and Sharpe, 1947; and Pintler et al., 1946). These investigators base their studies on the belief that a child's aggression toward a doll compares with his aggression in the real world. Some experimental support for this contention has been provided by Bach (1945); Sears (1951); and Sears et al. (1946), who found in their studies of sex differences that boys display a greater degree of fantasy aggression than girls and this finding is in accord with observations made of other behavior. Cohn (1962), in a review of studies employing doll-play aggression, concludes that doll play allows children to express aggression with less inhibition and that it is a valuable, if somewhat unrefined, research technique.

The idea that there is a carry-over of emotional behavior from early childhood to later years is shown by the data of Bronson (1966), obtained from a longitudinal study. She discovered that for boys, behavior problems, particularly in the first twenty-one months, are predictive of later emotional expressiveness. Her data indicated that an "expressive-outgoing boy" had been an infant who easily expressed his desires, while the "reserved-withdrawn boy" had been more passive as an infant. With girls, too, problem behavior in the first twenty-one months correlated with expressive-outgoing behavior in adolescence.

The question can be asked: Is aggression an inevitable consequence of feelings of anger? Socialization endeavors to channel emotions of various types into socially approved behavior. Accordingly, behavior associated with anger may be directed toward problem solving. Successfully coping with the stimulus and problem may result in behavior that does not involve overt aggression, even though the behavior began with feelings of anger.

In infancy, emotional expressions of fear are whimpering, crying, and perhaps holding the breath. By the end of the first year, a child becomes more attentive to stimuli that he deems benign or frightening. After motor development has taken place and the child is able to walk or run, avoidance and retreat become possible. As the child grows older and is less protected from falls, punishment, and hurts from accidents or other children, fear responses increase and the susceptibility to fear is enhanced.

In the second year of life, sensitivity to stimuli associated with fear, pain, and unpleasantness increases. Later, in the third and fourth year of life, as a result of emotional insecurity and traumatic experiences, some children develop a pervasive anxiety to such extent that learning and responsiveness are affected. In such instances, new experiences hold so much threat that the child tries to avoid them. Lacking the emotional support of close relationships with parents, some children withdraw, thereby laying a foundation for serious disorder in later life. In association with such conditions, an infant or young child sometimes develops a condition with characteristics of depression and shows little interest in events or changes in stimuli.

Fear and anxiety, however, do have some value, since these emotions may contribute to survival. A child who does not learn to be cautious about hazards or to fear danger is considered to have a disorder or to be incapable of coping with his environment. Therefore, the goal of parents in child training should not be to teach children to refrain from all fear responses because, in fact, some are necessary. Thus, some fear responses are appropriate and are part of a child's training to survive.

THE DEVELOPMENT OF LANGUAGE

As the child matures and acquires new learning, activity increases in complexity. This complexity makes possible a great deal of variability of response, and thus activity is no longer based primarily on physiological processes internally initiated but is increasingly influenced by external stimuli and events. In the early-childhood period, the incredibly complex activity of language is begun. Much of the future learning of the child is then related to language. Although a definition of language may well include all communication, sufficient information about nonverbal communication is presently unavailable. Therefore, discussion here is directed toward speech sounds, vocabulary, and language complexity. Language development occurs in four psychological stages, according to Beasley (1964): (1) a beginning stage consisting of purposeless oral sounds; (2) a second stage consisting of sounds having private meaning to the child, which primarily consist of "echo-reaction" to the mother's sounds; (3) a third stage which is reached when the child uses sounds to interest or control others; and (4) a final stage when language emerges as social behavior.

With the attainment of language as social activity, the child is able to express thoughts and feelings and can relate his behavior to environmental events and social interchange.

Vocalizing behavior, which may accompany infants' perception of the bottle, seems to be influenced by social conditions, as illustrated by the study of Weisberg (1963). This investigator in a study of three-month-old infants in an orphanage found that vocalization could be operantly conditioned by social actions, such as touching an infant's chin, smiling at him, or talking to him. Infants having this type of conditioning vocalized more than infants who had less social interaction.

The Mechanisms of Speech

Language begins in infancy with the early reflexive sounds associated with breathing, swallowing, and hiccoughing. In a strict sense, there is preverbal "language," as that which occurs when the mother shows the infant his bottle and he responds with sounds and body movements showing his anticipation of pleasure. Oral activity of sucking, biting, and chewing are precursors of the muscle activity necessary in language.

McCarthy (1952) emphasizes that the production of sounds parallels physical maturation. Speech sounds are related to the shape of the oral cavity—the front vowels emanate from the open area, but as the tongue matures the back vowels are made. The use of the tongue in gross movements for making vowels precedes the finer movements for making consonants. Dentition makes possible the formation of more words. Sitting erect and walking enlarges the thoracic capacity for more breath control in forming nasal sounds.

As language develops in accordance with over-all growth, an orderliness in the vowel and consonant usage is observed (Winitz and Irwin, 1958). Templin (1957) found that by four years of age, children have mastered initial and medial consonant sounds, but mastery of final consonant sounds has not been attained. At this age, most of the sentences used are functionally complete, although incomplete structurally.

Speech development may be measured by the use of phoneme types. (A phoneme is a minimal unit of sound without meaning.) The average infant has the ability to produce a number of these elementary sounds at a very early age. Most speech experts believe that new sounds are not learned directly, but rather result from vocal experimentation and general maturation of the child, with speech being achieved through the imitation of combinations of sounds. Because of the general vocalization by the infant, it is difficult to determine when the first word is said. Probably speech begins at around the age of eleven months or one year, although for some children it may be several months earlier. A child is able to learn a set of distinguishing phonemes from a small speech sample. This learning usually takes place in the very early years of life and aids a child in distinguishing between similar and dissimilar things and events (Berko and Brown, 1960; Brown and Hildum, 1956; Miller and Nicely, 1955).

A morpheme is a minimal unit of meaning in a language. The use of *un,* as in un*happy* or un*kind,* implying a negative element in both instances, provides an example of a morpheme. Another example of a morpheme is that of the final -*s* at the end of a word in conveying a common meaning In a list of words such as *dogs, cats, birds,* and *rabbits,* the final -*s* denotes plurality. Gradually, the child learns such units of language as he matures.

Language Forms

As early as two years of age, a child can usually use words in combination. At this time, he may even use short sentences. Sentences become common by the middle of the early-childhood period, although they usually lack certain language components. Sentences contain many nouns but few verbs, prepositions, and conjunctions. At about 2½ to 3 years, complete sentences consisting of as many as six or eight words are used, and the sentences include all the different parts of speech. But, as Templin (1957) indicates, at three years of age, the child's accuracy of articulation of speech sounds is a little more than half that of the eight-year-old.

By the close of the early-childhood period, a child can use most of the forms of sentence structure and all of the parts of speech, with language being advanced to the point that the child now greatly enjoys verbal communication and stories. Not only is there now understanding of the meaning of many more words, but also much more use is made of a wide variety of words. Sentences are complex in play and in interchange with others. Five-year-old children tell simple stories and can describe events in which they took part outside of the family experiences. Social learning is facilitated by the developing capacity for language, so that with their new knowledge it is possible for them to tell stories, to explain actions, and to relate experiences to adults.

Grammatical errors by children are quite common and many times are quaint and enjoyable. Although imperfections may persist and some authorities emphasize the necessity for correction, too much attention to the errors may bring about anxiety, causing speech disorders. In time.

corrections will be made by the child himself as he hears the proper language forms about him.

Speech Disorders

Because of the complexity of speech accomplishment, speech difficulties often occur in early childhood. Of all the speech difficulties encountered, stuttering perhaps is the most common. This disorder is characterized by involuntary repetition of sounds, syllables, or words. The etiology of the problem apparently lies in anxiety or emotional disturbance. Stuttering often begins at an early age, perhaps between two and four. During this period, parents demand or expect the development of other skills and if the child is unable to meet these demands, his consequent anxiety may cause a speech disorder. Where no abnormalities of an anatomical nature exist that would produce a speech disorder, it is probable that the problem arises from the parent-child relationship.

McCarthy (1953) has found that speech disorders are more frequent and more severe in boys. She relates this sex difference to the fact that language development usually begins in girls a little earlier than in boys and subsequent environmental influences, particularly in parental relationships, are more likely to cause disorders in boys. Girls have more opportunity to emulate their mother's behavior than boys to emulate their father's. Also, the father's voice is louder and deeper than any sounds that a small boy can produce. For these reasons, boys are approximately six months later in linguistic development than girls. They are slower also in beginning to read.

Sampson (1956, 1959) in the study of British children did not find evidence of a sex difference in beginning language. In a follow-up study, however, of the children at five years of age, some evidence of sex differences was found in that the linguistic fluency of girls exceeded that of boys.

Language, Learning, and Thought

Language facility depends not only upon maturation, but also upon the kinds of experiences that children have in the family. Rheingold et al. (1959) suggest that the vocalizing of infants and their social responsiveness is directly related to the responsiveness of adults to them. Irwin (1960) believes that during the second year of life, the infant's verbal experience (for example, when his parents read to him) considerably affects his rate of language growth. Such experience contributes to social-class differences and is a factor in the more rapid word acquisition of children in the middle class. As a child matures, he is called upon to solve problems of increasing difficulty; he discovers that language is basic to the solution of many problems, and thus, the rewards of language facility are increasingly apparent to him. He learns that language is necessary for the understanding of causality, categorization, and social effectiveness and that verbal exchange can be a source of pleasure in itself in activities with parents and peers.

Language facility is essential for reasoning processes. Piaget (1959), in his studies of the relationship of language to thought, found that in early verbalization the child tends to use language as a personal activity and for his own pleasure, but as he grows older he turns toward speech of a social nature and becomes aware of the response of the hearer and tries to influence him in verbal exchanges. Accordingly, Piaget described the child's early speech as repetitive and self-directed. As the socialization process continues, thoughts are exchanged with others and social learning progresses rapidly. The young child may use critical remarks, try to influence others by demands or threats, ask questions, or offer answers himself. Some observers differ with Piaget as to the balance between a young child's language directed toward himself and that directed outward; for example, the studies of McCarthy (1954) over the years led her to see the child as directing much of his speech outward.

Bernstein (1961) asserts that through language the diverse influences of the culture are reinforced: "Language, spoken language, powerfully conditions what is learned and how it is learned, and so influences future learning." He emphasizes that children in the middle socioeconomic class learn a "formal" language in which the language structure is difficult to predict for any one individual. This type of language allows different possibilities of sentence organization to clarify meaning or make meaning explicit. Middle-class children also learn a "public" language in which individual choice and selection is considerably limited. Because children in the lower socioeconomic class do not learn a formal language, they are limited in the opportunity to learn "extent and type" of object relationships.

In relating language experience and cognitive development to social class and training methods, Hess and Shipman (1965) found that cultural deprivation brings about a "lack of meaning" in reference to experience. Behavior in new situations is mediated and controlled more by rules than by elements of the situation, and culturally deprived children receive less help than middle-class children in learning the meaning of experience. This lack of training, according to these investigators, causes the culturally deprived child to be controlled but not reflective—the consequences of his behavior are considered in terms of immediate results rather than in long-term goals. Thus, limitation of verbal experience is a part of the total deprivation of children in adverse social circumstances and poverty.

THE ONTOGENESIS OF SOCIAL BEHAVIOR

Part of the stimulus field of experience of the infant is represented by those who care for him and contribute to his physical well-being. Usually, it is the mother who provides repetitive stimuli to which the child becomes conditioned; but it is difficult to determine initial response patterns of infants to stimuli and to describe them as the beginnings of social behavior. In a way, the response described earlier as a "quiescent" reaction after feeding can be termed a social response to the person providing satisfaction.

The term *social behavior* refers to patterns of response taking place in human interaction. Gradually, as the infant interacts with persons around him, he develops a pattern of response that can be defined as social behavior. Children, of course, often behave toward animals and inanimate objects as if they had human qualities.

Parent-Child Interaction as the Foundation of Social Behavior

Infants between two and three months of age will react to persons with a smiling response. Around the age of four months, an infant begins to discriminate between persons, and when he recognizes his mother he will respond with general body activity. At five or six months of age, a child often withdraws from strangers.

Sears (1951) explained social interaction as a dyadic sequence. A dyadic situation is one in which the behavior of each person is important to the goal-seeking behavior of the other. For example, the mother obtains satisfaction from the child's expressions of comfort, while the nurturant behavior of the mother satisfies the child. This important interaction between parent and child has been emphasized through studies of infants who have been deprived of their mothers. Schaffer (1966) has suggested that maternal or social deprivation has the least unfavorable effect on active infants and the most detrimental effect on passive, less-active infants. He concluded that reactions to deprivation are a function of organismic characteristics and are less affected by age or length of time of deprivation. The explanation that he advances for this difference is that the more-active infants encounter more environmental stimuli. Physiological functioning and general responsiveness are enhanced by activity, so that even more activity is engendered.

While the early interaction between the infant and the mother is difficult to describe and approach scientifically, it is nevertheless the foundation of later social response. The mother and her behavior represent symbols of satisfaction, and the infant's responses are reinforced time after time throughout the days of his early life. An infant learns quickly that human beings represent the fulfillment of his needs and learns to associate comfort with stimuli emanating from the mother's behavior. Thus, the early conditioning occurring in parent-child interaction has a profound influence on the developing and malleable response capacities of the infant and young child. In fact, it may be wondered how much of the misery of human kind with its fear and hostility stems from unfortunate experience in infancy and early childhood, when the organism is particularly susceptible to neglect, rejection, and harsh training methods.

Peer Associations

Transition from individual to cooperative play is gradual. By the time a child is one year old, he begins to show preferences for people and usually by this time has had opportunity to interact with persons other than his parents and siblings. The group play of two-year-old children is largely individual, although each child is often engaged in the same type of activity as the other children. For example, at this age children enjoy individually digging in sand and filling sand buckets, but often in this kind of play there is imitation of the behavior of nearby peers. Between three and five years of age, children may engage in cooperative activity, such as playing store or in building projects. In such activity, members in the project may come or go from time to time; consequently, the activity cannot be said to show well-defined and stable organization. In fact, organized group activity takes place only minimally in the early-childhood period. As children move through the early-childhood period, they develop friendships and preferences for certain companions, tend to engage in more cooperative activities, and find less satisfaction in individual play or the mere observation of others at play.

One of the concerns that adults have about peer associations in early childhood is aggressive behavior. The experiences and training in reference to aggressive behavior in the setting of a middle-class nursery school as opposed to the sidewalk in an urban poverty area are quite different, as Davis and Havighurst (1947) pointed out a number of years ago. In the middle-class nursery school, open and unprovoked aggression is disapproved by teachers; but in the more harsh environment of the city sidewalk, children see and experience much unrestrained physical aggression and there are few remonstrances about it. It may well be that aggression in the middle class is channeled into competitive activities and that middle-class children are taught to deal with aggression differently, although not necessarily to avoid it.

In the middle class, more aggression is tolerated in boys than in girls, and sex-oriented training toward passivity and dependence is given to girls (Kagan and Moss, 1962). In the middle class, confusion frequently exists about moral training in reference to aggression, particularly about teaching the child to respond appropriately to the aggressive behavior of another child. This confusion reflects lack of certainty in adult value systems and beliefs of the culture.

Moral Learning

Moral behavior can be defined as a response system developed as the result of perception of the pleasure and satisfaction occurring in other persons. It is likely that in early childhood, perhaps by the age of three years or earlier, the child comes to understand that some behavior brings parental approval and praise and other behavior brings disapproval or perhaps even disgust and anger. Verbal responses of the parent begin to describe behavior that is "bad" and behavior that is "good." The child during his first five years, however, can differentiate only minimally among types of behavior that might be termed "moral." Disapproval of taking a toy away from another child has moral implication for the parent; but for the child, the disapproval of such an act as immoral compared with disapproval of spilling milk from his cereal bowl without moral implication is beyond the child's understanding. Therefore, teaching about morality is in a context similar to that of teaching about other behavior, and the moral significance of behavior is only realized at a later age.

The fact that the child does not understand the significance of moral behavior does not mean that so-called "moral learnings" do not occur in early childhood; it simply means that the child does not differentiate moral behavior from any other taught behavior. However, a child does begin the internalization of emotional responses of others in association with actions labeled "good" and "bad." To some extent, then, he becomes empathic with others and learns to be concerned about their feelings in association with his actions. He learns even to disapprove of some of his own actions and to experience some of the feelings that others would have about them. Once he is able to make judgments about his own actions and predictions about his feelings of approval or disapproval as well as the feelings of others, he is able to make true moral judgments in reference to his own behavior and that of others. In some ways, moral learnings are the same as any other learned response system except that there is more emotion about them.

Piaget (1932) relates moral judgments in the child to a child's understanding of rules in a game. According to Piaget, three stages occur: the stage of *symbolism,* consisting of the learning of ritualistic acts, such as repeating gestures (about the end of first year); the stage of *egocentrism* (about three to five years of age), when the child plays to win the game but plays in an "individual" way; and *the social stage* (about seven to ten years old), in which the child seeks to learn the rules and takes special interest in social play. In this way, there is a gradual development of an internal frame of reference for behavior according to social demands.

One aspect of morality is "moral realism," or the judgment of behavior in reference to consequence instead of motives or causes. According to Piaget, children do not show much concern for motives until about the age of twelve. There is evidence that moral realism continues, however, until later years and that there are significant cultural differences in this area (Arnold, 1960; Johnson, 1962). (Further discussion about morality and "internalization" of values is found in Chapter 6.)

Development of Autonomy

As has been noted, at birth the infant becomes much more biologically autonomous. In the first few years of life, biological dependency lessens dramatically, so that by the time that the end of the early-childhood period is reached, a child can interact with the environment for increasingly long periods of time without the immediate presence of adults.

While biological autonomy is easier to define than social autonomy, the latter nevertheless grows out of the former. For example, when change from the activity of the mere ingestion of food to the activity of procuring one's own food occurs, an obvious lessening of dependency on another person for food takes place. And while social and emotional satisfactions are provided for the infant and young child, eventually he must learn to fulfill these needs for himself. Consequently, autonomy refers to the ability to fulfill one's own needs at least to some degree. In a way, autonomy is a meaningless term unless it is reserved for the more elementary biological processes, such as oxygenation, because human existence is preponderantly symbiotic—to an extent, every individual is dependent on another. The greatest satisfactions in human relationships involve dependency. A paradox therefore exists in the struggle of individuals to attain independence, since complete independence does not bring satisfaction nor can it be the kind of behavior tolerated in a social order. Autonomy, therefore, is relative and exists only in terms of opportunities to find satisfaction within dependency relationships and within a social order. Nevertheless, to some extent independence is of value in making choices about behavior and in choosing paths to satisfying goals. Therefore, children need to have some independence in problem solving and in goal-directed behavior within a culturally approved behavioral range of a dependent-independent axis. It should be clear, however, that the meaning of independence and the striving for it as a realistic goal are not easily attained. Meanings vary from culture to culture, from social class to social class, and from individual to individual. Parents and teachers are not consistent in their approval of independent and dependent behavior, neither is the legal system nor the social order in which the child develops.

It is not surprising, therefore, that scientific studies and measurements of behavior on a continuum ranging from dependence to independence are difficult to carry out. And, if an "independent" behavioral measure were obtained, no one child is consistently dependent or independent; hence, a label for him would be only partially descriptive. Several investigations support the view that a child's dependent behavior varies from time to time (Beller, 1955; Heathers, 1955). Despite these problems, certain behavior patterns probably could be cataloged or perhaps arbitrary definitions could be selected, and then normative behavior could be described for a particular culture. As yet, norms for dependence-independence have not been derived and a satisfactory catalog or definitional pattern has not been developed.

Excessively dependent children, feeling insecure about parental approval and favorable emotional response, seem to be less able to successfully engage in problem-solving behavior. Crandall et al. (1960) found that three- to five-year-old children who repeatedly and persistently attempted to accomplish tasks requiring skill and effort were generally less dependent on adults for help than those who were not persistent. Children experiencing support and freedom to explore new situations, to experiment, to develop new patterns of behavior, to expand their knowledge, and to develop new skills were seen not only to find satisfaction in social relationships, but also were observed to develop new ways of solving problems (Crandall et al., 1958).

Toward the end of the early-childhood period, some children develop what is described as "negativism." The negativistic child refuses to do things that he might enjoy or in which he might achieve satisfaction because he finds more satisfaction in thwarting his parents or some other adult. Some thwarting of parental or adult demands, of course, continues into adolescence or even later, based on the satisfaction gained in the assertion of self-demands. But extreme negativism hampers the attainment of social maturity and satisfaction and cannot be said to be within the normal course of the development of independence.

Overcompliance with a child's demands can bring difficulty, just as it is possible for too many parental demands to overinhibit the child's behavior. Whiting (1953) in a study of the Kwoma of New Guinea found that the mothers responded to their infants with great care and, according to this investigator, a "frustration-dependence" sequence was established, which ultimately seemed to bring about pathological behavior. Overdependency, according to Stendler (1954), can result from discontinuities in the socialization process during the critical age period of nine months to three years. Major upheavals in the social relationships of the family, such as those created by absence of the father, can create overdependency, but they do not inevitably have this effect. It cannot be said that unfavorable experiences in early childhood lay an irrevocable foundation that neither the individual nor circumstances can alter; but inadequate or unsuccessful response patterns established in this period can continue. Pathological conditions in adulthood often can be traced to adverse circumstances in early childhood (Mohr et al., 1958; Vandenberg, 1968).

Sex differences in behavior in reference to independence and dependence seem to begin in early childhood. Kagan and Moss (1962) indicate that dependent behavior for males is much less approved than for females. These investigators maintain that disapproval of dependent behavior is learned by the child through direct rewards and punishment, as well as through role models. Their study leads them to believe also that when child behavior in reference to autonomous behavior is congruent with accepted sex role characteristics, appropriate sex role behavior will be likely to continue, at least phenotypically, into adulthood. Girls, according to Lynn (1959), have more difficulty in identifying with the female sex role than boys have in identifying with the male role. He suggests that more females than males prefer the opposite sex role and that boys tend to identify with the culturally expected male role, while girls tend to reject certain aspects of their mother's role. Lynn sees that the lack of prestige afforded the feminine role as well as the lack of punitive factors for adopting some aspects of the masculine role weaken feminine identification. On the other hand, rewards and punishment strengthen boys' identification with the masculine role. This interpretation is in contrast to the hypothesis that because boys have less opportunity for contact with males in the early years, they have more role-identification difficulty. The issue will have to be decided on the basis of progress in research in human development.

In the latter part of the early-childhood period, most children in American culture begin the long educational climb to a social role by reaching out toward the world beyond the family and home. Most have made substantial progress toward independence in body cleanliness, in dressing, and in feeding themselves. They have acquired much information about their environment and have learned to communicate with others and to engage in some elementary cooperative behavioral patterns. Because of the recognition that many children profit from the expansion of their environment beyond the family, certain types of school experiences are often provided. Since the publication of the classic study of Skeels et al. (1938), indicating the benefits of certain types of preschool experiences, more and more emphasis has been given to the importance of the provision of creative activities and learning experiences that will help the child to accomplish the tasks set for him in the first grade of regular school. Not only has the expansion of experience in early childhood been considered beneficial for children who are obviously ready for new experiences, but also extension has been held to be essential for children who are culturally deprived and who come from families living in the poverty-stricken sections of large cities.

With support from the Federal government, programs have been established for three- to five-year-old children to help them enter regular school with a better outlook for success than they would have had otherwise. Accompanying these programs has been a rapid growth in research activity with the establishment of research centers in universities throughout the nation. In addition, a national laboratory in cooperation with certain universities facilitates multidiscipline research programs on the early-childhood period. Interest in early childhood, accordingly, is growing. It is increasingly seen as a period of rapid change and significant accomplishment, a period when the child changes from an infant to an individual who is representative of the culture and who will readily benefit from experiences beyond the home and family.

A POINT OF VIEW

In early childhood, the child gradually moves toward behavioral autonomy as dependence on the mother lessens. Autonomy is a relative term, however, in that human existence throughout the life span is always dependent to some extent. Autonomy meaningfully exists only in terms of opportunities for the individual to find satisfaction within a society.

While there are many important accomplishments in development in this period, probably the most important is the acquisition of language. As the child is required to solve problems of increasing difficulty, the acquisition and increase of language facility is of much importance since cognitive development and thought processes are apparently quite dependent on linguistic facility and behavior. The child learns language easily and effortlessly in the family where there is minimal emotional stress and great opportunity to explore the environment and freedom to express thoughts and feelings. Of much importance is the parents' continuing exchange with him and the extension of his experiences within a setting of language and verbal behavior. Such patterns of interaction and behavior lay the foundation for social and environmental interaction of the future.

REFERENCES

Ammons, R. B., and H. S. Ammons, 1949. "Parent Preferences in Young Children's Doll-Play Interviews," *Journal of Abnormal and Social Psychology,* **44**, 490–505.

Arnold, M. B., 1960. *Emotion and Personality*. Vol. II: *Neurological and Physiological Aspects*. New York: Columbia.

Bach, G. R., 1945. *Young Children's Play Fantasies*. Psychological Monographs, **59**, No. 2. Washington, D.C.: American Psychological Association.

Banham, K. M., 1950. "The Development of Affectionate Behavior in Infancy," *Journal of Genetic Psychology,* **76**, 283–289.

Beasley, J., 1964. "Language Origins and Development," In *The Child. A Book of Readings,* edited by J. M. Seidman, pp. 276–282. New York: Holt.

Beller, E. K., 1955. "Dependence and Independence in Young Children," *Journal of Genetic Psychology,* **87**, 25–35.

Berko, J., and R. Brown, 1960. "Psycholinguistic Research Methods," in *Handbook of Research Methods in Child Development,* edited by P. H. Mussen, pp. 517–557. New York: Wiley.

Berlyne, D. E., 1960. *Conflict, Arousal, and Curiosity*. New York: McGraw-Hill.

Berlyne, D. E., and F. D. Frommer, 1966. "Some Determinants of Children's Questions," *Child Development,* **37**, 176–189.

Bernstein, B., 1961. "Social Class and Linguistic Development: A Theory of Social Learning," in *Education, Economy, and Society,* edited by A. H. Halsey, J. Floud, and C. A. Anderson, pp. 288–314. New York: Free Press.

Bronson, W. C., 1966. "Early Antecedents of Emotional Expressiveness and Reactivity Control," *Child Development,* **37**, 793–810.

Brown, R. W., and D. C. Hildum, 1956. "Expectancy and the Perception of Syllables," *Language, 32,* 411–419.

Cohn, F. S., 1962. "Fantasy Aggression in Children as Studied by the Doll Play Technique," *Child Development, 33,* 235–250.

Crandall, V. J., S. Orleans, A. Preston, and A. Rabson, 1958. "The Development of Social Compliance in Young Children," *Child Development, 29,* 429–443.

Crandall, V. J., A. Preston, and A. Rabson, 1960. "Maternal Reactions and the Development of Independence and Achievement Behavior in Young Children," *Child Development, 31,* 243–251.

Davis, W. A., and R. J. Havighurst, 1947. *Father of the Man.* Boston: Houghton Mifflin.

Delgado, J. M. R., H. E. Rosvold, and E. Looney, 1956. "Evoking Conditioned Fear by Electrical Stimulation of Subcortical Structures in the Monkey Brain," *Journal of Comparative and Physiological Psychology, 49,* 373–380.

Despert, J. L., 1940. "A Method for the Study of Personality Reactions in Preschool Age Children by Means of Analysis of Their Play," *Journal of Psychology, 9,* 17–29.

Doll, E. A., 1953. *The Measurement of Social Competence.* Minneapolis: Educational Test Bureau.

Erikson, E. H., 1950. *Childhood and Society.* New York: Norton.

Gellhorn, E., 1957, *Autonomic Imbalance and the Hypothalamus.* Minneapolis: The University of Minnesota Press.

Gesell, A., and C. S. Amatruda, 1947. *Developmental Diagnosis,* 2d ed. New York: Hoeber-Harper.

Goodenough, E. W., 1957. "Interest in Persons as an Aspect of Sex Difference in the Early Years," *Genetic Psychology Monographs, 55,* 287–323.

Hartup, W. W., and E. A. Zook, 1960. "Sex-role Preferences in Three- and Four-year-old Children," *Journal of Consulting Psychology, 24,* 420–426.

Heathers, G., 1955. "Acquiring Dependence and Independence: a Theoretical Orientation," *Journal of Genetic Psychology, 87,* 277–291.

Hebb, D. O., 1949. *The Organization of Behavior.* New York: Wiley.

Hess, R. D., and V. C. Shipman, 1965. "Early Experience and the Socialization of Cognitive Modes in Children," *Child Development, 36,* 869–886.

Hollenberg, E., and M. Sperry, 1951. "Some Antecedents of Aggression and Effects of Frustration in Doll Play," *Personality, 1,* 32–43.

Inselberg, R. M., 1958. "The Causation and Manifestations of Emotional Behavior in Filipino Children," *Child Development, 29,* 249–254.

Irwin, O. C., 1960. "Infant Speech: Effect of Systematic Reading of Stories," *Journal of Speech and Hearing Research, 3,* 187–190.

Johnson, R. C., 1962. "A Study of Children's Moral Judgments," *Child Development, 33,* 327–354.

Kagan, J., and H. A. Moss, 1962. *Birth to Maturity.* New York: Wiley.

Kreitler, H., and S. Kreitler, 1966. "Children's Concepts of Sexuality and Birth," *Child Development, 37,* 363–378.

Lawler, C. O., and E. E. Lawler, III, 1965. "Color-Mood Associations in Young Children," *Journal of Genetic Psychology, 107,* 29–32.

Levin, H., and R. R. Sears, 1956. "Identification with Parents as a Determinant of Doll Play Aggression," *Child Development,* **27,** 135–153.

Levy, D. M., 1943. "Experiments in Sibling Rivalry," in *Child Behavior and Development,* edited by R. G. Barker, J. S. Kounin, and H. F. Wright, pp. 397–410. New York: McGraw-Hill.

Lövaas, O. I., 1961. "Interaction Between Verbal and Nonverbal Behavior," *Child Development,* **32,** 329–336.

Lynn, D. B., 1959. "A Note on Sex Differences in the Development of Masculine and Feminine Identification," *Psychological Review,* **66,** 126–135.

McCandless, B. R., C. B. Bilous, and H. L. Bennett, 1961. "Peer Popularity and Dependence on Adults in Preschool-Age Socialization," *Child Development,* **32,** 511–518.

McCarthy, D., 1952. "Organismic Interpretations of Infant Vocalizations," *Child Development,* **23,** 273–280.

McCarthy, D., 1953. "Some Possible Explanations of Sex Differences in Language Development and Disorders," *Journal of Psychology,* **35,** 155–160.

McCarthy, D., 1954. "Language Development in Children," in *Manual of Child Psychology,* 2d ed., edited by L. Carmichael, pp. 492–630. New York: Wiley.

Miller, G. A., and P. E. Nicely, 1955. "An Analysis of Perceptual Confusions among Some English Consonants," *Journal of the Accoustical Society of America,* **27,** 338–352.

Mohr, G. J., I. M. Josselyn, J. Spurlock, and S. H. Barron, 1958. "Studies in Ulcerative Colitis," *American Journal of Psychiatry,* **114,** 1067–1076.

Muste, M. J., and D. F. Sharpe, 1947. "Some Influential Factors in the Determination of Aggressive Behavior in Preschool Children," *Child Development,* **18,** 11–28.

Olds, J., and P. Milner, 1954. "Positive Reinforcement Produced by Electrical Stimulation of Septal Area and Other Regions of Rat Brain," *Journal of Comparative and Physiological Psychology,* **47,** 419–427.

Peters, H. N., 1963. "Affect and Emotion," in *Theories in Contemporary Psychology,* edited by M. H. Marx, pp. 435–454. New York: Macmillan.

Piaget, J., 1930a. *The Child's Conception of Physical Causality.* New York: Harcourt, Brace & World.

Piaget, J., 1930b. *The Child's Conception of the World.* New York: Harcourt, Brace & World.

Piaget, J., 1932. *The Moral Judgments of the Child,* translated by M. Gabain. London: Routledge.

Piaget, J., 1959. *The Language and Thought of the Child,* 3d ed., translated by M. Gabain. New York: Humanities Press.

Pintler, M. H., R. Phillips, and R. R. Sears, 1946. "Sex Differences in the Projective Doll Play of Preschool Children," *Journal of Psychology,* **21,** 73–80.

Plutchik, R., 1962. *The Emotions.* New York: Random House.

Rheingold, H. L., 1956. *The Modification of Social Responsiveness in Institutional Babies.* Monographs of the Society for Research in Child Development, **21,** No. 2. Lafayette, Ind.: Child Development Publications, Purdue University.

Rheingold, H. L., J. L. Gewirtz, and H. W. Ross, 1959. "Social Conditioning of Vocalizations in the Infant," *Journal of Comparative and Physiological Psychology* **52**, 68–73.

Ribble, M. A., 1965. *The Rights of Infants.* New York: Columbia.

Rosenblith, J. F., 1966. "Prognostic Value of Neonatal Assessment," *Child Development,* **37**, 623–631.

Sampson, O. C., 1956. "A Study of Speech Development in Children of 18–30 Months," *The British Journal of Educational Psychology,* **26**, 194–201.

Sampson, O. C., 1959. "The Speech and Language Development of Five-Year-Old Children," *The British Journal of Educational Psychology,* **29**, 217–222.

Schaffer, H. R., 1966. "Activity Level as a Constitutional Determinant of Infantile Reaction to Deprivation," *Child Development,* **37**, 595–602.

Sears, R. R., 1951. "A Theoretical Framework for Personality and Social Behavior," *American Psychologist,* **6**, 476–482.

Sears, R. R., M. H. Pintler, and P. S. Sears, 1946. "Effect of Father Separation on Preschool Children's Doll Play Aggression," *Child Development,* **17**, 219–243.

Sears, R. R., J. W. M. Whiting, V. Nowlis, and P. S. Sears, 1953. "Some Child-Rearing Antecedents of Aggression and Dependency in Young Children," *Genetic Psychology Monographs,* **47**, 135–236.

Skeels, H. M., R. Updegraff, B. L. Wellman, and H. M. Williams, 1938. *A Study of Environmental Stimulation: An Orphanage Preschool Project.* University of Iowa Studies in Child Welfare, **15**, No. 4. Iowa City, Iowa: State University of Iowa.

Solley, C. M., and G. Murphy, 1960. *Development of the Perceptual World.* New York: Basic Books.

Spitz, R., 1949. "Role of Ecological Factors in Emotional Development in Infancy," *Child Development,* **20**, 145–155.

Stendler, C. B., 1954. "Possible Causes of Over-Dependency in Young Children," *Child Development,* **25**, 125–146.

Tajfel, H., and D. G. Winter, 1963. "The Interdependence of Size, Number, and Value in Young Children's Estimates of Magnitude," *Journal of Genetic Psychology,* **102**, 115–124.

Templin, M., 1957. *Certain Language Skills in Children: Their Development and Interrelationship.* Minneapolis: University of Minnesota Press.

Tomkins, S. S., 1962. *Affect Imagery Consciousness,* Vol. I. New York: Springer.

Vandenberg, S. G., 1968. "The Nature and Nurture of Intelligence," in *Genetics,* edited by D. C. Glass, pp. 3–58. New York: The Rockefeller University Press.

Vinacke, W. E., 1951. "The Investigation of Concept Formation," *Psychological Bulletin,* **48**, 1–31.

Weisberg, P., 1963. "Social and Nonsocial Conditioning of Infant Vocalizations," *Child Development,* **34**, 377–388.

Wenger, M. A., F. N. Jones, and M. H. Jones, 1956. *Physiological Psychology.* New York: Holt.

Werner, H., 1948. *Comparative Psychology of Mental Development,* rev. ed. Chicago: Follett.

Whiting, J. W. M., 1953. "The Frustration Complex in Kwoma Society," in *Personality in Nature, Society, and Culture,* edited by C. Kluckhohn and H. A. Murray, pp. 137–145. New York: Knopf.

Winitz, H., and O. C. Irwin, 1958. "Syllabic and Phonetic Structure of Infants' Early Words," *Journal of Speech and Hearing Research,* **1,** 250–256.

Wolff, W., 1946. *The Personality of the Preschool Child.* New York: Grune & Stratton.

Young, P. T., 1967. "Affective Arousal: Some Implications," *American Psychologist,* **22,** 32–40.

[*five*]

Motivation and
Cognitive Development

Motivation is a term used to describe the "why" of human experience. It is an abstraction, covering the broad causes of behavior as well as explanations for various types of acts taking place in either social or isolated contexts. The origins of motivation are not completely understood, but internal, or physiological, conditions of the individual are certainly of significance in causing some behavior. Thus, a number of investigators define motivation in terms of physiological needs that stimulate or bring about behavior leading to a homeostatic state (Harvey, 1963; Young, 1967). Such a definition indicates that motivation is concerned primarily with antecedent conditions (needs).

Morgan (1957, 1959, 1965) postulates that motives come from an anatomical center, although he does not give its specific location. The center might be in the reticular formation or in the hypothalamus or some other place in the brain. Stellar (1954) believes that the center is in the hypothalamus and that the amount of motivated behavior varies directly with the amount of activity in the excitatory centers of the hypothalamus.

Morgan describes motivation as consisting of three stages: (1) stimulation of behavior, (2) maintenance of behavior, and (3) termination of behavior. The beginning of the behavior comes through stimulation of exteroceptors or receptors which, once started, may continue as a result of action within the organism itself. Termination comes through external removal of the stimulus or through the organism's behavior to bring about removal of the stimulus. A simple illustration of the stages can be found in the following episode. A child playing in his sandbox in his back yard was frightened when a large dog ran through the yard chasing a cat and barking furiously. The dog caused the child to cry (stimulation of behavior). The child continued to cry while the dog was in the yard (maintenance of behavior) and ceased crying when the dog ran on (termination of behavior).

Freud's theory about motivation, which asserts that all behavior results from stimulation or from some instinct, has been modified by some psychologists to the statement that all behavior results from a "drive." Hunt (1960, 1963), however, considers the assumption that organisms will become inactive unless stimulated to be of doubtful validity and takes the view that children engage in play even if they are "homeostatically satisfied" and, accordingly, their behavior is "unmotivated in the traditional sense." Another variation of the "instinct" view is supported by the work of Tinbergen (1951) and other ethologists.[1] Tinbergen hypothesized that innate behavior comes from a center in the nervous system which accumulates energy and that behavior takes place when appropriate external stimulation is present to release energy.

Ethologists attempt to follow their observations of behavior in the natural environment with experiments with animals. These experiments have led to two terms now adopted by those interested in investigation of instinctive behavior. One of these terms is *releaser stimuli*. Such stimuli, which may be objects, set off instinctive behavior and are in the nature of a trigger's setting off a response pattern that continues even after the "releaser" is no longer present. The second term of instinctive behavior developed by ethologists is that of *imprinting*. The often-cited experiment illustrating imprinting is one made with newly hatched ducks. Ducklings are shown a mechanical "mother" during their first few hours of life; then after this "imprinting," they will continue to follow the model even though they are allowed to associate with live adult ducks. Although work has been done primarily with animal subjects, imprinting as a concept may be applicable to child development, especially the acquisition of motor skills. Despite the interest shown in ethology by such investigators as Kovach and Hess (1963), Gray (1962), and Moltz (1960, 1963), making a clear distinction between innate and learned behavior is not easy.

[1] Ethology refers to the study of the natural behavior of species.

MOTIVATION AND EXPERIENCE

Although motivation cannot be readily separated into primary and social motives, it is convenient, nevertheless, in dealing with the problem of motivation to consider incentives for behavior that come from the social environment. Language is such an incentive and is particularly important as a source of social motives. Much of the child's behavior is influenced by parents' or teachers' verbalizations; and words, of course, have much influence on behavior at any age level, as reward and punishment. Words of praise and pleasure about a child's behavior reinforce behavior valued by the parents, just as words expressing displeasure and disappointment deter undesirable behavior.

While social motives are quite numerous, they cannot be studied on the same level as physiological motives nor is their categorization into generally agreed upon separate entities easily accomplished. Experimentation with social motives involving such psychological processes as perceiving and problem solving should lead to an increased understanding of the determinants of behavior that lie both in the physiological and social aspects of human behavior.

Two directions can be taken in the search for more understanding of motivation: (1) obtaining more information about bodily conditions or physiological states, and (2) obtaining more information about the range of conditions with which certain behaviors are linked. The latter type of effort, according to Brown (1961), has led to the development of such concepts as "intelligence" and "drives."

Developmental Dimensions of Motivation

For the child to come to know about his world and to learn the many skills required for living in a complex society, a willingness to seek and to deal effectively with new experiences is essential. Because of the importance of motivation to seek new experiences during the developmental years, a number of investigators have sought information about the motive to seek the "novel" and the "unknown." For example, several hundred children in the third, sixth, and ninth grades were asked to choose between a list of things with which a great many people are familiar and a list of things with which only a few people are familiar. The children indicated their choices and then wrote down the reasons for making their choices. They did not know that the two lists of items from which they chose were identical.

The results of the study showed that the preference for the list designated as "unknown" increased from the third to the ninth grade for both sexes. The investigators (Teeter et al., 1964) also determined the relationship of choice to IQ and found that children with lower intelligence test scores were as likely to choose the unknown list as those with higher intelligence test scores. Additional evidence from this study indicates that interest in unknown information increases with age and that interest is independent of sex and socioeconomic level. The investigators reported that children who preferred the unknown items were more independent, less preoccupied with comparison of themselves to others, had fewer feelings of inadequacy, and had more desire for difficult tasks than children who preferred the known items.

Apparently, unusual and unfamiliar objects hold a general attraction for children, and novel stimuli seem to arouse an active striving toward exploration. Information on this point was obtained in a study of six- and seven-year-old children through the use of a series of stimulus situations that contained "incongruity" or "conceptual conflict" or were considered "ambiguous." The results of the experiment indicated that novelty brought about "approach" behavior generally, but the results also indicated a sex difference in "approach" behavior. Girls tended to be more rigid and to choose the "familiar" when the opportunity was present. The investigators, Smock and Holt (1962), suggest that the sex differences in response to novelty arise from child-training practices in reference to sex roles. Parents, they believe, make more restrictive demands of girls. Further pursuit of information about such training and its effect on child behavior and development is obviously important. Such evidence as provided by the Smock and Holt study would suggest that girls' avoidance of novelty might well interfere with creative behavior. Such a conclusion, however, seems to be unwarranted at this time.

Motivation for learning in children is apparently significantly related to persistence in a task. Willingness to continue to explore objects, to obtain information, or to develop skills is an important part of development. Using the conditioning model to study persistence, Amsel and Ward (1965) postulated that persistence in a task exists on the basis of rewards. If the reward is not provided when anticipated, primary frustration results and a drive state characterized by aversion for the task often develops. They suggest that rewards can be used to influence and increase persistence and that individual differences in persistence can be explained by the individual's degree of success or failure in the attainment of rewards. In their study of children three through five years of age, Amsel and Ward found that the median persistence level increased with age. Other studies indicate that children who are only partially rewarded for success in tasks will improve their performance to a greater extent than children who are led to expect continuous reward (Penney, 1960; Ryan and Cantor, 1962). Similarly, some conditioning experiments suggest that children whose responses are partially reinforced (that is, not receiving rewards continually) resist the extinction of conditioned responses better than those children who receive continuous reinforcement (Bruning, 1964; Lewis, 1960).

The influence of adult approval on behavior is demonstrated in a study that involved the use of reinforcing stimuli consisting of adults' verbal expression of approval of the children's use of verbalization. Results of this study indicated that aggressive verbal behavior can be modified through the use of operant conditioning techniques. This study did not indicate that the factors of age and sex were of significant influence (Meyer et al., 1964).

While studying motivation through the use of rewards to determine their effect on children's motivation to perform tasks can provide information about motivation in children, much is yet to be learned. Often rewards used in current studies are pieces of candy or words of approval, yet the link of these rewards to theoretical constructs (for example, primary and social drives) still leaves many questions in doubt. Attributing children's motivation to develop more speed in performance of certain tasks to the desire for a small piece of candy may be giving much more value to the candy than is warranted. Furthermore, such experimentation as related to complex learning tasks, although contributory, is perhaps limited in theoretical value.

That it is possible to increase children's motivation to improve intellectual performance has been suggested by a number of writers (for example, Bloom, 1964; Hunt, 1961). Certain characteristics of the environment that have positive or negative effects on development and motivation to achieve have been described. For example, there is substantial evidence that intellectual functioning can be influenced by such environmental factors as child-rearing practices. Such evidence is illustrated by Bing's study (1963) in which it was found that children with much verbal behavior had had more verbal stimulation in early childhood than those children whose verbal behavior was minimal. The mothers of the more verbal children tended to remember more of their children's early accomplishments, they were more interested in their children's academic achievement, they had given their children more experience with books, and they had let them have a significant part in mealtime conversations.

In a comparison of the performance of middle-class and lower socio-economic class children on a task of sorting plastic toys by color and function, it was found that the performance of children from middle-class homes was well above that of children from lower socioeconomic class homes. The investigators, Hess and Shipman (1965), relate the teaching styles of the mothers to the performance of their children. The middle-class mothers gave better instructions to their children and permitted them to proceed with the task on their own; while, in contrast, mothers of the children in the lower socioeconomic class were much less explicit and much less successful in instructing their children for the task.

In general, the evidence indicates that when the backgrounds of children with superior intellectual ability are investigated, it is often found that the children come from homes where parents have shown interest in their development and have tried to increase their children's motivation to learn and to succeed and to persist in difficult tasks. Evidence also suggests that parents' efforts to increase verbal facility is particularly effective.

Achievement Motivation

The concept of achievement motivation is not easily defined; thus, it has not been used as a unitary concept in research studies. The concept of achievement motivation at least can imply motivation to accomplish tasks. It has been suggested that investigation of achievement motivation should emphasize the process by which achievement becomes an actuality and put less stress on the identification of potentially high achievers (Mc-Clelland, 1958).

Parental expectations have an important influence on a child's motivation to successfully complete tasks (Crandall et al., 1964; Katkovsky et al., 1964a and 1964b). For example, a high-achieving child is usually less emotionally dependent on his mother, despite the fact that his mother assiduously rewards his effort to achieve (Crandall et al., 1960). Strodt-beck (1958) believes that the family is a "power system" and that the son's success and acceptance in the family prepares him for success and achievement outside. Greater achievement is made by children who grow up in a family in which they can learn to believe in their own ability to control their own destiny and who are willing to leave home.

The influence of adult responses on children's achievement motivation is sometimes subtle and may be unrecognized by teachers, parents, and even some research investigators. For example, silence or "nonreaction" can have active reinforcing properties under certain conditions. When a mother or teacher praises a child for performance in a certain task and then in subsequent instances fails to praise him and responds to him with silence or nonreaction, the child may interpret the silence as holding disapproval and will endeavor to improve his performance. The silence arouses emotion that leads to further effort for achievement. On the other hand, if adults have complained about a child's performance and disapproved of his behavior, silence and nonreaction may also lead to further effort for achievement. In such instances a child, expecting negative reactions, may interpret silence as approval. Crandall et al. (1964) in a study of eighth-grade boys found that both positive or negative treatment preceding nonreaction produced changes in children's expectations of success. Despite available research studies and the advances which have been made in this area, a review of parental influence by Freeberg and Payne (1967) indicates that much more systematic research is needed in the area of achievement motivation before research findings can be effectively applied.

The effect of motivational differences on performance of school tasks is illustrated in the following story of Robert G., a son of a wealthy industrialist.

> Robert's grandfather, an immigrant to America, had established extensive business operations, which Robert's father had entered after completing college. It was easy to see that the family was "socially mobile" and much emphasis was placed on Robert's school achievement. Now in the third grade, Robert was having a great deal of difficulty with reading. If called upon by his teacher to read aloud, he stammered and was unable to respond. His mother tried to work with him at home but found her patience limited when Robert failed to read even very simple words. As money was no problem, tutors were hired and Robert was given extensive drill after school and on Saturdays. A "crash" program to get him to read was begun during the summer following the third grade. Instead of making progress, however, Robert seemed to lose the few words that he had learned. In desperation, his mother took him to a child guidance clinic.

> At the clinic, his mother was given an opportunity to talk generally about her concerns. In these talks, it was found that Robert's reading problem was only one of her several problems. Her husband spent a great deal of time in his father's business operations. And when he needed relaxation, he sought pleasure

by himself or with friends by going on extended fishing trips. He took little interest in Robert's problem and left its solution to her. She did not feel able to cope with it and, being lonely, turned to an active social life on her own.

At the clinic, it was found that Robert was very much interested in building model airplanes, and he was provided a number of them to build during his weekly visits to the clinic. There, with a clinician who put no pressure on him to read, he worked diligently on the models. Gradually, the models were increased in difficulty until Robert needed the instructions accompanying the kits in order to put them together. In his interest to complete the models and unaware of his actions, Robert read the instructions sufficiently well to complete the complex tasks of building the models. Thus, it was discovered that Robert could read when he was not preoccupied with his feelings of inadequacy and when reading served his own desires. It was noted, too, that Robert referred to the "instructions" as "corrections." Apparently, reading material had for sometime held a threat and he usually expected to be corrected. Robert, it seemed, thought he had never met the requirements of reading without being corrected and thus he inadvertently called the instructions accompanying the model kits "corrections." Eventually, Robert found he could read without anxiety and without undue concern about being corrected. By building on his own interest and motivation in completing the models he was helped to face the more difficult tasks of the school.

Motivation and Social Learning

Experience with peers determines not only motivation to achieve, but also motivation to behave in ways that are accepted by and conform with group standards. By providing a four-year-old nursery-school boy with approval of responses acceptable to peers, Scott et al. (1967) were able to change his status in a group. Similarly, a young girl's isolate behavior in a nursery school was changed by giving her attention when she played with other children and by withholding it when she engaged in solitary play. In this experiment, it was possible to markedly increase social interaction with other children, while at the same time it was possible to reduce interaction with adults (Allen et al., 1964).

In a study of a three-year-old boy in a laboratory preschool, an effort was made to aid in the development of motor skills by social reinforcement of a physical activity. At the time of the study, the child engaged in physical activity to only a limited extent and he wandered from one area to another, seldom joining other children in play. He particularly avoided climbing equipment and a large climbing frame. Although teachers had tried to help him in dealing with his problems of social behavior, he had, however, received little attention in reference to the climbing frame. Having neither physical nor social skills, he was a disruptive factor in the school's activities. A period of "reinforcement" training was begun, which consisted of a teacher standing near the child watching, speaking to, smiling at, or touching him each time he approached the frame. During the second reinforcement period, the child spent over one-half of his time playing on the climbing frame. Other results that were not a part of the study were observed: The child showed improved skill with other play equipment as well as an increase in social interaction with the other children (Johnston et al., 1966).

Motivation for nurturant behavior would be expected to be influential in a child's acceptance in his peer group. That is, if other children perceive him to be helpful and contributing to their satisfaction, his presence and participation in activities would be sought. Social acceptance could well be a reinforcement for motivation to be nurturant and to engage frequently in that type of behavior. There is evidence that even with preschool children nurturance giving is positively related to sociometric status in the group. Children who provide nurturance for others have been found to be more frequently chosen as companions by other children, suggesting that the motivation for nurturant behavior is reinforced by social acceptance. Conversely, less nurturant children tend to be rejected. In the latter case, such children may have less motivation to engage in nurturant and socially acceptable behavior (Moore and Updegraff, 1964).

Another aspect of motivation in social learning is the observed tendency of young children toward imitative behavior An important question arises in relation to such behavior: Is it generalized or does it occur in specific situations? For example, does imitation of a parent in one situation also occur in other situations? And if a child learns to imitate his father (a like-sex model), will he also imitate other male adults? The generalization of imitative behavior has been of interest for many years since the publication of the book by Miller and Dollard entitled *Social Learning and Imitation* (1941). A number of studies have contributed additional information over the years. A study of imitative behavior in children three to five years of age using a doll-play technique is illustrative. In this study, it was found that very early some children have strong motivation toward engaging in imitative behavior and that such behavior is generalized across models with little evidence to support the view that it is "situation-specific" (Hartup, 1964).

Expectations related to sex roles provide motivation toward certain behavior. In our society, men are expected to take greater risks than women, and such expectation is likely to cause a child to perceive a man's role as one showing much courage. That risk taking for boys emerges at an early age is supported by a number of studies of children's performance in decision-making tasks. In one study, subjects ranging in ages from six to sixteen were seated before a panel of ten switches. Each child was told that nine of the switches were safe, but the tenth was a "disaster switch." The disaster switch was assigned randomly to each of the switch positions on the panel. If the child pulled a safe switch, he was allowed a certain amount of candy. He was then required to decide whether to pull another switch or to stop and eat the candy he had obtained. If he decided to try for additional candy and happened to pull the disaster switch, a buzzer sounded and he lost the candy that he had already earned. Since the probability and magnitude of loss increased with the number of switches pulled, continuance was labeled a form of risk taking. It was found that boys generally took more risks than girls (Slovic, 1966).

Cultural Influences on Motivation

With cultural differences it might be expected that there would also be differences in motivation, especially in relation to value given to rewards. For example, a study of children in the middle socioeconomic class showed that they had about the same level of achievement motivation on receiving information about having reached a standard as they did when they were promised a sum of money. Subjects in the lower socioeconomic class showed much less motivation when money was not promised and the only reward was information about reaching the standard (Douvan, 1956). In another study of five-, six-, ten-, and eleven-year-olds from the middle and lower socioeconomic class it was found that children in the middle socioeconomic class learned an experimental task more quickly with the nonmaterial incentive, in contrast to children in the lower socioeconomic class, who learned more quickly with the material incentive (Terrell et al., 1959). Conclusions, however, about achievement motivation in children in reference to material and nonmaterial reinforcement should be only tentative at this time.

At the beginning of this discussion of motivation, views of various investigators about motivation indicated that many saw motivation as basically organic in origin and as resulting from drive or instinct. A solely biological view, however, is unsatisfactory because, as with all of human behavior, there is the modifying influence of experience. Thus, the complexity of human behavior allows limited understanding about the "why" of it. Even with animals, the modifying influence of experience on what can be termed "instinctual behavior" is apparent. Harlow (1958) and Mitchell et al. (1966) in their experiments illustrate such modification particularly well.

Fundamentally motivation is the struggle to fulfill organic needs, but obviously these needs gradually extend into affective and social needs so that separation of motivating factors according to origin or to unitary and isolated needs now seems impossible.

COGNITIVE PROCESSES IN DEVELOPMENT

Childhood is looked upon by some as primarily a time of preparation, a time to acquire knowledge and experience, and therefore satisfactions are of relatively little consequence. Nevertheless, childhood does have its own intrinsic rewards and satisfactions, exemplified by freedom from certain responsibilities and by time for pursuit of pleasure. When adults consider childhood, however, they cannot help but dwell upon the aspect of preparation and emphasize the importance of the child's acquisition of experience.

"Cognition" refers to the processes through which the child comes to know about himself and his world and is part of the preparation for adulthood and wider participation in the culture. These processes include organization of sensory and perceptual capacities, perceptual learning, the formation of concepts, and problem solving. In the past, motivation and emotion have not been considered as cognitive processes, but it is difficult to separate them from the processes through which the child acquires experience.

Organization of the Child's Sensory and Perceptual Capacities

The organization of sensory and perceptual capacities is a process in which the child becomes aware of objects, events, qualities, or relations of things and events. Such awareness comes through the sense organs. Thus, perception is not an experience in which the child remains passive while stimuli come to his sense organs; instead, once the sense organs are stimulated, the child's own individuality significantly influences perceptual organization and processes.

Essentially, the environment consists of surfaces and spaces in a context of time. Patterns of stimuli from the environment come to the child primarily through the visual and auditory organs, and it is these organs that provide the most complex perceptual experience. Stimuli, or events and objects in the environment, do not affect the sense organs as a whole—only the energy from the stimuli reach the sense organs. These forms of energy from stimuli are photic, phonic, thermal, and the like. The environment thus provides sources of energy to which the child can respond, but he is not actually aware of the objects themselves or even of their properties. He can only be aware of the energy coming from them.

The patterns of energy reaching the sense organs are transformed in such a way that the nerve pathways leading from the sense organs can transmit impulses to the brain. The information about stimuli is contained in the energy that is carried along the neural pathways. This complex process of transformation and transmission of energy through neural pathways involves timing and thresholds, as well as other factors influenced by electrical or chemical reactions contributing to the functioning of the nerve cells. As characteristic energy reaches the brain, part of the brain's function is to assign meaning to the energy associated with the objects or events in the environment.

In brief, the sense modalities mediate between the external events and the internal events or ongoing behavior of the organism. In sensory processes, significant behavioral steps are detection or awareness of the energy by sense organs, a transformation of this energy so that the nervous system of the body can manage it, and direction of the transformed energy into certain pathways or tracings. Sometimes difficulty arises in the study of some aspects of perception because individual perception of stimuli cannot be absolutely determined. Interpretation is variable for the child, for things are not what they seem to be: What seems to be a hard, smooth top of a table is actually not solid at all, but is composed of small elementary particles moving in patterns.

Conclusive information about the initial development of perception is not at hand, since studies of infancy and subsequent developmental periods have not established facts beyond doubt about perceptual development. It is probable that the perception of form is primary; that is, discriminations by young children are first made on the basis of form rather than color or context. The findings of a study by Kagan and Lemkin (1961) support this view. Children aged three to eight years use principles based on form more often than color in matching geometric stimuli.

Evidence for developmental changes in the perception of form seems substantial. Early perceptions are often vague and diffuse and later become more specific. And, apparently, changes in the perception of form occur at different rates during development. For example, specificity of recognition in reference to contextual situations seems to change with age and maturation. A series of longitudinal and cross-sectional studies concerned with the perceptions of children at different ages indicated that younger children tend to be relatively "field-dependent"; that is, they experience surroundings in global fashion rather than experiencing objects as discrete from their backgrounds. Older children, on the other hand, tend to be more "field-independent" (Witkin et al., 1962).

The meaning of field-independence as described by Witkin can be gained from a description of one of his experimental situations. In his "rod and frame test," the subject is seated in a darkened room before a luminous square frame that is tilted at 28 degrees (at the beginning of the experiment). At the center of the frame, a luminous rod is fixed on a pivot so that the subject can tell the experimenter the direction to move the rod. The test is to move the rod to the vertical while the frame remains in its original and tilted position. Field-independent behavior is moving the rod to a vertical position regardless of the position of the frame. On the other hand, field-dependent behavior consists of moving the rod in alignment with the frame. A child who is field-dependent seems to have limited ability for differentiation of other aspects of his environment, according to the studies of Witkin and his associates (Witkin et al., 1966).

Further, the ability to recognize familiar stimuli in unusual positions also seems to be related to age and maturation. Children aged three to seven shown forms usually seen in a particular orientation recognized significantly more figures if they were in their characteristic right-side-up positions. Older subjects, however, recognized figures equally well in all positions (Ghent, 1960). In a later study, Ghent and Bernstein (1961) obtained the same results with geometric forms.

Another kind of specificity was found in Gollin's (1960) study of recognition of line drawings by children and adults. Young children required more completeness of the outlines of fragmented drawings for recognition than did adults.

Information from such studies are in accord with the conclusions of Wohlwill (1960), who reports in his view of developmental studies of perception that errors in children's perceptual judgments sharply decrease as age increases.

Other differences in perception that may not be directly related to chronological age and developmental sequence may stem from disorders in development. In other words, specificity and dealing with details on a quantitative basis can be difficult for children who have various types of disorders. For example, 449 children (275 normal, 68 with behavior disorder, and 106 with a central nervous system disorder) were compared on the basis of their drawings of the human figure and the number of essential parts of the body that were included. While differences among groups of children in the use of the number of essential parts were encountered, no one essential body part was omitted characteristically by members of any group. The normal children, however, used the largest number of body parts and the children with the central nervous system disorder used the least. A quantitative difference thus was found among the groups of children in their drawings, suggesting that specificity and the perception of details were more difficult for the children with disorders (Alexander, 1963).

In addition to the perception of the form, or boundary, of an object, other aspects may be perceived, such as depth or solidity. For a child, it seems that the most common perceptions relate to objects characteristically surrounding him: the members of his family, the furniture of the house, the pictures on the wall, his cup, his plate, his spoon, his bed, and so on. Such objects are perceived as units, but clues to their identity come from surface, depth, and the variations in planes or lines bringing differences to light. In perceiving an object, the child usually depends upon cooperation from several senses. For example, in perceiving his pet dog he may depend on several sources of stimuli, such as seeing him, hearing him, and feeling him. The cooperation among the senses is such that separation is virtually impossible.

As has been suggested, the use of detail in perception is important in establishing the identity of the perception. For example, although perceiving a square requires that it be seen as a totality or as a unit, attention must be given to details so that they can be grouped not only to establish unity, but also to establish identity. In the perception of an inkblot, such as one of those comprising the Rorshach inkblot test, it has been found that some individuals see the blot as a whole and that their perceptions have unity. Although such individuals may eventually move to a description of details of the blot, they still see the details as related to the whole. And in the process they are able to identify the unity as being some object. Some children, however, concentrate on the details and go from one detail to another without ever trying to see the perception as a whole. One might say that the details are perceived as wholes in themselves. However, the ability to organize these smaller bits into a larger whole is lacking. If a child, then, is confronted with a new situation, the failure to see the unity of the details as comprising a large pattern or whole can interfere considerably with problem solving. Often, a perception of the entire problem to be solved will greatly facilitate activity toward a solution; on the other hand, concentration upon the details of a problem may inhibit solution.

Another way of looking at the problem of the relationship to figure and ground or totality and details is in terms of context. Dember (1960) prefers to use the term *context* rather than *background*. He emphasizes that all perceptual activity takes place in some context, that it occurs with some other activity, and that none is independent. Contextual aspects in a situation must be controlled or maintained in a neutral way, as it has been found that context or background influences the perception of a figure. A gray figure on a black background may appear to be lighter than a gray figure on a white background, yet both may be identical. Hence, the perception of details, figures, or parts of the unit are influenced by the background. Hebb (1949) asserts that in perception of figure and ground there really are two processes: perceiving "unity" and perceiving "identity." He means that the awareness of the existence of the figure standing out from the background is the perception of the unity, whereas if the child can say that this is an object, such response contributes to identity in that it is seen as a class of figures. A higher level of identification would take place if the figure was described as a square. Unity may be innately determined, but identity is dependent upon experience.

Unity is important in interaction with the environment in a number of ways. Unity is related to essential components, in that in order to achieve unity or totality, one must select the essential elements comprising it. Unity is important in terms of memory in that it is much easier to remember a figure if there is some unity or perception of the figure as a whole; if the figure is broken up and the perception consists of various parts, remembering without unity is much more difficult.

Some research directed toward understanding perceptual processes has involved effort to find principles of perception having some universality (Wohlwill, 1960). For example, some investigators have been concerned with "cognitive controls," or factors that determine the ways in which individuals organize and pattern their perceptions of the environment (Gardner et al., 1959). The organization of information is not only dependent upon availability and environmental characteristics, but is also determined by experiences and conditioned responses growing out of interaction with the environment. The development of individual differences as influences on perceptual processes will be discussed in the next section on perceptual learning. Here it is appropriate to emphasize the importance of the fact that children acquire controls and characteristic approaches in their day-by-day efforts to organize perceptual experience.

Santostefano and Paley (1964) studied two types of cognitive controls in reference to age. They used six-, nine-, and twelve-year-old children as subjects. One type of cognitive control was characterized by the way in which a child attended to and concentrated upon a stimulus field. The task used to determine a subject's approach to a stimulus field required that judgments be made about the comparative size of circles printed in pairs on cards. The investigators assumed that if a child approached the problem of making judgments about the size of circles in an unsystematic way (for example, by examining one circle for a long period of time and another only briefly), he would overestimate the size of the circle on which he spent the most time. The investigators found that the younger children in the study did make more errors than the older children. The second type of cognitive control was characterized by the ability to attend to stimuli without being distracted by intrusive stimuli. Two large cards with 50 colored drawings of fruit (apples, bananas, etc.) were used. On one of the cards, small achromatic drawings of other objects were placed beside each of the fruits. The achromatic drawings were used as intrusive stimuli in the task of saying aloud the colors of the fruits. In this part of the study it was also found that the younger children had more difficulty, presumably because of the intrusive stimuli, than the older children.

Jackson and Messick (1962) describe stylistic response as an important personality trait. By "response style," for example, they indicate that a person who is required to make a response to a stimulus situation and who is inclined to acquiesce, regardless of the appropriateness or necessity, has a characteristic style. In this sense, acquiescence is characterized as stylistic behavior (Messick and Jackson, 1961).

Perceptual Learning

With increasing age, it seems reasonable to expect that a child's perception and responses to a stimulus field will become more systematic. And, as experience becomes more complex, further perceptual learning will take place in association with maturation and physical development.

Children apparently can distinguish visually between geometric forms in the first year of life and can complete a simple formboard by the age of two; yet, producing geometric forms in drawing cannot be done until several years later. Maccoby and Bee (1965) believe that children involved in perceptual learning tasks that require them to distinguish among a variety of stimuli comprising either visual or auditory patterns find it easier to make such distinctions than it is to do reproductive matching, such as is required in copying a square. Drawing may be more difficult in part because visual or auditory distinction is possible by attendance to only a few attributes, while reproduction (drawing) requires attendance to all of the attributes of the model or pattern.

Developmental changes in relation to certain perceptual processes have been found, particularly in response to ambiguous stimuli (Elkind, 1964; Elkind and Scott, 1962). Individual age-group differences were significant among groups ranging from nursery school through sixth grade. As children develop, perception becomes more active and the perceptual field is structured into new patterns. It has been noted in perceptual learning that children can perceive differences in stimuli coming from others before they can make similar distinctions in their own behavior. Berko and Brown (1960) described the request of a child, David, to go to the "mewwy-go-wound." Another child in a teasing voice said, "David wants to go to the mewwy-go-wound." "No," said David, "you don't say it wight." Similarly, a little girl in pronouncing the word *Hudson,* said "Huddon" but her friend in an effort to correct her said, "Mary, it isn't Huddon—it's Hudsunt."

Does one sense modality provide a better means of perceptual learning than another? Some information in regard to this question is provided in a study of the rates of learning by auditory and visual modalities of seven- and eight-year-old children (Budoff and Quinlan, 1964). The children were to learn via paired-associate tasks in which it was necessary for the subjects, on seeing or hearing a stimulus word, to say aloud the other word of a pair of words. The results of this study showed that in the performance of this type of task, aural presentations were learned with less effort than were visual presentations. Further research in reference to this problem, however, is needed, particularly studies of a longitudinal nature.

The Child's Formation of Concepts

In the cognitive processes, complexity increases in moving from sensory experiences to perceptual learning, and then to organization of percepts into concepts. A concept is a way of developing order and serves to link stimuli or energy from the environment to those processes which take place inside the individual. Kendler (1961) defines concept formation as "the acquisition or utilization, or both, of a common response to dissimilar stimuli." E. B. Hunt (1962) sees a concept as a mental image involving generalization from particulars.

Classification and organization of percepts into concepts is an activity in which the individual seeks to determine specific elements in a situation and to describe these elements in a particular way—the search for similar elements is part of the concept-formation process. An organization of meanings or symbols into a concept brings about the possibility of further symbolic activity, since the grouping can then be given a verbal label and comes to stand for a much more complex experience. Associated with this complex experience are the various qualities of objects and events characterized by the perceptual process of the individual. Through this organization, then, children learn to make judgments and determine their responses to stimulus complexes rather than to just one stimulus itself.

A concept may be termed an "experiential filter" through which the stimuli from the environment are selected, sorted, and evaluated, with responses being determined on the basis of this filtering process (Harvey et al., 1961). Through concepts, standards against which the stimuli in the environment may be judged are set up subjectively, and the relevance and significance of the environment for the individual is thereby determined. Since concepts provide a way of dealing with the vast numbers of stimuli present in the environment, they provide an important adjunct to the environmental interaction process.

Piaget's theory of intellectual development from infancy to adolescence is linked to language development and is characterized by stages. Each stage lays the foundation for its successor. In the stage from birth to two years, the child learns that objects persist even when removed from his perceptual field. In the second stage, from two to seven years, the child uses language and becomes able to internalize actions. From seven to eleven years, the third stage, the child has the ability to perform concrete operations that belong to the logic of classes. The fourth stage, from eleven to fifteen years, is a precursor to adult logic and is marked by the appearance of the ability to reason by hypothesis.

The importance of language to concepts is easily seen when an object and a verbal response go together—a mother repeatedly points to her child's shoe and says the word *shoe* until the child associates the verbal response with the object. This type of learning is widespread and begins very early in the child's life, continuing through the formative years into many types of experiences with objects and events. Only gradually during development is the word separated from the object and the usefulness of symbolization comes into play. As the child matures, his language ability gradually comes to assist in the regulation of his behavior and after the age of five the child expresses himself more by language than by any other behavioral form.

The most extensive use of symbols, accordingly, is that of language, since it aids in differentiation, description, and classification of objects, situations, and relationships. As experience increases, the child depends more and more on symbolization in order that he may manage association and reasoning in relation to problems encountered. Symbols in themselves become responses in that the child must go through the process of conditioning and the association of the symbolic behavior with the object. The creation, then, of a symbol is in itself a response and yet at the same time the response or symbol is used as a stimulus in order to bring about other responses. Hence, in the assignment of meaning and in the use of symbols, individual variations can and do occur.

Bruner et al. (1956) list a number of steps in the attainment of a concept. First, the individual encounters an array of "instances," or stimuli described in terms of color, weight, and other "attribute values." The second step involves a tentative prediction or decision as to whether or not the problem can be further divided. The third step is a decision about whether a decision is correct, incorrect, or indeterminate. The fourth step provides information by limiting the number of attributes and attribute values. The fifth step involves a number of decisions that take the individual toward a solution of the problem and is described as "strategy." It includes objectives to appraise the information, to reduce a strain on the individual, and to appraise the risk involved if the individual fails. The final step includes decision in reference to the consequences of success or failure.

Developmental information about concept formation is difficult to obtain, although some information is available. Elementary forms of concepts begin quite early, certainly in the preschool years. The grouping of meanings into complex concepts probably takes place in the early school years, although such grouping begins in the preschool years (Lee and Bingham, 1959).

In a study of the utilization of concepts in preschool children Lee (1965) found that six-year-olds tend to depend less upon concepts of color and size than younger children. This investigator believes that this tendency is adaptive in that the kindergarten child is learning that form discrimination has more relevance than color or size for many of the school tasks. For example, the size of the letter *C* is not important in its recognition or use and neither is the color in which it is written. Since concepts are developed in order to deal with the environment, there may well be developmental shifts in dependency.

When a young child looks at the stars they all seem to be at the same distance, but he learns eventually that some stars are many times farther away than others. In modern cultures, much training in reference to perception of space is given to children but such is not the case among primitive societies. If some of the primitive people in New Guinea are asked about distances from one place to another, they are unable to give an accurate answer since they have had little training and no real interest in measurement; their answer is, "not far."

The perception of time also is influenced by learning and those primitive people who have no way of reckoning time are unable to describe their experience in reference to time nearly as well as does a child in Western culture. Even so, a child in this culture does have difficulty in concepts of time. If his mother tells him that he can go to play at a neighbor's house for an hour and to return at the end of this time, he may become so absorbed in play that he loses his usual capacity to reckon time—the time allowed him seems to go in only a few minutes. On the other hand, if he is anticipating a pleasurable activity and is told that he will be allowed to go out to play in an hour, the time passes very slowly and he is unable to understand that the length of time is similar to that which he saw pass so swiftly.

Some types of concepts come late in the developmental years—middle childhood or early adolescence. Shifts in conceptual orientation seem to be difficult for children in the fourth and fifth grades, but come easily within the capacities of adolescents.

Problem Solving

Problem solving refers to behavior that is more complex than is usually included under the term of sensorimotor, or labeling activity. Problem solving involves an awareness of characteristics of a stimulus complex, gathering of information so that comparisons, contrasts, and evaluations can be made, and a response pattern or sequence of related response patterns. The arrival at a response pattern in a complex problem usually involves prediction of the future in two ways: (1) the combination of past experience and present facts into a predicted or abstract situation, and (2) the matching of this abstraction with an appropriate response.

Since energy from many sources in the environment reaches our sense organs, problem solving involves discriminatory or selective activity. Out of a vast number of sources of energy, an individual must select a source to which he will attend or respond. Capacity for response allows only a small number of types of energy to be involved; thus, much of an individual's experience is directed and limited.

The child, on the basis of experience, responds to what he considers to be or has been taught to consider essential elements of the problem situation in the environment. He must be selective and attend only to those stimuli that seem to hold the key to the appropriate or necessary response. Learning to make this type of response involves the learning of those aspects of a situation that are essential to a successful or appropriate solution to the problem. It is easy to see that the teaching of the child, his experience in the family, and his association with peers have a great deal of influence on his selection of essential elements of the environment.

As explained in Chapter 4, "set"—the tendency to respond in a predetermined way—is important in the perceptual process and in the utilization of experience. Patterns of perception and response are established early, and the child soon learns to approach even quite different problems with predetermined response; that is, he has learned to deal with problems and new situations on the basis of past experience and already chosen responses. Some evidence suggests that set becomes better established developmentally in some aspects of behavior than in others (Reese, 1963a and 1963b).

Set may or may not be an advantage. It can be an advantage if it is linked to the appropriate type of response. For example, if a child is told, "Get ready to catch the ball" and if there is a set for attention and motor readiness, he is much more likely to catch the ball. If a certain set is maintained by a boy to make a certain type of dive into the water, but he is suddenly told by his coach to make a different one, his performance may be hampered by the sudden change in instructions. His set would then be a disadvantage or inhibitory. Thus, it is possible for a child to approach new experiences by distorting them in the perceptual process into ones appropriate for a particular favored set. A child who continues to distort the perceptual world in terms of his own needs or his own way of seeing it or responding to it, obviously will have much difficulty in solving problems.

Problem solving involves movement from specific responses closely related to the problem at hand to responses that are more abstract and which involve generalization. Accordingly, children in their problem solving seek to develop rules that may be applied to related problems. Older children and those with greater intellectual ability move more quickly to the development of rules and self-instructions than do younger children and those with less intellectual ability. A study by Neimark and Lewis (1967) is illustrative. These investigators used a problem-solving task involving geometrical designs in which children, aged nine to sixteen, were to identify patterns by uncovering as few elements of each pattern as possible on a problem-solving board. In this study, it was found that even the youngest children developed "self-instructions" that controlled their behavior. Often the self-developed rules were said aloud as an aid in solving the problem.

Investigators in the study of the processes involved in problem solving must try to take into account many variables that are difficult to control. Neimark and Lewis point out that in many research studies on this topic a lack of control of intervening variables is in evidence. However, in their study they sought to reduce the influence of the factors of "specific school training, content knowledge, and verbal fluency." Other significant variables, such as differences in visual capacity, energy levels related to metabolic processes, the possible presence of chronic diseases, nutritional deficiencies, and fatigue may also be of consequence.

A different approach to the investigation of problem solving was described by Alexander et al. (1964). In this study of children five to twelve years of age, investigation was made of their problem-solving efforts in dealing with ambiguous stimuli on cards containing figures which could be interpreted as being in a number of different relationships and conditions of social interaction. It was found that there was a relatively normal distribution on a continuum of problem-solving approaches. Some children were able only to enumerate and describe the perceptual experience; others were able not only to describe but also to reason about the "why" of the events they described; and still others were able to respond in even more complex ways with description, causation, and a prediction of events that would follow. The latter response to the stimuli with which they were confronted was believed by the investigators to indicate much more complex and effective problem-solving behavior.

It can be seen that the concept of cognitive processes is a broad and inclusive one. In many ways, separation into components and separate processes is helpful only to a limited extent. Even in perception of environmental stimuli, motivation or bodily conditions may determine the selectivity process and therefore "input." With input determined, a response pattern may then be predetermined, and thus what might cursorily be considered a free perceptual experience is in reality to some extent already predetermined. Perhaps this view is similar to Freud's view of behavior, as well as his ideas about the influence of the unconscious. The more knowledge about cognition that is gained, the greater is the complexity that is discovered.

A POINT OF VIEW

While motivation and cognition are abstractions that are difficult to define as concepts, motivation (the reasons for behavior) and cognition (knowing) are closely related in organismic functioning. Accordingly, although motivation and cognition are organic processes depending much on individual characteristics, they are continually being modified by experience during development.

Through experience, an individual comes to exclude what he considers as irrelevant stimuli and to base responses on channelized perceptions. Changing such perceptual or behavioral patterns, even in a very young child, is quite difficult not only because of motivation, but also because past conditioning over time has led to a certain selectivity and response complex.

To bring about change in behavior, motivation, of course, must be seen as fulfilling a child's needs. In using reinforcement to bring about change, it is easy to be misled and interpret a reward according to an adult value system. While the child ostensibly may wish to have the reward, his desire actually may be for adult emotional exchange, so that almost any type of material reward will do. Judgments, thus, about hierarchy of types of effective rewards between groups or among individuals need to be made with much caution.

REFERENCES

Alexander, T., 1963. "The Effect of Psychopathology in Children's Drawing of the Human Figure," *The Journal of Psychology,* **56,** 273–282.

Alexander, T., R. B. Kugel, B. Cushna, and B. Snider, 1964. "Studies of Complex Behavior: I. The Processes of Perception, Association, and Prediction of Response," *The Journal of Psychology,* **58,** 23–32.

Allen, K. E., B. Hart, J. S. Buell, F. R. Harris, and M. M. Wolf, 1964. "Effects of Social Reinforcement on Isolate Behavior of a Nursery School Child," *Child Development,* **35,** 511–518.

Amsel, A., and J. S. Ward, 1965. "Frustrations and Persistence: Resistance to Discrimination Following Prior Experience with the Discriminada," *Psychological Monographs: General and Applied,* **79,** No. 597.

Berko, J., and R. Brown, 1960. "Psycholinguistic Research Methods," in *Handbook of Research Methods in Child Development,* edited by P. Mussen, pp. 517–557. New York: Wiley.

Bing, E., 1963, "Effect of Childrearing Practices on Development of Differential Cognitive Abilities," *Child Development,* **34,** 631–648.

Bloom, B. S., 1964. *Stability and Change in Human Characteristics*. New York: Wiley.

Brown, J. S., 1961. *The Motivation of Behavior*. New York: McGraw-Hill.

Bruner, J. S., J. J. Goodnow, and G. A. Austin, 1956. *A Study of Thinking*. New York: Wiley.

Bruning, J. L., 1964. "Effects of Magnitude of Reward and Percentage of Reinforcement on a Lever Movement Response," *Child Development*, **35**, 281–285.

Budoff, M., and D. Quinlan, 1964. "Auditory and Visual Learning in Primary Grade Children," *Child Development*, **35**, 583–586.

Crandall, V. C., S. Good, and V. J. Crandall, 1964. "Reinforcement Effects of Adult Reactions and Nonreactions on Children's Achievement Expectations; A Replication Study," *Child Development*, **35**, 485–497.

Crandall, V. J., A. Preston, and A. Rabson, 1960. "Maternal Reactions and the Development of Independence and Achievement Behavior in Young Children," *Child Development*, **31**, 243–251.

Crandall, V. J., R. Dewey, W. Katkovsky, and A. Preston, 1964. "Parents' Attitudes and Behaviors and Grade-School Children's Academic Achievements," *Journal of Genetic Psychology*, **104**, 53–66.

Dember, W. N., 1960. *The Psychology of Perception*. New York: Holt.

Douvan, E., 1956. "Social Status and Success Striving," *Journal of Abnormal and Social Psychology*, **52**, 219–223.

Elkind, D., 1964. "Ambiguous Pictures for Study of Perceptual Development and Learning," *Child Development*, **35**, 1391–1396.

Elkind, D., and L. Scott, 1962. "Studies in Perceptual Development: I. The Decentering of Perception," *Child Development*, **33**, 619–630.

Freeberg, N. E., and D. T. Payne, 1967. "Parental Influence on Cognitive Development in Early Childhood: A Review," *Child Development*, **38**, 65–87.

Gardner, R. W., P. S. Holzman, G. S. Klein, H. B. Linton, and D. P. Spence, 1959. "Cognitive Control: A Study of Individual Consistencies in Cognitive Behavior," *Psychological Issues*, **1**, No. 4.

Ghent, L., 1960. "Recognition by Children of Realistic Figures Presented in Various Orientations," *Canadian Journal of Psychology*, **14**, 249–256.

Ghent, L., and L. Bernstein, 1961. "Influence of the Orientation of Geometric Forms on their Recognition by Children," *Perceptual and Motor Skills*, **12**, 95–101.

Gollin, E., 1960. "Developmental Studies of Visual Recognition of Incomplete Objects," *Perceptual and Motor Skills*, **11**, 289–298.

Gray, P. H., 1962. "Is the Imprinting Critical Period an Artifact of a Biological Clock?," *Perceptual and Motor Skills*, **14**, 70.

Harlow, H. F., 1958. "The Nature of Love," *American Psychologist*, **13**, 673–685.

Hartup, W. W., 1964. "Patterns of Imitative Behavior in Young Children," *Child Development*, **35**, 183–191.

Harvey, O. J., 1963. "Overview," in *Motivation and Social Interaction*, edited by O. J. Harvey, pp. 3–17. New York: Ronald.

Harvey, O. J., D. E. Hunt, and H. M. Schroder, 1961. *Conceptual Systems and Personality Organization.* New York: Wiley.

Hebb, D. O., 1949. *The Organization of Behavior.* New York: Wiley.

Hess, R. D., and V. C. Shipman, 1965. "Early Experience and the Socialization of Cognitive Modes in Children," *Child Development,* **36**, 869–886.

Hunt, E. B., 1962. *Concept Learning.* New York: Wiley.

Hunt, J. McV., 1960. "Experience and the Development of Motivation: Some Reinterpretations," *Child Development,* **31**, 489–504.

Hunt, J. McV., 1961. *Intelligence and Experience.* New York: Ronald.

Hunt, J. McV., 1963. "Motivation Inherent in Information Processing and Action," in *Motivation and Social Interaction,* edited by O. J. Harvey, pp. 35–94. New York: Ronald.

Jackson, D. N., and S. Messick, 1962. "Response Styles and the Assessment of Psychopathology," in *Measurement in Personality and Cognition,* edited by S. Messick and J. Ross, pp. 129–156. New York: Wiley.

Johnston, M. K., C. S. Kelley, F. R. Harris, and M. M. Wolf, 1966. "An Application of Reinforcement Principles to Development of Motor Skills of a Young Child," *Child Development,* **37**, 379–387.

Kagan, J., and J. Lemkin, 1961. "Form, Color, and Size in Children's Conceptual Behavior," *Child Development,* **32**, 25–28.

Katkovsky, W., A. Preston, and V. J. Crandall, 1964a. "Parents' Attitudes toward their Personal Achievements and toward the Achievement Behaviors of their Children," *Journal of Genetic Psychology,* **104**, 67–82.

Katkovsky, W., A. Preston, and V. J. Crandall, 1964b. "Parents' Achievement Attitudes and their Behavior with their Children in Achievement Situations," *Journal of Genetic Psychology,* **104**, 105–121.

Kendler, T. S., 1961. "Concept Formation," in *Annual Review of Psychology,* edited by P. R. Farnsworth, pp. 447–472. Palo Alto, Calif.: Annual Reviews.

Kovach, J. K., and E. H. Hess, 1963. "Imprinting: Effects of Painful Stimulation upon the Following Response," *Journal of Comparative and Physiological Psychology,* **56**, 461–464.

Lee, C. L., 1965. "Concept Utilization in Preschool Children," *Child Development,* **36**, 221–227.

Lee, D. M., and A. Bingham, 1959. "Intellectual Processes," *Review of Educational Research,* **29**, 185–195.

Lewis, D. J., 1960. "Partial Reinforcement: A Selective Review of the Literature since 1950," *Psychological Bulletin,* **57**, 1–28.

McClelland, D. C., 1958. "Issues in the Identification of Talent," in *Talent and Society,* edited by D. C. McClelland, A. L. Baldwin, U. Bronfenbrenner, and F. L. Strodtbeck, pp. 1–28. Princeton, N.J.: Van Nostrand.

Maccoby, E. E., and H. L. Bee, 1965. "Some Speculations Concerning the Lag Between Perceiving and Performing," *Child Development,* **36**, 367–377.

Messick, S., and D. N. Jackson, 1961. "Acquiescence and the Factorial Interpretation of the MMPI," *Psychological Bulletin,* **58**, 299–304.

Meyer, W. J., B. Swanson, and N. Kauchack, 1964. "Studies of Verbal Conditioning: I. Effects of Age, Sex, Intelligence, and 'Reinforcing Stimuli,' " *Child Development,* **35,** 409–510.

Miller, N. E., and J. Dollard, 1941. *Social Learning and Imitation.* New Haven, Conn.: Yale.

Mitchell, G. D., G. C. Ruppenthal, E. J. Raymond, and H. F. Harlow, 1966. "Long-term Effects of Multiparous and Primiparous Monkey Mother Rearing," *Child Development,* **37,** 781–791.

Moltz, H., 1960. "Imprinting: Empirical Basis and Theoretical Significance," *Psychological Bulletin,* **57,** 291–314.

Moltz, H., 1963. "Imprinting: An Epigenic Approach," *Psychological Review,* **70,** 123–138.

Moore, S., and R. Updegraff, 1964. "Sociometric Status of Preschool Children Related to Age, Sex, Nurturance-Giving, and Dependency," *Child Development,* **35,** 519–524.

Morgan, C. T., 1957. "Physiological Mechanisms of Motivation," in *Nebraska Symposium on Motivation,* edited by M. R. Jones, pp. 1–35. Lincoln, Neb.: University of Nebraska Press.

Morgan, C. T., 1959. "Physiological Theory of Drive," in *Psychology: A Study of Science.* Vol. I: *Sensory, Perceptual, and Physiological Formulations,* edited by S. Koch, pp. 644–671. New York: McGraw-Hill.

Morgan, C. T., 1965. *Physiological Psychology,* 3d ed. New York: McGraw-Hill.

Neimark, E. D., and N. Lewis, 1967. "The Development of Logical Problem-solving Strategies," *Child Development,* **38,** 107–117.

Penney, R. K., 1960. "The Effects of Nonreinforcement on Response Strength as a Function of Previous Reinforcements," *Canadian Journal of Psychology,* **14,** 206–215.

Reese, H. W., 1963a. " 'Perceptual Set' in Young Children," *Child Development,* **34,** 151–159.

Reese, H. W., 1963b. " 'Perceptual Set' in Young Children: II," *Child Development,* **34,** 451–454.

Ryan, T. J., and G. N. Cantor, 1962. "Response Speed in Children as a Function of Reinforcement Schedule," *Child Development,* **33,** 871–878.

Santostefano, S., and E. Paley, 1964. "Development of Cognitive Controls in Children," *Child Development,* **35,** 939–949.

Scott, P. M., R. V. Burton, and M. K. Yarrow, 1967. "Social Reinforcement under Natural Conditions," *Child Development,* **38,** 53–63.

Slovic, P., 1966. "Risk-Taking in Children: Age and Sex Differences," *Child Development,* **37,** 169–176.

Smock, C. D., and B. G. Holt, 1962. "Children's Reactions to Novelty: An Experimental Study of 'Curiosity Motivation,' " *Child Development,* **33,** 631–642.

Stellar, E., 1954. "The Physiology of Motivation," *Psychological Review,* **61,** 5–22.

Strodtbeck, F. L., 1958. "Family Interaction, Values and Achievement," in *Talent and Society,* edited by D. C. McClelland, A. L. Baldwin, U. Bronfenbrenner, and F. L. Strodtbeck, pp. 135–194. Princeton, N.J.: Van Nostrand.

Teeter, B., D. L. Rouzer, and E. Rosen, 1964. "Development of a Dimension of Cognitive Motivation: Preference for Widely Known Information," *Child Development,* **35,** 1105–1111.

Terrell, G., K. Durkin, and M. Wiesley, 1959. "Social Class and the Nature of the Incentive in Discrimination Learning," *Journal of Abnormal and Social Psychology,* **59,** 270–272.

Tinbergen, N., 1951. *The Study of Instinct.* Fair Lawn, N.J.: Oxford.

Witkin, H. A., R. B. Dyk, H. F. Faterson, D. R. Goodenough, and S. A. Karp, 1962. *Psychological Differentiation.* New York: Wiley.

Witkin, H. A., H. F. Faterson, D. R. Goodenough, and J. Birnbaum, 1966. "Cognitive Patterning in Mildly Retarded Boys," *Child Development,* **37,** 301–316.

Wohlwill, J. F., 1960. "Developmental Studies of Perception," *Psychological Bulletin,* **57,** 249–288.

Young, P. T., 1967. "Affective Arousal: Some Implications," *American Psychologist,* **22,** 32–40.

[*six*]

Behavioral Development in Middle Childhood

The middle years of childhood, those between the ages of six and twelve, are the years during which the child makes the transition from the beginning of life to adulthood. At the beginning of this period, the child can look back at his great dependence upon his parents, and at the end he can look forward to increasing independence and the threshold of adulthood. The two great events of this period come at the beginning and the end: at the beginning, the entrance into the educational system and the demands for considerable and immediate accomplishments; at the end, the beginning of adolescence with its significant physiological and social changes. The middle years are those years in which the child completes the training of elementary school. These are the years in which the child acquires a great deal of information and many new skills; he learns much more about the demands of adults, the kind of society in which he lives, the expectations of his peers, his capacity, ability, and the opportunities within his culture. Within this period, the child discovers many of the realities that have important influences on his destiny: He discovers the importance of his family's financial standing and its meaning for his social status and place in society; he sees the experiences in his home as influencing his performance in school; and he sees the significance of his own physical development and health, the color of his skin, the origins of his family, the place where he lives, the condition and quality of his clothing, the religious group to which he belongs, and the acceptability of his own interests and desires. Not only does he come to see himself as having both favorable and unfavorable characteristics, but also he learns of the feelings of his peers toward him.

In peer associations during this period, sex differences in behavior become clearly established. Boys and girls tend to show indifference and at times hostility toward the other sex. Freudian theory holds that middle childhood is a "latency period" in which there is repression of sexual matters resulting from anxieties about the Oedipus complex (Baldwin, 1967). According to this theory, sexual impulses are kept under control by rules and regulations.

Intellectual curiosity of this age period is seen, however, as a repressed form of behavior related to sexual interest. Despite the fact that sex interest and activity is much more limited in this age period than in adolescence, there is still considerable interest in sex matters and the pushing and shoving of the opposite sex is a form of sex play. One ten-year-old girl when asked what she did for fun at school answered, "Chase boys."

PHYSICAL DEVELOPMENT

Middle childhood is a time when there are relatively steady changes. Increments in height and weight are virtually the same each year. Some of the precarious chemical balances of early childhood no longer exist and the biochemical processes steadily approach the characteristics of adulthood.

Growth in Middle Childhood

The importance of growth in the development of the child has stimulated a great deal of research on developmental change. Considerable attention has been given to the comparison of individual children with their age-mates in reference to growth and normative data.

In middle childhood, growth becomes slower, occurring in uniform increments rather than uneven spurts. At the beginning of the period, the average child is about 46 inches in height and approximately 46 pounds in weight. Height during middle childhood increases at the rate of about 5 per cent per year and weight something over 10 per cent. At the end of the period, the average child is about 5 feet tall and weighs nearly 100 pounds. During the early part of the period, boys are slightly taller than girls, but around age ten, girls become taller and remain so on into adolescence. Weight follows a similar trend, and up until the tenth or eleventh year the boys are somewhat heavier than girls, but after that the girls' weight increases beyond the boys' until adolescence.

During the middle-childhood period, the proportions of the child's body are similar to the adult's, since the earlier infantile disproportions of the body have decreased. Some of the changes in body proportion occur in the trunk, which elongates and becomes more slender; in the chest, which becomes broader; and in the neck, which grows longer. The shoulders drop somewhat, and the size of the pelvis increases. These changes in the bodies of children during middle childhood bring about the possibility of better coordination and strength, as well as more rapid reaction time and, as a result, greater complexity in motor behavior. Boys usually surpass girls in reaction time and in the capacity for gross body movements.

Although much research has been carried on in the study of children's growth, much is yet to be known. Evidence now available indicates that children grow somewhat faster and attain maximum height earlier than children did fifty years ago. The maximal height, however, is not believed to have changed greatly. Nutritional factors and prevention of childhood ill-nesses are believed to be contributory to this change in growth pattern. Nutritionists and pediatricians have not conclusively established dietary boundaries in reference to an inadequate diet, despite acknowledgment of some principles about the needs for vitamins, minerals, calcium, starches, proteins, and fats. Complete agreement on the proportions of these nutrients necessary for an adequate diet, however, has not been obtained.

Constitutional and physical characteristics need to be kept in some perspective. Sometimes parents overemphasize body changes and, by follow-ing a child's growth very closely, bring about a preoccupation in the child with his changing body. As children grow at different rates and according to their own individual patterns, undue emphasis on growth and its changes can have undesirable effects on the child. To a large measure, the child has little control over these changes, despite the fact that some parents try to relate growth directly to conformity to health rules.

Development of Physical Skills and Abilities

The development of motor skills and ability is especially important in middle childhood, for the child's success in school and on the playground depends on his ability to acquire skills in activities valued by his peers. If he is unable to engage in activities or cope with peer expectations, he may withdraw or his peers themselves may exclude him.

Many skills are learned, involving gross as well as fine motor coordination. Generally, boys are more adept in skills involving the larger muscles: throwing a basketball, kicking a football, running, and broad jumping. Girls, on the other hand, are more adept in skills using finer muscles, as in painting, sewing, and other similar tasks. By the time a child enters middle childhood, he has acquired the skills associated with eating, cleanliness, and dressing, and he seldom needs help. In many ways, however, performances are not up to adult standards, and parents continue through the years to warn, plead, and threaten about the way the child eats, keeps his clothes, or washes himself.

In school, the child learns the skills of writing, drawing, singing, dancing, and in many schools the construction of things with tools. In the community at large, at home, or at school in association with social activities, skills such as skating, swimming, craftwork, and bicycle riding are perfected. Children outstanding in some of these activities seem to make better adjustment in school (Havighurst, 1953).

The use of the right or left is established by the time the child reaches school, and dominance is usually not a problem (Benton, 1959). After this age, a shift from one hand to the other is infrequent. However, a child who uses his left hand exclusively often has difficulty because equipment in our society is constructed for people who use their right hand; in addition, as the teacher writes on the board or explains tasks and problems, the demonstrations will appear differently to the child oriented to the left.

> Bill Keller on entering kindergarten used his left hand. As he began drawing and printing exercises, he became confused and could not decide at which margin to begin to print. When he entered first grade, Bill became even more confused. Even in making his letters, he turned them sometimes from left to right and then from right to left. Examination revealed that Bill could use either hand equally well and, for example, could draw with his right hand as well as with his left. If he were asked which was his left or right hand, he was unable to answer. General coordination in both fine and gross motor tasks was relatively equal.
>
> When he was about four years of age, Bill's mother had thought his right hand to be weak and had encouraged him to use his left. But, apparently, righthandedness was dominant for Bill and as he grew older, confusion resulted. If his mother had realized that he could do equally well with his right hand and had therefore allowed him to use his right hand, he would probably not have developed his difficulty in school.

Confusion about handedness becomes a greater problem by the time a child enters school if preference has not been firmly established.

Changes in Anatomy and Physiology

Internal organs change during middle childhood and increase in size. The left ventricle of the heart develops, and with the descent of the diaphragm, the heart assumes a more vertical position. The heart rate gradually decreases as the vagus nerve gains functional control. In relation to weight, the blood volume does not change very much throughout the life span.

Growth of the kidneys lags somewhat behind anatomical growth. After infancy, the ureters increase in length, and the bladder descends into the pelvis (Watson and Lowrey, 1962). In middle childhood, the capacity to tolerate chemical disturbances related to illness increases. The tendency toward severe acidosis and toward problems resulting from infection is much less.

The reproductive organs grow slowly during middle childhood. The periods of greatest growth of the testes are in infancy and in adolescence. The ovaries double their weight in the first few months of infancy, but their weight is not again doubled until adolescence. The uterus reduces in weight after birth and does not regain its relative weight until the latter part of middle childhood.

Information about metabolism in children is used in nutritional studies, particularly in determining the number of calories needed in good health. Information about metabolism is also important in diagnosis of some abnormal conditions such as over- or underactivity of the thyroid gland. The term *metabolism* refers to chemical reactions taking place constantly in the cells and the body. All tissues in their chemical reactions in the body produce heat, with the skeletal muscles and liver producing the most. The liver alone produces about 20 per cent of the body's heat. Metabolic processes are usually divided into those activities in which substances are synthesized—*anabolism*—and into those activities where there is dissimilation and chemical decomposition—*catabolism* (Carlson et al., 1961). In anabolism, increases in protoplasm are associated with growth; however, the process continues independent of growth, as the production of protoplasm in the cells of the body is continuous. Such production replaces proteins and other compounds destroyed in the catabolic process. These processes of anabolism and catabolism require energy, which is obtained through respiration. Metabolism, thus, can be measured by measuring the oxygen used, since the amount of oxygen used is an indication of cell and body activities. Metabolic rate decreases throughout middle childhood. At the beginning of middle childhood, the rate is nearly double that of the adult, but it continues to lessen through adolescence.

Health in Middle Childhood

Acute Illnesses. Acute illnesses are divided into infective and parasitic illnesses, respiratory illnesses, digestive illnesses, miscellaneous acute conditions, and injuries. In general, as children grow older their health improves, and there is a steady decrease in the rate of acute illnesses. In early childhood, about three acute illnesses can be expected per child each year. During middle childhood, the rate drops to approximately two acute episodes of illness each year. (See Figure 6-1.) Of the illnesses in childhood, more than half the acute illnesses in children under fifteen are respiratory disorders. In middle childhood, however, the number of respiratory illnesses drops sharply. Of the children under fifteen who go to the hospital, almost half have surgery. Tonsillectomies account for nearly half of the operations. (See Figure 6-2.)

At the beginning of middle childhood, in the early school years, children often have what are called "children's diseases": mumps, chicken pox, measles, and others. A number of the more severe and dread infectious diseases are now prevented by immunization. Such diseases as whooping cough, diphtheria, and poliomyelitis have been greatly limited. Then too some diseases have become less serious because of advances in medical treatment and the availability of new drugs. For example, pneumonia and tuberculosis are no longer as feared as they were a few years ago. Death from these diseases is now very unlikely if the child has the opportunity for adequate medical care.

Chronic Diseases. Although much progress has been made in the treatment of acute illnesses in children, many children suffer from chronic diseases. Chronic diseases are those of a continuing nature and include hay fever, asthma, or other allergies, respiratory diseases, paralysis and orthopedic impairments, and diabetes. Contrary to the acute illnesses in children, chronic diseases increase with age. The highest incidence is found in the early part of adolescence. However, hay fever, asthma, and other allergies have their highest incidence earlier. (See Figure 6-3.)

Some sex differences are found in the incidence of chronic diseases. While about one-third of the chronic diseases consist of hay fever, asthma, and other allergies in both boys and girls, the rate for asthma in boys is almost twice that for girls. Diseases such as sinusitis and bronchitis also have a higher incidence among boys than girls. (See Figure 6-4.)

Injuries. Injuries continue to be an important problem in childhood.

Children have more acute illnesses than adults

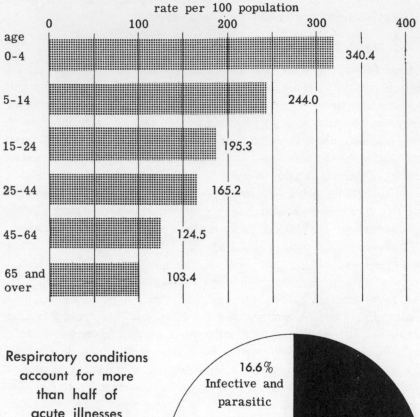

rate per 100 population

age	
0-4	340.4
5-14	244.0
15-24	195.3
25-44	165.2
45-64	124.5
65 and over	103.4

Respiratory conditions account for more than half of acute illnesses among children under fifteen

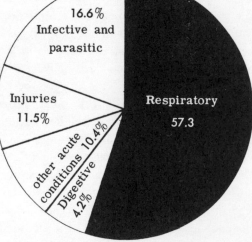

16.6%
Infective and parasitic

Injuries
11.5%

other acute conditions 10.4%

Digestive 4.2%

Respiratory
57.3

Based on U.S. National Health Survey data for period July 1966 to June 1967.

Clara G. Schiffer and Eleanor P. Hunt, *Illness Among Children,* U.S. Department of Health, Education and Welfare, Children's Bureau Publication No. 405, 1963. Data for Figures 6-1 through 6-5 were brought up to date by the National Center for Health Statistics, courtesy of Drs. Philip Lawrence and Charles S. Wilder.

Figure 6.1.

Tonsillectomies play an important part
in the hospitalization of children

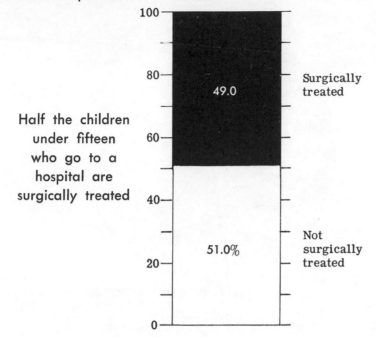

Half the children
under fifteen
who go to a
hospital are
surgically treated

49.0 — Surgically treated

51.0% — Not surgically treated

Almost half the operations on children
under fifteen are tonsillectomies

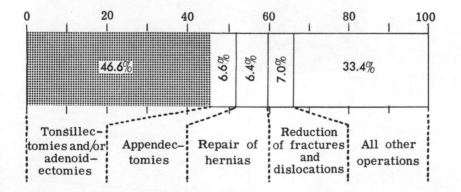

46.6% 6.6% 6.4% 7.0% 33.4%

Tonsillec-tomies and/or adenoid-ectomies | Appendec-tomies | Repair of hernias | Reduction of fractures and dislocations | All other operations

Based on U.S. National Health Survey data as reported in interviews during period
July 1963 to June 1964.

Figure 6.2.

Hayfever, asthma, and other allergies account for one-third of all chronic conditions reported for children under seventeen

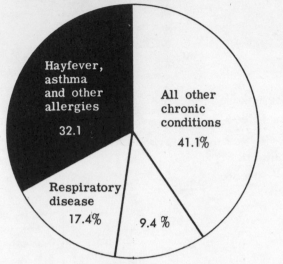

Paralysis and orthopedic impairments

Nearly one-fifth of the days reported lost from school because of chronic conditions are due to asthma

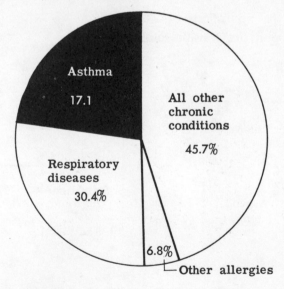

Based on U.S. National Health Survey data as reported in interviews during period July 1964 to June 1966.

Figure 6.3.

The rate of chronic conditions reported among children under seventeen increases with age

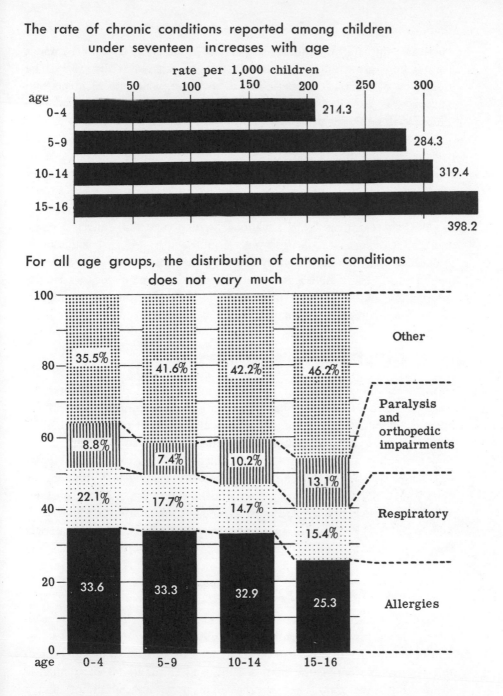

rate per 1,000 children

age		
0-4		214.3
5-9		284.3
10-14		319.4
15-16		398.2

For all age groups, the distribution of chronic conditions does not vary much

	0-4	5-9	10-14	15-16
Other	35.5%	41.6%	42.2%	46.2%
Paralysis and orthopedic impairments	8.8%	7.4%	10.2%	13.1%
Respiratory	22.1%	17.7%	14.7%	15.4%
Allergies	33.6	33.3	32.9	25.3

Based on U.S. National Health Survey data as reported in interviews during period July 1964 to June 1966.

Figure 6.4.

About two-thirds of all injuries are suffered in the home by children under five. As boys grow older, they tend to have more injuries than girls. The proportion of home accidents decreases with age, while the accidents and injuries away from home increase. (See Figure 6-5.) Only a small percentage of the injuries of children is caused by motor vehicles.

Avoidance of hazards is difficult for those who have serious cerebral dysfunction and impairment of the brain, because they are unable to recognize hazards and consequently have more accidents. On the other hand, some children because of emotional characteristics seem to deliberately seek hazardous activity. Behavior that is impulsive and lacking in sufficient reasoning about situations holding potential danger may be another factor in causation. Restraints established to reduce hazards often are unsuccessful because they increase the child's resentment or negativism, and he then intentionally seeks the forbidden activity and disregards danger. Information about "accident proneness" in children from the standpoint of research investigations is limited.

LANGUAGE AND BEHAVIOR

Most investigators agree that by the beginning of middle childhood the basic structure of language has been learned. Accordingly, further language development consists of advances in all aspects of repetitive linguistic behavior and, as a result, patterns of response become so well learned that they are almost reflexive. Ervin and Miller (1963) explain that regular patterns of speech are carried over from early years and that although the child knows a correct language form, he may not use it because of insufficient practice and experience. It remains necessary for children in middle childhood to acquire grammatical patterns associated with complex language, such as passive transformations and construction related to causal events.

Vocabulary Development

Brown and Berko (1963) conducted an experiment to test the degree to which change in word association is of consequence to a child's organization of vocabulary into parts of speech. Subjects for the study relevant to this discussion were in the first, second, and third grades of a middle-income residence area. They were given a word association test and a usage test. The results of the study showed that the scores from tests of association and word usage were closely related and that the scores improved according to age. The conclusion reached by the investigators was

Most childhood accidents occur at home

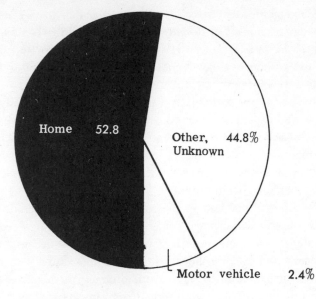

Home   52.8

Other,   44.8%
Unknown

Motor vehicle   2.4%

The proportion of home accidents decreases
as children grow older

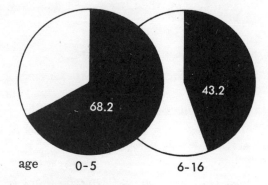

68.2

43.2

age   0-5   6-16

"Other" includes accidents occurring in public places such as
schools and playgrounds, adverse reactions to immunizations, etc.

Based on U.S. National Health Survey data for period July 1966 to June 1967.
Figure 6.5.

that the change in word association and the ability to use new words is a result of organization and development of the child's vocabulary into English syntax. Ervin and Miller (1963) believe that while studies of the complexity and grammatical development of language in children are available, adequate norms for development are still lacking.

Vocabulary size is particularly valuable in learning to read, and children who have had experience with books and whose parents have read to them find that in school this background of learning is of particular help. At the beginning of middle childhood, the child likely understands 20,000 to 24,000 words, and by the end of the middle-childhood period, he usually has more than doubled this number.

The number of children in the family and birth order do not seem to influence the rate of language development. Only children seem to acquire more extensive vocabularies than others, perhaps because they emulate adult speech and because the parents spend more time with them. On the other hand, twins seem to have more difficulty in language development than do other children. Twins sometimes may have slower language development because of central nervous system disorders. Such disorders occur more frequently in twins than in other children. Another possibility is that twins seem to depend on nonverbal communication with each other as a means of satisfying social needs. Their close association leads to imitation of each other's speech rather than adult speech. However, differences in language skill disappear rapidly when twins enter into the wider social contacts of school (Mussen, 1963).

Oral and Written Language

The differences between children's oral and written language were studied by Harrell (1957). Two age levels of subjects, nine and eleven years, were used. In this study, the children were shown two brief motion-picture sequences. Following the first one, the children were asked to write stories about it. Several weeks later they viewed the second picture and were asked to tell oral stories.

Harrell found that both the oral and written stories of older children were longer than those of younger children. However, written stories were not as long at each age level as the oral ones. The length of clauses showed no appreciable change with an increase in age, but there were differences in types of clauses used by older children.

Language and Memory

Not only does the child in the middle-childhood period learn many words from his parents and teachers, but he also learns many from his peers.

Experimentation with words, secret codes, passwords, and the like become part of his play with his age-mates. Secret symbols and signs help him to feel that he is accepted by others of his own age. At the beginning of this period, the child is able to use nearly every type of sentence, and as he moves through the middle-childhood period, his sentences increase in length, becoming somewhat shorter again as he enters adolescence.

Language, of course, is useful in memory; apparently saying aloud the names of objects is an aid to recalling the names later. Rosenbaum (1962) studied the memory of children aged ten to twelve by determining the extent of their recognition of previously shown common objects. At a later date, when the subjects were given a test listing the previously shown objects, it was found that saying the name while being shown the object facilitated its later recognition.

Sex Differences in Language Development

Studies of language development have generally indicated that girls acquire greater language facility and larger vocabularies than boys, particularly up to the age of ten (McCarthy, 1954). Some studies, however, indicate little evidence of sex difference in verbal ability (Templin, 1957; Winitz, 1959); others indicate boys of lower socioeconomic level exceed girls (Alexander, et al., 1968). Environmental differences probably account for variance in reports of studies.

Language and Speech Disorders

Many children who have had speech defects and disorders in early childhood begin to improve markedly upon entering school. By the time the age of seven is reached, most of the defects have disappeared. After reaching middle childhood, speech defects and disorders are not likely to develop. However, if stuttering and stammering have begun earlier, anxiety associated with the child's efforts to meet the requirements of the school may increase his speech problem. Fewer speech defects are encountered among girls than among boys (McCarthy, 1954).

Blanton (1965) believes that stuttering should not be considered a speech defect because it does not occur at all times and does occur only in certain situations. He sees it as a form of social maladjustment. Johnson (1956) asserted that the greater incidence of stuttering in boys than in girls, four times as many boys as girls, is because boys develop more slowly than girls and because of the confusion in teaching boys sex role behavior. The latter reason is based on the fact that while boys are expected to be aggressive, they often are punished for aggression.

A number of physical conditions affect language development adversely.

Hearing loss can be an important factor in preventing normal language development; even slight hearing handicaps may interfere. If language is impaired as a result of hearing deficit, the child's general acquisition of knowledge and information is also delayed.

Language disorders often associated with other types of developmental disorders of an organic nature, such as auditory aberrations, mental retardation, and CNS disorders, may result in aphasia (Lennenberg, 1964). Organic disorders also may have emotional components, in that any physical or anatomical impairment may increase anxiety and thereby cause various types of speech disorders.

Other difficulties that can affect language development are defects in the structures necessary for speech. A cleft palate, for example, interferes with the formation of sounds, and because of the difficulty in communication, a child may tend to avoid verbal exchange with others. Some types of impairment of the central nervous system also affect speech and language acquisition. Such problems come from impairment of innervation structures or from defects in the brain center controlling speech.

Bilingualism

Bilingualism, or the acquisition of two languages, can present several problems. Some children who live in a home or community where more than one language is spoken seem to make slower progress than the child who has to learn only one language. Language is not separated from culture, and if a child lives in a home where two languages are spoken, it is likely that there are differences in cultural influences also. It is difficult, therefore, to attribute the child's problems with language and his associated problem behavior alone to the fact that he must learn two languages. Each language is associated with certain customs, ways of thinking and behaving, which provide a basis for conflict. Thus, in addition to learning a second language, the child must learn related customs and attitudes that may be in conflict with the culture of the first language. In addition, he must be able to sort out the appropriate responses for each cultural environment when they are required. Cultural differences create problems in association with peers, since a child may be teased or rejected by the peer group because of differences in speech forms. Learning another language is a different situation when children learn it in school or in travel; then a second language is an addition to their own language and the culture of which they have become a part.

A problem in the consideration of bilingualism is the meaning of the term. According to Soffietti (1955), three possible conditions of bilingualism are encountered: (1) bicultural-bilingualism—in which a child participates intimately in two cultures (an example would be that the immigrant parents of a child insist that the child retain cultural behavior of the old culture to a major extent); (2) bicultural-monolingualism—in which a child is of an immigrant family which has given up one language or whose native language is English but which keeps the customs of another culture; (3) monocultural-bilingualism—in which a child learns a second language in school or lives with parents who are bilingual and choose to speak to the child always in a foreign language.

Problems seem to result from emotional conflict accompanying separation of the child's loyalties resulting from life in two cultures. While Darcy (1963), in a review of a decade of research in reference to intelligence test scores and bilingualism, cautions about generalization, her review indicates that bilingual children more often receive lower scores than do monolingual childen.

Peal and Lambert (1962), however, concluded from their research with ten-year-old children in six French schools in Canada that bilingual children performed significantly better than monolingual children on both verbal and nonverbal tests of intelligence. These investigators attributed the superior performance of the bilingual children to the parents' favorable attitudes and encouragement. They found that the bilingual children were superior in concept formation and in having a wider range of mental abilities than the monolingual children.

The conflict about the favorable or unfavorable effects of bilingualism probably results from problems of definition and varying conditions studied. Yamamoto (1964), for example, believes that bilingualism does not have to have an unfavorable effect, particularly when one language is not deemed inferior to the other and when the child can learn both languages spontaneously.

Cultural and Social-Class Influence

The lack of opportunity for communication with others is another factor adversely affecting the acquisition of language. Children away from families in an institution and deprived of the opportunities for a normal amount of verbal exchange have much difficulty. Most experts in language development believe that environmental opportunities for acquisition of vocabulary and language complexity is of greater importance as the child advances in years. As with other skills, maturation and learning go apace, the one influencing the other. Social class undoubtedly affects language development. It may have the most significant effect, for example, on the acquisition of grammatical forms acceptable in middle class by children from lower socioeconomic class. In general, lower-class children have many difficulties in meeting the school requirements, but they are particularly handicapped from the standpoint of their limited vocabulary, the lack of experience in the use of language in solving of problems, and in their lack of experience in utilizing language to influence people.

Children from lower socioeconomic conditions often have been found to have more vocabulary and language deficiencies in comparison with children in upper income brackets. Children living in deprived social conditions are not as advanced in some forms of speech development as children living under more advantaged conditions (Alexander et al., 1968). Much more information about language development will be available in the next few years as the result of large governmental programs in university research centers that have been established to study developmental problems of children born into deprived conditions.

In a study of children's speech comprehension in the first and fifth grades, Peisach (1965), using the technique of requiring children to fill in deleted words of sentences in order to supply meaning, found little difference between Negroes and whites but found that socioeconomic class differences were greater in older children. This investigator found that girls in fifth grade surpassed boys in the use of proper grammatical structure. It was found that middle socioeconomic class boys and girls generally were equal in language performance but boys of lower socioeconomic class were inferior to the girls of lower socioeconomic class. This investigator suggested that this latter sex difference reflects motivation and training.

EMOTIONAL BEHAVIOR

In middle childhood, children derive satisfaction from activities with others, as well as satisfaction from isolated enterprises. Children may gleefully stamp with others in a puddle of rainwater or they may enjoy an amusing story book alone. Appropriateness of behavior associated with feelings, however, changes in middle childhood. Certain kinds of behavior tolerated in the small child, such as stamping his feet and crying when thwarted, are not usually allowed in middle childhood by teachers or parents. Accordingly, as the child grows and change comes about in other areas of his behavior, so must change take place in his emotional behavior.

During middle childhood, positive emotions are easily observed and much carefree behavior or *joie de vivre* is seen. Children leave the school's doors for recess with shoving, laughing, shouting, and excited anticipation.

Laughter comes easily and an almost total enmeshment in mirth often takes place. Sometimes the carefree behavior of children in middle childhood brings disapproval from parents. Such behavior, however, may be a reflection of parental behavior as was exemplified in the actions of Yvonne.

Yvonne, an attractive ten-year-old girl, enjoyed many activities but did not take any of her responsibilities seriously at home or at school. She enjoyed the activities in which she engaged, but if tasks were not completed and if some other activity proved more desirable or interesting, she quickly abandoned the assigned tasks. Scolding or remonstrances with Yvonne failed to upset her. She accepted the criticism with a pleasant expression and happily continued in her own choice of activities. As her behavior was upsetting, particularly to her mother and her teacher, the parents had a conference with Yvonne's teacher. The father realized that Yvonne's behavior was similar to his own. He said, "Yvonne seems to enjoy life—and, as a matter of fact, so do I." On making this observation, he laughed loudly and easily. His wife agreed that Yvonne was very much like her father. As the father considered Yvonne's behavior, he found he was quite pleased with her and that her behavior was far from distasteful to him. As the mother thought about Yvonne's behavior, she too saw that the similarity to her husband's behavior was also attractive to her. She thought that she herself worried too much. As they both thought about Yvonne's behavior and its similarity to her father's, they decided that they would enjoy Yvonne as she was.

Types of Emotional Behavior in Middle Childhood

Although affection is a source of comfort and satisfaction in very young children, it is acceptable especially to boys in middle childhood only under certain conditions. In this period, both boys and girls are more undemonstrative and engage in less affectionate exchange. They will, however, show affection for their dogs and other pets. With peers, they express affection through desire for close association.

Some negative emotions during the period of middle childhood result from stress encountered in the socialization process in a complex society. Resentment sometimes accompanies social learning, and children in this age period have difficulty in learning to deal with resentment as they cannot express it directly toward parents, teachers, and others in authority. They can, however, express resentment in interaction with other children, especially with those who are younger or who have less capacity for fighting back or protecting themselves.

In a study of anxiety in relation to the learning of nine- and ten-year-old children, Horowitz and Armentrout (1965) concluded that such emotional response is closely related to type of task, difficulty, and type of reinforcement. Such findings suggest that in the normal course of development anxiety tends to be specific and less generalized. Kagan and Moss (1962) found some consistency in behavior in dealing with anxiety lasting into adulthood. Children who withdrew from anxiety-arousing stimuli tended to continue such behavior as adults.

Sears (1961) found sex differences in aggression. For example, girls showed higher scores on measures revealing feelings of fear about and dislike of aggression. They also had higher scores on measures indicating use of aggression in socially approved ways. Boys, on the other hand, scored higher on measures indicating acceptability to them of socially disapproved forms of aggression. Jeering, teasing, fighting, and other acts of hostility are, of course, not unusual. Sometimes the behavior of children is harsh and in later childhood, especially in adolescence, extremes of cruelty by way of social ostracism and ridicule are encountered.

Socioeconomic-Class Influence on Emotional Behavior

Angelino et al. (1956) in a study of 1,100 children found that socioeconomic background was an important factor in the types of expressed fears. The number of fears in both the lower and higher socioeconomic groups was similar. The kinds of fears differed, however: Boys from the lower-class groups tended to fear matters of violence, while boys from the higher group feared car accidents and storms; the girls from the lower-class group feared animals, strangers, violence, and drunk people, while girls from the higher group feared kidnappers, heights, and the like. In school, the boys from the lower-class group tended to be more afraid of teachers, while the boys in the higher groups tended to be more concerned about grades and school achievement.

Emotions and Physiological Processes

The behavior of Emory illustrates how a child's emotions in reference to his relationship with his parents can influence his physiological processes.

> Emory, an attractive and pleasant child, found that certain behavior in reference to his body processes helped him to gain sympathy and concern from his parents. Most of the time Emory

conformed to his parents' wishes and, even though only six years old, kept his room very neat.

The parents were pleased with his behavior in all but one area —his behavior at mealtime. When Emory, his parents, and his two older brothers sat down to eat, the problem would begin. As the meal progressed, Emory would say, "Mother, I think that I am going to spit up." His father would order him to continue to eat and not spit up. Sometimes his father would take him to the bathroom. At other times, the parents tried to distract him with conversation so that he would forget about his warning. At still others, his father would ask him to wait and see if he would really find it necessary to regurgitate his food. Whatever the response of his parents, however, Emory would eventually warn his parents and would regurgitate the food he had eaten. He would then return to the table and continue his meal. He usually ate the rest of his food without having a similar episode. These episodes occurred only at breakfast when all of the family was together and during the evening meal. As this behavior continued, his parents became increasingly annoyed and struggled with him to prevent regurgitation. Nevertheless, Emory had learned to control the process and could regurgitate the food that he had eaten at will. The sequence of the behavior was first to give a warning, then listen to suggestions of both his parents that he try to wait, and next to give a final warning: "Dad, I am going to have to spit up." The parents learned that when this final warning came, they would have to acquiesce.

In the parents' efforts to utilize conversation which they thought might interest Emory, they failed to see that their exchange still excluded Emory's contribution. Unwittingly, they contributed to the problem, because when Emory found that he was left out of the conversation, he could always bring attention to himself by his warning.

His parents were not certain that he was not ill nor that he did not have some anatomical problem, thus they tried to avoid punishment and demands that he remain at the table. The regurgitation of food served Emory by giving him some control over his parents—in fact, it became a powerful threat by which he could upset them and at the same time gain their sympathetic interest. Emory's problem was not resolved until the parents were willing to lessen their demands upon Emory and actually leave the problem of regurgitation to Emory for solution. When he found it was not necessary to give his warning, that he could leave the table or not as he liked, and that he would be included in conversation without his problem behavior, the regurgitation ceased.

SOCIAL BEHAVIOR

In middle childhood, influences outside the family are increasingly influential on the child's behavior. Peers particularly are a source of emulation and emotional support in a wide range of emotional behavior. Patterson and Anderson (1964), as a result of their study of social relationships of children in middle childhood, found that older children showed more marked changes in preference for behavior reinforced by peers than did younger children. Older children in the second and third grades were particularly influenced by their friends.

Interaction with Peers

A child's standing in the esteem of his peers becomes increasingly important to him as he moves away from the family and becomes more independent. Peers provide sources of emotional support and influence a child's feelings about himself and his accomplishments.

> Maurice's problems with his peers or age-mates had become of such great concern to him that he refused to play with the children at school and preferred to stay indoors at recess. At home he watched TV or engaged in other sedentary activities. Maurice was so overweight that he walked with difficulty. His peers called him "Fatty" and teased him whenever he appeared. He resented their ridicule and name calling, but his age-mates found it satisfying to see his anger and resentment. Finding himself unsuccessful in coping with the teasing, he sought to avoid contact with them.

> Maurice's mother enjoyed cooking and often cooked more than the family consumed. She offered the excess to Maurice so that he ate much more than he needed. He pleased his mother by eating and enjoying her food. His mother had decided that his overweight came from some abnormality; actually, it stemmed from a complex family situation. His mother had had prolonged depressive episodes associated with the illness of her own mother. Apparently, Maurice's mother had depended upon her own mother for emotional support since she and her husband had not been close. Maurice's appreciation of her talent in food

preparation had been particularly satisfying to her and she unwisely depended too much upon Maurice for emotional support. When his mother found satisfaction and emotional support from other sources, she then was able to help Maurice to decrease his food intake.

In middle childhood, adult values are only part of the child's value system, because his peers also provide sources of behavior for emulation. The very fact that the peer-valued behavior differs from that desired by adults has in itself some intrinsic appeal—an appeal for independence from adult or parental control. A child is thus in some conflict—he does not wish to throw off all parental values, yet he feels he must conform to peer values too. In later childhood, precursors of adolescent conflict are in evidence, providing a background for the "storm and stress" so common in adolescence in our society.

Development of Moral Judgments

Behavior, particularly social behavior, of children in middle childhood is increasingly determined by what has been called "moral judgments." The influence of such judgments is complex and results in part from the child's sensitivity and responsiveness to complex stimuli from others. Grinder (1964) concludes as the result of a study of children in second, fourth, and sixth grades that compliance with social standards is more a function of social learning than maturation of mental structure. This view, according to the investigator, differs from Piaget's about the significance of cognitive development in reference to moral judgments. Whiteman and Kosier (1964), in a study of moral judgments in relation to age, sex, and IQ in middle childhood, concluded that the ability to form judgments about behavior is a function of higher levels of intelligence test scores. Johnson (1962) believes that age is significantly correlated with moral judgments and that ability to form moral judgments gradually increases as the child moves through middle childhood. Mischel (1958) believes that the willingness of children to forego immediate rewards for future ones is related to their age, social class, culture, and family structure. The conclusions were based on studies of American, West Indian, Negro, and East Indian children.

On the other hand, Boehm and Nass (1962) with their subjects, children aged six to twelve in the lower and middle socioeconomic class of average intelligence, found no social-class or sex differences in moral judgments but did find age level of significance.

Studies of moral judgment present many problems to the investigator, particularly in reference to other investigators, because of the difficulty of definition of the abstract terms of *moral judgment, conscience,* and *social behavior.* Finding tasks which measure or which are directly related to abstractions is so difficult that comparison of methodologies and resultant findings is often impossible. Furthermore, testing of theoretical generalizations and broad principles in reference to morality is yet to be satisfactorily achieved. Despite such difficulties, those individuals who are involved in the study of human development and social processes are increasingly aware of the importance of investigation of the acquisition of values and the adherence to a value system.

The Educational System's Influence on Behavior

In middle childhood, the school becomes of great consequence in the child's life: It supplements and extends the teachings of the family and, in fact, provides experiences for the child that he has never had in the family. Before the beginning of school, the child's training is largely that which he received from his parents and many of the family requirements were kept within his capacity to learn; but moving outside of the family into the school usually holds many new problems. The many rules of the school, for example, are not only difficult for the child to accept, but also they have little meaning for him in terms of necessity. Gump and Kounin (1961) found in a study of several hundred first-grade boys and girls that the children had difficulty in explaining reasons for the school rules.

A child's response to the new experience of school and his ability to utilize it, in a large measure, are determined by his earlier experiences. Parents are sometimes dismayed and confused by the fact that the experiences they provided within the home failed to give their children the proper background to meet the school's requirements. Hersov (1960), in a study of children afraid to go to school, found that while they were overinhibited at school, they were very demanding at home.

Children with better than average intellectual ability and physical well-being are better able to meet the demands of the school; thus, characteristically, such children have less anxiety and express more positive emotional feelings about themselves than do those less favored. Cowen et al. (1965), in a study of nine-year-old children, found that lower anxiety tended to be related positively to IQ and achievement scores, and high anxiety tended to be positively related to teachers' rating of maladjustment.

The educational system's influence on behavior is indicated in a study by Kagan (1964). This investigator assumed that children are more willing to master school tasks when the tasks are believed to be appropriate to their sex. In this study of second- and third-grade children he found that many school objects were associated with femininity and the suggested reason was that the woman teacher used the objects. Kagan concluded that girls were more motivated to accomplish school tasks because of the congruence of their perception of these tasks with their sex. This study suggests that there are many complex and subtle influences in the school which influence the development of children.

Toward the end of the first school year, most children are ready to go on to the next grade. Of those who are not, poor general health and physical defects are important factors in failure. A direct relationship between constitutional defect and school achievement, however, cannot always be established. And, although general agreement exists that children from the lower class have more health as well as behavior problems, Mensh et al. (1959) found in their study of boys from the upper social class that many had problems also. Difficulties listed were aggressiveness, withdrawal, destructiveness, speech disorders, sleep disturbances, fears, temper tantrums, daydreaming, and stealing.

FAMILY RELATIONSHIPS IN MIDDLE CHILDHOOD

To some extent, as Hurlock (1968) explains, family relationships contain more friction as the child moves through the middle childhood period. Sometimes, to the usual differences between parents and child are added other sources of conflict and disordered relationships. These sources affect to varying extent the child's learning and development, but they are nearly always deleterious.

> Barbara, the youngest of three children, had difficulty with arithmetic. She did quite well in her other studies, but she did not seem to be able to achieve in arithmetic as well as her classmates. Both parents worked with Barbara each night on her homework. She nevertheless made poor grades and fell further and further behind the other children in her class. In the fourth grade, she began to have pains in her abdomen because of an intestinal disorder; she finally became so ill that she could not attend school. Although Barbara's father described her ability to do arithmetic as "horrible," her parents realized that she had not failed in any of her subjects since beginning school and that the teachers had always been satisfied with Barbara's work. Despite her satisfactory record, both parents had worked diligently each night with Barbara in order to help her to achieve a higher

level in arithmetic. Barbara's ability, however, was only average and her parent's insistence that she achieve at a higher level was more than could reasonably be expected. While the apparent cause of Barbara's difficulty was her achievement in school, in actuality the problem was much greater. At the onset of her serious intestinal disorder, which was in part associated with her anxiety, her mother was placed in the hospital for a serious mental disorder, extreme depression. The problem of Barbara in school, as well as her trouble with her parents and her teacher, were all symptomatic of the far greater family problems.

Family Constituency

The preferred size of the family is influenced by religion, education, social class, and the parents' own experiences in early life (Hurlock, 1968). The size of the family also is dependent upon the adults' investment in children and the extent of satisfaction derived from a large number of children. Large families in modern society, however, place considerable strain on the time, energy, and financial resources of parents.

In addition to early experience, social-class backgrounds also contribute to different feelings toward parenthood and family size. The middle- and upper-class parents see parenthood as a part of the attainment of life goals and view their children as possibilities for fulfillment of some of their own dreams and hopes. Lower-class parents often view their parenthood as the result of their sexual activity and do not see their children as holding possibilities for achievement of their own goals.

The family makeup affects later choices about marriage, friendship, and vocation. The absence of the father seems to have certain specific effects. Lynn and Sawrey (1959) in a study of Norwegian children in middle childhood whose fathers were absent from the family found that the boys tended to react with more compensatory masculinity and more often seek to identify with the father than children whose fathers were in the family. Girls in such families tended to be more dependent on the mother than girls in families having the father present.

Parental Conflict

Tension and conflict between parents usually adversely affect the child's behavior and emotional development. Vogel (1960) believes that a disturbed child often is the child who becomes a "scapegoat" in marriages on the verge of breakup. Although parents in emotional turmoil themselves usually deny that their own problems affect the child, their training, however, is usually more unsuccessful (Altman, 1958; Becker et al., 1959).

Conflict between the parents affects a child's ability and willingness to meet requirements outside the family, particularly in school. In seeking solutions, parents concentrate all too often on the child's problems when in reality the solution lies in changing family conditions, as is illustrated in the following two stories.

> Janice was an exceptionally attractive girl in the fourth grade. Her family had recently moved to a new town. Her parents thought the move had upset Janice, since she had not wanted to leave her old school. In the new school, although she had superior ability, she refused to do some of her work, especially her language studies. Her teacher and parents, of course, were displeased about her failure to study, but Janice was adamant in her decision. She refused to do her work, although she was frequently threatened with punishment. Her problems, however, were more complex than her parents thought, as Janice realized that her parents were on the verge of separation. Her mother had threatened to take the children and leave the father because of the continuing quarrels. Both parents thought that they had kept their quarreling from the children, but Janice was aware of their unhappiness and the turmoil provided a background of unhappiness which prevented Janice from meeting the school's requirements.

> Darlene, eight years old and in the third grade, was affected differently by her parents' conflict. At home, Darlene would not accede to the demands of the parents: She quarreled with her sister, was petulant and demanding, and at times would stamp her feet and cry if she did not receive the attention or objects that she wished to have. If she was asked to perform some task, she would shake her head and stamp her feet while saying "no." Her defiance and sullen expressions upset her parents.

> Darlene's parents had been on the verge of divorce for six years. Her mother had continually threatened to leave her father, although the father wished to hold the family together. When his wife threatened to leave him, he became quite disturbed. Darlene's mother also often became distraught by the children's behavior and quarreling and sought medication from her physician in an attempt to control her emotions. Darlene's parents saw themselves as failing as parents and as failing each other.

> Neither, however, saw clearly the extremely deleterious effect that the family's instability was having on Darlene. Although

Darlene was a talented child, she did not do her work in school nor did she show the promise of her potential capability. Darlene's difficulties were only a part of a much larger problem.

A child with central nervous system dysfunction, orthopedic difficulties, visual, or auditory impairment, is particularly devastated by parental conflict. He lacks the opportunity for emotionally satisfying relationships, which provide the courage to complete tasks more difficult for him than the ordinary child. Psychological effects of physical defect are greatly increased by parental unhappiness and conflict.

Many of the deleterious effects upon children of parental conflict and family dissolution are obvious, but some are subtle. Defamation of the absent parent by the one with whom the child lives after divorce is particularly confusing. On the other hand, a child may seek to give all of his devotion to the parent with whom he lives and completely separate himself emotionally from the parent from whom he is separated; yet this effort is not without cost to the child in anxiety and guilt.

Schaefer and Bayley (1963), in a report of a longitudinal study lasting from infancy through adolescence of 54 children, sought to analyze the relation of maternal behavior to the social and emotional behavior of the child. The findings of the study indicate that emotional relationship with the mother is significantly related to positive social and emotional responses. A higher correlation was found between mothers and sons than between mothers and daughters. In general, the investigators believe that their study supports the belief that the mother's emotional relationship to the child is of significance in the child's success in social interaction.

In a report of research on the influence of social class and children's perception of parents, Rosen (1964) indicated that parents of the middle socioeconomic class were perceived to be more positive in competence than were lower-class parents. The parents of lower socioeconomic class were perceived as being "shy, nervous, and worried." Middle-class parents were reported to be more interested in performance or success in school and were more responsive to requests for attention. Although lower-class mothers were less interested in their sons than middle socioeconomic class mothers, they were more interested than the fathers. In this study, all the subjects were boys.

Bailyn (1959) reported research indicating that family and socioeconomic class have considerable influence on social role models that the child selects. The occupation and education of fathers were satisfactory bases for predictions relative to the boy's vocational aspirations. Girls' vocational choices, however, were more independent of socioeconomic class position.

A POINT OF VIEW

In middle childhood, a child learns about "homework," extended times of study, and long-term pursuit of educational assignments. Parents too become involved in the educational experiences of their child and often express concern about the quality of the school as they believe the educational system to be a significant determining factor for both the welfare of the child and that of the social order.

The child's activities and behavior in this age period are more easily controlled than in either the early-childhood or adolescent periods, and thus he may not feel he is free to express his feelings or demands. Since at this time the child is closely related to the family and is still primarily emotionally dependent on adults, the period is an impressionable time in reference to control and to cultural values both subtly and openly taught to him. Also of much significance is the fact that the period is the prelude to adolescence with all of this latter period's conflict so prevalent in most cultures of the world today. Research studies in middle childhood, accordingly, need to be extended to study family life and school experiences, particularly in reference to affective exchange and the teaching of values important to cultural continuity.

REFERENCES

Alexander, T., J. Stoyle, and C. Kirk, 1968. "The Language of Children in the Inner City," *Journal of Psychology, 68,* 215–221.

Altman, C. H., 1958. "Relationship Between Maternal Attitudes and Child Personality Structure," *American Journal of Orthopsychiatry, 28,* 160–169.

Angelino, H., J. Dollins, and E. V. Mech, 1956. "Trends in the 'Fears and Worries' of School Children as Related to Socio-Economic Status and Age," *Journal of Genetic Psychology, 89,* 263–276.

Bailyn, L., 1959. "Mass Media and Children: A Study of Exposure Habits and Cognitive Effects," *Psychological Monographs, 73,* 1–48.

Baldwin, A. L., 1967. *Theories of Child Development.* New York: Wiley.

Becker, W. C., D. R. Peterson, L. A. Hellmer, D. J. Shoemaker, and H. C. Quay, 1959. "Factors in Parental Behavior and Personality as Related to Problem Behavior in Children," *Journal of Consulting Psychology, 23,* 107–118.

Benton, A. L., 1959. *Right-Left Discrimination and Finger Localization.* New York: Hoeber-Harper.

Blanton, S., 1965. "Stuttering," in *New Directions in Stuttering,* edited by D. A. Barbara, pp. 3–17. Springfield, Ill.: Charles C Thomas.

Boehm, L., and M. L. Nass, 1962. "Social Class Differences in Conscience Development," *Child Development,* 33, 565–574.

Brown, R., and J. Berko, 1963. "Word Association and the Acquisition of Grammar," in *Research Readings in Child Psychology,* edited by D. S. Palermo and L. P. Lipsitt, pp. 351–361. New York: Holt.

Carlson, A. J., V. Johnson, and H. M. Cavert, 1961. *The Machinery of the Body.* Chicago: The University of Chicago Press.

Cowen, E. L., M. Zax, R. Klein, L. D. Izzo, and M. A. Trost, 1965. "The Relation of Anxiety in School Children to School Record, Achievement, and Behavioral Measures," *Child Development,* 36, 685–694.

Darcy, N. T., 1963. "Bilingualism and the Measurement of Intelligence of a Decade of Research," *Journal of Genetic Psychology,* 103, 259–282.

Ervin, S. M., and W. R. Miller, 1963. "Language Development," in *Child Psychology,* National Society for the Study of Education, Sixty-second Yearbook, Part I, pp. 108–143. Chicago: The University of Chicago Press.

Grinder, R. E., 1964. "Relations between Behavioral and Cognitive Dimensions of Conscience in Middle Childhood," *Child Development,* 35, 881–891.

Gump, P. V., and J. S. Kounin, 1961. "Milieu Influences in Children's Concepts of Misconduct," *Child Development,* 32, 711–720.

Harrell, L. E., 1957. *A Comparison of the Development of Oral and Written Language in School-age Children.* Monographs of the Society for Research in Child Development, 22, No. 3. Lafayette, Ind.: Child Development Publications, Purdue University.

Havighurst, R. J., 1953. *Human Development and Education.* New York: Longmans.

Hersov, L. A., 1960. "Refusal to Go to School," *Journal of Child Psychology and Psychiatry,* 1, 137–145.

Horowitz, F. D., and J. Armentrout, 1965. "Discrimination-Learning, Manifest Anxiety, and Effects of Reinforcement," *Child Development,* 36, 731–748.

Hurlock, E. B., 1968. *Developmental Psychology.* New York: McGraw-Hill.

Johnson, R. C., 1962. "A Study of Children's Moral Judgments," *Child Development,* 33, 327–354.

Johnson, W., 1956. "Stuttering," in *Speech Handicapped School Children,* edited by W. Johnson, S. J. Brown, J. F. Curtis, C. W. Edney, and J. Keaster. New York: Harper & Row.

Kagan, J., 1964. "The Child's Sex Role Classification of School Objects," *Child Development,* 35, 1051–1056.

Kagan, J., and H. A. Moss, 1962. *Birth to Maturity.* New York: Wiley.

Lennenberg, E. H., 1964. "Language Disorders in Childhood," *Harvard Educational Review,* 34, 152–177.

Lynn, D. B., and W. G. Sawrey, 1959. "The Effects of Father-Absence on Norwegian Boys and Girls," *Journal of Abnormal and Social Psychology,* 59, 258–262.

McCarthy, D., 1954. "Language Development in Children," in *Manual of*

Child Psychology, 2d ed., edited by L. Carmichael, pp. 492–630. New York: Wiley.

Mensh, I. N., M. B. Kantor, H. R. Domke, M. C. L. Gildea, and J. C. Glidewell, 1959. "Children's Behavior Symptoms and Their Relationships to School Adjustment, Sex, and Social Class," *Journal of Social Issues*, **15**, 8–15.

Mischel, W., 1958. "Preference for Delayed Reinforcements: An Experimental Study of a Cultural Observation," *Journal of Abnormal and Social Psychology*, **56**, 57–61.

Mussen, P. H., 1963. *The Psychological Development of the Child*. Englewood Cliffs, N.J.: Prentice-Hall.

Patterson, G. R., and D. Anderson, 1964. "Peers as Social Reinforcers," *Child Development*, **35**, 951–960.

Peal, E., and W. E. Lambert, 1962. "The Relation of Bilingualism to Intelligence," *Psychological Monographs*, **76**, No. 27.

Peisach, E. C., 1965. "Children's Comprehension of Teacher and Peer Speech," *Child Development*, **36**, 467–480.

Rosen, B. C., 1964. "Social Class and the Child's Perception of the Parent," *Child Development*, **35**, 1147–1153.

Rosenbaum, M. E., 1962. "Effect of Direct and Vicarious Verbalization on Retention," *Child Development*, **33**, 103–110.

Schaefer, E. S., and N. Bayley, 1963. *Maternal Behavior, Child Behavior, and Their Intercorrelations from Infancy through Adolescence*. Monographs of the Society for Research in Child Development, **28**, No. 3. Lafayette, Ind.: Child Development Publications, Purdue University.

Sears, R. R., 1961. "Relation of Early Socialization Experiences to Aggression in Middle Childhood," *Journal of Abnormal and Social Psychology*, **63**, 466–492.

Soffietti, J. P., 1955. "Bilingualism and Biculturalism," *Journal of Educational Psychology*, **46**, 222–227.

Templin, M., 1957. *Certain Language Skills in Children: Their Development and Interrelationship*. Minneapolis: University of Minnesota Press.

Vogel, E. F., 1960. "The Marital Relationship of Parents of Emotionally Disturbed Children: Polarization and Isolation," *Psychiatry*, **23**, 1–12.

Watson, E. H., and G. H. Lowrey, 1962. *Growth and Development of Children*. Chicago: The Year Book Medical Publishers.

Whiteman, P. H., and K. P. Kosier, 1964. "Development of Children's Moralistic Judgments: Age, Sex, I.Q., and Certain Personal–Experiential Variables," *Child Development*, **35**, 843–850.

Winitz, H., 1959. "Language Skills of Male and Female Kindergarten Children," *Journal of Speech and Hearing Research*, **2**, 377–386.

Yamamoto, K., 1964. "Bilingualism: A Brief Review," *Mental Hygiene*, **48**, 468–477.

[*seven*]

Intellectual Development

THE BRAIN

The human brain has been called the most complex organ of all creation
and its capacity has no challenge from even the largest computer. If a
model of the brain were to be constructed, thousands of cubic feet would
be required for the location of electrical sources of power and at least a
million kilowatts of electricity would be required to operate it. The quarter
of a kilogram-calorie provided each minute by oxidation of glucose in the
brain is sufficient for its function. A human brain has much more storage
capacity than present-day computers, since it records experiences moment
by moment and day by day in a never-ending stream. The system of filing
and recall are beyond understanding, for the brain can obtain instantaneously
extremely small details with many associated meanings. In some ways,
however, a computer is analogous to a human brain. For example, a computer for radar control of some military weapons makes corrections for
error and, similarly, the brain through "feedback" improves the chances
of achieving a goal. The basic units of the nervous system are neurons—
microscopic cells that number in the billions in the brain. Each of the
larger neurons has thousands of connections (synapses) to other neurons.
Brain, receptors, and effectors are joined in such a way that a receptor
stimulates an effector and an effector then can in turn stimulate a receptor
(Bailey, 1962). Thus, the brain's cortex, with its vast number of nerve

nets connected together in an infinite number of ways, changes and fluctuates operationally until the individual reaches a goal.

The Brain's Capacity

The brain develops rapidly after birth and modifies its functional organization by its exposure to constant conditions of stimulation. In association with the stimulation, problem-solving and intellective processes are functionally directed by activity in the associational areas in the frontal lobes. Processes here are dependent upon visual images, which become the basis for an "internal conversation." By such conversation, tentative solutions can be sought by projecting the results and by comparison with memory and "stored input." New solutions judged to be more effective than older ones can thus be tried out and evaluated without the organism as a whole committing itself to action. Hence, such a process delays "output" and increases the effectiveness of behavior, while at the same time conserving organismic energy. Foresight against either wear and tear on the brain or threat to the welfare and safety of the entire organism is thus a part of the brain's functioning.

The term *mental processes* cannot refer just to brain activity; it must also take into account other parts of the total complex activity of the individual—in one sense, mental processes involve the whole behavior of the individual. This totality of behavior is, in turn, a part of the social interaction and matrix of society and culture in which an individual lives (Cantril, 1962). Emotions, too, can be a significant part of intellectual functioning. The functioning of the brain, therefore, can be seen as a dynamic system, consisting of the internal processes of thought, emotional processes, and external activity (behavior).

During development, an individual needs to be socially conditioned because behavior of a social creature cannot be entirely directed toward his own welfare. Social behavior, however, needs continuing reinforcement during the developmental years. Through such reinforcement, the brain's cortex is conditioned to respond to a symbol related to a social goal, and the individual system of behavior becomes part of a larger system composed of the interrelated behavior of others. Hence, mental processes during development are a part of an ever-widening system of interaction.

In accordance with the above reasoning, it follows that effective functioning of the brain depends upon social interaction of the organism with the environment. Disappointment, for example, may reduce feelings of hunger and hence affect nutrition. Or, group exchanges may induce euphoria and feelings of well-being, which bring about behavior leading to further accomplishment. Experiences thus influence the efficiency of the organism and, indeed, in turn influence the efficiency of the mental processes themselves within the cortex (Bruner, 1964). Experiments with animals have demonstrated the importance of early environmental inter-action in the developing of effective behavior (Masserman, 1962). For example, infant chimpanzees kept blindfolded for a while after birth are found to engage in "stupid" behavior and may never learn to "see"; and young goats separated from their mothers for only a short time on the first day after birth develop persistent difficulties that may result in death several months later.

Use of Capacity

Does man use his brain's capacity to a greater extent today than during the days of the Roman Empire? Such a question cannot be answered perhaps, but evidence does not suggest that he does. Despite the great progress in science, health, and knowledge about the environment, we do know that there is much difficulty in the way individuals manage their lives and cope with the stresses of the present-day society. Man today is still baffled by many social problems and still resorts to war to solve them. And despite the great efficiency in death-dealing weapons, peace keeping based on social problem solving apparently has not made much progress.

New methods must be devised in education to bring about increased use of the brain's capacity. It has been estimated that the average person does not use more than 2 to 5 per cent of his capacity for abstract thinking and problem solving. How many original ideas come to the average person? How much time is spent in reflection or in the exploration of the meaning of life and of directions to which effort might be devoted? How well can individuals express their views orally or in writing? Many problems of modern life lie outside the area of technology in areas where the use of the brain and individual mental processes can provide the only answers (Gallup, 1964).

INTELLIGENCE AND THE MIND

While psychologists have tended to hold the term *mind* as lacking in specific and scientific meaning, the term probably is no less definable than the term *intelligence*. "Mind" is often used in a somewhat broader way than "intelligence," so that it includes feelings, motives, and activities (Glad, 1962). It may well be that a better conception of intelligence and mind than is now available can contribute to an understanding of human development and behavior. One important way would be for the definition to help in understanding integrative activities and the kinds of experiences that would enhance them.

Definitions and Meanings

A definition of intelligence and mind can be limited to "integrating activities" alone, but a broad definition seems more appropriate, as is illustrated by the following example.

> A young man dropped out of college because he felt at odds with all about him, particularly with his dominating parents. He was dependent on them but resented them and their influence on his life. Seeing no solution to his problem, he drove out on a long bridge to end his life. He had lost interest in making his life fit together—it could be said that he had lost his *mind* as he desired to lose his life.

Subsequently, in the process of psychotherapy, the young man in the above story was helped to find his "mind" and his life by developing a sense of adequacy and the motivation and ability to organize his activities to live courageously and independently. The mind, accordingly, may be seen as concerned with the functioning of the organism as a whole and as an integrating system that assists the individual in dealing with disequilibrium. The child during the course of development should learn to reduce tension effectively, and, in this sense, mental ability can be evaluated in terms of success in reducing tensions associated with needs.

Awareness, the central characteristic of the mind, grows out of experience and the evaluation of stimuli in terms of the likelihood of meeting needs. As discussed in earlier chapters, in infancy only elementary awareness of external stimuli is present, but as experience is gained, differentiation among stimuli is increasingly accomplished. Mental capability and the ability to be aware of essential stimuli develop simultaneously, and in such a manner experience contributes to mental development.

In dealing with these concepts of the mind, it is useful to relate them to concepts usually associated with definitions of intelligence. Vernon (1960) sees three types of definition: biological, psychological, and operational. The biological definition describes intelligence as an inherited and general capacity that gradually increases in flexibility and complexity. A possible difficulty with this definition from the standpoint of human intelligence is that there does not seem to be a close relation between brain size and intelligence. In animals, adaptation, even of a complex nature, develops according to species and thus mental functioning seems to be more closely related to brain structure. In humans, the psychological definitions, however, emphasize such qualities as judgment, abstraction, and perception of new relationships, while the operational definitions avoid a theoretical definition and describe intelligence as that quality of behavior that "intelligence tests measure." As satisfactory definitions of intelligence need to provide explanations of why a child is either superior or deficient in effective behavior, operational definitions are too narrow and avoid dealing with essential questions about human behavior.

Recently, in seeking the meaning of intelligence, the developmental approach of Piaget has been given increasing attention. Piaget sees life as a continuing interaction between the organism and the environment, with the child becoming increasingly capable of dealing with stimuli more and more separated from him in space and time. Intelligence can be viewed in such a way as a "central process" that develops in relation to a child's interactions with the environment. Since the way in which development is influenced by the environment is only partially understood, Piaget's view offers only a beginning.

The Place of Genetics in the Definition of Intelligence

Before World War II, intelligence as a concept was generally believed to be inherited and fixed. It was seen as an "inborn" characteristic and without possible modification by individual effort or training (Burt et al., 1934). This view that intelligence is fixed and essentially genetically based grew from an emphasis on the developing science of genetics, beginning around the first of the century, which in turn developed from the impetus of Darwinian theory. Behavior and intellectual capacity were believed to unfold in development through maturation of the body and the brain. Support for this view also came from new observations and theoretical formulations in biology and comparative psychology. Coghill's (1929) studies, for example, indicated that behavioral development of salamanders followed the principles of body development already accepted. Similarly, Shirley's (1933) emphasis and description of the sequential development of infant behavior provided additional support.

The inheritance theory also was supported by the finding that a child's IQ remains relatively constant; that is, it was found that as children grow older, they still tend to score in a similar way on the tests. Thus, the mean IQ for groups was found to be relatively constant. Hunt (1961) maintains, however, that the constancy merely results from the way that test items were chosen.

Other evidence cited as supporting the view that intelligence is inherited is that intelligence tests predict school achievement quite well. Correlation of intelligence tests with academic achievement and ratings by teachers of children's capacity for problem solving is high. Such findings give some support to the view that the tests show evidence of innate ability. Again it should be emphasized, however, that the intelligence test items in many instances are similar to school tasks and a high correlation is to be expected. Hunt thus suggests that behavioral scientists wish to see their work in testing as measuring a fixed trait, and if intelligence is fixed they can feel that their effort is more scientific in character than if it involves measurement of a changing and illusory trait.

Finally, stimulus-response theory and the search for laboratory methods of behavioral experimentation are better suited to a genetic approach. However, as Hunt has asserted, stimulus-response methodology based on the stimulus-response theory has brought about a revision in the original theory, with a present emphasis on the study of "intervening variables"—factors which influence and change an ordinarily expected course of behavior.

The Place of Environmental Influences in a Definition of Intelligence

A number of research activities have brought serious doubts about the view that intelligence is fixed and primarily genetically determined. Hunt sees such a change of view as coming from three types of investigations: (1) studies of identical twins raised apart in different homes, (2) longitudinal studies where intelligence tests show variation in children during development, and (3) studies indicating the influence of training on children's intelligence test scores.

Studies of identical twins over the years have been of much interest because such twins have the same genetic basis for behavior. They develop from one egg and sperm. Therefore, if intelligence differs, it is argued, environmental influences account for the differences. Newman et al. (1937) as a result of their studies decided that environmental influences did indeed account for differences in the performance of twins on intelligence tests.

Data from longitudinal studies, such as those done by Bayley (1949) and by Honzik et al. (1948), have indicated that as time between testing of a group of children increases, the correlation between the earlier and later tests decreases. Tests given in the early years have a low correlation with those given in early adulthood. It might be argued that the low correlation occurs because of a lack of similarity of items and that the tests, at least, have been shown to be reliable within a small age period.

Studies of the effect of training on intelligence test scores were given considerable impetus by research with young children at the University of Iowa (Skeels et al., 1938). Investigators there established a nursery school at an orphanage, so that one group of children could have several hours of training each day. The findings of improved intelligence test scores brought not only further investigation but also additional controversy about the "constancy of the IQ." Recently, however, with the establishment of a research program of national scope for children in the poverty areas of large cities as well as in isolated, economically depressed areas, it has been found that Head Start or preschool programs can, in fact, be effective in increasing the intelligence test scores of children who live in deprived environments. In one such study concerning the effects of a governmentally supported preschool program for children from the poverty sections of one large city, investigators found that the children improved not only in intelligence test scores, but also in the specific area of vocabulary (Alexander et al., 1968).

The controversy about the constancy of the IQ has lessened, and most behavioral scientists believe that "experience" can change performance on intelligence tests. What influence experience has on actual structure and physiological processes within the brain still is unclear, but it is not inconceivable that experience can modify neurological and biochemical processes. At present, knowledge is rapidly being extended about environmental interaction and total somatic functioning.

In dealing with environmental influences, it is necessary to return to topics discussed earlier about the relationship of specific influences to development in the first few years of life. Most external events have influence only when the individual assigns some significance to them. Consequently, learning and experience have much to do with what is experienced. To this end, and to some degree, each child begins to control his destiny and even the development of his capacity as he selects events to which to assign importance. The resulting experience accordingly influences the utilization of other experience.

The definition of the concept of intelligence is of such a nature and the knowledge of genetic factors associated with intellectual behavior is so limited that it is easier to give attention to environmental factors and environmental interaction. Accordingly, the intellectual capacity of a child is defined at the present time in terms of his performance in school. Before he enters school, demands for performance on complex tasks are limited; but upon entering the school system, the child finds himself classified according to his performance on complex tasks. Such classification varies in terminology according to his degree of success in coping with the school tasks, but it is likely that if he has difficulty, he soon will be designated as a "slow learner" or "retarded."

For all practical purposes, then, an individual during the developmental years is described as intellectually "gifted" or intellectually "retarded" according to his success in performing school tasks. In addition, because success in obtaining education is viewed in Western culture as the gateway to a successful social role, intelligence—even for functioning in segments of society far removed from educational institutions—may still be judged on the basis of past performance in an educational institution. Hence, it is predicted that a child successful in an educational institution will likely be successful in a social role, and one who is unsuccessful in school is likely to continue to be unsuccessful throughout his life span.

It should be seen that such a definition of intelligence is a relatively modern one and that it has developed in association with scientific developments, technological change, and widespread social role complexity. In American society, with the passing of the frontier and the change from a largely agrarian economy to one of urban complexity with its great interdependence of social roles, the opportunities for individuals who have been unsuccessful in the educational system have steadily declined. Accordingly, the lowest group of people economically, are also, in general, the lowest educationally or "intellectually."

As a corollary to this definition it follows that regardless of the source of the factors causative in bringing about poor performance in school, an individual is likely to be given a designation that indicates an inferior endowment of intellectual ability. Thus, in some ways, differentiation between whether or not an individual is genetically or culturally inferior in reference to school performance is academic, since, the truth is, his hope for a successful social role is indeed limited if he does not do well in school. The differentiation is even more academic if one subscribes to the view that capacity for performance in any individual is only partially used.

Most adults concerned with child development, then, place considerable emphasis on success in the educational system. Evaluation of the validity of this view is difficult. Just how many individuals leave the school system after a largely unsuccessful stay in it and later find satisfactory opportunities in society, is unknown. But it seems to be a rare exception at the present time to find an individual achieving success in a social role who had not been successful in the educational system. Conversely, graduation from certain schools in certain programs of specialization practically guarantees success in a social role, including immediate social status, salary, and extended opportunities. While social scientists are disturbed by a definition of intelligence based only on success in school tasks, the trend in our society toward equating intelligence and school success is increasingly clear.

Another important consideration in the definition of intelligence is the relationship of intelligence to socioeconomic class. A number of studies over several decades have indicated that children in the lower socioeconomic class tend to perform at lower levels both on intelligence tests and on school tasks. Among Negroes, who have had difficulty in moving out of the lower socioeconomic class, the findings are that many children have a generally lower performance on intelligence tests than do white children (Shuey, 1966). Also characteristically, Negro children have had difficulties in meeting school demands. It has been found that Negro children in early childhood who grow up in deteriorated parts of large cities have lower scores on intelligence tests than the tests' age norms. One specific deficit of such children on intelligence tests is that of vocabulary. Experiences within their environment apparently have prevented them from learning the meaning of many words that children on whom the tests were standardized have learned. It can be seen, therefore, that the practical definition of intelligence is related to socioeconomic class.

Despite the generalization that children born into the lower socioeconomic class can be expected to perform below average on intelligence tests and on school tasks once they enter the educational system, some children, however, do perform above average. It would be helpful to look into the environment of these children to find the factors that have offset the adverse influences that tend to prevent children in the lower socioeconomic class from performing adequately.

Much research currently supported by the Federal government is directed toward studying very young children to determine the environmental conditions causing them to perform so poorly in school and which continue to cause them to accomplish less than most of their classmates. Some of these children's difficulties come from the child-rearing practices of their parents. A number of years ago, Davis and Havighurst (1946, 1947, 1948) compared children from the lower socioeconomic class with children from the middle socioeconomic class and indicated certain differences in child-training procedures. Such differences in parent-child interaction have been substantiated over the years.

The school performance of the child from the lower socioeconomic class suggests that early deficits are not usually offset by the school experience and, as Masland et al. (1958) suggest, the deficits continue to be a problem as the child moves through the school system. Thus, the effects of early training and environmental differences continue; and it seems that some of the training of the middle socioeconomic class child prepares him to cope with the changing types of tasks required by the school, whereas, the child from the lower socioeconomic class has increasing difficulty. The early experiences of the child in the family and environment are of so much consequence that although the child has lived only a fraction of his life in the deprived conditions, he is already marked by his culture. Subsequently, it is apparently difficult to offset these early disadvantages by later ameliorative efforts within the general curricular pattern of the school.

The life story of Henry Brink is illustrative and provides an example of a child's life in a deteriorated part of a city.

> Henry's family moved frequently but always lived within the same level of poverty and deprivation characterized by filth, decay, and the prevalence of rats and mice.
>
> In the evening when the rodents became more active, Henry's father, usually in a state of drunkenness, would throw his shoes at them, while shouting profanity and obscenities. Henry and his many brothers and sisters learned to stay out of their father's way and to avoid thrown objects, for the father frequently struck any child within reach, as well as his wife.
>
> Henry's playground was the sidewalk, where he learned the language, emotional expressions, and ways of the big city slums. "The Law" was a policeman. If a policeman remonstrated with a band of older boys loitering at the corner, Henry learned to join in yelling obscenities at the officer after he had moved down the street. Here on the dirty sidewalks and in the alleys Henry learned about fighting, the cruel violence, and the principles of survival in the "concrete jungle."
>
> Because of the family's frequent moves and the indifference of his parents, Henry did not begin school until he was seven. There for the first time he discovered that some people were concerned about dirt on his face and body. He also became aware for the first time of his worn shoes and buttonless and soiled clothing. Before beginning school, Henry had learned to forage for food, and so he soon discovered that scraps from the school cafeteria could be taken from the garbage cans in the alley at the back of

the school. One day on being seen by a teacher while taking scraps, Henry was assigned free lunches, and for the first time in his seven years he had regular food and meals of a balanced nature. Because of eating in the school lunchroom, he learned for the first time to wash his hands before he ate and was thereby first introduced to the middle-class interest in cleanliness.

Henry found that some of his usual behavior would not be tolerated at school. His speech was the language of the section of the city in which he lived, but many of the words were not allowed at school and he was ridiculed and punished for utterances that went unnoticed at home. At home, he had always appropriated the property of others when it was unattended (he thought of property of others as belonging to those who could defend it), but in school he was scolded frequently for taking items belonging to other children. At home, Henry had always resorted to physical violence when he was frustrated or whenever it would serve his needs of defense or attack; but in school, physical attack, even in the face of wrongdoing on the part of a class-mate, was not allowed. Thus, although Henry often felt justified in fighting back, he was surprised and chagrined to receive disapproval and punishment from the teacher.

Although the teacher was often patient with Henry, he tended to regard her, like the policeman on the beat, as a person to be avoided if possible and one whose wishes were to be respected only during the moments when she attended to him individually. Henry had little motivation to accomplish the school tasks, and he avoided completing them as much as possible. Despite the fact that for the next three years he was moved from grade to grade, he increasingly fell further behind the children in his class. Because of his school failure, Henry was given an intelligence test. His teacher's appraisal of his ability was substantiated when she was told that he had "borderline" mental ability and that he would very likely be unable to do high school work.

After a few years Henry was found to be not only mentally limited but also mentally disordered. Medical records of his early years showed that at the age of two he had deliberately banged his head until bloody on cement floors and sidewalks, and that he had continued to be enuretic into his school years. Ultimately, in early adolescence, because of his thievery and aberrant sex behavior, he was sent away to a training school in the hope that a change in his environment would bring about a change in his behavior.

From the story of Henry's life it can be seen that his early years did not equip him to deal with school tasks. Then, after some years of failing in them, Henry was considered to be lacking in sufficient intellectual capacity to meet them. Furthermore, whatever help Henry received in trying to meet the tasks, clearly proved to be inadequate. The unfavorable conditions of his early life were definitely not ameliorated. As the years passed, Henry's behavior and person became less and less acceptable to the school. It is difficult to say at what point Henry became destined to fail, but unfortunately his ultimate failure in school could have been predicted from his family background and the cultural level from which he came.

THE DEVELOPMENT OF MENTAL ABILITIES

Much research has been carried out to learn about changes in mental ability throughout the years of childhood, middle life, and old age. The value of the information gained from much of this research rests upon a definition of intelligence based on tasks purporting to show intellectual capacity. Measurement is indeed a considerable problem, in part because behavior, activities, and social roles vary according to chronological age. The criteria on which a definition of intelligence might be based at fifteen could differ considerably from criteria deemed appropriate at twenty-five. Thus, neither the means of measurement of intelligence nor its definition are sufficiently developed to provide definite age comparisons. On the other hand, it seems that the evidence from research studies does support the view that a developmental approach is of value in reaching some generalizations about an intellectual growth curve.

The Growth of Intelligence

In the first few years of life, intelligence tests show a positively accelerated growth in intelligence. However, as children enter school around six years of age, the curve becomes negatively accelerated; that is, the growth of intelligence is less and less as the individual grows older.

Inhelder and Piaget described three stages in development (Inhelder, 1963). The first stage, from birth to eighteen months, is called the sensorimotor stage of development. Included in this stage are reflexes, motor habits and perceptions, the beginning of intentional acts, substitute behavior, and the like. The second stage lasts from about eighteen months to eleven years. In this second stage, there is the beginning of symbolic thought growing out of earlier sensorimotor experience and "mental actions," or definite

problem-solving patterns of behavior. In the third stage, intellectual behavior is characterized by the use of hypotheses and thinking processes
that take place in the abstract.

Another way of defining the development of intellectual behavior is in
terms of acquisition of certain developmental skills. For example, the
acquisition of language increases the complexity of behavior and of intellectual processes and makes possible the lessening of dependence upon
trial-and-error types of solutions. Through a series of tests, early experiments by Rey in France demonstrated the problem-solving abilities of
children at different age levels (Viaud, 1960). The first test consisted of
a bottle containing an object, such as a small block with a screw eye in it.
The child was given a piece of wire that he could use as a tool to form a
hook with which to lift out the block. The experimenter found that children
from three to five cannot arrive at the solution of bending the end of the
wire into a hook. However, by the age of six and a half, most children can
arrive at the solution.

In another test, the problem was to balance a platform with a weight at
one end on top of a fulcrum. Four solutions to the balancing problem were
possible: remove the weight, add an equal weight at the other end, place a
support under the weighted end, or tie down the unweighted end. Very
young children try to balance the board with their hands. Between ages
four and six, children by trial and error discover that they can use a prop
to maintain the board in a level position. After the age of seven, most
children find a correct solution almost at once.

A third type of experiment involved the search of a room for a hidden
object. In comparing solutions by children and adults through the use of
"actograms" (diagrams of movements about the room), Rey found that
a young child depends on the random behavior of running back and forth.
Rey described the child's behavior as being "similar to an amoeba in a
drop of water." An adult, on the other hand, searches the room systematically.

According to Viaud the very young child's type of intellectual behavior
can be characterized as *organic* and in this sense is similar to Piaget's
sensorimotor category. The child uses his body, for example, in balancing
the board with his hands. As he grows older, he uses objects instead of
his body, as in using a stick as a prop in the balancing problem. At a later
age, a child begins to use abstract thinking and reasoning in the solution
of problems; and after the age of four, language and formation of concepts greatly increase the child's problem-solving ability. Reliance on
abstract thought is mastered only gradually, and the very young child

depends on methods of trial and error and impulse rather than on symbolic thought processes or projected possible solutions. Highly intelligent behavior involving a minimal use of trial-and-error solutions and the use of reasoning instead of impulsive efforts at solution comes with growth and maturation.

The Progression of Mental Growth

While it is important to see the growth of intelligence as related to over-all growth of the body and maturation of body organs and functions, certain problems become immediately apparent upon even a cursory analysis of the concept of an intellectual growth curve. First, the quality and content of intellectual function changes and, accordingly, concept, definition, and measurement must be altered as chronological age increases. Second, as Vernon (1960) has indicated, growth in intelligence is not linear throughout childhood nor does it stop at some specific age. There is little basis for the assumption that intellectual growth between the ages of three and four is the same as the growth between the ages of twelve and thirteen. (The use of IQ and intelligence tests makes such an assumption, however.)

In view of these two reasons, it is clear that at present there is theoretical and technical difficulty in describing a growth curve of intelligence. Furthermore, general developmental studies indicate that the development of no one individual is absolutely smooth—there are rapid increments as well as plateaus; thus, education, experience, physiological factors of health, and emotions all have significant influence and all change from time to time. A child, for example, who moves from a rural to an urban environment is likely to improve in test scores after being in the urban environment for a while.

The Problem of Racial and Cultural Comparisons

Since the earliest days of testing, the problem of racial and cultural comparisons of intelligence test scores has been a source of controversy. Vernon views the trend of tests as indicating the following order of intellectual ability from high to low: Jews, American whites and northwest Europeans, southern Europeans and English-speaking Chinese and Japanese, American Negroes, and primitive peoples, such as Australian aborigines. In a famous investigation done many years ago, Klineberg (1935) studied Negroes who had lived for various lengths of time in New York. He found that the longer they lived in New York, the greater the increase in IQ. For example, those who lived in New York less than a year had an average of 81 and those who lived there more than four years had an average of 87. However, the IQ's did not continue upward to reach the national average for whites.

Performance tests have been used in various parts of the world in the belief that such tests as a maze would not reflect cultural and educational influences as much as verbal tests. It is likely, however, that children in a complex cultural environment have many experiences that are related to performance tasks and are of value to them in solving such a problem as a maze.

Differences among cultural groups are less in very young children, but as children grow older the differences among cultural groups tend to increase. Scott (1966) suggests that intelligence test scores of children living in poor and disadvantaged environments tend to decrease as they get older. This same view also was suggested more than thirty years ago by Sherman and Key (1932).

Some investigators believe that intelligence tests discriminate unfairly against children of lower socioeconomic class and that a child in the lower socioeconomic class (or for that matter, one from other cultures) may not do well on the many abstractions and verbal items making up modern intelligence tests. Children in the lower socioeconomic class, it is suggested, must deal with more practical and concrete problems in their environment than middle-class children. In an extensive study, Haggard (1954) changed abstract items on tests into more concrete terms. He found that the children in the lower socioeconomic class did better on his so-called "culture free" test, but so did the middle-class children. Thus, other factors were deemed to be of significance in the performance of middle-class children, such as experiences related to test taking and motivation. It thus can be seen that the questions about racial and cultural differences are not unequivocally answerable. It is to be hoped that the large-scale testing of very young children in various conditions of poverty in connection with the national program of research carried out on children in Head Start will provide more information about socioeconomic class differences.

The Measurement of Intelligence

As suggested earlier, the basic problem in the measurement of intelligence relates to definition. If intelligence is considered to be a unitary trait, then measurement instruments should consist of homogeneous items. If intelligence is seen as consisting of a number of factors, then an intelligence test must be complex and varied and the resulting measurement is likely to be approximate. Also, if a number of factors are involved, arrival at a numerical index that will indicate a level of complex functioning and reflect individual variation is very difficult and perhaps impossible. Nevertheless, people who work with children wish to have some indication about an individual child's level of intellectual performance other than their own judgment of his ability. Hence, it would be convenient to have some way of dealing with the question of amount of ability. Because of this need, tasks that have some similarity to tasks performed in everyday life or in the educational system have been chosen as a way of obtaining a sample of a child's behavior. The selection of these tasks is based on the assumption that these tasks are generally indicative and characteristic of the child's behavior in problem-solving situations. An intelligence test, thus, should be considered as a measurement of *samples of behavior* and not as a measurement of total performance.

Present-day intelligence tests include such tasks as fitting blocks into a formboard, following directions given by the examiner, defining words, memorizing numbers, perceiving spatial relationships, and the like. Such tasks related to concepts of intelligence are based on the belief that intelligence is composed of abilities to make adaptations, to deal with complex and abstract elements, to deal with novel situations, and to use symbols.

The use of intelligence tests began in Paris, France, around the turn of the century. Concern about children who were unable to learn effectively in the schools of Paris instigated the research. Binet, a psychologist, was asked to aid in finding a way to separate those children who could learn from those who could not. The Binet scale was later published with Simon and subsequent revisions were made in this country (Goodenough, 1954; McNemar, 1942; and Terman and Merrill, 1960).

Originally, Binet did not begin with the idea of constructing a so-called "intelligence" test; his intent was to find a way of distinguishing between those children who had the capacity to meet the school's requirements and those who would have difficulty. Test items were selected by determining the percentage of children who could pass and complete each test at each age level. Another criterion for selection of specific tasks was a high correlation with other tasks already selected and deemed appropriate for each age level. Terman at Stanford University added other criteria for the selection of tasks: ease of administration and scoring, variety, and tasks within the experience of most children. In the development of intelligence tests, the importance of relating a child's performance to his chronological age was soon realized, and the concept of mental age was devised to meet this need. The term *mental age* now refers to the sum of items passed on a test such as the Stanford-Binet.

In Table 1 an example of the scoring of test results for a four-year-old child is shown.

TABLE 1

Computation of MA Score for a Four-year-old Child

Year level	Number of tests passed	Months' credit per test	Total credits	
			Years	*Months*
III	6 (Basal age)	—	3	—
III–6	5	1	—	5
IV	3	1	—	3
IV–6	2	1	—	2
V	2	1	—	2
VI	1	2	—	2
VII	0 (Ceiling age)			0
			3	14
			Mental Age Score, 4–2	

From the Manual for the Third Revision, Form L-M of the Stanford-Binet Intelligence Scale by Lewis M. Terman and Maud A. Merrill (used by permission of Houghton Mifflin Company, Boston).

It should be noted from this example that the four-year-old child passed all the tests at the three-year-old level and thus obtained a basal age of three years. He failed one test at the three years-six months level and continued to fail an increasingly larger number of items until, at the level of seven years, he failed all of the items. Notice that at age six, two months' credit is given for each yearly test passed. By taking the three-year basal age and adding to it the months' credits allowed, he obtained a mental age of four years and two months. Thus, if his chronological age is four years and two months, he has an IQ of 100. The standard way of computing IQ is as follows: IQ = (MA/CA × 100). (However, in the tables in the manual provided with the scale, some adjustments have been made in this formula.)

A child receiving an IQ of 135 on the Stanford-Binet scale will exceed 98 per cent of other children, and he certainly should be able to do very well in school in learning to read, to write, to comprehend arithmetic, and to acquire a great deal of information. Thus, scores on verbal and mathematical items on intelligence tests provide the best-known method of prediction of academic achievement (Chauncey, 1958).

Another type of intelligence test devised in recent years is the Wechsler Intelligence Scale for Children (WISC), designed for use with children between the ages of five and fifteen. It is divided so that there are five verbal items and five performance items, which are the same for children of all ages. Wechsler does not approve of the concept of mental age and therefore uses the child's performance in comparison with other children of his age group. An intelligence quotient is derived from the percentile rank. Although differences in construction and in derivation of IQ are to be found between the Binet and the WISC, a high correlation exists between the two tests. In 1967 Wechsler provided another test for younger children, the Wechsler Preschool and Primary Scale of Intelligence (WPPSI).

Another frequently used test over the years is the Goodenough Intelligence Test devised by Florence Goodenough, which is based on children's drawing of a man. Points are given for the inclusion of details, coordination, proportion, and the like. This test is widely used in connection with other tests and new normative data have been made available by other investigators (Harris, 1963).

Limitations in the Measurement of Intelligence

One of the basic limitations of intelligence measurement is that the value of the test is dependent upon the cooperation elicited from the child. The value of the score rests on the assumption that the child performs at his highest level of capacity and potentiality on every test item—a precarious assumption at best, but particularly so in dealing with young children. A child's temperature or blood pressure may be taken without his cooperation and even under protest, but such is not the case in the measurement of intelligence. Moreover, intervening influences are many—fatigue, disinterest, anxiety, and distraction by stimuli other than those comprising the test are only a few. Another basic limitation lies in the construction of the test itself; that is, the range of items that are selected to represent intelligence. It is probable that other items could be found that would reveal important capacities of some children better than the present items do.

Another problem of intelligence tests is the fact that items on the Binet-type scales vary from year level to year level. Consequently, scores obtained at an earlier age reflect the performance of tasks which are different from those used at later ages. For example, the very young child is asked to place beads on a string, but at a later age he is asked to arrange pictures in a complex order. Such changes in tasks probably cause the test to measure different types of capacities at different age levels.

Physiological Correlates of Intelligence

Although thinking processes are seen as primarily the function of the brain, the brain's functioning cannot be separated from other body processes.

Therefore, much attention has been given to the effect of body states on intellectual functioning. Physiological conditions associated with such an emotional state as anxiety affect the efficiency of the entire functioning of the individual and thus to some degree are determinants of the level of intellectual behavior (Ruebush, 1963; Wallach and Kogan, 1965).

Studies using intelligence tests in relation to various physiological characteristics have seemed to indicate that a low positive relationship between height and weight and intelligence can be found (Abernethy, 1936; Olson and Hughes, 1943; Paterson, 1930; Shuttleworth, 1939). Eichorn (1963) believes that it is important to consider behavioral consequences of variations at the cytological level or the level of life processes in the cells. For example, Kubala and Katz (1960) found a relation between concentration of ascorbic acid in the blood and performance on group intelligence tests and that test performance over a time correlates with changes in ascorbic acid. The functioning of other organ systems, such as the circulatory system and the endocrine gland system, affect the brain and its ability to carry on its processes. In one sense, a measurement of intelligence might be considered to some degree as measuring the effectiveness of the functioning of the pituitary or thyroid glands.

In recent years, study of new means of lessening limitations imposed upon an individual's effectiveness by so-called "emotional" states has been carried on with psychoactive drugs. The possibility now exists that drugs can be found not only to reduce emotional agitation and anxiety, but also to specifically improve the functioning of the brain and central nervous system itself. Many drugs currently available are purported to influence behavior in beneficial ways and to contribute to over-all interaction of the individual with his environment. Some of these drugs are now being used with children who have both behavior and central nervous system disorders. It is possible that a child who is found to be lethargic and depressed may be brought to a much more active and efficient level of functioning by the use of certain drugs.

An example of the effectiveness of certain medication on the improvement of general functioning of a child is found in the help provided for a child having convulsive seizures in school. Such a child is aware that others respond to him differently, and it is likely that his anxiety is heightened, thus jeopardizing his school performance. Once the seizures are controlled by medication, however, the child is no longer under the threat of the seizure episodes that are so terrifying to others, and thus his whole functioning in school can be improved.

Despite the extensive research in various types of drugs and the wide use of many kinds, much research still needs to be done. The complexity of evaluation of even one product is great (Kugel and Alexander, 1963), but much more progress will undoubtedly be made in the next few years.

A POINT OF VIEW

Two points of emphasis in considering intellectual development seem desirable. First, a concept of "mental process" cannot be confined to the functioning of the brain or central nervous system alone, since other body systems affect functioning and environmental interaction. Consequently, the term *mental process* is too limiting. A concept including the totality of organismic functioning seems to be a necessity, but such a concept is difficult to formulate either practically or theoretically.

Second, concern about early developmental experience as a determinant of an adequate level of capacity for future environmental interaction seems increasingly justifiable. In fact, evidence now is pointing to the view that constitutional development is to some extent determined by environmental opportunities; thus, prevention of early deprivation through the provision of adequate experiences in the early years is being recognized as an effort of major importance.

REFERENCES

Abernethy, E. M., 1936. *Relationships Between Mental and Physical Growth.* Monographs of the Society for Research in Child Development, 1, No. 7. Lafayette, Ind.: Child Development Publications, Purdue University.

Alexander, T., J. Stoyle, and C. Kirk, 1968. "The Language of Children in the Inner City," *Journal of Psychology,* 68, 215–221.

Bailey, P., 1962. "Cortex and Mind," in *Theories of the Mind,* edited by J. M. Scher, pp. 3–14. New York: Free Press.

Bayley, N., 1949. "Consistency and Variability in the Growth from Birth to 18 Years," *Journal of Genetic Psychology,* 75, 165–196.

Bruner, J. S., 1964. "The Course of Cognitive Growth," *American Psychologist,* 19, 1–15.

Burt, C., E. Jones, E. Miller, and W. Moodie, 1934. *How the Mind Works.* New York: Appleton-Century-Crofts.

Cantril, H., 1962. "A Transactional Inquiry Concerning Mind," in *Theories of the Mind,* edited by J. M. Scher, pp. 330–353. New York: Free Press.

Chauncey, H., 1958. "How Tests Help Us Identify the Academically Talented," *Journal of the National Education Association,* 47, 230–231.

Coghill, G. E., 1929. *Anatomy and the Problem of Behavior.* New York: Macmillan.

Davis, A., and R. J. Havighurst, 1946. "Social Class and Color Differences in Child Rearing," *American Sociological Review*, **11**, 698–710.

Davis, A., and R. J. Havighurst, 1947. *Father of the Man*. Boston: Houghton Mifflin.

Davis, A., and R. J. Havighurst, 1948. "The Measurement of Mental Systems," *Scientific Monthly*, **66**, 301–316.

Eichorn, D. H., 1963. "Biological Correlates of Behavior," in *Child Psychology*, National Society for the Study of Education, Sixty-second Yearbook, Part I, edited by H. W. Stevenson, pp. 4–61. Chicago: The University of Chicago Press.

Gallup, G., 1964. *The Miracle Ahead*. New York: Harper & Row.

Glad, D. D., 1962. "Mind as an Organismic Integration," in *Theories of the Mind*, edited by J. M. Scher, pp. 519–532. New York: Free Press.

Goodenough, F. L., 1954. "The Measurement of Mental Growth in Childhood," in *Manual of Child Psychology*, 2d ed., edited by L. Carmichael, pp. 459–491. New York: Wiley.

Haggard, E. A., 1954. "Social Status and Intelligence: An Experimental Study of Certain Cultural Determinants of Measured Intelligence," *Genetic Psychology Monographs*, **49**, 141–186.

Harris, D. B., 1963. *Children's Drawings as Measures of Intellectual Maturity*. New York: Harcourt, Brace & World.

Honzik, M. P., J. W. McFarlane, and L. Allen, 1948. "The Stability of Mental Test Performance Between 2 and 18 Years," *Journal of Experimental Education*, **4**, 309–324.

Hunt, J. McV., 1961. *Intelligence and Experience*. New York: Ronald.

Inhelder, B., 1963. "Criteria of the Stages of Mental Development," in *Psychological Studies of Human Development*, edited by R. G. Kuhlen and G. G. Thompson, pp. 28–48. New York: Appleton-Century-Crofts.

Klineberg, O., 1935. *Negro Intelligence and Selective Migration*. New York: Columbia.

Kubala, A. L., and M. M. Katz, 1960. "Nutritional Factors in Psychological Behavior," *Journal of Genetic Psychology*, **96**, 343–352.

Kugel, R. B., and T. Alexander, 1963. "The Effect of a Central Nervous System Stimulant (Deanol) on Behavior," *Pediatrics*, **31**, 651–655.

McNemar, Q., 1942. *The Revision of the Stanford-Binet Scale: An Analysis of the Standardization Data*. Boston: Houghton Mifflin.

Masland, R. L., S. B. Sarason, and T. Gladwin, 1958. *Mental Subnormality*. New York: Basic Books.

Masserman, J. H., 1962. "Ethology, Comparative Biodynamics, and Psychoanalytic Research," in *Theories of the Mind*, edited by J. M. Scher, pp. 15–64. New York: Free Press.

Newman, H. H., F. N. Freeman, and K. J. Holzinger, 1937. *Twins: A Study of Heredity and Environment*. Chicago: The University of Chicago Press.

Olson, W. C., and B. O. Hughes, 1943. "Growth of the Child as a Whole," in *Child Behavior and Development*, edited by R. G. Barker, J. S. Kounin, and H. F. Wright, pp. 199–208. New York: McGraw-Hill.

Paterson, D. G., 1930. *Physique and Intellect*. New York: Appleton-Century-Crofts.

Ruebush, B. K., 1963. "Anxiety," in *Child Psychology*, National Society for the Study of Education, Sixty-second Yearbook, Part I, edited by H. W. Stevenson, pp. 460–516. Chicago: The University of Chicago Press.

Scott, R., 1966. "First to Ninth Grade I.Q. Change of Northern Negro Students," *Psychology in the Schools*, **3**, 159–160.

Sherman, M., and C. B. Key, 1932. "The Intelligence of Isolated Mountain Children," *Child Development*, **3**, 279–290.

Shirley, M. M., 1933. *The First Two Years of Life*, Vol. II. Minneapolis: The University of Minnesota Press.

Shuey, A. M., 1966. *The Testing of Negro Intelligence*, 2d ed. New York: Social Science Press.

Shuttleworth, F., 1939. *The Physical and Mental Growth of Girls and Boys Age Six to Nineteen in Relation to Age at Maximum Growth*. Monographs of the Society for Research in Child Development, Vol. 4, No. 3. Lafayette, Ind.: Child Development Publications, Purdue University.

Skeels, H. M., R. Updegraff, B. L. Wellman, and H. M. Williams, 1938. *A Study of Environmental Stimulation: An Orphanage Preschool Project*. University of Iowa Studies in Child Welfare, Vol. 15, No. 4. Iowa City, Iowa: State University of Iowa.

Terman, L. M., and M. A. Merrill, 1960. *Stanford-Binet Intelligence Scale*. Boston: Houghton Mifflin.

Vernon, P. E., 1960. *Intelligence and Attainment Tests*. New York: Philosophical Library.

Viaud, G., 1960. *Intelligence: Its Evolution and Forms*. New York: Harper & Row.

Wallach, M. A., and N. Kogan, 1965. *Modes of Thinking in Young Children*. New York: Holt.

[*eight*]

Imagination
and Creativity

Through imagination a child can make things as he would like them to be. Thus, imagination is an important source of pleasure in childhood, and the value of pleasant pastimes spent in using imagination is never outgrown. Adults rarely are aware that imagination has an important influence in their everyday lives. For example, they continue to enjoy plays and motion pictures with which they can identify and feel strong emotions even though they know that what they see is only "make-believe." Novels, poems, musical compositions, and moments of reverie are part of imaginary experience. Moreover, imagination leads to creativity, and with imagination things can be arranged in infinitely different ways so that doors are opened to new patterns of thought and new possibilities of achievement.

IMAGINATION AND THE
DETERMINATION OF REALITY

In observing the play of a young child, one sees that the child makes his possessions into what he wishes them to be. The porch railing becomes a spirited steed on which he chases Indians across the plains; in a flash it is transformed into a jet fighter plane streaking across the sky in pursuit of an enemy; and only a few seconds later it will become a racing automobile roaring around the track at Indianapolis. The child's imagination frees him—it is an Aladdin's lamp with which all the world's treasures can be brought to his own door. The child does not limit his imagination only to the attainment of possessions; he also uses imagination as a vehicle of expression for his feelings. For example, he will often endow his pet dog with the same feelings of joy or sadness that he himself experiences. Even inanimate objects will be given human characteristics of understanding and sympathy so that the child can become attached to them as well. By enabling pets or toys to share the range of his own emotions, the child is provided with much satisfaction by them. In fact, he derives so much pleasure from his possessions and toys that adults enjoy giving him possessions; they in turn receive vicarious pleasure in the joyful satisfaction the child obtains in using them imaginatively.

The child, of course, uses imagination in other ways, for it helps him to explain and understand the realities of the world. The very young child has considerable difficulty in understanding reality, since reality involves attainment of definite concepts of time, space, relationships, skills, or methods. In fact, the child cannot understand the world of reality as does the adult because he does not have the experience, training, or capacity for integration of the various concepts that are a part of the adult's creation of reality. The young child, too, has difficulty understanding the past or the future; even the present for him differs from that of adults.

The child's perception of stimulus situations in the environment is different from that of the adult since adults have been conditioned to perceive reality in specific order and patterns and, in fact, tend to see their environment in terms of past experience. The adult, as a result of his experience, can respond more effectively and instantaneously to situations requiring quick action without the usual exploration of the problem. The child, on the other hand, has not established either the skills or patterns of response; thus, to substitute for experience, the child must use his imagination.

In addition, the child has not had experience in understanding the feelings of others, and so he attributes to others his own feelings. It is hard for him to understand others except in reference to himself. Not only does he have difficulty in understanding the feelings of others, but also he tries to interpret causality in the actions of others in terms of his own experience. For example, Mary's father was reading to her from a storybook at the end of the day. While the story held considerable interest for Mary, her father nearly fell asleep and at one long pause in the story due to his momentarily falling asleep, Mary remarked, "Why did you stop, Daddy, don't you know the word?" She, in her first-grade experience, found that some children stopped reading the story because they did not know the word, and she thought her father had the same problem. Because even adults will project their feelings and experiences onto objects and things in the environment, there has been an age-old struggle to determine the bounds of imagination. Man has always used his imagination to some extent in explaining events and things about him. For example, the stars, sun, and moon—a part of man's experience previously difficult for him to investigate—have long been explained by imagination. Only in modern times has science been able to push away the imaginative explanations about the heavens.

Adults learn to respond to an object according to its characteristics. In part, perception involves an analysis of the characteristics of the stimulus situation; by associating past understandings with the aspects of the new stimulus situation, the adult seeks to comprehend its meaning. The child, however, usually responds without this careful analysis and uses his imagination to supply that which is lacking from the immediate experience.

A child in a society must behave in accord with its mandates and customs and he increasingly orders his behavior externally in accordance with the expectations of others and the boundaries set by others. But in imagination he can create his own environment, seeing and feeling as he himself wishes. Some children find the pressures for conformity too great and feel the necessity for escape into an imaginary world. Accordingly, the imaginative play of the young child may be carried over into middle childhood or even adult life.

In the enculturation process the child must only conform to the extent that his behavior is acceptable and in accord with the customs of his culture—what he actually thinks or imagines otherwise can be his own affair. He need only accept the language, symbols, explanations, and mandates necessary to avoid conflict; within himself he can be individualistic. This individuality, however, is progressively limited as he grows older, and the child tends more and more to adopt the explanations, concepts, and traditions of the environment and of the culture in which he lives. Each individual, however, organizes and interprets what happens about him in his own way, and he carries on his own life in accordance with the way he sees the world. Accordingly, one person does not know how another perceives reality, and learning, of course, does not lead to a standard perception, organization, or understanding of stimuli. Thus, each child develops the uniqueness that is his, and only occasionally and to the astute observer does this individuality reveal itself.

In the main, however, a child struggles to be like others—he talks like others, wears similar clothing to others, and seeks to be a part of the society or culture in which he grows up. At the same time, though, he may create his own world and in so doing develop problems that he is unable to resolve. A considerable gap can exist between his external behavior and the way he actually feels himself to be. Although outwardly presenting the picture of confidence and success, he may inwardly feel defeated and without hope. And while pretending that he sees the world according to the description of his peers, in reality he only makes the approved responses. Needless to say, an extreme gap between how the child perceives himself and how he feels he is or should be perceived by others causes devastating conflict and anxiety.

Perceptual Modes and Imaginative Behavior

It is particularly important in a technological society such as ours that the imagination of children is not stifled to the point that creativity is impaired. It is possible that teaching modes of thinking related to specifically perceived realities will interfere with children's freedom to use imagination to achieve a better way of life. Schachtel (1959) in his discussion of the two modes of perception—the autocentric and allocentric—provides some guides in understanding the child's perceptual development in reference to creativity. In differentiating between his two modes, Schachtel explains that the autocentric, subject-centered mode is one in which emphasis is on a feeling in reference to perception and upon the sensory quality of pleasurable and unpleasurable feelings; that is, the perceiver reacts to stimuli impinging upon him in terms of emotion. In the allocentric mode of perception, the perceiver is more objective and seeks to deal with objects on the basis of understanding. Development is largely away from the autocentric mode in infancy to the more objective kinds of perception as maturation progresses.

The development of human potentiality for effective behavior depends upon conditions which allow exploration. But conditions also can interfere with an "openness to experience," so that a child's reality is determined by his family or society. Schachtel believes that for some people allocentric interest in objects decreases, particularly in the latter part of the life span. It is important for the culture to encourage spontaneity, interest, and openness in children as they approach and respond to their environment because these qualities are part of the creative experience and allow the individual to use his capacities.

Emotion and Imagination

Emotion often accompanies imaginary experience, and thus in reading a story or seeing a play, identification with the characters often brings a range of emotion. Emotion may be partially related to external surroundings or entirely separated. Hence, an external stimulus may cause a child to have an emotional experience, although the external stimulus in itself can be entirely innocuous. Parents often wonder why their child becomes upset or what has caused his mirth. Yet an external stimulus need not be present at all, and in imagination the child can experience a range of human emotions from despair to hilarity. In such ways emotions are associated with imaginary experience of everyday life.

Parents teach their children about emotion and often will try to teach them to project feeling into external stimuli. For example, parents in trying to teach their child to be aware of the welfare of others, ask, "How would you feel if this were done to you?" In such an instance, they are asking the child to project his own feelings onto another so that he will better understand the principle involved. Such projection is largely individualistic. Only gradually are these feelings modified in terms of experience and the teachings of parents. On the other hand, a child may learn to disregard the feelings of others or to control and repress his own feelings so that emotions come to be of little significance in his life.

As a child grows older, however, he must learn the appropriateness of emotions and he must somehow relate his imagination and accompanying emotion to the reality of his culture. Laughing inappropriately or crying without relation to external stimuli brings the child into conflict and difficulty. And, if he continues to experience emotion unrelated to external events, he usually learns to mask the feelings so that at least outwardly his behavior is in accord with external events. And, as Torrance (1962) indicates, being different is a problem for the creative individual. Little research has been done on the effect of our training and teaching of children about their imagination and emotions.

The relationship of imagination to motivation coming from body conditions is quite difficult to ascertain. A hungry child, for example, may in his imagination see and taste the delights of apple pie or ice cream, and by imagining the pleasure brought by such food he then may try to obtain such food. Imagination, too, can play an important part in motivation coming from acquired needs. A child on seeing a motion picture about a drama in a courtroom and as a result of imagining himself in one of the dramatic roles, decides to make law his profession. In the latter instance, as he struggles through the long course of training, his imagination creates for him the possibilities of satisfaction yet to be enjoyed. Similarly, the adolescent girl on seeing a motion picture starring a handsome hero endows the boy next door with the same heroic characteristics. Thus, imagination leads to aspiration and an emulation of adult roles. As the child anticipates and perceives himself in a satisfying adult role, pleasurable feelings encourage him to meet the requirements to achieve it. Such feelings about a perceived role are illustrative of Schachtel's autocentric mode, or feeling about a perception.

Some children who feel defeated and hopeless seem to have little motivation to change and cannot see themselves in successful roles. On the contrary, they imagine failure and associate past failure with the present and expect unfavorable situations and events to occur. Children must see the possibility of satisfying social roles so that under favorable circumstances their imagination can provide motivation for valued kinds of behavior.

Since children's play allows them to disregard rules and barriers encountered in their daily lives, popular roles for small boys are those of Indians, robbers, pirates, and others who defy law and order with impunity. On the other hand, they do have representations of the "forces of good" by playing policemen, sheriffs, soldiers, and the like, and they take turns in the roles. A child can thus play out the struggle between being as society wants him to be and being what he wishes to be.

In disturbed children and those who have been deprived of a normal family life, the struggle may be clearly in evidence, as is illustrated in the following story.

Bill Harverson, twelve years old, a large and strong boy, had been adopted, but not legally, by lower socioeconomic class parents. In time, his parents came to reject him, and he was abused and neglected. As a result, Bill believed no one valued or cared for him; and because of the abuse and the harsh treatment, he developed much resentment and hostility toward everyone. In psychotherapeutic sessions, Bill had an opportunity in his imagination to be a powerful person. Having watched many television programs about robbers and gangsters and having read many comic books about Western "bad men," his sessions in the children's clinic revealed his confused feelings about such roles. He was unable to decide which was more satisfying to him—to be the powerful outlaw who inspired fear in those around him and who could easily overcome the sheriff, or to be the sheriff on the side of right who would overcome the powerful outlaw. In his play with his therapist, Bill vacillated between the roles; he often took the part of the robber and after having bound the sheriff to a chair with an imaginary rope and having struck him several times over the head with an imaginary pistol, he would rob the safe. Sometimes, however, in the midst of robbing the safe, Bill would decide to switch roles and would demand that the therapist be the robber. Then Bill would be the sheriff, who would loosen his bonds and by trickery as well as great strength overcome the robber in a furious battle. At other times, the robber would bind and imaginatively beat the sheriff in order to escape with the money. These episodes were played again and again in a confusion of the roles. Although he could not quite decide which one to be, Bill was sure, however, that he wished to be a powerful person whom others could not ignore.

Normal children, too, in emulating adult roles can make themselves brave and powerful. Sometimes it is not clear just what forces the children see themselves as overcoming. Two five-year-olds were pretending to be hunters. As they approached a group of trees near their backyard, they stood holding their toy guns as if they were ready to shoot on a moment's notice. The nature of the game which they were stalking, however, was unclear. Suddenly one called to the other in an excited manner, "There goes a great big bad . . ." he hesitated, ". . . thing!" With this comment, he began to shoot at it with great abandon, "bang, bang, bang!" The other boy was not sure of the game either but was quite willing to join in the firing at the imagined evil creature.

Imagination and Imitative Behavior

Parents listening to children's play and emulation of adult roles often hear their own words repeated. For example, two young children in playing doctor and patient will act out an inoculation. The child to be inoculated is told, "Hold still, it won't hurt." Both children apply adult words to the situation and at the same time reveal their own anxiety and fear. Piaget's theoretical formulation about the functions of *accommodation,* the adaptation to changing conditions in the environment, and of *assimilation,* a taking of external conditions into behavioral patterns so that behavior can be adapted to new circumstances, is relevant to the understanding of the child's emulation of adult roles. Piaget believes that accommodation depends upon the extent of the child's interaction with the environment and that motivation grows out of this interaction, since the more the child experiences, the more experiences he desires.

Children's play can be a source of valuable data for the investigator of child behavior. For example, children in play with dolls can endow dolls with various roles and since the behavior given to the dolls will reflect the child's perceptions of his own experiences, the play is particularly valuable in providing sources and origins of the child's own behavior.

In Levin and Sears' study (1956) of 241 five-year-old children, the following hypotheses were made: (1) The more that a child identifies with a parent, the more his doll play will approach the level of aggression he perceives in that parent; (2) the level of aggression of the like-sex parent will be the most significant influence in determining the aggressive behavior with the dolls; (3) boys will show more aggression in doll play than girls; (4) more aggression will be shown in doll play when there has been more punishment of the child; and (5) when there is severe punishment for aggression, more aggression will be shown in doll play when the like-sex parent is the principal disciplinarian. To obtain data, each child was given two 20-minute sessions to play with dolls. The activity with the dolls was scored on units of behavior involving aggression and neutral or positive acts. Aggression for the study was defined by the investigators as "action intending to irritate, hurt, injure, punish, frustrate, or destroy dolls or equipment." Verbal aggression was also included. Information was also gained from interviews with mothers and was rated and categorized so that three measures were obtained: (1) degree of identification with the parent, (2) severity of punishment of the child for expressing aggression, and (3) sex of parent who usually punished the child. The results of this study indicated that boys who identified with their fathers and who were usually punished by their fathers showed the highest frequency of aggression of all subjects. Identification for girls was related to high aggression only when there was severe punishment by mothers. This study also indicated that boys were more aggressive than girls but that there were no differences in aggression based on socioeconomic status of the families. A study of this type illustrates the value of information obtained in a study of children's imaginative behavior. The children, in attributing to dolls the behavior they had seen and experienced in the family, showed in imagination their feelings about and perception of family interaction.

Gilmore and Zigler (1964) in an investigation of children aged five to eight hypothesized that the children in their play would show differences in the influence of early parental child-rearing practices. The differences in practices were thought to be related to the differences in experience of children who are firstborn and those who are not. Expected excessive social reinforcement of firstborn children, for example, would be expected to interfere with the development of independence and would not encourage them to seek new ways to solve problems or persist in tasks. The findings of the study indicated that firstborn children showed less persistence in the experimental game than did later-born children when there was social reinforcement by the experimenter. However, other investigators indicate that firstborn children seem to be more creative than younger siblings.

In a study of play preferences of children nine to twelve years of age, Sutton-Smith and Rosenberg (1960) found that the choices of games of highly anxious boys were feminine and "immature" and those of highly anxious girls were masculine and "mature." Such findings, if supported by subsequent research, suggest that emotional factors are influential even in the free choice of divergent and imaginary activities.

Dreams and Imaginary Creations

As with the child's imaginary play, dreams provide outlets for expression of wishes and feelings. Some evidence indicates that a child dreams by the time he is three years old. By this time, language has become important and some symbolization is possible. Then too by this time demands have been made for responsibility in control of his body processes and for attainment of self-care skills. He also has experienced many of the frustrating and prohibitive aspects of cultural training, as well as the interference of peers with the fulfillment of needs. And he has learned sources of satisfaction for the development of themes in play which provide a basis for dreams.

It is likely that children dream more than adults and that wishes appear more openly in the dreams of young children. Foulkes and Vogel (1965) found that dreamlike activity occurs at several stages of sleep. Jersild (1968) asserts that however untrue a dream may seem, it comes from the dreamer's thoughts. Consequently, dreams have been studied in an effort to understand a child's behavior. Freud's (1956) emphasis on the disguised elements of dreams as related to events and meanings in a dreamer's life brought about interest in the investigation of dreams and clinical application of findings. Jersild et al. (1933) listed the frequent content of children's dreams, which included possession of objects, adventure, daily activity, apparitions, strange people and places, physical injury, and being chased. It is probable that content has changed since these studies, particularly as a result of the influence of television.

Influences on a child's dreams come from his experiences during the day, his physical condition, his capacity to symbolize and express himself through language and thought, his age, and the emotional satisfactions and dissatisfactions in his life. Foulkes (1966) asserts that conforming individuals have much more difficulty in recalling dream material than do nonconforming individuals. Apparently, nonconformists either have more dreams or feel more at ease in describing their dreams than those who seek to follow rules and customs.

Singer and Streiner (1966) studied the imaginative content of dreams and fantasy of blind and sighted children. The study was made of 20 blind and 20 sighted children with an age range of eight to twelve years. These investigators wished to obtain some information about the degree to which imagination and fantasy are related to innate capacity or to influences in the child's environment. They were also interested in obtaining information as to the extent of the influence of the deprivation of visual stimuli on imaginative development. These investigators hypothesized that the complexity of content of the blind children's responses would reflect the limitations imposed on them by their blindness and that the children with vision would show more flexibility and creativity in their responses. In interviews, data were obtained through the children's account of their own play, examples of their fantasies, and their descriptions of night dreams. Ratings were made about flexibility of space-time relations, variety of characters, and originality of content. Ratings indicated the degree of imaginativeness expressed in fantasy and night dreams. Results of the study indicated that sighted children were found to have more imaginativeness than the blind children. Despite more opportunities for introspection and fantasy forced upon them by their handicap, the blind children did not reveal as much imagination and fantasy as the children with vision. If the groups used in this investigation were comparable, then visual interaction with the environment would seem to be of consequence in the development of imagination and fantasy. Also, if imagination is considered to be significant in cognitive development, then specific effort is needed to help blind children and, in fact, any group of children lacking in the ability to respond imaginatively.

The contents and themes of children's dreams change as they grow older, since their feelings about themselves change as does their knowledge about their environment. Until about the age of five, it is not unusual for a child to have difficulty distinguishing that which he has dreamed and that which actually happened to him. In a young child's dream, he usually sees himself as the most important person. As he grows older, his dreams become more complex and he is not necessarily the central figure, although identification of feeling with this central figure is likely. Children in middle childhood have more frightening dreams and probably more nightmares. In their dreams, animals figure prominently, and dreams often consist of fear episodes where they are pursued by some dangerous beast. By the time the child reaches middle childhood, he is able to distinguish his dreams from real life and recognizes experiences that have been dreamed and those that have actually been experienced. As with the child's imagined play, dreams can be an expression of wishes. In dreaming while asleep, imagery is probably more complex and feelings probably are stronger than in reverie while awake.

Sarason (1944) in studying and comparing dreams of adolescent girls found that their dreams while sleeping were similar in thematic content to stories told about pictures given to them while awake. Not only are dreams related to waking reverie at times, but also they are often symbolic, so that a person does not see what a dream means as he disguises his real feelings, needs, or desires in it. Also, dreams do not usually occur in logical sequence, but are distorted or organized symbolically according to time, place, objects, and people, and action takes place in brief intervals of time with little relationship to reality or to coherency. It is likely that the basis for most dreams is tension and unfulfilled needs which the person seeks to achieve through his dreams.

Sometimes parts of a dream are brought into the waking world. This continuance of the dream is seen in the child's creation of a companion in his imagination. Children who have imaginary companions usually create these in the latter part of the early-childhood period, before they go to school. Sometimes, however, imaginary companions continue into the early part of the middle-childhood period and the early school years. Some imaginary companions are even given names and have a definite place to sit. Such a companion can serve as a hero to the child in performing acts of daring that the child himself is afraid to perform. At other times the imaginary companion is the scapegoat and by blaming the imaginary companion for the misbehavior, the child thus hopes to escape punishment.

An imaginary companion grows out of the need of a child for emotional exchange and affection. The creation of imaginary companions sometimes upsets parents, since this fantasy seems to indicate to them an unrealistic and disturbed state. However, not all children who have imaginary companions are emotionally disturbed nor is the creation necessarily a pathological development. A creation of an imaginary companion is not far removed from imaginary identifications such as emulation of a famous Indian fighter or war aviator. In these instances, a child finds little difficulty in projecting his feelings into either type or role since he can feel more powerful. As a child's satisfaction in interaction with others grows and as he finds playmates with whom he can express his feelings in imaginative play, he usually finds it unnecessary to continue the fantasy.

In order to obtain information about imaginary companions and fantasy related to play, Singer (1961) studied a group of children in the middle-childhood period. One of the procedures in the study was to tell the children that the experimenters were seeking spacemen for the future and that, since spacemen must sit in isolated and cramped conditions, it was important to know which individuals could sit quietly in their chairs as long as possible. Singer found that children who had been given high ratings in reference to fantasy, daydreams, and make-believe in their play were able to sit longer in place. It was also found that children rated high in fantasy activity were given high ratings for creativity in stories that they told.

Singer (1966) concludes from his studies that environmental stimulation is consequential in the development of fantasy and dream behavior and that a child who has had considerable environmental stimulation continues to explore and deal with his environment in fantasy as a pleasurable pursuit. Singer also sees the daydream as activity producing internal stimuli that may be a basis for other new stimuli which introduce novelty and at the same time involve little threat. A child may develop individualistic patterns of fantasy and stylistic behavior. Such characteristic behavior is suggested by the work of Witkin et al. (1962).

DIVERGENT BEHAVIOR AND CREATIVITY

Creativity means the bringing about of something new, a rearrangement of materials, events, actions, or relationships of people. It may be something that will contribute to the pleasure of other people—a musical offering, a painting, a sculpture, a new source of power, a new type of material, instrument, or machine. Fromm (1959) believes that creativity should be defined in simple terms, as the "ability to respond." Fromm apparently means that many individuals who show little creative behavior tend to respond to a stimulus by correctly classifying it or labeling it and fail to go beyond this limited response to an appreciation of the implicit meaning of the stimulus and of its potential associations.

Rogers (1959) believes that to be creative an individual must develop some "observable product." The creative production will be in terms of something that others can perceive and will bear the mark of the person who created it, indicating his individuality. A creative product is not necessarily something absolutely new; that is, creativity usually consists of a rearrangement of old patterns and out of old patterns new conceptions, arrangements, and combinations are achieved. Unusual facts and items are placed in juxtaposition with boundaries of time, space, and limitations of material disregarded. Symbols or abstractions can be brought quickly into play, and images and parts of past experience are projected into new experiences at a different place or time. Infinite explorations, superimpositions, and associations are made, with novel configurations and patterns being thus obtained. Images evoke other images, thoughts evoke other thoughts, and reorganization follows reorganization, all taking place in fractions of time. In the repatterning of perceptions and associations, it is important that integration take place in order that a result, a conclusion, or a product can be translated into a reality to which others can respond.

Developmental Aspects of Creative Appreciation

Some evidence is available that suggests that preference for creative objects and creations follows a developmental sequence. Machotka (1966) in a study of children's preferences for certain paintings in a group by famous artists believes that he found three developmental levels: (1) preferences based on subject matter and color (ages six to seven years); (2) preferences based on representation, clarity, and on contrast and harmony of colors (ages seven to eleven years); and, (3) preferences based on interest, style, composition, etc. (ages twelve and above). Choices based on the first category, Machotka asserts, depend upon the child's identification with the picture and his identification with the activities of the people depicted. Also, in the first category, the preferences depended upon the emotions or "affect" that the child attributed to the pictures. Preferences based on the second category (clarity) do not seem to depend on relationships among objects, and Machotka thinks maturation is a factor. Preferences in the third category (style, composition) seemed to be based on "formal operations in the thought of the child." In the later developmental levels, it seems that the child loses interest in realism and thinks of several styles at once. This investigator concludes that vocabulary becomes important at the more advanced levels. It is likely that not only vocabulary but also language facility and ability for verbal expression affect the placement of the child's responses into the categories.

Motivation and Creativity

Schachtel (1959) believes that motivation for creativity comes from the need to relate to the environment and that this need is in evidence in the child's exploration of objects in his environment. A child does not want to remain in a closed and familiar place but wishes to explore the novel and strange. According to Schachtel, the type of experience that leads to creativity is one in which there is openness, attention, thought, and feeling in the play of the child. The motivation for creativity can be related also to Schachtel's two modes of perception, particularly the autocentric mode.

Motivation for group conformity does not seem to be significant, since creative children do not seem to be unduly influenced by behavior of their peers in terms of making certain choices. For example, Yamamoto and Genovese (1965) found that creative fifth-grade children depended very little on group norms for making choices. Thus, motivation to make choices in accord with others did not seem to be present.

Wallach and Kogan (1965) believe that there are two classes of properties in the perception of the environment. One class refers to information about form, color, configuration, and the like and seems to be similar to Schachtel's allocentric mode. The other refers to the emotional significance of environmental stimuli and is thus similar to Schachtel's autocentric mode. Emotions such as joy, anger, or fear in association with stimuli are referred to as "physiognomic properties." The term has its origin in the idea of discovering a person's character from his facial features or form of his body. Now the term is used in reference to properties discernible externally which give clues to feelings or affect states. Werner and Kaplan (1963) believe that physiognomic sensitivity may well be genetically based and not necessarily all learned. Wallach and Kogan think that it may be both inherited and learned. These latter investigators explain that a child's response to physiognomic properties involves a simile. For example, if a child says that the front grille of an automobile looks as if it is frowning, he is giving indication of physiognomic sensitivity. In so doing, Wallach and Kogan believe, the child is perceiving an identity relation between a visual configuration and feeling. Such behavior may in itself be creative, but it may also lead to active creation of new relationships among things or between people and things.

In his studies of creative people and in his discussion of intelligence, Guilford (1950, 1957, 1959, 1967) sees creative characteristics as the ability to perceive difficulties and incomplete aspects of problems, to maintain a fluency of thinking, to verbalize, and to utilize associative experience. The ability to use associative experience means that the creative individual has the ability to use other experiences that are appropriate and helpful in solving problems. In addition, Guilford emphasizes an expressional fluency and illustrates this capacity by the test to measure the production of phrases and sentences. Other types of fluency that he thinks are important are *ideational fluency,* or an ability to produce a large number of ideas; *flexibility,* an avoidance of persistently seeking a solution that at first looks satisfactory but which does not provide the proper direction;

and *unusual or original types of solutions in association,* the ability to remove oneself from usual or conventional methods.

Many investigators of creativity in recent years maintain that children generally are creative and open to new experiences. Children seem to possess in common with creative adults a willingness to investigate new situations, expend energy in unknown and puzzling conditions, and to remain unfrightened by ambiguous stimuli. Another characteristic seen in some creative adults and characteristic of children (to the distress of some mothers) is the tolerance for disorder, inexact, approximate, and uncertain conditions (Barron, 1958). This tolerance is often translated into a lack of concern for rules, regulations, and direction.

Students of child development have long been interested in the apparent ability of some children to show an encompassing recall of a collection of objects. In Jaensch's early work (1930) he found that children's imagery depended upon the perception and a pure memory image, or *eidetic image.* Some children, according to Jaensch, can see the images of a briefly seen configuration of stimuli as real projections on a surface. This image seemed to be equal to the experience of actually perceiving the configuration. For example, such children describe in great detail the contents of a store window from a memory image as well as if they were actually looking at the window. Such an ability does not seem closely related to intelligence, and wide individual differences seem to occur. Apparently, it is much more common in the early-childhood period. As the child matures, effective behavior seems to be much more dependent upon the use of abstractions and symbols rather than upon the recall of irrelevant details. Consequently, as the child grows older he likely finds that such imagery is of less and less value to him. That is, interaction with the environment becomes increasingly complex and dealing with it is facilitated by abstract and symbolic thought rather than a great deal of specificity. On the other hand, Doob (1965) found that adolescents in Africa were shown to possess eidetic imagery. It did not appear to this investigator that the images aided immediate or longer recall but did aid in remembering drawings or photographs.

It is important in considering eidetic imagery to take into account Werner's belief that eidetic imagery is more prominent in young children and primitive people. He suggested that primitive people are much more subject to visions suggested by shapes in their environment, such as trees and rocks, and that "visionary appearances" are given significance and supersede the reality of day-to-day life. He also pointed out that the memory for natural forms in the environment approaches the same type of behavior seen in eidetic imagery in children. For primitive people it may be that memory of natural aspects, mountains, rivers, and plateaus is necessary and that such imagery common in childhood continues to serve; whereas, in more complex cultures, abstractions and symbols are necessary in order to reduce complexity to more manageable groupings for thought processes.

Child-Rearing Practices and Creativity

That child-rearing practices in the family will affect the development of creativity in children seems to be a reasonable assumption. In a study of creative children in the fourth grade, Weisberg and Springer (1961) examined certain characteristics of parental behavior in an effort to delineate influential environmental factors. The children were first selected on the basis of a high score on an intelligence test and then further selection on such tests as the tin-can test in which the children were asked to give as many uses as possible of a can. Projective tests and interviews were also used in selection. It was found that the child scoring high on the test for creativity was frequently the oldest child in the family. The families of the selected creative children were described by the investigators as not being "close." The most creative ones came from families where the children were "not dominated" and where conformity to parental values was not stressed. In the family structure, the father was seen to exercise authority both in his work and at home.

In a study investigating the relation of children's experiences in the family to differences in extent of differentiation, Dyk and Witkin (1965) found that less "differentiated" children were likely to have less differentiated mothers. Differentiation is seen to be related to creativity in that it refers to the perceptual organization, such as the ability to separate figure from ground. Dyk and Witkin assert that since the significance of stimulus objects and the organization of the perceptual field come from the initial teachings of the mother, mothers who are able to provide examples and teach their children in a "differentiated" way are more likely to produce children who have the ability to separate figure from ground. Further, such children can organize a perceptual situation and impose structural organization on a stimulus field in which little structure exists. Socioeconomic class differences are not clear, but Busse (1968) concluded from a study of fifth-grade Negro boys that there was evidence of a "general flexible thinking" factor in the subjects of his sample.

Creativity and Intelligence

In a study seeking to differentiate among different types of intellectual characteristics, Getzels and Jackson (1962) investigated differences between subjects who were determined to be highly intelligent and subjects who were highly creative. They selected two experimental groups—one high in intelligence but not high in creativity and one high in creativity but not high in intelligence. The groups were determined on the basis of intelligence tests and on a series of five creativity tests indicating ability to deal inventively with verbal and numerical symbols and with object-space relations. The tests were a Word Association Test, a Uses for Things Test (subjects had to give as many uses as possible for a common object, such as a brick), a Hidden Shapes Test (subjects had to find a geometric figure in a complex pattern), a Fables Test (subjects had to compose endings for fables), and a Make-up Problems Test (subjects had to make mathematical problems from given information). In examining the results of this research, Getzels and Jackson reported that despite the 23-point difference in mean IQ between the highly creative subjects and the highly intelligent subjects, achievement test scores were very similar (both groups were high). The creative subjects, however, were not as much preferred by teachers as were the subjects with high intelligence test scores. In reference to personal qualities, the creative subjects favored personal qualities that had no relationship to those qualities believed to be necessary for success in adult life and to some extent the preferred qualities were the reverse of those which they believed their teachers favored. The investigators also found that the creative subjects made greater use in fantasy of humor, incongruities, and playfulness. In reference to career aspirations, the highly creative subjects had much more preference for unconventional careers. In general, the creative subjects were seen as individuals who freed themselves from the usual and were divergent from the expected. They also showed enjoyment of the unknown.

The relationship of intelligence test scores and academic achievement and creativity is not as yet clearly established. Cicirelli (1965) found that achievement and creativity had a "weak relationship." His study led him to conclude that IQ and creativity are additive in their effect on academic achievement. In a study of fifth-grade children, Yamamoto and Chimbidis (1966) used the Minnesota Test of Creative Thinking and the Stanford Achievement Test. They compared test results and found that IQ predicted school achievement best. They found little support for the idea of a threshold of intelligence; that is, beyond a certain minimum of intelligence, academic achievement is more closely related to creativity than intelligence.

The distinction between creativity and intelligence is still open to question according to Wallach and Kogan (1965), despite the data presented by Getzels and Jackson. For example, Wallach and Kogan point out that they see Getzels and Jackson's data as failing to indicate that the tests of creativity were independent of general intelligence. Furthermore, the five tests of creativity were no more highly correlated with each other than they were with intelligence. Consequently, grouping the five creativity measures into a combined score as if they represented something distinct from general intelligence is unwarranted. Thus, Wallach and Kogan maintain that a specific and characteristic definition of the concept of creativity cannot be obtained from the Getzels and Jackson data.

Hudson (1966) approached the problem of creativity by studying boys whom he classified as "divergers" and "convergers." The convergers were boys who did well on multiple-choice, or structured, tests, and divergers were those who did better on "open-ended tests." He found that boys who tended to prefer subjects in the arts were those who were more successful on the open-ended tests than the structured tests. Boys in the sciences were the convergers and did not do as well on the open-ended tests as those preferring the arts. Hudson believes that his findings have implications for the selection and training of scientists and raises questions also about the definition of creativity tests and their interpretation.

Getzels and Jackson had other concerns about intelligence and creativity, and they reasoned that excellence on intellectual tasks of the school or creative activity in relation to such tasks was not the only form of excellence relevant to society. Consequently, they sought information about "moral" and "adjustment" behavior and undertook to see if it were possible to differentiate between children who were outstanding in "adjustment" and outstanding in "moral character." They listed seven characteristics which they saw as defining the moral person. One item, for example, was as follows: "chooses the ethical rather than the expedient alternative when faced with an interpersonal dilemma." To get such information about their subjects, they developed a test of 25 problem situations, each having four alternative courses of action. The investigators also used a "Personal Opinion Questionnaire" and a "Descriptive Words Test." The latter involved choices by subjects as to words which they would like to have applied to themselves.

To obtain information about adjustment, Getzels and Jackson used the California Test of Personality, a test with such items as "Do you find that your mother and father are difficult to please?" They also used two sentence-completion tests and a test consisting of 30 statements, such as "I sometimes say unpleasant things about a person that I would not tell him to his face." Two groups were selected with one high on morality and the other high on adjustment. They found negligible correlations between the morality and adjustment measures. It was found that despite similarity in IQ, the moral subjects were superior to the adjustment subjects in both numerical and verbal achievement. But the adjustment subjects were more satisfied with their school achievement than the moral subjects. It was found, too, that the mothers of the moral subjects were more critical of their children and the relation of the children to the family seemed to be more distant.

The investigators have summarized by saying that the highly moral individual seems similar to the highly creative individual as being somewhat rejecting and rejected. On the other hand, Getzels and Jackson see the high IQ group and the adjusted group as "insiders" and as people who engage in behavior approved by the social order. These research workers conclude that the school ought to be sure not to reject any of the four groups (the creative, the highly intelligent, the moral, and the adjusted), as all of these types of "giftedness" are much needed by society.

A POINT OF VIEW

As with a number of other topics in psychology, definitions of "imagination" and "creativity" are difficult to achieve. Hence, behavior that should be approved or disapproved on the basis of that which is imaginative and creative is difficult to describe. In almost any social role, both convergent and divergent thinking occurs. It seems reasonable to say that at times it is prudent, desirable, or helpful to engage in convergent thinking and equally the same can be said for the necessity for divergent thinking. Making generalizations about the desirability for one or the other in reference to both self and society is likely to be related to adjustment and morality, as Getzels and Jackson have suggested. In fact, concepts of adjustment and morality should be included in a holistic approach to human behavior. The preceding comments, it should be noted, have some similarity to psychoanalytic, or Freudian, concepts of the structure of personality and the relationships of the id, ego, and superego.

A reasonable perspective of individual behavior should include both divergent and convergent thought in reference to social roles, because distinct polarities rarely exist in human behavior. While the use of the Objects Use Test may help to distinguish between students in the arts and sciences, with apparently the divergent thinkers being more prevalent among the students in the arts than in the sciences, conclusions as to whether or not this is as should be are to be doubted. In a way, as is found in so much of human behavior, a paradox is encountered. A social order, even a profession or a social role, is dependent on convergent thinking; on the other hand, social progress in both the arts and sciences must be made to some extent by divergent thinking. Some resolution is likely possible by allowing flexibility within roles and social demands for behavior.

As far as the Objects Use Test is concerned, the stimulus presented may not be appropriate to the interests of every individual. For example, a brick may not arouse a creative response in a physics student but a complex electronic circuit might. Accordingly, while present-day leads are helpful, more study is needed in this interesting and important area of human behavior.

REFERENCES

Barron, G., 1958. "The Psychology of Imagination," *Scientific American,* **199**, 150–170.

Busse, T. V., 1968. "Establishment of the Flexible Thinking Factor in Fifth-Grade Boys," *Journal of Psychology,* **69**, 93–100.

Cicirelli, V. G., 1965. "Form of the Relationship between Creativity, IQ, and Academic Achievement," *Journal of Educational Psychology,* **56**, 303–308.

Doob, L. W., 1965. "Exploring Eidetic Imagery among the Kamba of Central Kenya," *Journal of Social Psychology,* **67**, 3–22.

Dyk, R. B., and H. A. Witkin, 1965. "Family Experiences Related to the Development of Differentiation in Children," *Child Development,* **36**, 21–55.

Foulkes, D., 1966. *The Psychology of Sleep.* New York: Scribner.

Foulkes, D., and G. Vogel, 1965. "Mental Activity at Sleep Onset," *Journal of Abnormal Psychology,* **70**, 231–243.

Freud, S., 1956. *The Interpretation of Dreams,* translated by A. A. Brill. New York: Modern Library.

Fromm, E., 1959. "The Creative Attitude," in *Creativity and Its Cultivation,* edited by H. H. Anderson, pp. 44–54. New York: Harper & Row.

Getzels, J. W., and P. W. Jackson, 1962. *Creativity and Intelligence.* New York: Wiley.

Gilmore, J. B., and E. Zigler, 1964. "Birth Order and Social Reinforcer Effectiveness in Children," *Child Development,* **35**, 193–200.

Guilford, J. P., 1950. "Creativity," *American Psychologist,* **5**, 444–454.

Guilford, J. P., 1957. "Creative Abilities in the Arts," *Psychological Review,* **64**, 110–118.

Guilford, J. P., 1959. "Traits of Creativity," in *Creativity and Its Cultivation,* edited by H. H. Anderson, pp. 142–161. New York: Harper & Row.

Guilford, J. P., 1967. *The Nature of Human Intelligence.* New York: McGraw-Hill.

Hudson, L., 1966. *Contrary Imaginations.* New York: Schocken.

Jaensch, E. R., 1930. *Eidetic Imagery.* New York: Harcourt, Brace & World.

Jersild, A. T., 1968. *Child Psychology.* Englewood Cliffs, N.J.: Prentice-Hall.

Jersild, A. T., F. V. Markey, and C. Jersild, 1933. *Children's Fears, Dreams, Wishes, Daydreams, Likes, Dislikes, Pleasant, and Unpleasant Memories.* New York: Teachers College, Columbia University.

Levin, H., and R. R. Sears, 1956. "Identification with Parents as a Determinant of Doll Play Aggression," *Child Development, 27*, 135–153.

Machotka, P., 1966. "Aesthetic Criteria in Childhood: Justifications of Preference," *Child Development, 37*, 877–885.

Rogers, C. R., 1959. "Toward a Theory of Creativity," in *Creativity and Its Cultivation,* edited by H. H. Anderson, pp. 69–82. New York: Harper & Row.

Sarason, S. B., 1944. "Dreams and Thematic Apperception Test Stories," *Journal of Abnormal and Social Psychology, 39*, 486–492.

Schachtel, E. G., 1959. *Metamorphosis.* New York: Basic Books.

Singer, J. L., 1961. "Imagination and Waiting Ability in Young Children," *Journal of Personality, 29*, 396–413.

Singer, J. L., 1966. *Daydreaming.* New York: Random House.

Singer, J. L., and B. F. Streiner, 1966. "Imaginative Content in the Dreams and Fantasy Play of Blind and Sighted Children," *Perceptual and Motor Skills, 22*, 475–482.

Sutton-Smith, B., and B. G. Rosenberg, 1960. "Manifest Anxiety and Game Preferences in Children," *Child Development, 31*, 307–311.

Torrance, E. P., 1962. *Guiding Creative Talent.* Englewood Cliffs, N.J.: Prentice-Hall.

Wallach, M. A., and N. Kogan, 1965. *Modes of Thinking in Young Children.* New York: Holt.

Weisberg, P. S., and K. J. Springer, 1961. "Environmental Factors in Creative Function," *Archives of General Psychiatry, 5*, 554–564.

Werner, H., 1948. *Comparative Psychology of Mental Development.* Rev. ed. Chicago: Follett.

Werner, H., and B. Kaplan, 1963. *Symbol Formation.* New York: Wiley.

Witkin, H. A., R. B. Dyk, H. F. Faterson, D. R. Goodenough, and S. A. Karp, 1962. *Psychological Differentiation.* New York: Wiley.

Yamamoto, K., and M. E. Chimbidis, 1966. "Achievement, Intelligence, and Creative Thinking in Fifth-grade Children: A Correlational Study," *Merrill-Palmer Quarterly of Behavior and Development, 12*, 233–241.

Yamamoto, K., and C. T. Genovese, 1965. "Creativity and Norm Conformity in Fifth-grade Children," *Exceptional Children, 32*, 257–258.

[*nine*]

Socialization

Socialization is the process of training through which a child becomes a part of society. Through the process the child learns to find satisfaction within the social order and to become a member of it, to contribute to it, and to insure its continuity. If behavior is patterned so that a child is accepted as a member of a society, then it follows that his behavior will be, within limits, characteristic of that society.

Socialization among human beings always takes place in a context established by a society. In addition, all societies have some activities common to others. For example, the members engage in certain behavior in order to provide food, shelter, and clothing. These activities are within a framework of organization that makes it possible for the members of the society to engage in cooperative endeavor (Asch, 1952). Since the very beginning of social organization, activities such as singing, dancing, wearing ornaments, and making art objects have characterized man's social behavior. These skills and arts have been passed on to the young as part of the socialization process.

Although one may observe or describe group behavior, a society's beliefs and activities must be conceptualized ultimately in terms of individuals, because individuals make the tools and objects and establish the relationships within the social order. A child becomes what he is not simply because of the contact with the objects and forces in his environment, but also through his contact with other human beings. Thus, in the developmental process from birth to maturity, a child discovers that he is a human being and that with infinite intricacy he is bound to his species and to a particular group or society.

It may be possible to study the socialization process by selecting a specific type of behavior, carefully describing it, obtaining and compiling normative data about it, and determining the frequency with which it occurs within a society. From such information, hypotheses and perhaps even a theory of socialization could be developed. Experimental methods in the establishment of a body of scientific information about socialization would be desirable but, at present, information probably can be better obtained through observational and descriptive methods because of certain limitations of the experimental method. Control of child training is not absolute, because one would not want to interfere with what is considered to be favorable experiences just to prove that some kinds of experiences are unfavorable. The favorable development of a child obviously cannot be jeopardized for the sake of experimentation; thus Dubin and Dubin (1965), after a review of a large number of studies dealing with childrens' social perceptions, concluded that available evidence considerably limits generalitions about socialization.

One important principle, however, has come from research and especially from the work of social anthropologists: Although man's behavior varies sometimes greatly from one social order to another, the variability is largely due to cultural influences rather than genetically based influences (Child, 1954; Mead, 1939; Whiting, 1951).

Increasingly, current cultural interchange is tending to reduce extreme variations. The realities of everyday activities and events in one culture are consequently not isolated but are related to activities or events in others. For example, some of the results of a man's labor in terms of money go for taxes that, as foreign aid, are shared with another man in another society on the other side of the earth.

THE SOCIALIZATION PROCESS

Why does the child become socialized? The most widely accepted view at the present time is that the child makes the effort to accept the standards of the parents because conformity fulfills the child's needs. A child soon learns that pleasurable sensations can be provided by the mother, and he learns to elicit such desired behavior from her. She will say to him, "Because you have been such a good boy today, I baked cookies for you."

As he conforms and stays within the framework of behavior that pleases his mother, he reduces both biological (desire for food) and acquired needs (desire for approval). Thus, such a principle is based on the thesis that a child learns a response on the basis of some need or drive. The learning of a response is much more likely to take place if it is reinforced or rewarded, and the more often a reward is associated with a response, the more likely the response is to recur. The exceptions, where the child does not seek reduction of tension through acceptable behavior patterns, are discussed in Chapter 13.

Social Motives

The acquisition of social motives, according to the drive or need point of view, is based on the theoretical approach dependent on the principle of reinforcement. Parents may convey to their child the thought, "If you develop behavior that is in accord with the standards I have adopted and which are part of the culture, I will reward you." The converse also exists: The parents may say in effect to the child, "If you do not conform, you will be punished."

Child-training methods or socialization can be divided into four dimensions, according to Sears et al. (1957). These investigators interviewed nearly 400 American mothers about their child training. In the study, four dimensions of child training were categorically devised. The first dimension is *action versus learning*. This term means that, in infancy and while the child is quite young, much of the mother's work with the child consists of controlling him and caring for his physical needs and that the mother seeks to increase independence and to help the child learn the necessary developmental skills.

The second dimension is called *impelling versus directing*. This means that the child must be "impelled" to do what the mother wishes. Training depends upon impelling events within the child, such as hunger, and at the same time the mother must provide direction so that the child is fed within the framework of her regulations. The third dimension described is that of *positive versus negative control*. Positive control consists of rewards as an incentive for the child to ally with the mother in conforming to the desired behavior; but with negative control, the mother may make an effort to change the child's behavior by threat of punishment. The fourth dimension is that of *love orientation versus object orientation*. The authors mean by this classification that the mother can reward the child with the promise of affection and a close emotional relationship with her, and similarly she can provide the child with objects (desired toys).

The child will generalize and to some extent perceive the opportunities for satisfaction and the world about him as he has been conditioned by the parent. For example, if a great deal of his experiences and rewards are associated with objects and if he is taught that when he conforms he will be rewarded with objects, then objects will assume great significance in the child's life and he will tend more toward obtaining satisfaction through acquisition of material possessions than through acquisition of satisfaction in social relationships.

Perceptual Selectivity in Socialization

Selectivity of stimuli in interpersonal interaction is a complex process requiring revision as a result of experience and in accord with the success or failure of one's own responses to stimuli and to favorable or unfavorable responses from others. Children seek to become increasingly successful in the utilization of cues and stimuli from others so that more satisfying interaction will be achieved.

Responses of a child are, of course, to certain selected stimuli, since he has found as a result of experience that if a particular stimulus situation exists, a particular response must be made. On the other hand, if a child considers himself to be generally unsuccessful, he may then make little effort to find or select appropriate stimuli. Some unhappy children avoid contact with people and feel that interaction is not rewarding; while others, angry and hostile, disregard the rights and feelings of other people in order to strike back at a world perceived as depriving.

Ordinarily, but to varying degrees, children learn to make appropriate responses and to order their behavior so that it will fulfill the needs of others too. Such behavior is characterized as "unselfish" or "other oriented," but since they receive satisfaction through the satisfaction of others, mutual benefit has led some theorists to a deterministic explanation of behavior, that is, all behavior is determined by needs and thus is ultimately directed toward self-satisfaction.

CULTURAL INFLUENCES DURING
SOCIAL DEVELOPMENT

In considering cultural influences on development, attention should be given to the concept of cultural norms, the significance of cultural change, and social class.

Because conformity to a group is one of the goals of socialization, from the standpoint of the group as well as the individual, social conflict can be avoided through conformity. Hence, if a child receives the approval of his parents and others, it is reasonable to expect that emotional tensions and frustrations are lessened. Conceptions of conformity can be constructed from behavior approved by the culture, and these standards may control individual behavior. A social order undergoing rapid change makes the socialization process particularly difficult for both children and parents by causing doubt about parental values and by causing the child to alter behavior acquired through much effort. Social-class differences may cause difficulty, because things learned, for example by children for the the lower socioeconomic class during their early life, may have to be altered once they enter school.

Cultural Norms and Cultural Change

Sherif (1935) developed the term *social norms,* which he defined as values, or standards, of a group established for the benefit of the individuals in it. Once established in a group situation, a social norm continues to influence the individuals, even though they may subsequently meet the same situation outside group influences. All societies have social norms, some being more flexible than others in their requirements for members. A great deal of effort in the socialization process is directed toward teaching the child to conform to the norms established by his culture and society. And, because the child learns to value culturally approved behavior, social norms in one sense become motivating influences for individual behavior.

Asch (1952) has advanced the concept of cultural relativism in reference to standards of behavior: Judgment of what is right or wrong is relative, and standards differ according to cultures and societies. Thus, a child's socialization in one society will lead him to approve certain behavior, but later in adulthood he may be surprised to find that in another society and culture, another individual is equally certain that his own behavior, although quite different, is appropriate.

Sherif (1961) believes that tolerance for deviance ranges in extent according to the relationship of the deviant behavior to group welfare. The more significance the behavior has for the group, the narrower is the range for deviance. Thus, if a type of behavior is of little consequence to the group, the variability allowed in behavior tends to be much greater. Hence, in child training, parents tend to be more strict in their demands if the child's behavior is of importance to group welfare. A changing society, with its age-old traditions being destroyed and with new ones not yet taking their place, might well be expected to hold hazards for individuals growing up in it. To obtain information about the effect of cultural change in a society under stress, Alexander and Anderson (1957) studied children of the

Northern Cheyenne Indians living on the Tongue River Reservation in Montana. These Indians lived behind fences and administrative barriers on a large tract of range and forest land given to them as a reservation in the latter part of the nineteenth century. The territory was the one on which they had hunted game in the days of the buffalo. At the time of the study, part of the aboriginal culture still persisted to the extent that cultural change was rather slow despite the fact that new institutions were growing out of old ones.

Child-training methods were similar to those used in the aboriginal days. The parents did not strike their children, but the children were given orders to behave and were taught to sit quietly and to listen when in the company of their elders. The beliefs of the past relating to the supernatural were taught and were epitomized by the sun dance, the healing activities carried on in the sweat lodges, the symbolism of the bison skull near the east entrance of the cabin, and the wearing of amulets. Although these practices all tied the people to the past, the past was fading and compromise now was taking place. Supernatural beliefs of the past had become merged with modern beliefs into a new religion called the "peyote cult." The Cheyenne faced two ways—toward the past with its ties and to the present with its change. Thus, the children were trained in a setting of cultural conflict. As might be expected, a frequent phrase heard was "We are distressed."

Endeavoring to discover the effect of the stress of cultural change on children, Alexander and Anderson used a technique similar to the test used by Henry (1947). They presented pictures about Indian life showing scenes within the experiences of the Indian children. Seven Cheyenne children between the ages of ten and fourteen were studied.

One of the stimulus cards depicted a small boy seated in the doorway of a log cabin with his elbows on his knees and his chin in his hands. (See Figure 9-1.) A child, Susan Sunwalking, told the following story about the picture: "That little girl is sitting outside. Maybe her mother died and maybe she never did eat and she got no shoes. I guess she was alone and she was so lonesome and her father had die too. They live out in the forest and the girl stays out in that forest. The end."

The child mistakenly called the boy in the picture a girl. It will be noted that there were no pleasant emotional expressions in the story and the child in the picture was described as "lonesome." The theme of the story is one of deprivation. Susan spoke of death, her mother and father, not being able to eat, having no shoes, and being alone.

The stories of the seven subjects studied by Alexander and Anderson included elements selected from their experience: human beings, the things

Figure 9.1. Card No. 1 used in the study by T. Alexander and R. Anderson, "Children in a Society under Stress," *Behavioral Science,* vol. 2, 1957, pp. 46–55.

human beings make, and the rocks, hills, and rivers about them. The emotional expressions were predominantly negative; the children frequently mentioned death and the adverse forces of nature and were usually concerned with feelings of sadness and anxiety with no descriptions of beneficent human activity. Analysis of the data indicated that the children did not have strong affectional bonds with their parents. The characteristic responses were those of submission and the denial of feeling about difficulties.

Other evidence of difficulty that children have in a changing culture was found in a study carried out in East Africa by Ainsworth and

Ainsworth (1962a, b, c, d). The subjects were 355 African children in secondary schools. The children were given a specially designed projective test, the Rosenzweig Picture-Frustration Test and the Draw-A-Person Test for which the subjects were asked to draw both a European and an African figure.

It was found that about two-thirds of the children drew the European person larger than the African, and the authors believe this size preponderance indicated that the children saw Europeans as more dominant than Africans. The children who had more contacts with Western teachers or administrators were more negative in their attitude toward authority. Other conclusions of the investigators are as follows: Those subjects with more European contacts experienced more frustration than those with fewer contacts; those with more contacts were more discontented with the then-present political situation; and those with more contacts were more aggressive than those with fewer contacts.

Although present intercultural studies have theoretical and methodological limitations, available information indicates that children in a society where drastic cultural changes are taking place will have many difficulties in the socialization process.

Social-Class Determinants

Socialization may be seen as varying according to a stratification of social classes. For example, the following is a study by Hollingshead (1949):

> Hollingshead classified a town's population into five classes and distinguished each class by specific characteristics. In Class I, membership was relatively stable from one generation to another through the combination of lineage and accumulated wealth. Since the members of this class had their position through inheritance, the prestige of their positions was not obtained as a result of their own efforts. Their accumulated wealth was invested so that the people had income with relatively little work. Thus, pleasure rather than labor was the goal and much of their leisure time was spent with other members of their class. This group encouraged marriage within their own class, thereby bringing together estates of the different families. They desired few children so that the estates would not be broken up by too many allotments. The children were carefully educated according to the station of the scions of the old families. Hollingshead divided Class I still further by placing those families who had been in the community for a number of generations in one group and those who had recently entered Class I in another group.

The people in Class II differed from the people in Class I in that they had their positions in the class as a result of their own efforts. Prestige accruing to the members of Class II rested as much upon their community activity as upon economic success. The family's income came from the head of the family, who usually practiced in a profession or operated a family business. Although this group appreciated wealth, security was the goal. Hollingshead found that the most highly educated people were in Class II and education was viewed as an important requisite for success. Therefore, the parents in this group sacrificed time, energy, and their own pleasure to give their children the advantages of education.

Class III families had sufficient income for the conveniences and comforts of life but had little left to invest in wealth-producing activities since most of their income was spent on consumer goods. More children were born to parents in Class III than in Class II. Although Class III parents were mutually concerned about their children's future, success was viewed as depending on individual effort. People in Class III were not as well educated as people in the upper classes and usually they looked to these upper groups for community leadership.

The people in Class IV were aware of their inferior prestige position and they realized that the upper classes saw them as contributing to the community only through their jobs. Class IV was viewed by the upper classes as being poor, hard working, and financially unsuccessful. The family stability in Class IV was less than in the upper classes, and many of the homes were broken by separation and divorce.

Class V was the lowest-ranking group among the classes, and since many of the Class V families were known to the law enforcement agencies as chronic offenders, they were seen by the upper classes as a group with no respect for the law and as living in unwholesome conditions where crime and delinquency were rampant. Periods of unemployment and illness cut into income, and jobs were left with little consideration. Family conditions often were unfavorable because of the many children and relatives who inhabited the same residence and who, because of overcrowded conditions, had many quarrels and fights. Those in Class V had little interest in education and believed that they had no opportunity to improve their position. The socioeconomic conditions and parental levels of education of each of these classes influenced the training of the children in them.

Before entering school, a child is taught the ways of behaving characteristic of his social class. The behavioral patterns acquired in the home are similar throughout a given neighborhood because neighborhoods are usually comprised of people in the same class; thus, behavior is reinforced in the peer group as the child moves out of the family.

That contrast with middle-class children exists in the training and experiences of children in the lower socioeconomic class was shown in an early study by Davis and Havighurst (1947). Children in the lower class who grew up in tenements had, from the earliest days, patterns of behavior in contrast to those of middle-class children. As a lower-class child grew older, he could fight if he felt angry and laugh if he won; he learned from his family and peers not to be afraid to fight and not to be afraid of those in authority, such as a teacher or a policeman.

Middle-class children are not free of problems in the socialization process either. Much of the difficulty arising between parent and child from infancy through adolescence in middle-class homes comes from the demands of the parents. This pressure exerted by parents is not seen by the children, nor are the children or parents aware of the resulting emotional effects on the child. Rebellion and difficulty with children, according to Davis and Havighurst, come from the large number of "cultural injunctions" imposed by the parents.

Class differences are also in evidence in other cultures than American. Thomas and Surachmad (1962) investigated social-class differences in Indonesian mothers' expectations for their children. They hypothesized that the class differences would be similar to the social-class differences found by Davis and Havighurst in America. They expected to find that middle-class mothers would wean their children earlier and would expect their children to be more precocious in school work than would the lower-class mothers. They also expected that lower-class children would be allowed to play away from home without supervision at an earlier age than would middle-class children. Social class was defined by neighborhood type and housing, with two neighborhoods being chosen as representative of lower and middle class. The results of the study showed that Indonesian middle-class mothers did in fact expect their children to be weaned earlier than did the lower-class mothers, and this finding was similar to that of Davis and Havighurst (1947) in their study of American mothers. They found that both groups of mothers had similar expectations about age of reading and writing, but lower-class mothers expected their children to count earlier.

Greek mothers were found to have similarities with American mothers in child training in that both middle-class American mothers and middle-class

Greek mothers tended to be more permissive with young children than their lower-class compatriots (Prothro, 1966). Prothro (1961) suggests that the pattern of child rearing in Greece and Lebanon may be indicative of that in other transitional societies which have a traditional peasantry and urban class.

Hollingshead, although writing over two decades ago, emphasized that consideration should be given to the class system and its influence on the child's development. He maintained that material acquisition is the criterion for success, because people with little money occupy the low-prestige positions in the structure and a few with much money occupy the higher positions. Most people desire the *status quo*. Those who have been successful in the competitive system wish to retain it and those who are not successful become anxious when confronted with social change. Hollingshead questioned the view that a person in the competitive process can always be successful merely through his personal attributes and hard work, and he also questioned the view that the failure of those in the lower class to reach a high position in the social structure stems from their lack of ability. The social-class system obviously does not provide all with equal opportunities.

SOCIAL LEARNING MODELS

The term *social learning models* is used here in association with imitative behavior. Sears et al. (1957) see imitative behavior as "role practice" and Emmerich (1959b) sees it as a "tendency to behave like another person in fantasy." Imitative behavior of models might be termed "indirect training," in that the child is not specifically "told" or "taught." Bruner (1965) makes this point in his discussion of films made of "King Bushman of the Kalahar" because no instances were observed where children were told how to perform a task. The children learned by being shown and through imitation in play. Bruner explains, however, that the instruction of children in complex societies depends on "telling" and abstract teaching, because the breadth of knowledge makes it impractical to depend on "showing."

Imitative Behavior and Indirect Learning from Models

Indirect learning is illustrated by a comparative study of Israeli and American children (Rabin, 1959). Data were obtained by the use of a sentence-completion test with items relating to the following words: *father, abilities, goals, future, fears, friend, family, mother,* and *guilt*. The responses were then categorized as being "positive" or "other" (negative or neutral). Israeli children tended to idealize the family less than American children and were more suspicious of friends. They also showed more guilt, less optimism about the future, and were less confident of their own abilities. The results of the study suggest that certain cultural conditions produced the differences between the groups. For example, the Israeli child assumes adult responsibilities at an earlier age than the American child and thus has more opportunity for critical appraisal of his parents. Another difference influencing the results, according to Rabin, is that nationalism of the people of Israel goes beyond the confines of the family circle to the nation as a whole. Apparently, the differences found in the two groups of children came from experiences in the family, although not from direct teaching by parents.

A young child begins to identify with his family by imitating his parents, his brothers, or his sisters. For example, a little girl observing her mother putting on a hat may imitate such behavior by placing a handkerchief or other piece of cloth on her own head. Identification and imitative behavior are particularly in evidence in play and fantasy, in which most young children take adult roles. In play with dolls, a little girl will reward them, isolate them, spank them, and otherwise deal with them in accordance with her own experiences.

Sex Role Learning

Research workers have found the study of children's imitative behavior in doll play especially revealing of sex role identification. For example, Hartup (1964) studied imitative responses of preschool children through the use of a doll-play interview consisting of 51 two-choice problem situations. He especially sought information about sex identification in parent and peer imitation. He found that like-sex imitation was "moderately" generalized, but opposite-sex imitation was not. Similarly, Emmerich (1959a) found that the like-sex parent was used more than the opposite-sex parent as an identification model for boys; however, such was not the case for girls. Emmerich thus concluded that the boys were more aware of sex-appropriate behavior than were girls.

Parent dolls are used more extensively by children of both sexes in play representing adult behavior. Such play can reveal children's ideas about authority roles of parents. Ucko and Moore (1963) found that their subjects before the age of six gave parent dolls more positive and authoritarian roles (but not more negative roles); and at six, the children tended to see a mixed role pattern for parents.

The question of whether or not there is a convergence of the two sex roles in American society in contrast to other societies having a more clear-cut role delineation was investigated by Rabin and Limuaco (1959). These investigators compared the sexual differentiation of 129 American boys and girls, ages ten and eleven, and a similar sample of 159 Filipino children. The Filipino children tended to differentiate more between sex roles than did the American children. For Filipino children, the mother is the model initially (both sexes), but boys change to masculine identification at an early age. This shift for boys is made to masculine identification because of the rewards offered by both the parents and peers.

A child tries to experience through his own behavior what it is like to be another individual. Observations seem to indicate that, in taking a role, the child tries to express the feelings, values, and actions of the person whom he imitates. In identification and through role practice the child acts as if he were another person. For example, a child concerned about a parent's affection and approval can reassure himself by playing the parent's part as he would like it to be.

Children also imitate irrelevant or undesirable social behavior. Parental inadequacies, emotional instabilities, prejudice, and unethical and immoral behavior, although not directly and specifically taught, may nevertheless be emulated. In such a way, children unknowingly engage in the kind of behavior that may be useless or which has involved their parents in social conflict. A study of such behavior was done by Bandura and Huston (1961), who investigated specifically the imitation of "nonfunctional" behavior in a group of nursery school children. The children were given a "diverting" problem with a model who engaged in unnecessary behavior and the children, as hypothesized, reproduced the useless behavior of their model.

A child can have difficulty in learning new forms of behavior through imitation. Since the mother is the model for much of the early training of the child, her perception of herself as an effective person and as one who is respected or held in high esteem by the members of the family is of significance. If the father is critical of mother's child-training methods or sees her as unsuccessful, she will be likely to approach many of the difficult problems of child training with anxiety. Where parental roles are sharply divided and the father sees himself as oriented primarily toward supporting the family and attaining success in an occupational role and sees the mother as primarily responsible for the home and the rearing of the children, criticism of her competency is particularly devastating to her success in child training. The problems of the Ellison family illustrate how lack of emotional support by the father for the mother creates problems in the child training process.

> The profession of the father took much of his energy and time. He had told his wife that he could only allow her and the children one hour of his time each day. For a while, his wife tried to use the allotted time to talk over the problems she had with the children. Her husband, however, told her that he dealt with people's problems during the day and he did not wish to be faced with his own family problems at night. The most troublesome family problem was the Ellison's four-year-old son who was not completely toilet trained and frequently wet his clothing during the day. The mother's concern was increasing because their son was to enter kindergarten the next year. The father refused to help the mother with the problem because he thought that the child's difficulty grew out of her failure in training him.

> The difficulties in the Ellison family involved more than the son's problem. Mrs. Ellison felt that she was not only unsuccessful as a mother, but also that she was failing as a wife. Although she realized the necessity for her husband's long hours, she believed that if she were more important to him, he would spend more time with her and with the family. As her son's problem continued, she approached it with more anxiety and her lack of confidence was an important factor in the child's own failure.

> Mrs. Ellison eventually came to recognize that she had feelings of guilt, anxiety, and resentment toward both her child and her husband and a feeling of disappointment and failure about herself. It was obvious that the child's training would not be successful until the relationship between the parents changed. Progress was made when Mrs. Ellison decided to make the one hour her husband allowed her a pleasant occasion and one in which to avoid family difficulties. Demanding more of her husband's time or his attention to the family had not been successful, so she tried to make the time as pleasant as possible.

> As she used this approach, Mrs. Ellison was pleased to find that the husband then was willing to spend more time with her and the family. As her relationship with her husband improved and as she came to feel more successful as a wife, she then faced the child's difficulty with more confidence and eventually achieved success in his training.

In identification, a child learns very early to direct behavior in reference to the facial expressions of the mother so that if she "looks cross," demands can be avoided until she gives cues which will lead to possible satisfaction. In considering such conditioning, it can be seen that it is possible for an individual to interpret cues and stimuli unrealistically. For example, a child may see other people as threatening when actually they are not; in such cases, these children will often make little effort to fulfill needs in interpersonal interaction because of the threatening perception, as in the case of Nina Sue.

> Nina Sue, a shy and anxious girl in fourth grade became easily upset if the teacher spoke abruptly to her. One day several teachers told Nina Sue that they disapproved of her bringing lunch instead of eating the food available in the cafeteria. Her teachers were not angry, but Nina Sue thought they were and she left the school crying. From then on Nina Sue began to have increasing difficulty with her stomach. In the morning before she went to school, her stomach hurt and pains became so intense that she was unable to go to school—usually there were fits of vomiting. Gradually during the day, however, Nina Sue began to feel better. Later in the day she could eat the evening meal and participate in family activities or watch television. In the morning again, Nina Sue would become ill and would be unable to attend school. Her perception of the teachers and the school situation was such that although the teachers were interested in helping her and were even kind to her, she saw them as threatening.

SOCIAL LEARNING THEORY AND SOCIALIZATION

Social learning theory has grown out of a combination of Freudian theory and stimulus response theory, according to Baldwin (1967). Social learning theory began with the combination in reference to the development of the child's social relations. The fundamental aspect of the theory is that the behavior of the individual, in the main, is learned. Thus, it is easy to incorporate in the theoretical approach the anthropological view that the child is a creature of his culture and that he is trained according to cultural precepts. As Baldwin emphasizes, social learning theory holds that similarities of behavior among children result from learning processes and from that which is common in their environments. Environments are similar for children to the extent that they will encounter physical laws, such as injury in falling from a high place. Further, there are certain child-rearing customs, such as weaning and toilet training, which are common to all cultures. Characteristically, then, socialization is the process of changing behavior patterns of a child over the developmental years into the kind of behavior expected from an adult.

BEHAVIORAL CHANGES CHARACTERISTIC OF THE SOCIALIZATION PROCESS

Out of physical dependence of the infant on the mother there come psychological needs associated with the dependence on the mother for physical sustenance and care. This psychological relationship, according to the psychoanalytic theory of Erikson, develops from an expectancy for need fulfillment, which is a mixture of trust and mistrust. This sense of basic trust is an important factor in early development (Maier, 1965). If the sense of trust develops, the child will extend it to new situations and reinforcement of favorable expectations occurs with each verification of justification of trust, although, because of some failure, some mistrust and anxiety inevitably result. Trust is a conditioning kind of experience that brings about social responsiveness and social spontaneity. This point is illustrated by Rheingold (1956) in her study of institutional infants in which she found that infants who had much social stimulation scored higher on a series of social responsiveness tests than her control infants. While social learning theory, particularly its psychoanalytic root, emphasizes the concept of psychological dependency, the concept of dependency and its favorable or unfavorable aspects is difficult to analyze. Developmentally, it seems, the child should move toward both physical and psychological independence, but in reality progress is limited. The child becomes a social creature, and psychological dependence on the mother is only transferred to peers and, in adulthood, ordinarily to one member of the opposite sex. Therefore psychological independence, to any great extent, does not seem to be a reasonable goal of the socialization process.

The social learning of the child is not a smooth and ordered process. A number of discontinuities occur: Things formerly learned must at a later time be discarded; biological and social needs are blocked; and, at times, emotions resulting from frustrations interfere with effective problem solving. Certain kinds of behavior become, at some point in time, no longer useful and must be discontinued; thus, the child is required to exert additional effort to learn new kinds of behavior. If the child is reluctant to relinquish behavioral patterns established earlier in his development, he is likely to encounter ridicule, disapproval, and even punishment. This necessity for changing his behavior continues through the developmental years.

Social conflict is common in human affairs at all age levels. It is sur-

prising that a problem so common to man has not led to a better understanding of its origins or to better ways of dealing with it. Some social
conflict evolves out of early experiences of the child in the family, and study
of the socialization process to see whether or not social conflict could be
ameliorated seems desirable. By providing experiences in which a child
might learn to solve basic problems in human interaction, better solutions
could perhaps be achieved.

Apparently, socialization involves some frustration, denial or postponing
of need fulfillment, and restrictions of fulfillment to only certain ways. A
child wishes to eat with his fingers, but his mother insists that he use a
spoon; he enjoys throwing food on the floor, but he must keep it on his plate;
he prefers one particular type of food to the exclusion of another, but he
finds he is forced to eat the other; he must learn to control his body
processes, even though he does not wish to do so. As his mobility increases
and he explores his living space, the child finds restrictions associated with
objects that he wishes to explore. In all such situations, the child encounters
much disapproval and even punishment if he does not conform to the desired behavior pattern. So, from the earliest days of infancy, the channeling
of behavior and the denial of the child's freedom to fulfill needs as he wills
are part of the socialization process. Does the child learn in these early
experiences that need fulfillment grows out of struggle with others and
that some feelings of hostility toward those who interfere always occur?
It seems that most children learn many ways of dealing with those who
interfere with their pursuit of desired goals. For example, a child may find
that if he screams or even strikes his mother, she will relent and grant his
demands; finding such behavior successful with his mother, he uses it
with siblings or peers. In such episodes in the child's training, socially conditioned responses may be established which will persist into adulthood.

Reaction to Frustration in Socialization

In socialization, a certain amount of frustration will occur, in that some
needs must be fulfilled in prescribed ways and other needs must be denied
or fulfillment postponed. Therefore, an emotional reaction involving anger,
anxiety, and hostility often occurs. A young child is seldom allowed to
strike his mother or to use her as an outlet for aggressive feelings. He does
learn, however, that he can partially discharge the emotional tension
through verbalization; although his mother may not allow him to strike
her, she may allow him to express his feelings in verbal protest. However,
if his mother is not nearby, the child will often strike a sibling, destroy
toys, or even attack another child as other means of reacting to frustration.

Not only can feelings of hostility be discharged unrealistically against people, but they can also be discharged unrealistically against objects. To some extent, hostility is cumulative and builds up to a point where some children appear to be generally hostile, and in almost every human interaction they will search for ways of discharging their unpleasant emotions through hostile expressions and activity.

In the usual course of development, a child begins to search for channels to reduce feelings of hostility in acceptable and tolerated ways. The methods that he learns and devises become increasingly complex and, as he grows older, he finds opportunities for reducing his hostile feelings through words, poems or slogans, nonconforming dress, humor, ridicule, membership in certain groups, and so on. In adolescence, some groups are formed with the express purpose of opposition to other groups, thereby providing outlets for individual hostility.

Since hostility often is a by-product of the socialization process, efforts to deal with the problem by those concerned with human development have been directed in two ways: First, it is suggested that some hostility be prevented so that the total does not overwhelm the individual and, second, that the hostile feelings that cannot be avoided be discharged in acceptable and socially approved types of activities or expressions.

Child training, however, has been carried out through the centuries with little consideration being given to the ultimate effect of various methods upon the development of hostility. Thought has been given to the ultimate goals, but methods whereby the goals are achieved have received little attention. For example, the mores of many societies require that a child be taught to refrain from taking objects belonging to others. However, methods of teaching the child to learn such a concept include deprivation of objects valuable to the child, ostracism, ridicule, threats of removal from the family, actual removal from the family, incarceration, and physical punishment in various forms. Although these measures are undertaken with the express purpose of teaching the child that he should not take things belonging to others, little thought is given to the hostility and resentment that such methods can engender.

The urgent social problems of our time need to be considered in reference to the socialization process. War is still used in human interaction as much as or more than it was a thousand years ago; man has the paradox of struggling to value human life and psychological freedom from anxiety and fear, while at the same time devoting much of his resources to destruction of human life and the bringing about of anxiety and fear. It would be unreasonable to say that man's adult social behavior is unrelated to his socialization processes. Consequently, the study of socialization of the child is a significant effort of man, even though it seems that he has benefited little from its study thus far.

A POINT OF VIEW

Socialization, or the training of the child in the ways of the family and culture, is not at present related to an explicit body of knowledge nor to guidelines for parents or teachers. A body of basic principles is thus unavailable despite both demands and needs for it. Still, there should be some attempt at formulations based on information currently available. A beginning could be made with a series of statements such as the following:

1. Exemplary models (female and male) should be available to all children.

2. Exploration of environment according to interests should be possible even though some areas deemed important might be neglected by the child.

3. The learning process should be individualized with opportunity for the child to explore "stimulus-input" according to desires.

4. Direct reward and punishment should be minimized; motivation should be based on internal factors as much as possible.

5. Tolerance for divergent thinking should be encouraged in both family and school and at the same time some convergent behavior should be expected.

6. A value system should be apparent with adult models realistically and emotionally committed to it.

7. The child should experience in social interaction affective exchange that will provide modeling behavior for the establishment in adolescence and adulthood of significant and lasting relationships outside the family.

REFERENCES

Ainsworth, L. H., and M. D. Ainsworth, 1962a. "Acculturation in East Africa. I. Political Awareness and Attitudes Toward Authority," *Journal of Social Psychology,* **57**, 391–399.

Ainsworth, M. D., and L. H. Ainsworth, 1962b. "Acculturation in East Africa. II. Frustration and Aggression," *Journal of Social Psychology,* **57**, 401–407.

Ainsworth, L. H., and M. D. Ainsworth, 1962c. "Acculturation in East Africa. III. Attitudes toward Parents, Teachers, and Education," *Journal of Social Psychology,* **57**, 409–415.

Ainsworth, M. D., and L. H. Ainsworth, 1962d. "Acculturation in East Africa. IV. Summary and Discussion," *Journal of Social Psychology,* **57**, 417–432.

Alexander, T., and R. Anderson, 1957. "Children in a Society Under Stress," *Behavioral Science, 2*, 46–55.

Asch, S. E., 1952. *Social Psychology*. Englewood Cliffs, N.J.: Prentice-Hall.

Baldwin, A. L., 1967. *Theories of Child Development*. New York: Wiley.

Bandura, A., and A. C. Huston, 1961. "Identification as a Process of Incidental Learning," *Journal of Abnormal and Social Psychology, 63*, 311–318.

Bruner, J. S., 1965. "The Growth of the Mind," *American Psychologist, 20*, 1007–1017.

Child, I. L., 1954. "Socialization," in *Handbook of Social Psychology*, edited by G. Lindzey, pp. 655–692. Reading, Mass.: Addison-Wesley.

Davis, W. A., and R. J. Havighurst, 1947. *Father of the Man*. Boston: Houghton Mifflin.

Dubin, R., and E. R. Dubin, 1965. "Children's Social Perceptions: A Review of Research," *Child Development, 36*, 809–838.

Emmerich, W., 1959a. "Young Children's Discriminations of Parent and Child Roles," *Child Development, 30*, 403–419.

Emmerich, W., 1959b. "Parental Identification in Young Children," *Genetic Psychology Monographs, 60*, 257–308.

Hartup, W. W., 1964. "Patterns of Imitative Behavior in Young Children," *Child Development, 35*, 183–191.

Henry, W. E., 1947. "The Thematic Apperception Technique in the Study of Culture-Personality Relations," *Genetic Psychology Monographs, 35*, 3–135.

Hollingshead, A. B., 1949. *Elmtown's Youth*. New York: Wiley.

Maier, H. W., 1965. *Three Theories of Child Development*. New York: Harper & Row.

Mead, M., 1939. *From the South Seas*. New York: Morrow.

Prothro, E. T., 1961. *Child Rearing in the Lebanon*. Harvard Middle Eastern Monographs. Cambridge, Mass.: Harvard.

Prothro, E. T., 1966. "Socialization and Social Class in a Transitional Society," *Child Development, 37*, 219–228.

Rabin, A. I., 1959. "Comparison of American and Israeli Children by Means of a Sentence Completion Technique," *Journal of Social Psychology, 49*, 3–12.

Rabin, A. I., and J. A. Limuaco, 1959. "Sexual Differentiation of American and Filipino Children as Reflected in the Draw-A-Person Test," *Journal of Social Psychology, 50*, 207–211.

Rheingold, H. L., 1956. *The Modification of Social Responsiveness in Institutional Babies*. Monographs of the Society for Research in Child Development, 21, No. 2. Lafayette, Ind.: Child Development Publications, Purdue University.

Sears, R. R., E. E. Maccoby, and H. Levin, 1957. *Patterns of Child-Rearing*. New York: Harper & Row.

Sherif, M., 1935. "A Study of Some Social Factors in Perception," *Archives of Psychology, 187*, 5–60.

Sherif, M., 1961. "Conformity-Deviation, Norms and Group Relations," in *Conformity and Deviation*, edited by I. A. Berg and B. M. Bass, pp. 159–198. New York: Harper & Row.

Thomas, R. M., and W. Surachmad, 1962. "Social-Class Differences in Mothers' Expectations for Children in Indonesia," *Journal of Social Psychology,* **57,** 303–307.

Ucko, L. E., and T. Moore, 1963. "Parental Roles as Seen by Young Children in Doll Play," *Vita Humana,* **6,** 213–242.

Whiting, J. W. M., 1951. *Becoming a Kwoma.* New Haven, Conn.: Yale.

[*ten*]

Adolescence

Adolescence begins with puberty and sexual maturation. Usually, for girls adolescence begins at about thirteen years and for boys at about fourteen years; but sexual maturation is gradual, and the time varies from individual to individual. Since boys reach puberty at a later age than girls and therefore enter the adolescent period later, the duration of adolescence for them is less than that for girls.

The adolescent period is often a time of difficulty in which a number of problems develop not only because of factors arising during the period of adolescence, but also because of factors incipient during the earlier part of the individual's life (Adams, 1968; Chansky, 1967; Freud, 1962; Gordon, 1962; Quay and Quay, 1965; Wattenberg, 1955). The period of adolescence is also one in which the adolescent must change his behavior within a short period of time from that characteristic of childhood to that which has more similarity to adult behavior.

The most important concept in reference to adolescence is that this is a period during which the individual is confronted not only with body change, but also with change in the cultural demands on his behavior. Because of the significant changes now taking place in the social order, such demands become sources of further difficulty. Consequently, as an adolescent searches for realities about himself and about his environment, he must do so from a changing point of reference. In a study of adolescent development and behavior, therefore, it must be understood that the adolescent period is one of two during which most marked changes occur and that adolescents need help in dealing with altered conditions within themselves and in their environment, so that continuity in identity of self and in cultural values can be achieved.

PHYSICAL DEVELOPMENT
Growth in Height and Weight

In adolescence it is obvious that height and weight increase markedly. In boys, the acceleration in growth, often called the "growth spurt," takes place between the twelfth and fourteenth years; in girls, this acceleration occurs between the tenth and twelfth years. Growth in height usually precedes increase in weight. While the growth of boys slows down between the seventeenth and nineteenth years, it may continue for some time until after the twentieth birthday.

At thirteen years of age, an average girl is about 5 feet 2 inches in height and weighs about 100 pounds. At seventeen, she is about 5 feet 4 inches tall and weighs about 117 pounds. For girls, the largest gain in weight is usually close to the onset of menarche. Usually growth ceases in girls between the sixteenth and nineteenth years (Bayley, 1943; Meredith, 1957; Shuttleworth, 1951).

At fourteen, the average boy is about 5 feet 4 inches tall and weighs about 105 pounds; by the time he is seventeen, he is about 5 feet 8 inches tall and weighs nearly 137 pounds (University of Iowa Growth Charts, 1949). The increase in weight, of course, is due not only to fat, but also to increase in bone and muscle tissue.

Growth norms in curves are useful since an individual's measurement can be compared with a pattern of growth for a group of individuals his own age. Normal growth means that the child maintains his relative position with regard to his age group. His individual growth curve plotted with the norm will reveal any deviations from the norm. Once the individual's height and weight are plotted on a chart, any significant deviation from the curve can be noted and causes sought.

Body Proportions

In addition to changes in height and weight, body proportions also change, although not all parts of the body increase in size at the same rate. Some parts change very slowly; for example, from ages fourteen to twenty head circumference increases by less than an inch. Developmentally, the face grows first in length and then in width, with the upper part of the face changing before the lower: The forehead becomes higher and wider; the nose becomes longer and wider; and finally the growth of mouth and jaw is completed. As a result of such facial changes, a boy's face becomes more angular, while a girl's becomes more oval (Tanner, 1962; Watson and Lowrey, 1962).

The trunk changes in adolescence consist of broadening of the hips and shoulders and the development of the waistline. Usually the shoulders of boys are broader than the hips, while girls' hips are usually wider than their shoulders. The legs grow proportionately at a more rapid rate than the trunk. The arms too begin to grow before the trunk, with the growth of both legs and arms apparently being related to the age of maturing.

Psychological concomitants of growth are of consequence and a number of investigators have sought to discover relationships. For example, one investigator in a longitudinal study reports that boys who mature early generally meet society's expectations and are relatively free from neurotic symptoms. Boys reaching puberty at a later time were seen as more "tense" and as engaging in "attention-getting behavior" in the high school years (Jones, 1965).

Growth in adolescence is sometimes inhibited by a number of factors, but determination of causes is difficult and individual variations must be taken into account (Vaughan, 1964). Most adolescents, in spite of variation, reach a satisfactory adult state, and it is important psychologically that adolescents do not place undue concern upon their rate of growth.

Strength and Activity

Sometimes adolescents seem to be lethargic and prone to avoid physical activity, but if an activity involves doing things that they enjoy, they usually display boundless energy and strength. Since many physiological changes and individual variations in body processes are taking place during growth, generalizations about an individual's capacity for activity should be made with caution. It is probable that activity is related to physiological states part of the time and part of the time to psychological or psychosocial factors. In general, adolescence is an active time in which individuals go from one activity to another from early morning to late at night.

Health and Nutrition

Investigators in the field of nutrition have long maintained that the quality and quantity of food are important factors in the health of children and adolescents and that diet affects not only growth, but also energy availability and resistance to disease. Because of the significant physical changes in adolescence, nutrition would indeed seem to be very important at this age period. For example, in all adolescents there is an increased requirement for calcium and potassium by the heart, digestive system, and nervous system; and for girls after menarche, there is increased need for nitrogen and calcium.

Nutritional requirements in adolescence vary widely, particularly in the amount of caloric intake brought about by metabolic changes during growth. Although inadequate caloric intake will allow growth in height to take place, it will occur at some cost to protein generally available for building body tissues (Watson and Lowrey, 1962).

The basal rate of metabolism decreases over the growth span, except for an increase at puberty. This reversal at puberty results from an increase in thyroid gland activity, which brings about the need for caloric increase (Johnston, 1964). The adequacy of caloric amounts is difficult to determine because of variations in activity and physiological changes in growth, but judgments are probably best based on appetite and growth rate. For an adolescent, 15 per cent of the total caloric intake should come from proteins, which are necessary for maintenance and growth.

The largest supply of calories comes from carbohydrates, although these make up less than 1 per cent of the total body weight. Carbohydrates, which are obtained from foods consisting mainly of sugars and starches, supply energy for body heat and muscular activity. Carbohydrates not burned by the body are stored as fat. Carbohydrates can protect against protein deficiency; if the fat in the diet is too low for use as a source of energy or body heat, the body uses carbohydrates instead of using the protein needed for tissue building. The percentage of the diet devoted to carbohydrates remains relatively consistent throughout development, with needs being between 40 and 60 per cent of the total calorie intake.

The adolescent's need for fat varies greatly. Sources of fats in the diet are butter, oil, lard, and meats. The sources of fat include, in addition to the direct intake of fatty food, the body's conversion of carbohydrates and protein into fat. The value of fat in the diet lies in its utilization for energy, building of tissues, and as an aid in the use of vitamins, particularly A, D, E, and K. Thus, fats, in addition to protein and carbohydrates, are important in good nutrition, and particular attention should be given to the adolescent's percentage of fat intake. Often the adolescent cannot be relied upon to adjust to changing body requirements.

Minerals are essential for human nutrition, but no requirement is peculiar to adolescence. Minerals that must be ingested for good health because the body cannot produce these substances are contained in most foods as inorganic salts. As far as is known, children require 12 particular minerals important in human nutrition at any age level. These minerals are sodium, potassium, calcium, magnesium, phosphorus, chlorine, iodine, iron, zinc, manganese, cobalt, and sulfur (Breckenridge and Vincent, 1960). Of these 12 necessary minerals, three are particularly important—calcium, sodium, and phosphorus. These minerals are needed in large quantities for skeletal growth; they also influence the elasticity and the irritability of muscles and nerves (Wohl and Goodhart, 1955). Calcium has a special part in the function of mineral metabolism of the body by being essential in the coagulation of the blood (Miller and Goode, 1960).

Vitamins too, as is well known, are essential for adequate nutrition. Most nutrition specialists believe that a diet in the fundamental food types will be adequate in vitamin content, and therefore supplementing the diet with vitamin preparations (except in infancy and under conditions of illness) is unnecessary.

Absolute nutritional requirements are difficult to determine in children and particularly in adolescents not only because of growth variations, but also because of lack of knowledge about the subject generally. No absolute method of determining a child's nutritional status exists, and even normal growth rates do not prove to be an adequate basis for judgment. In inadequate nutrition, maturational processes, such as menarche, may be delayed; but when the child returns to an adequate diet, growth and development take place again. Although proper nutritional levels cannot be fully determined, the effects of deficiencies can be observed. One of the effects of such deficiencies is an increased susceptibility to disease. For example, if protein is lacking, production of antibodies may be inhibited. In adolescence, it seems to be particularly important to guard against deficiencies of protein and calcium. A lack of these substances in the diet will cause the adolescent to be especially vulnerable to infectious disease.

Emotional and cultural teachings affect food intake. As everyone has recognized, peers influence adolescent food choices, and among adolescents food fads are common. The food preferences of different groups of adolescents are remarkably similar and are linked to certain social activities and places. Hamburgers, malts, and French fries are high on the list of most adolescent food preferences. During adolescence, appetite increases and some active boys seem to be insatiable. Between-meal snacks seem necessary, but they may interfere with proper food balance at mealtime.

Psychological relationships of diet and body proportion to emotions and self-perception are relative to family and environment, as the following story about the Evans family illustrates.

Amy Evans was born and reared on a large farm. She grew up in the midst of abundance of good food, which her mother took pride in preparing. Family meals were pleasant occasions during which the enjoyment of food was emphasized. Needless to say, all the family members were overweight. However, the weight was distributed over large frames, which made the overweight less obvious.

During her adolescent years, Amy was taken to a hospital for a physical examination and a condition was discovered that caused the physician to recommend that she reduce her weight. On subsequent visits, the physician became alarmed that her weight had increased rather than decreased. When Amy and her parents were confronted with the evidence of her lack of progress, Amy burst into tears and exclaimed that she did not think that she was overweight. Her father, placing his hands on his own ample abdomen, protested, "We are all big people and Amy doesn't seem overweight to us." The physician wisely decided that the overweight would provide less hazard to Amy than would the psychological conflict resulting from the effort to reduce.

BEHAVIORAL CHARACTERISTICS

Adolescence is a period when increased emotionality is observed, and expressions of emotions often seem to be extreme. Outwardly at least, adults usually demonstrate emotional stability and show a tendency toward controlled elation over the immediate and present circumstances, if favorable, and less of a tendency toward extreme depression if circumstances are unfavorable. From experience, adults have found that feelings about success and failure come and go as a part of life. On the other hand, adolescents are just beginning to be exposed to social forces outside their families, and their limited experience leads them to have much more concern for the immediate.

Emotional Behavior

Emotional security may be defined as a feeling achieved through learned perceptions of the environment and of oneself that enables an individual to believe that he is capable of fulfilling essential needs. If some needs are momentarily unfulfilled, a relatively secure person will not become depressed or so frightened that he is unable to take effective action. Perhaps the reason adolescents so often seem insecure is that they have not had sufficient opportunities to rely on their own resources and to perceive themselves as persons capable of fulfilling needs or avoiding deprivation; perhaps, similarly, in periods of elation, they abandon themselves to the feeling of the moment without attending sufficiently to future possibilities.

A further factor in the emotional variation of adolescence involves experience in control. In a complex social order, uncontrolled emotional behavior is impossible, but emphasis on emotional control generally varies with the culture. Some primitive societies emphasize emotional control as an important virtue, while others are more tolerant of uncontrolled emotional behavior. In American society, an adolescent's anger and resentment at unfair punishment or scolding by a teacher or parent cannot be expressed directly to the parent or the teacher without consequent disapproval and possible punishment. Hence, it is often difficult for the inexperienced adolescent to deal with feelings of anger.

Emotional instability is sometimes increased because of unreal perceptions of certain persons as being able or willing to establish emotional relationships. In fantasy, a person—perhaps a teacher, or a youth group leader—is endowed with desirable characteristics and an imagined emotional relationship is assumed to be a possibility; but when the real characteristics and real possibilities of relationship are perceived, disappointment and depression sometimes occur.

Adolescent Interests

Adolescent interests have been studied by some investigators. One method of research involves a generation comparison. For example, Harris (1959) compared the interests of adolescents in 1935 and in 1957. He found that interest in money ranked high for both boys and girls in 1935, as well as in 1957, although boys were more interested in money than girls in both periods. Health, rated high as a problem in 1935, was not seen as such in 1957, although boys had more interest in it than girls. Study habits were ranked low in interest and were more of a problem in 1957 than in 1935. Home and family relations were ranked higher in importance by girls than boys in 1957, with manners and courtesy being more of a problem in 1957 than in 1935. Attractiveness ranked as both a problem and an interest for boys and girls in both periods.

Kuhlen and Houlihan (1965) used a sociometric questionnaire to compare the choices of a group of adolescents with the choices of adolescents made 21 years earlier. These investigators found evidence to support the view that adolescents now have a greater heterosexual interest than they did a generation ago. They reasoned that because of more interaction between the sexes, the subjects made more choices from the opposite sex than were made years before in the earlier study.

In a study of the interests of 674 eleven- to sixteen-year-old adolescents, Amatora (1962) found that television, cooking, and family members respectively were the first choices as sources of interest for girls; television, members of the family, sports, and hobbies respectively were important as the first choices for boys.

Most adolescents usually desire money and will try to find part-time jobs where they can earn it. Part-time work experience is often valuable to adolescents both from the standpoint of vocational experience and because such experience makes the transition to adulthood easier (Harris, 1961). Often adolescents will take part-time or temporary work, hoping as the result of experience or more education to eventually obtain positions suitable to their interests and abilities. Adolescents sometimes are envious of others who have jobs or even of adults who can earn money, since they have a difficult time securing employment and have little opportunity to assume the responsibilities and the perspectives of wage earners. However, an interest in a vocation seems to be of most concern between the ages of fifteen and sixteen years (Norton, 1953). Those adolescents who go on past high school to college usually modify earlier vocational choices, and although a number of factors are important in determining a vocation or choice, the family is of primary importance. Students whose parents are college trained prefer vocations with prestige and those which require a college education (Moser, 1952).

In high school, interest in the school's program lessens and often adolescents find little satisfaction in the high school's curriculum. They are interested, however, in participation in the social relationships and the activities provided by the school. Those individuals who are rewarded by approval and recognition of superior academic ability find satisfaction, and this smaller number shows more interest in their studies than those who are less successful. However, as adolescents in general move closer to adulthood, many tend to lose interest in education.

In a study of boys outstanding in their accomplishments in athletics, science, fine arts, leadership, and academic achievement, the one trait common to all was that of higher intelligence. Other traits examined were skeletal age, physique, strength, speed and agility, interests, and the like (Clarke and Olson, 1965).

THE PLACE OF THE ADOLESCENT IN THE CULTURE

Adolescents have an ambiguous place in the social structure, in part because clearly described behavioral codes are lacking. Too frequently, adolescents are told what should *not* be done rather than being given guides to follow in complex and often conflicting interactional patterns of social behavior. Since the attitude of society toward adolescents is frequently one of deprecation and hostility, adolescents themselves feel that, as a group, they are too often criticized and devaluated by adults.

Perceived Characteristics of Adolescents

Although adolescent behavior is characterized as stereotypic, irresponsible, and antisocial, one study indicates that adolescents (as well as their parents) view themselves generally in a "mildly favorable manner," although they feel they have an unfavorable reputation. The results of this study also revealed that parents see adolescents as having a tendency to undervalue adults (Hess and Goldblatt, 1960). According to this investigation, adolescents tend to mistrust and misunderstand adults, while adults tend to mistrust and misunderstand adolescents.

According to Medinnus (1965), the self-perception of older adolescents (eighteen-year-olds) is related to parents' attitudes toward them and affection for them. He found that those adolescents who had favorable perceptions of themselves perceived their parents as being affectionate and concerned for their welfare. Evidence was also found in this study to support the view that the mother's child-rearing practices were more important than the father's and that the self-perceptions of boys were more closely correlated with the child-rearing attitudes of the mother than was the self-perception of girls.

The Adolescent and Peers

As is well recognized, age-mates of adolescents have a significant influence on behavior, and the extensive reliance of adolescents on peers is regarded by some to be symptomatic of the struggle for independence from parents. Investigators believe that an adolescent's association with others who are also in the struggle for independence and who have similar problems provides much emotional support. Some evidence exists, however, that adolescents' interests in participation in peer groups rather than in activities with their families is not because of rebellion against parents but because the cultural attractions of the peer groups are more appealing (Burke and Grinder, 1966).

Adolescents gain satisfaction in several ways from the peer-group associations: They learn to define a role for heterosexual behavior, to establish an emotional relationship with another person that can be a model for marriage, to form a value system, and to begin some type of vocational orientation (Hurlock, 1968). On the other hand, adolescents can have difficulties in peer groups. Sometimes problems result from behavior that they think will increase their popularity or acceptance but which they subsequently find is unacceptable. Also, not all of their efforts to seek peer approval are wise. Sometimes, for example, believing that daring behavior will bring acceptance, adolescents engage in dangerous behavior or in activities that bring them into conflict with the law; and, in some instances, they seek sexual relationships in the hope that they can thereby achieve admiration or acceptance.

The significance of the influence of the peer group is questioned by Douvan and Adelson (1966), who believe that the importance of peers is much exaggerated. These investigators see important differences existing between boys and girls in relationships to peer groups. Boys perceive their peer groups as a source of emotional support, while girls see their peer groups as an opportunity to find close friendships. Douvan and Adelson believe the effects of the family on adolescent behavior continue to be strong and consistent regardless of type of family structure and discipline. These generalizations, they believe, apply similarly to all social classes.

In adolescence, girls are increasingly concerned with their attractiveness to boys, but because they mature earlier they usually become interested in boys before boys show interest in them. As a result, girls in association with physically younger boys usually feel some doubts about themselves. It may be that some of the antagonistic interaction between the sexes in the intermediate grades comes from girls' unreciprocated interest in boys. Harris and Tseng (1957) in a study of children from the third to the twelfth grade, using the sentence-completion technique, found that although both boys and girls were predominantly favorable in their feelings toward their peers, at every age they were more positively oriented to peers of their own sex than to their peers of the opposite sex. Kagan and Freeman (1963) found that girls who reject "traditional feminine sex role behaviors" tend to have higher scores on intelligence tests than girls who behave in "traditional" sex-typed ways. These investigators suggest that intellectual achievement is associated with a rejection of heterosexual relationships.

ADOLESCENCE AND A MORAL CODE

Morality, consisting as it does of customs and patterns of behavior approved by a group or social order, serves as a regulation of conduct of the adolescent by himself, not only out of consideration for his own welfare but also in order to enhance the welfare of others. Morality involves a recognition of the consequences of behavior and the way it affects others. Over the years, moral concepts have grown out of social concern for the welfare of the group—behavior that interferes with the need fulfillment of others is considered to be "wrong" by the group and that which enhances the opportunities for need fulfillment for others is "right."

Although scientific investigation of moral concepts is quite difficult, most scientists would agree that moral behavior is an important element in human behavior. In young children, moral behavior is of particular concern to middle-class parents, and the child is taught about "right" or "wrong" in accord with the concepts of the social order. If a young child takes a toy belonging to another to fulfill his own needs without regard for the rights of others, he is admonished by his parents and told that he must leave the toy alone. By the time he reaches adolescence, however, he is expected to have learned that even though property is unattended and even though he can take it with none to know, still he must not take it because taking it is considered "wrong." Such behavior controlled and regulated by the individual himself in accord with the customs and sanctions of the social order is considered to be "moral."

Morality and a Moral Code

The developing individual must learn not only society's moral code, but must also learn to reason and to decide the part of the code that is applicable in particular situations. The individual's moral response is further complicated by necessity to obey the code even though it may conflict with fulfillment of his own needs or desires. Additional complication results from a necessity for an individual to believe in the value of a moral code so that his conformity is not based upon fear of punishment, but instead upon his own reasoned value of the code.

Kohlberg (1963) questions the belief that the child merely "internalizes" the moral standards. In his research, he studied 72 boys, ages ten, thirteen, and sixteen, using "lengthy free interviews" so that they could describe their responses to hypothetical moral dilemmas. The results of his studies have led him to believe that morality grows out of the interaction of the child with his environment rather than from an external code imposed upon him.

Kohlberg devised three levels of morality: (1) a premoral level, (2) morality of conventional role conformity, and, (3) morality of self-accepted moral principles. Within each of these three levels, he saw two types of moral behavior. An individual moves from Type I, a punishment and obedience orientation, to Type VI, a morality of individual principles of conscience. More advanced individual types of morality occur as age increases. Kohlberg believes that conceiving of morality as a simple process of internalization of the external cultural customs is too simple and sees rather a "series of internally patterned or organized transformations of social concepts and attitudes" and that these transformations constitute the "developmental process."

Motivation toward Morality

Although concern is currently expressed about adolescents' lack of morality and adherence to cultural values, it is evident that many adolescents are "idealistic." Some of the present-day problems of moral behavior in adolescence come from the developmental changes in perception and insight, in the attainment of independence, and in new relationships with parents, peers, and institutions of society and do not stem just from a lack of idealism or morality.

Moral behavior is derived from specific and immediate situations, and adolescents often need assistance in generalizing from experience to create a personal moral philosophy. Havighurst and Taba (1949) expressed the belief some years ago that adolescents welcome opportunity to abide by moral values and that antisocial behavior comes from sources other than a desire to disobey moral sanctions. It is reasonable to assume that moral behavior is related to parental teaching and methods used to coerce children into specific patterns of moral conduct. Hoffman and Saltzstein (1967) in a study of children in early adolescence sought to relate discipline techinques to moral behavior. They placed discipline techniques into three categories: (1) power—the assertion of authority, (2) nonphysical expressions of anger, and (3) teaching about the consequences of the child's action on others. The results of the study indicated that moral development of children in the middle class was closely linked with teaching about the consequences of action.

During adolescence, a serious questioning of the moral code begins, perhaps as a result of discovering people who verbally ascribe to a code yet who, in reality, do not adhere to it. An adolescent then may rationalize:

If others do not find the code of significance and value, why should I? This period is, therefore, a time for an examination of moral values that heretofore were unquestioned. It is also a period for the discovery of faults and inconsistencies in the system itself. For example, at one time an individual follows the prevailing moral code, which disapproves of a certain type of behavior; he subsequently discovers that at a later age the behavior is approved by the same moral code. Not only does inconsistency exist within the code itself in relation to specific demands for each individual, but inconsistency for group behavior also exists. Inconsistency undoubtedly arises from increased mobility, increased material possessions, changes in transportation, and other factors inherent in a rapidly changing society.

Adolescents growing up in a modern culture and exposed to many media of communication seldom can avoid seeing discrepancies and inconsistencies in adult moral behavior. Inconsistency and a changing moral code obviously lead to a logical questioning of the code, and the adolescent is tempted to rationalize that if the moral code is shortly to be changed, then one can hasten the change for the sake of convenience. Consequently, individual judgment, interpretation, and reasoning are important and necessary for moral behavior.

THE ADOLESCENT AND THE FAMILY

Adolescence is a time when family relationships are changed significantly. Dependence upon parents for affection or support lessens, and adolescents increasingly seek emotional alliances outside the family. The emotional satisfactions of both parents and children are thus disrupted.

Not all of the problems of the adolescent in the family are of an intrapersonal nature, since many come from the parents' feelings about independence and the way expectations of family, school, and society are imposed. Some difficulties seem to be unavoidable, and many social expectations for adolescent behavior do seem to be too complex. Undoubtedly, part of the reason that Mead found the transition from childhood to adulthood in Samoa easier than in this country lies in the many differences in behavioral requirements. A complex society requires acquisition of many more skills, the mastery of much more information, and the facing of many more frustrations than does a simple society.

Parental Expectations

Parental expectations, although sometimes an extension of personal ambitions, account for some of the problems of adolescents. Indeed, most parents' expectations come from their experience in a competitive society, which makes them keenly aware of the necessity to strive for achievement. Those parents who have attained vocational and social prominence wish their children similarly to achieve.

One of the factors causing an adolescent to turn away from parental expectations for achievement is that most young people growing up in our society must live within a competitive system in which only a few are at the top in an occupation or profession. An adolescent is expected to learn to live in a competitive system and continue to strive for a goal that he has slight hope of attaining. Furthermore, if an adolescent does reach parental goals and achieves the highest grades in his school, his achievement often brings little satisfaction to him. While his parents may derive considerable satisfaction, the satisfaction accruing to him is mixed with regrets since he finds that academic achievement is not as valued by his associates as it is by his parents. Discovering this situation, the adolescent may then show a lack of interest in finding a place in society, in meeting the requirements of the school, or in preparing for a vocation.

Adolescent Behavior and Adult Disapproval

Adolescents incur adult disapproval in a number of ways. In order to assert their independence and express themselves, they sometimes adopt extreme hair styles, exaggerated makeup, and unusual clothing styles.

Adolescents also frequently encounter disapproval of their treatment of property. The very young child is restricted in his access to valued family property, but the adolescent is allowed access to it. The family's money, its valued possessions, household appliances, car, treasured books—all are open to the adolescent's use. Despite earlier teaching about the care of property, the adolescent is often careless. Part of this behavior results from the fact that he is inexperienced and unaware of the consequences of inadequate care and part of the difficulty comes from the fact that he gives attention to other matters or to his own feelings. Thus, the adolescent's behavior is often described as "unthinking." He is at a loss himself to understand why his carelessness resulted in damage.

Adolescents sometimes neglect assigned tasks and chores and therefore adults are upset at the failure to carry out tasks. An adolescent is not necessarily unwilling to expend energy, since some peer-organized work groups provide evidence of much effort; but many assigned tasks hold little appeal, and adults eventually realize that adolescents find limited satisfaction in assignments.

Another area of behavior in which the adolescent incurs adult disapproval is in his sex behavior. The adolescent usually has had insufficient teaching about sex, although in recent years this lack is being remedied. Apparent lack of concern about moral limits shown by some adults or by society at large is applied by adolescents to sex behavior, and some adolescents proclaim there is no reason to conform to social expectations. To complicate the problem further, the whole area of sexual behavior is one in which social requirements and expectations are changing. Adults are confused, since the values they have been taught are at present being overthrown and a definite or practical listing of social rules about sexual behavior is not available.

Family Conflict

Some conflict comes in the family because of the parents' concern about the grave consequences that can accompany adolescent misbehavior. The adolescent may not understand the changed consequences of his behavior— if a sixteen-year-old steals from a store or deliberately destroys property, his behavior is viewed as much more serious by society than when he was a nine-year-old. In addition, heterosexual behavior is much more controlled in adolescence; while smaller children can engage in sex play with little opprobrium, similar behavior is disapproved in adolescence.

Apparently, sex differences are found in relation to the problems of adolescents. For example, Lansky et al. (1961) investigated sex differences in aggression in a longitudinal study of 54 adolescents between thirteen and eighteen years of age. The investigators found that generally accepted concepts of sex differences about aggression were supported by their data, which indicated that boys were more aggressive than girls and more preoccupied with efforts to achieve independence.

Three main types of conflict occur between adolescents and their parents according to Hurlock (1955, 1968): One type of conflict stems from the use of discipline that the adolescent feels is not deserved; a second type of conflict comes from the adolescent's response to the parents, his siblings and his home; and the third type of conflict comes from the adolescent's belief that his parents, because of their own differences and disparity in age, do not understand his problems. According to Hurlock, parents become more conservative as they grow older and find it difficult to deal with the radical views of adolescents. In a questionnaire study of 1,278 middle-class high school boys with an age range of thirteen to eighteen, Meissner (1965) reports that in all age groups the boys showed a consistent tendency to feel more often misunderstood by the father than the mother.

Becoming discouraged, some parents discontinue their effort to understand their child, but this rejection can have only deleterious effects. Adolescents experiencing rejection by parents become resentful of any disapproval by members of the community because the disapproval extends their feelings of rejection experienced in the family (Bandura and Walters, 1959). Similarly, Peck (1958), in reporting findings from the extensive study of Prairie City, a Midwestern town, explains that much adolescent behavior reflects reactions to parental emotions and behavior.

Some conflict with parents seems to be unavoidable in that the adolescent must experiment with rebellion. Some rebellion may even be necessary to prepare the adolescent to deal with his peers. If a child is conditioned too much to conform to demands of others, he may be unable to say "no" to peers when asked to engage in obviously unwise behavior. Adolescents thus need some experience in rebelling and in behaving counter to the wishes of those around them. To this end, the opportunity to rebel safely within the family provides an important experience in learning. However, sometimes conflict with parents becomes so severe and the frustrations so great that adolescents try to escape by deperate courses of action. Elaine Rogers took such action.

> Elaine lived with her mother, who was divorced from her husband. Because the mother worked and because much of Elaine's time was spent in school and with friends, an insufficient exchange took place between mother and daughter. On one very cold winter evening after a quarrel with her mother, Elaine left her home and made her way through the snow to a highway where she sought a ride. Elaine was not in good health and had become very cold from exposure. At last a man stopped and offered her a ride to the next town. On reaching the next town, her benefactor stopped at a phone booth and told Elaine he would wait for her to call her mother. He waited for her to go to the phone booth. He did not know, however, that she pretended to make the call. On emerging from the booth, she explained that her mother had promised to come to get her. After the man had driven on, Elaine wandered aimlessly down the street and came to a drug store where she bought a package of razor blades. On the street corner in the shadow of a building, she cut both wrists and then began walking on down the street.

> A boy passing in a car offered her a ride. She accepted and after a few minutes the boy discovered that she was bleeding and he hurriedly took her to a physician. By having treatment in time, Elaine narrowly escaped death. The physician contacted her mother, and Elaine had no choice but to return home.

Conflict between the parents is particularly detrimental to the child during the developmental years. If the conflict results in a breakup of the home during adolescence, the separation is devastating because it comes at a time when adolescents are not sure of themselves socially or of their capacity to attain independence. They are caught in the highly emotional struggle between the parents and divided in loyalty because, as children, both parents were a part of their emotional life, values, and beliefs. In divorce and separation, the adolescent is expected to give his loyalties unswervingly to the parent with whom he lives. It is difficult, if not impossible, for an adolescent to hold to the values of parents who are separated and who have failed to work out problems in their own lives. The usual course of action of the adolescent in such families is to seek satisfaction away from the home.

ADOLESCENTS AND SOCIAL CHANGE

Adolescents are having increasing influence generally in society and culture throughout the world. This influence may be considered a social phenomenon of modern times and is occurring in diverse cultures in both the Western and Eastern worlds. This age group has influenced fashion, art, music, and economic, political, and educational values and beliefs. In recent years, administrative officials and policies of educational institutions and even national governments have been altered by the demands of young people.

Long-standing values of the cultures of a number of societies have been rejected and groups of adolescents have refused, at least temporarily, to follow approved paths into cultural roles. *Drop-out* has become a term for the rejection of education and preparation for ordinary or generally acceptable social roles. Society often is characterized by materialism and hypocrisy. Ideals of self-actualization by freedom to pursue one's desires in any direction and "love" instead of hate and competition are avowed. Groups have formed to provide housing under communal arrangements, so that freedom of action can be found without the proximity of adult control or knowledge. Disregard of conventional modes of dress, food preparation, sex behavior, and even hygienic regulations is the rule.

Protests are common, and a general "distrust of anyone over thirty" is characteristic of many. Protests against the social standards are diverse and directed toward quite varied cultural modes such as food prices, grading policies, institutional administrative actions, dormitory hours, alcoholic beverage regulations, and military demands.

Sometimes the adolescent causes are well articulated and clear, but at other times the causes and explanations of protests are unclear. Causes can be quickly espoused and with considerable aplomb quickly changed enroute to a demonstration site. Protests also occur for protest's sake, apparently. But most of the time the protests are idealistic and point to moral issues or the failures of society.

Perhaps nowhere has the influence of adolescents been more effective than in the issues of American policy about the Viet Nam war. Changes in national policy were brought about in part by the behavior and protests of young people.

American society, however, is not the only society affected. Many European and South American governments have been shaken or changed by student throngs. And even in China and Japan, the young people have had a profound effect on the modern social order.

While in revolutions in the past, the young often have been used or led by adults or political opportunists, in the modern world the young now frequently provide both the leaders and the cause.

The reasons for this kind of change are obscure and complex: Science and technology have brought many more opportunities for social roles and social diversity, there is now a rapid change of cultural values and a questioning of religious beliefs, less concern is necessary for food and shelter, generalized anxiety exists about nuclear war and is related to uncertainties about national policies, changes have taken place in amounts of leisure time available, mobility has increased through developments in transportation, and extensive opportunities for social interaction have come through new forms of communication media. All of these and more are factors in the changed place of adolescents in the social order.

There are a number of behavioral life styles of youth in the latter part of the adolescent and early adulthood years. Because of both the forced and empathic concern on the part of society, it is important to categorize, delineate, and determine the origin of these behavioral life styles. In general, life styles can be placed under three broad categories: the alienated, the activists, and the socially oriented.

The Alienated Youth

Adolescents and young people appropriately placed in the category of the alienated unequivocally reject authority and social values. They do not wish to work toward a social role or to continue their education. They wish to remove themselves from society and "opt" out. They are called "the beat generation" or the "hippies." While rejecting society and its values, they follow no ideological or philosophical constructs. However, they are interested in self-expression and various kinds of experiences sometimes associated with oriental mysticism and sometimes with various drugs. Certain characteristics of alienated youth are described by Keniston (1965) and Block et al. (1968). While sympathizing with their mothers' unrealized ambitions, they resent domination by them. They see their fathers as men oriented to success but emotionally indifferent. Their early adolescence was a time of turmoil and it was then that they began to question the parents' values and those of society. Keniston believes that such youth are estranged from both family and society, as do Watts and Whittaker (1966).

The Activists

Generally, student activists are deemed to be in the upper range of socio-economic status in American society (Flacks and Neugarten, 1967). Block et al. (1968) believe that the rejection of many social values, laws, and customs of society does not necessarily reflect conflict with parents because parents often support their children in their rejection of social values. The activists are often rebellious, restless, and contemptuous, particularly in reference to university administrative regulations and programs. They claim for themselves idealism and social concern, demand participation in decision-making processes, especially those affecting what they consider to be their own welfare, and speak of achieving their goals by harassment and forceful demands.

These young people view their own rearing as permissive and see their parents as having used a reasoning and explanatory approach. Consequently, they demand a "meaningful dialogue" with authority and expect that their protests will be heard and given attention. They are not inhibited and seek participation in many areas of society or university life where they believe they can contribute to change in many forms.

The Socially Oriented

Most youth today are not alienated or actively rejecting society—most have adopted to varying degrees the social values of their parents and do not see themselves in conflict with authority to any great extent. Many are interested in idealistic enterprises such as the Peace Corps and other social organizations. If society is perceived as being in need of change, they would rather work within its framework and with authority than to reject it outright.

The youth in this category are not necessarily without criticism of the "establishment," but they usually express disapproval in a well-articulated manner. Many youth today believe in openly expressing their feelings and at times will endorse or listen attentively to the activists. On the other hand, most pursue educational programs with some commitment both to the educational institution and to the social framework leading to careers in the social order.

A POINT OF VIEW

Despite the problems of the adolescent period, adolescent influence is contributing to the dynamic aspects of social change. The energy and idealism of individuals in this age period are useful to society. On the other hand, negativism, hostility, and destructiveness can adversely affect man's present condition and hinder hope for progress only painfully and slowly achieved. A social order must have some cohesiveness and structure, with individuals in it assuming some responsibility to maintain it. Also, reason and practical knowledge must undergird it. Thus, society should somehow integrate the hopes and abilities of adolescents into its structure and function, yet at the same time provide opportunities for adolescents to evaluate and to change cultural continuities appropriately.

REFERENCES

Adams, J. F., 1968. "An Introduction to Understanding Adolescence," in *Understanding Adolescence,* edited by J. F. Adams, pp. 1–12. Boston: Allyn and Bacon.

Amatora, M., 1962. "Home Interests in Early Adolescence," *Genetic Psychology Monographs,* **65**, 137–174.

Bandura, A., and R. H. Walters, 1959. *Adolescent Aggression.* New York: Ronald.

Bayley, N., 1943. "Size and Body Build of Adolescents in Relation to Rate of Skeletal Maturing," *Child Development,* **14**, 47–90.

Block, J. H., N. Haan, and M. B. Smith, 1968. "Activism and Apathy in Contemporary Adolescents," in *Understanding Adolescence,* edited by J. F. Adams, pp. 198–231. Boston: Allyn and Bacon.

Breckenridge, M. E., and E. L. Vincent, 1960. "Nutrition and Growth," in *The Adolescent,* 2d ed., edited by J. M. Seidman, pp. 128–139. New York: Holt.

Burke, R. S., and R. E. Grinder, 1966. "Personality-oriented Themes and Listening Patterns in Teen-Age Music and Their Relation to Certain Academic and Peer Variables," *School Review,* **74**, 196–211.

Chansky, N. M., 1967. *Untapped Good.* Springfield, Ill.: Charles C Thomas.

Clarke, H. H., and A. L. Olson, 1965. "Characteristics of 15-Year-Old Boys

Who Demonstrate Various Accomplishments or Difficulties," *Child Development,* **36**, 559–567.

Douvan, E., and J. Adelson, 1966. *The Adolescent Experience.* New York: Wiley.

Flacks, R., and B. Neugarten, 1967. "The Liberated Generation: An Exploration of the Roots of Student Protest," *Journal of Social Issues,* **23**, 52–75.

Freud, A., 1962. "Adolescence," in *The Causes of Behavior: Readings in Child Development and Educational Psychology,* edited by J. P. Rosenblith and W. Allinsmith, pp. 240–246. Boston: Allyn and Bacon.

Gordon, I. J., 1962. *Human Development—From Birth Through Adolescence.* New York: Harper & Row.

Harris, D. B., 1959. "Sex Differences in the Life Problems and Interests of Adolescents, 1935 and 1957," *Child Development,* **30**, 453–459.

Harris, D. B., 1961. "Work and the Adolescent Transition to Maturity," *Teachers College Record,* **63**, 146–153.

Harris, D. B., and S. C. Tseng, 1957. "Children's Attitudes Toward Peers and Parents as Revealed by Sentence Completions," *Child Development,* **28**, 401–411.

Havighurst, R. J., and H. Taba, 1949. *Adolescent Character and Personality.* New York: Wiley.

Hess, R. D., and I. Goldblatt, 1960. "Status of Adolescents in American Society: A Problem in Social Identity," in *The Adolescent,* 2d ed., edited by J. M. Seidman, pp. 321–332. New York: Holt.

Hoffman, M. L., and H. D. Saltzstein, 1967. "Parent Discipline and the Child's Moral Development," *Journal of Personality and Social Psychology,* **5**, 45–57.

Hurlock, E. B., 1955. *Adolescent Development,* 2d ed. New York: McGraw-Hill.

Hurlock, E. B., 1968. *Developmental Psychology.* 3d ed. New York: McGraw-Hill.

Johnston, J. A., 1964. "Adolescence," in *Textbook of Pediatrics,* 8th ed., edited by W. E. Nelson, pp. 163–171. Philadelphia: Saunders.

Jones, M. C., 1965. "Psychological Correlates of Somatic Development," *Child Development,* **36**, 899–911.

Kagan, J., and M. Freeman, 1963. "Relation of Childhood Intelligence, Maternal Behaviors, and Social Class to Behavior during Adolescence," *Child Development,* **34**, 899–911.

Keniston, K., 1965. *The Uncommitted: Alienated Youth in American Society.* New York: Harcourt, Brace & World.

Kohlberg, L., 1963. "The Development of Children's Orientations Toward a Moral Order. I. Sequence in the Development of Moral Thought," *Vita Humana,* **6**, 11–33.

Kuhlen, R. G., and N. B. Houlihan, 1965. "Adolescent Heterosexual Interest in 1942 and 1963," *Child Development,* **36**, 1049–1052.

Lansky, L. M., V. J. Crandall, J. Kagan, and C. T. Baker, 1961. "Sex Differences in Aggression and Its Correlates in Middle-Class Adolescents," *Child Development,* **32**, 45–58.

Medinnus, G. R., 1965. "Adolescents' Self-Acceptance and Perceptions of Their Parents," *Journal of Consulting Psychology, 29*, 150–154.

Meissner, S. J., 1965. "Parental Interaction of the Adolescent Boy," *Journal of Genetic Psychology, 107*, 225–233.

Meredith, H. V., 1957. "A Descriptive Concept of Physical Development," in *The Concept of Development,* edited by D. B. Harris, pp. 109–122. Minneapolis: The University of Minnesota Press.

Miller, B. F., and R. Goode, 1960. *Man and His Body.* New York: Simon and Schuster.

Moser, W. E., 1952. "The Influence of Certain Cultural Factors Upon the Selection of Vocational Preferences by High School Students," *Journal of Educational Research, 45*, 523–526.

Norton, J. L., 1953. "Patterns of Vocational Interest Development and Actual Job Choice," *Journal of Genetic Psychology, 82*, 235–262.

Peck, R. F., 1958. "Family Patterns Correlated with Adolescent Personality Structure," *Journal of Abnormal and Social Psychology, 57*, 347–350.

Quay, H. C., and L. C. Quay, 1965. "Behavior Problems in Early Adolescence," *Child Development, 36*, 215–220.

Shuttleworth, F., 1951. *The Adolescent Period: A Pictorial Atlas.* Monographs of the Society for Research in Child Development, *14*, No. 2. Lafayette, Ind.: Child Development Publications, Purdue University.

Tanner, J. M., 1962. *Growth at Adolescence.* Oxford: Blackwell Scientific Publications.

Vaughan, V. C., 1964. "Growth and Development in the Infant and the Child," in *Textbook of Pediatrics,* 8th ed., edited by W. E. Nelson, pp. 14–60. Philadelphia: Saunders.

Watson, E. H., and G. H. Lowrey, 1962. *Growth and Development of Children.* Chicago: The Year Book Medical Publishers.

Wattenberg, W. W., 1955. *The Adolescent Years.* New York: Harcourt, Brace & World.

Watts, W. A., and D. N. E. Whittaker, 1966. "Free Speech Advocates at Berkeley," *Journal of Applied Behavioral Science, 2*, 41–62.

Wohl, M. G., and R. S. Goodhart, 1955. *Modern Nutrition in Health and Disease.* Philadelphia: Lea & Febiger.

[eleven]

Social Learning and Authority

The child's first experiences with the functioning of authority are in association with parental control, and these experiences are the beginning of learning about constituted authority. During the developmental years, much of a child's training is in reference to authority, and the interaction between himself and authority figures affects his emotions about himself, his peers, and those who are in a position to fulfill or deny his needs.

Modern authority and its exercise developed in the Middle Ages, and with the advent of the Renaissance man glimpsed the satisfactions lying in freedom; with this, the modern trend toward certain patterns of relationships with authority began. The divine rights of kings and their traditional authority over their subjects lessened, the long accepted authority of feudal lords over serfs in economics and politics began to topple, and demands for freedom of religious, political, and economic activity accompanied new scientific exploration. At the same time, the arts began to flourish throughout European societies.

CATEGORIES OF AUTHORITY

In addition to the traditional or medieval type of authority, authority can be placed in two other categories: (1) legal-rational authority, which is based on patterns of legality in which the person in authority is given the right under regulations to give certain orders (Peters, 1965) and (2) "charismatic" authority (Weber, 1946). The latter type (associated with such a person as DeGaulle) is so successful that it has even been suggested that a mysterious quality occurs in a person's makeup that exerts a force on other people and causes them to conform to his wishes.

Historians and political scientists have called attention to the specific effort of the founders of the American form of government to establish laws and regulations to avoid giving too much authority to one person. They intended that authority should rest on the consent of the governed and that it should be granted to an abstraction or to an office but not to a specific person; a person, however, may temporarily hold this office and symbolically carry out and represent the authority invested in the office. In the modern era while new concepts of freedom have developed, it is now realized that freedom, in reality, can only exist in juxtaposition to authority. Once freedom is achieved, there is no authority. Such a premise leads to the conclusion that man desires and seeks authority, but at the same time wishes to be "free" of it (Hendel, 1958).

Man's behavior in reference to authority has remained much the same over the centuries since rules prescribed by the culture have been readily accepted. But now in the modern era cultural institutions are being altered and beliefs cherished in the past as sacred are in many instances being discarded. The questioning and discarding of customs and beliefs have brought problems other than those associated with the change in customs. If one cannot depend on authority then one must examine the nature of things for oneself and, for some individuals, much anxiety about this responsibility develops.

CHANGES OF AUTHORITY IN THE FAMILY

The patriarchal system and the absolute rule of the father is no longer characteristic of the American family (Bronfenbrenner, 1961; Nimkoff, 1957; Parsons, 1961). Today parents turn to each other for support in meeting the problems of living as well as in the training of the children. One of the important factors in bringing about the change in family authority patterns is the independence of women and their entrance into activity in the community (Hart and Allen, 1957; MacIver and Page, 1960). Also, because in modern families the father often leaves early in the morning and docs not return until evening, it is impractical for him to be the "head" of the household, and many decisions and activities must take place in his absence. Furthermore, just as the father moves out to his work in the morning and stays away most of the day, so do other members of the family. The children go to school and often activities after school keep them away almost as long as the father. The mother, with the many changes in the management of the house, also engages in activities outside of the home. Accordingly, the family members go their ways separately and the control of family activities by one person is no longer feasible.

The present role of the father also results in the training and instruction of children in this culture being carried on largely by women, not only at home, but in school as well. Boys, consequently, turn to peer groups, although these groups are an inadequate substitute for a father since they cannot provide the emotional support or adequate adult models. Then too, the value system of peers is not always in accord with parental desires or even the culture as a whole. Hence, present-day trends in the father's role in the family seem to increase the problems of growing up.

To understand the effects of different authority systems in the family, it is important to have information about children's perceptions of family authority. Hess and Torney (1962) sought such information by using a questionnaire in a study of nearly 2,000 children between the ages of seven and fifteen. These investigators reported that the boys in their study perceived the father as the dominant authority more frequently than the girls. However, the older children in the study less frequently saw the father as dominant. Where mothers are controlling, the methods of discipline are likely to be indirect (Droppleman and Schaefer, 1963).

In one study of the perception relationship of parental roles by children, Henry (1957) found that the eldest child tends to see the father as the principal disciplinarian, while the youngest child tends to see the mother as such. He also found that daughters tend to perceive the mother more as the disciplinarian than do sons. Similarly, Mosher and Mosher (1965) found in a study of adolescent delinquent girls in the lower socioeconomic class that the mothers' use of authority was of particular significance. As a result of information obtained about child-rearing practices from the mothers and also from the adolescents themselves, it was concluded that the authoritarian attitudes of the mothers were reflected in the attitudes of the daughters.

That children generally perceive the mother's role in the family as being more of a helping nature and that the father seems to be seen as an interfering person is indicated in a study by Emmerich (1959). Girls saw the mother as more powerful than the father but saw themselves as less powerful than boys. The findings of Kagan and Lemkin (1960) also lend support to the view that children see their fathers as more punitive and fear-provoking than mothers. So, evidence is available that suggests that children in this society are generally in some conflict about the father's authority and that these perceptions of the father and associated conflict would influence concepts of authority and the child's own behavioral development.

The problems attendant upon the modern structure of the family and the father's pursuit of a social role in a highly competitive society, however, are not of such a character that a return to a predominantly patriarchal system where the father is "master of the house" and the entire center of authority is desirable. It may be, though, that with the increasing opportunities for leisure, the father in the future can assume increased responsibility in child training.

In some ways, authority has biological origins. The complete dependency of the infant upon the mother for life itself represents an example of one human being's existing under the complete dominance and authority of another. Only gradually does a child discover that some of his biological functioning is not subject entirely to the authority of the mother. It is important to see in this early and largely biological setting, involving the dependence of the infant upon the mother, that a conflict begins—the young child seeks to behave as he wishes, yet at the same time he derives satisfaction from his conformity. In the conflict, the young child in making demands upon the parents—or for him, "authority"—finds that at times the authority refuses to accede to his demands; thus, he develops negative feeling about authority. He sees the parents as not only powerful, but also tyrannical, since the parents' actions are perceived as the unjustified exercise of authority. And, in this conflict, the child discovers that he can thwart the demands of his parents. Hence, what to him had been an absolute and fearsome authority gradually becomes one over which he has some influence. The child's beginning experience with authority, then, is one of struggle and is accompanied to some extent by confusion about authority as represented by his parents, since at one moment the parents are comforting and fulfilling needs and, at another, are interfering with the child's self-directed interaction with the environment.

Parental authority, of course, is usually described as benign, and parents explain their interference with the child's behavior as being "for his own good." Nevertheless, their authority interferes with action impelled by forces within the child and, in fact, they use their authority to thwart the child's pursuit of his own goals. "Parental authority," of course, has no meaning or function unless it does interfere. Since freedom cannot exist without authority, the child's struggle for freedom of choice about his behavior in actuality is a struggle against authority; he cannot feel free unless he thwarts some authority. Accordingly, if we teach children to "love freedom" they will find satisfaction in both the existence of authority and the defiance of its resulting interference.

Authority, of course, can be comforting and useful to a child; it helps him to avoid responsibility, it is protective, and it provides a solution to problems when solutions are impossible for him. In addition, authority is useful to the child indirectly, since, when he sees himself successful in overcoming authority, he then sees himself growing toward being an authority in his own right. In such growth, the child can test his courage and his developing wisdom. He therefore learns to respect authority and at the same time, he resents it and seeks to circumvent it.

EMOTIONAL BEHAVIOR ASSOCIATED WITH AUTHORITY

Sometimes conflict with authority comes about not necessarily because authority interferes with satisfaction or that it unrealistically limits the child, but rather because conflict becomes an outlet for displaced feelings. Feelings of frustration and disappointment resulting from failure to achieve are directed against an authority figure or even against a system of rules. The authority then is only a means to an end—an outlet of hostile and negative feelings because some limiting or interfering factor has brought unhappiness. All authority is then resented and is subject to hostility. Permissive, sympathetic, and generally benign adults sometimes are the object of more of a child's hostility than are adults who are severe, oppressive, and powerful. The child finds it safer to rebel or attack the less frightening symbol of authority rather than to confront the more formidable one. Sometimes the people who are the object of such displaced hostility or aggression are at a loss to understand the reason for the behavior, which, of course, seems grossly unfair to them.

Generalization of Emotion in Reference to Authority

Not only do children displace their feelings toward individuals or regulations that are not in fact the cause of their frustration, but also they may endow authority or parental figures with unreal characteristics. Parents' restrictions are often seen as unrealistically stemming from a lack of sympathy and understanding; but in order to justify their own intense feelings of hostility, children may give inappropriate or undesirable characteristics to parents to put them in an unfavorable light. The child to some degree can then avoid guilt and feel justified in hostile or destructive behavior. Accordingly, parents or teachers at times become symbols of unyielding and punitive authority, as exemplified by the following conversation between two first-grade boys who were seated on the edge of a fountain and pool in front of an administration building of a university. One reached down into the water and made several efforts to seize one of the goldfish in the pool. The other boy viewed the behavior with trepidation and finally cautioned his friend: "You'd better watch out," he said, glancing over his shoulder at the columns of the administration building, "there might be a principal in there!" For this child, the principal was an almost omnipresent authority who interfered with boyish pranks.

Adults who are the objects of displaced resentment often can help by recognizing the child's feelings and by being sympathetic to the child who has the hostile outbreaks. Some limits, nevertheless, must be placed on the hostile behavior, so that the destructive behavior does not become extreme. Recognizing the feelings of the child and his upset and at the same time delineating the limits for his hostile actions will help the child over the emotional crisis. If a child is allowed freedom within some limits, he can much better deal with the feelings driving him toward destructive and hostile behavior. Such is the conclusion of Watson (1957), who studied children with strict and permissive parents. He found that the children with the greater freedom showed more initiative, independence, cooperation, spontaneity, and originality and at the same time expressed much less hostility than did the children with strict parents.

One of the important aspects of the experience in psychotherapy for children is the opportunity to express hostility openly and with limited restrictions. A child in such an experience can break objects, scatter paint on the wall or playthings, spill water on the floor, and scatter sand from the sandbox; at the same time, he must respect the person of the therapist, he cannot strike or harm him, and he cannot destroy valuable property. He can, however, do many things not allowed in the ordinary course of living. By having this freedom to display feeling, the child can then control his hostility and outburst of feeling to a greater extent in other situations. Some children who are never destructive in their homes or at school, find a release in psychotherapy for a great deal of resentment that they feel against inhibiting individuals or rules (Alexander, 1963).

Identification with Authority

Some children seek to live within the framework of authority and, in fact, to go to great lengths to be allied with it. Thus, a child will not only endeavor to live within the rules of authority but also seek an emotional alliance with the authority. In part, this alliance is sought so that if the child is unable to meet the requirements he can then hope for some tolerance and his anxiety about conformity can thereby be lessened. This type of behavior, in which the child seeks to identify with authority or seeks to have an emotional tie with it, is exemplified by the old idea of taking an apple to the teacher in order to lessen the possibility of wrath for infractions or failure. Those individuals engaging in such behavior feel the necessity for protection, approval, affection, as well as leniency if wrongdoing is discovered.

AUTHORITY AND THE CONTROL OF BEHAVIOR

Authority is, of course, an abstraction; once an authority uses an external force upon an individual, it becomes action of some type. In this sense, authority is not active, but action in reference to it is taken over by some person for whom the authority exists. It is true, of course, that in the background authority often has power and can call upon power to enforce whatever it stands for; however, once that power is invoked, it becomes a force embodying aggression, punishment, or whatever else one can appropriately term it. Authority therefore is closely aligned to the concept of "conscience." A child is concerned about conformity to authority and thereby directs his own behavior.

Authority and the Exercise of Power

Although force can be used to achieve the goals for which authority was originally set up, punishment is also an added factor, in that it is a protection for generalized authority. Thus, if a child demurs but is forced to carry out a task for which an order is given and is also punished for demurring, then the punishment theoretically is used to instill in the child the respect for authority (not merely to get the task done). Punishment is given to insure that the next time there is a request from authority, the desired behavior will take place.

Not only protection but also revenge may be present in the enforcement of authority. Revenge in a way is denied by those who use force, in that others may view it as primarily benefiting the person using the force and not benefiting the person on whom revenge is taken. Punishment, theoretically, is for the benefit of the person who has defied authority in some way, since it will supposedly bring about conformity without further force on another occasion. Revenge, on the other hand, is action taken to make the person using the force feel better. A person harmed feels that those in authority are responsible for his protection, and he also wishes to see justice as uniform; thus, he desires that the person who has wronged him be punished just as he expects to be punished for his own wrongdoing. To this extent, then, an element of revenge in punishment exists. The complexity, therefore, of the problem of force and punishment in relation to authority is easily apparent.

In a different approach to the data from the same families obtained in an earlier study, Hoffman (1963b) studied the personal needs of parents in relation to their assertion of power over the child. The research techniques used consisted of a questionnaire developed by Levinson and Huffman (1955), a projective test consisting of cards from the Thematic Apperception Test by Murray, cards from Alexander's Adult-Child Interaction Test (1955), and other selected pictures. Hoffman hypothesized that the parents' authoritarian characteristics and their need for power would be associated with their means of dealing with their children's behavior. The findings, however, indicated that personal authoritarian characteristics of the parents were associated with approaches to controlling the child only in the case of middle-class mothers and lower socioeconomic class fathers.

Authority and "Discipline"

The term *discipline* is usually applied to force used to bring about the compliance with and respect for authority. The use of such a term means that action should be taken toward the child which interferes with the pursuit of goals that the child has set himself. The term *discipline* is used because the force is considered to be for the benefit of the child by teaching him to conform to authoity. Discipline, however, is in reality based on fear or anxiety, since the child is conditioned and forced to learn that if specific behavior does not take place in accordance with the expectations of authority then unfavorable events will occur. In such a situation, the child's own desires are disregarded and are held to be erroneous or of no consequence. The authority sets the standard, and the child must conform or suffer the consequences. Common usage of the term *discipline* leads to the conclusion that it refers to "action"and therefore it is to be differentiated from authority. It is a way of insisting that the child conform to a pattern of behavior for which the parent stands as the authority, albeit as a representative of the culture.

A child's behavior is channeled by two types of forces exerted upon him. One type of force is impersonal and can act in a way similar to the personal one of punishment. For example, if primitive man built a fire in his log hut, was careless with it, and did not follow certain patterns of behavior with it, his house was destroyed. Or if a child walks along the top of a wall, he must conform to certain physical laws or suffer the consequences of falling and being injured. As the child grows, he learns these physical laws and limitations for his safety and well-being and he will avoid hazards and the consequences, which in a way act as punishment for transgression of these laws.

The second type of force is personal coercion. Adults seek to set up a sequence of events similar to the action of impersonal forces. That is, a body of rules and regulations is set up that the individual must learn; as a consequence of going against these regulations, he is made uncomfortable in some way. The most common reasons for punishment given by parents are for infractions of rules that they have made, for disobedience of orders and demands made upon the child, and for accidents that result in harm or damange that might have been avoided by the child through either anticipation or care.

Some parents resort to indirect forms of discipline, such as denial of pleasurable activities at later times. Parents who use this form of discipline believe it helps them avoid facing the issue of whether or not to punish their child. The confusion of parents about punishment and the *indirect* exertion of power, however, can also cause problems with their children. Greenfield (1959), in an investigation of people who were diagnosed as having mental disorders, found that a majority of subjects had experienced indirect discipline. The control group with which they were compared was shown to have had direct forms of discipline. This investigator believes that the parents' failure to arrive at satisfactory forms of discipline had a deleterious effect on the patients as children and perhaps had some bearing on the later development of psychopathology. The use of indirect forms of punishment is perhaps most deleterious because of the confusion of the child as to why he is being punished and because the forms of punishment are unreasonable as far as the child is concerned.

There is some evidence to suggest that parents who exercise rigid control over their children tend to create more anxiety in their children than parents who are permissive. In a study of 22 preadolescent boys, Tiffany and Shontz (1963) used a technique consisting of 48 pictures of parent-child interaction situations. Each subject was asked to sort the pictures according to his perception of his family on the basis of permissiveness or control. The subjects also were given five minutes to think of and write down the consequences of Mother Hubbard's finding her cupboard bare.

Then judges ranked the responses according to the degree of physical danger in the stories. It was found that children who indicated by their choices that their parents were very rigid showed in their stories more fantasy about danger in their environment than did children whose parents were more flexible.

Hoffman (1963a) investigated parental discipline and control of children's behavior from a "positive point of view" and studied the development of a "consideration of others." He based his study on the assumption that a positive affective orientation for other people develops in children who have an affectionate relationship with parents and who have freedom for the expression of impulsive behavior. Subjects for the study were 22 families, each of which had a child in nursery school. The data for the study were obtained from the parents in recorded interviews and from the children through observations of their behavior in school.

The parent interviews were categorized and coded according to overt interaction between mother and child and the "influence" techniques used by the mother to change the behavior of the child. Three categories of interaction were devised: (1) *acceptance of the child,* defined as the amount of time the mother spent with the child in pleasurable interaction in which no attempt was made to change the child's behavior contrary to his wishes; (2) *consequence-oriented discipline,* meaning the use of techniques which pointed to the consequences of the child's behavior and which were intended to caution him that when he behaved in certain undesirable ways, unfavorable events would occur; and (3) *other-oriented discipline,* defined as the techniques for changing the child's behavior by giving an explanation of the significance of the child's behavior for another person; that is, when the child does something which adversely affects another person, the likely feelings of the person are pointed out to the child. The observational data of the children were analyzed according to two categories. The first, *consideration for others,* was used to obtain the incidence of behavior in which the child gave unsolicited help to another child in distress. The second category was called *positive affective orientation* and included behavior in which emotions were positive; for example, as indicated by expressions of affection for peers. The investigators found a significant relaship between parental acceptance and the child's *positive affective orientation* but did not find a significant relationship between the parent's influence techniques directed toward making the child aware of the consequences of behavior toward others and the amount of the child's overt positive affect.

Although parents insist that discipline or punishment is important for children and that it is an essential practice of child training, many will say that they find punishment unsuccessful. Parents of children who have various types of constitutional inadequacies or who are emotionally upset find that punishment and the infliction of pain actually increase the problems of the child and of themselves. Some children with pathological conditions in the brain engage in behavior that has the outward appearance of disobedience or a disregard for rules; as a result, their parents, not understanding the child's problems, resort to punishment. Parents of such children usually discover for themselves that the effects of punishment are unfavorable and do not in reality change the child's behavior in a conforming direction. Similarly, parents of children who are emotionally upset, disobedient, failing in school, and generally recalcitrant find that punishment of any type only increases the child's negativistic or asocial behavior.

Children sometimes seek to have punishment given others as a means of securing justice. When in conflict with peers, a younger child, according to Durkin (1959), tends to resort to authority and to seek retribution or justice from the authority figure. The demands from the younger child for justice usually disregard the concern for others or the circumstances that brought about the problem in the first place. After children reach middle childhood, they make fewer demands that others who cause trouble receive the same amount of trouble that they themselves have received. Durkin's study seems to indicate that perceptive and highly intelligent children understand better the concepts of justice and the factors bringing about disputes. Concepts of justice in child training, of course, are the reflections of the concepts of their society. An increasing tendency to understand the factors of human behavior alters the concepts of what is "just" and what needs to be done to the individual. Earlier concepts of justice involved punishment and retribution for infractions against society, but now a countertrend is in evidence that maintains that the individual's behavior is a result of forces that brought him to the behavior and that he needs more than mere justice or retribution.

CULTURAL AND SOCIAL DIFFERENCES IN SOCIAL LEARNING

Authority and its place in the social order varies according to culture and even within cultures. All cultures have some concept of authority and, consequently, children in every culture must learn to understand and act in accord with certain principles. Understanding authority in different cultures may be of value in seeking its place in the socialization process. Similarly, the differences in the social learning process of children in the lower socio-economic class can provide a basis for understanding their feelings about authority.

Authority in Primitive Societies

In the world today, those peoples who have the simplest cultures are the food gatherers and hunters, such as the Eskimos, Indians of the Shoshone tribe, the pygmies and bushmen in Africa, or the Australian aborigines (Hoebel, 1958). Hoebel sees the Eskimos as representatives of these primitive societies and describes authority as resting in two social roles and in the individuals in those roles: One is that of "headman" and the other that of "shaman." The authority of the headman comes from his prowess as a hunter as well as his energy and activity. The others in the group find that by following him, the hunt is successful. He, however, does not give commands or orders, but is the leader through example and perhaps suggestion. The other type of authority, the shaman (the Eskimo term is *angakok*), derives his authority from his relationship with supernatural beings. He determines who has violated taboos and who therefore has kept valuable animals away from the hunters. He also decides the type of penance to be done. The angakok's authority is coercive, while the headman's comes through example.

In these simple societies the authority results from superior knowledge or a special relationship to the supernatural, but both help in interaction with the environment. Both types of authority are ambiguous and both are somewhat indirect. Neither is tyrannical. Hogbin (1934) concluded that in many primitive societies of Polynesia, authority comes from religious origins. In cultures at a somewhat more complex level, such as those that existed among the Plains Indians, authority, while more direct, rested in a council in which important decisions about war and peace were made.

In primitive societies, as in other cultures, the child first learns about authority through child training and later learns about political authority. To primitive peoples, authority is personal and comes about through performance rather than through inheritance. In large, segmented societies, such as those in primitive Africa, authority rests in a system of clan headmen, and the central power is complex and related to magical, religious, military, economic, charismatic, and kinship factors. Jules Henry (1954) found that in some primitive societies, especially in that of the people of Alor, conformity to authority is attained through punishment and that children often run away from the village in order to escape punishment. Kardiner (1945) reported that the children on the island of Alor were not to think well of themselves but were constantly impressed by their parents with the imminence of punishment.

In the main, however, in the simple societies, authority is more benign and is brought about through examples of prowess, knowledge, or by special relationships with the supernatural. Generally, authority is not based on inheritance or tyranny but is created in part because of the group's struggle to maintain itself in a specific environment.

Social Class and Authority

Within American society, social-class differences are found in the individual's relationship to authority. Children from the lower socioeconomic class who have not internalized the teachings and expectations of middle-class culture view authority in terms of a person—one who interferes or imposes his will upon them.

McCord and McCord (1958), in a study of lower-class boys whose criminal records were examined twenty years later, found that if boys were rejected and if there was a criminal role for a model, the boys would likely become criminals. The hostility of such individuals is displaced and is directed not only against the police but also sometimes against a teacher, principal, or others who represent authority to them.

Some children develop much resentment and thus endeavor to thwart adult authority but still live within the authority mandates of their own peer group. If such children come in conflict with the law and are punished, the feelings of hostility that they have about authority are reinforced. Many individuals with such experiences during adolescence fall into a life of crime. Having no emotional deterrents, they uninhibitedly defy authority and seek to cope with the forces of a society that they see as hostile and depriving. Adams (1960) in a study of 2,000 children in middle childhood and early adolescence found that the delinquent children in his sample were the least conforming individuals in the study.

Some basis exists for believing that lower socioeconomic status and little education provide a favorable environment for the development of extremist and intolerant forms of political and religious beliefs. Lipset (1959) suggests that the reason for the development of such beliefs is that individuals with low socioeconomic status and little education fail to understand causal relations and are driven by feelings of insecurity to seek to better their condition through dependence upon some authoritarian individual.

The role of the mother in the lower-class family in relation to authority seems to be particularly significant. In a study of 12 middle-class and 10 working-class families having children in attendance at a nursery school,

Hoffman (1960) found that the mother's use of unqualified power brought more hostility than the father's. His study also showed that lower-class parents more frequently resorted to power enforcement than did middle-class parents. In a study by Zuckerman et al. (1960), a large group of mothers and fathers from the lower socioeconomic class were compared with parents in a control group. The findings in this study were similar to those of Hoffman in that lower-class mothers were found to have more authoritarian attitudes toward their children than did middle-class mothers.

AUTHORITY AND GROUP PROCESSES

Conclusions about the effects of authority on the behavior of children and productive effort in groups should be relative to situations. For example, one study indicates that individuals who accept authority are more productive and efficient in activity in groups where the situation contained rules from authority and that individuals who are less acceptant of authority are more productive in group situations where less authority is in evidence (Shaw, 1959). Anderson (1959), after reviewing a large number of studies, also concluded that neither authoritarian nor democratic situations led consistently to higher productivity, although White and Lippitt (1960) found that more general satisfaction was obtained in group participation in democratically led groups than in autocratically led groups. Individuals who tend to rely on authority and have not learned to rely on themselves or assume responsibility are often at a loss in situations where no authority is exercised. A group of such individuals usually turns to a search for someone to direct them or to prescribe the course of action to follow. If such direction is not obtained, anxiety develops and the effectiveness of the group is greatly impaired.

Productivity of Individuals in Groups

The problem of the individual's behavior in groups has wide ramifications not only for social interaction in children's groups, but also in adult and family life. Asch (1956) found in a study of independence and conformity in groups that had supported an obviously wrong proposal that many individuals who conformed did so because of fear of exposure of personal inadequacy and because of fear of group disapproval.

It is impossible in a way to demonstrate empirically which type of group experience provides the best opportunity for children since their past experiences have much to do with their ability to profit from different types of group leadership and structure. For example, a child who has had experiences in the family that help him to communicate with others will be more successful in group interaction than those children who have had little opportunity to communicate (Leavitt, 1958); and children who have had little opportunity to demonstrate creative thinking, when first placed in a group where they are expected to profit from freedom and self-direction often are unable to do so. On the other hand, if children who have experienced freedom and less direction are placed in groups where more direction is given than they want, they too are in conflict and feel resentful against the unwarranted direction of their affairs.

On the assumption that boys who perceive their parents as coercive and themselves as having a high degree of autonomy will be successful in school, Hoffman et al. (1960) studied boys in the third through the sixth grade. They found that boys who reported a high degree of coerciveness by the parents and a high degree of autonomy were, as they hypothesized, successfully assertive in school. The autonomy was seen as facilitating the expression of hostility aroused by parental coerciveness, and the resulting assertiveness brought success in school in the areas of academic performance, social influence, and friendship.

Thus, the types of activities of groups may alter experience of members and the acceptance of authority. Studying the attributes of leaders elected by children ranging in age from eight to thirteen, Clifford and Cohn (1964) found that as the activities changed, the personal attributes perceived as necessary for the leader roles also changed. Most people agree that children need some direction, but most also agree that excessive control or influence can be deleterious.

Sherwood (1966) suggests that the basis of morality which Piaget describes for the young child also is similar to that of an authoritarian adult. Accordingly, it may be that authoritarianism is an earlier stage in the development of specialized human behavior and that social maturity consists of a reduction of a personal need to be authoritarian.

A POINT OF VIEW

It is important to see that authority in its most elementary form is in reality biologically based, that it is present in human life at its very beginning, and that the struggle even for biological independence requires the removal of authority when the new organism need no longer be subject to it. At the same time, although the parental yoke may ostensibly be removed, the training and enculturation of the child takes place in society in such a way that at times he respects authority and at other times rebels against it. In a complex and changing society, not only must an individual adjust to a changing relationship to authority inherent in the individual process of human development, but also he must, as a result of varying social conditions, adjust to a changing of the relationship to authority in every area of human affairs—what is approved and acceptable behavior on this day becomes disapproved or changed on the next.

While it is apparent that most of today's youth are not alienated or inclined to be destructive of authority, an increasing number of adolescents seem to be, and in fact, the unrest of American youth has spread to Asia, Europe, Latin America, and the Middle East. The actions of American youth have affected not only educational institutions, but also governmental policies, organizations, and the careers of public figures. Therefore, increasing attention is being given to the origin of such restlessness and protest.

One explanation given for adolescent unrest is that parents have been too permissive, that parents, by using the "rational approach," have not instilled in their children a respect for authority. That is, during the child-rearing period, reasons for rules were explained to the child and often in reference to the welfare of others. And, rules and punishment were not strictly enforced by the parents. Hence, adolescents face difficulty when confronted with authoritarian policies for which they receive no explanation or about which they have no opportunity to express their feelings.

This approach to an explanation of adolescent unrest and rejection is perhaps too simple. Although child rearing and the place of authority, particularly that of the father, in the American family has changed increasingly as the twentieth century has advanced, there are other factors to be considered. While there has been a movement away from authoritarianism and punishment by middle-class parents, the change has been accompanied by a loosening of family relationships and emotional interaction. The social and occupational roles of fathers have become increasingly complex and demanding and at the same time mothers, because of technical change, have engaged in more activities outside the home. And further, children have become more involved in education and social activities associated with the schools. Consequently, children have turned to the peer group for emotional exchange partly because they spend more time with the peer group than with the family. For some children, the minimal emotional support gained from parents, the lack of appropriate adult models, and the insufficient teaching about behavioral values and abstractions contribute to an estrangement from the family at an early age and cause an unrealistic reliance on peers. It is an easy step from estrangement from the family and its values to an estrangement from the social order at large. Accordingly, the permissiveness and rational approach of the parents is not in itself the cause: The difficulty lies in the lack of close emotional interchange between parent and child—an interchange that is necessary and of paramount significance for any pattern of child rearing to be successful.

REFERENCES

Adams, A. A., 1960. "Identifying Socially Maladjusted School Children," *Genetic Psychology Monographs,* **61**, 3–36.

Alexander, T., 1955. *The Adult-Child Interaction Test: A Projective Test for Use in Research.* Monographs of the Society for Research in Child Development, **17**, No. 2. Lafayette, Ind.: Child Development Publications, Purdue University.

Alexander, T., 1963. *Psychotherapy in Our Society.* Englewood Cliffs, N.J.: Prentice-Hall.

Anderson, R. C., 1959. "Learning in Discussions: A Resumé of the Authoritarian-Democratic Studies," *Harvard Educational Review,* **29**, 201–215.

Asch, S. E., 1956. *Studies of Independence and Conformity. I. A Minority of One Against a Unanimous Majority.* Psychological Monographs, **70**, No. 9. Washington, D.C.: American Psychological Association.

Bronfenbrenner, U., 1961. "The Changing American Child," in *Values and Ideals of American Youth,* edited by E. Ginzberg, pp. 71–84. New York: Columbia.

Clifford, Clare, and T. S. Cohn, 1964. "The Relationship Between Leadership and Personality Attributes Perceived by Followers," *Journal of Social Psychology,* **64**, 57–64.

Droppleman, L. F., and E. S. Schaefer, 1963. "Boys' and Girls' Reports of Maternal and Paternal Behavior," *Journal of Abnormal and Social Psychology,* **67**, 648–654.

Durkin, D., 1959. "Children's Concept of Justice: A Further Comparison with the Piaget Data," *Journal of Educational Research,* **52**, 252–257.

Emmerich, W., 1959. "Young Children's Discriminations of Parent and Child Roles," *Child Development,* **30**, 403–419.

Greenfield, N. S., 1959. "The Relationship between Recalled Forms of Childhood Discipline and Psychopathology," *Journal of Consulting Psychology,* **23**, 139–142.

Hart, H., and F. R. Allen, 1957. "Major Problems Arising from Social Change," in *Technology and Social Change,* pp. 435–451. New York: Appleton-Century-Crofts.

Hendel, C. W., 1958. "An Exploration of the Nature of Authority," in *Authority,* edited by C. J. Friedrich, pp. 3–27. Cambridge, Mass.: Harvard.

Henry, H., 1957. "Working Paper on Creativity," *Harvard Educational Review,* **27**, 148–155.

Henry, J., 1954. "The Problem of Invariance in the Field of Personality and Culture," in *Aspects of Culture and Personality*, edited by F. L. K. Hsu, pp. 139–171. New York: Abelard-Schuman.

Hess, R. D., and J. V. Torney, 1962. "Religion, Age, and Sex in Children's Perceptions of Family Authority," *Child Development*, 33, 781–789.

Hoebel, E. A., 1958. "Authority in Primitive Societies," in *Authority*, edited by C. J. Friedrich, pp. 222–234. Cambridge, Mass.: Harvard.

Hoffman, M. L., 1960. "Power Assertion by the Parent and its Impact on the Child," *Child Development*, 31, 129–143.

Hoffman, M. L., 1963a. "Personality, Family Structure, and Social Class as Antecedents of Parental Power Assertion," *Child Development*, 34, 869–884.

Hoffman, M. L., 1963b. "Parent Discipline and the Child's Consideration for Others," *Child Development*, 34, 573–588.

Hoffman, L. W., S. Rosen, and R. Lippitt, 1960. "Parental Coerciveness, Child Autonomy, and Child's Role at School," *Sociometry*, 23, 15–22.

Hogbin, H. I., 1934. *Law and Order in Polynesia*. New York: Harcourt, Brace & World.

Kagan, J., and J. Lemkin, 1960. "The Child's Differential Perception of Parental Attributes," *Journal of Abnormal and Social Psychology*, 61, 440–447.

Kardiner, A., 1945. *The Psychological Frontiers of Society*. New York: Columbia.

Leavitt, H. J., 1958. "Some Effects of Certain Communications Patterns on Group Performance," in *Readings in Social Psychology*, 3d. ed., edited by E. E. Maccoby, T. M. Newcomb, and E. L. Hartley, pp. 546–563. New York: Holt.

Levinson, D. J., and P. E. Huffman, 1955. "Traditional Family Ideology and Its Relation to Personality," *Journal of Personality*, 23, 251–273.

Lipset, S. M., 1959. "Democracy and Working-Class Authoritarianism," *American Sociological Review*, 24, 482–501.

McCord, J., and W. McCord, 1958. "The Effects of Parental Role Model on Criminality," *Journal of Social Issues*, 14, 66–75.

MacIver, R. M., and C. H. Page, 1960. "Changing Techniques and Changing Society," in *Social Change*, edited by J. E. Nordskog, pp. 25–41. New York: McGraw-Hill.

Mosher, D. L., and J. B. Mosher, 1965. "Relationships Between Authoritarian Attitudes in Delinquent Girls and the Authoritarian Attitudes and Authoritarian Rearing Practices of Their Mothers," *Psychological Reports*, 16, 23–30.

Nimkoff, M. F., 1957. "Technology and the Family," in *Technology and Social Change*, pp. 305–323. New York: Appleton-Century-Crofts.

Parsons, T., 1961. "A Sociologist's View," in *Values and Ideals of American Youth*, edited by E. Ginzberg, pp. 271–287. New York: Columbia.

Peters, R. S., 1965. *Authority, Responsibility, and Education*. New York: Atherton.

Shaw, M. E., 1959. "Acceptance of Authority, Group Structure, and the Effectiveness of Small Groups," *Journal of Personality,* **27,** 196–210.

Sherwood, J. J., 1966. "Authoritarianism and Moral Realism," *Journal of Clinical Psychology,* **22,** 17–21.

Tiffany, D. W., and F. C. Shontz, 1963. "Fantasized Danger as a Function of Parent-Child Controlling Practices," *Journal of Consulting Psychology,* **27,** 278.

Watson, G., 1957. "Some Personality Differences in Children Related to Strict or Permissive Parental Discipline," *Journal of Psychology,* **44,** 227–249.

Weber, M., 1946. *From Max Weber: Essays in Sociology,* translated and edited by H. H. Gerth and C. W. Mills. New York: Oxford University Press.

White, R. K., and R. Lippitt, 1960. *Autocracy and Democracy.* New York: Harper & Row.

Zuckerman, M., B. H. Barrett, and R. M. Bragiel, 1960. "The Parental Attitudes of Parents of Child Guidance Cases: I. Comparisons with Normals, Investigations of Socioeconomic and Family Constellation Factors and Relations to Parents' Reactions to the Clinics," *Child Development,* **31,** 401–417.

[*twelve*]

The Child
and Society

The development of many children is significantly influenced by certain organizations within the social order. These specialized social organizations and institutions are more likely to influence children's development in urban areas than in rural areas. Despite the fact that these organizations are established for children's welfare, children often view them with hostility and as inimical to their welfare. Thus, not only must some children cope with a modern and changing society with many types of social organizations created by adults, but also they must cope with certain social organizations established with beneficent intention but which they perceive as interfering.

Examples of social organizations which may influence a child in development can be seen in the life of an adolescent who has a chronic disease and who lives in the deteriorated part of a large city.

> The boy, Harvey Allen, is seventeen years old and has been known to have had diabetes since it was discovered in a community health clinic two years ago. For the last two summers, Harvey has attended summer camps for children with diabetes. He was sent to these camps on money raised by a local business and professional men's organization. Years ago, his father had deserted the family and as his mother has been receiving welfare

payments for as long as he can remember, Harvey has always been well acquainted with case workers. At sixteen, Harvey dropped out of school and now is receiving "on the job training" under a Federal program administered by the state. Also, he is taking some night courses at a local high school. Two years ago, Harvey was apprehended by police while dismantling an old car parked on a side street. At the time, he was with a group of boys known as the Jets, a peer social organization. Taken before a juvenile court judge, he was placed on probation and directed to see a juvenile court counselor periodically.

In the above story, at least ten different types of organizations influenced Harvey's behavior and opportunities in society. These organizations were cooperative in varying degrees in their efforts to help Harvey, but all affected in different ways his feelings about himself and the world in which he lives. Some are likely to have had considerable influence on his attainment of a satisfactory social role.

THEORETICAL APPROACHES TO UNDERSTANDING THE CHILD IN SOCIETY

The causes of the difficulties that some children have in becoming a part of society have been explained in a number of ways. These explanations provide some theoretical approaches to understanding and are useful in providing a base for scientific investigation of the etiological factors of some of the difficulties that children have. These approaches can be put in two categories: those related to social organizations and those related to psychological factors associated with certain social conditions. Although these approaches are described as "theories," in reality they are not true theories because they lack a system of sufficient complexity.

Approaches Related to Social Organizations

Three theoretical approaches have been used in explaining a child's difficulty in developing in accord with the regulations and customs of society's organizations. These approaches seek to explain the cause of the problems that arise during the developmental years and which bring dissatisfaction to the child and to society. The three approaches are the ecological theory, the subcultural theory, and the mirror theory.

The Ecological Theory.   An ecological approach to the understanding of the variability of child behavior has been used for many years. For example, in the city of Chicago it was found that the behavior of children and adolescents varied according to specific geographic areas (Park et al., 1925; Shaw, 1929). The implication of such findings is that predictions can be made about the behavior of a child on the basis of his residence in a particular area of a city. Furthermore, the geographical area in which the child lives can be used as a basis for the prediction of his ultimate social role in society. For example, a young child living in the deteriorated section of a large city is likely to develop certain problem behavior and to come into conflict with certain social organizations and institutions of society. On the other hand, a child growing up in an area at the periphery of the city is likely to find satisfactions in a social role as a conforming member of society.

Because the variability of behavior according to geographic area has been known for some time, the characteristics of the differing geographical areas have been analyzed. The findings have led some investigators such as Merton (1962) to believe that the social system of an area producing problem behavior in children is inconsistent and lacks definitiveness. Consequently, children growing up in such an area cannot find consistent behavioral models or teachings that will aid them in the acquisition of behavioral patterns in accord with the broad patterns of behavior of society at large. Appropriate social behavior, accordingly, can be acquired by a child only in a situation where the environment around him is organized and consistent.

The Subculture Theory. The view that certain geographical areas of the city have disorganization and inconsistency has been challenged. Whyte (1955), for example, has asserted that there is organization—a subculture —but that it is in conflict with the society at large. Cohen (1955) also sees a subculture existing in deteriorated areas of the city and that this subculture serves a child in a number of ways: (1) it compensates for the denial of social status that he experiences in the school system; and (2) it offers opportunity for achievement at least within its framework. Further support for this view has been provided by the studies of Short and Nye (1958), who found that similar geographical areas in different cities produced similar behavior.

In the study of children in River City by Havighurst et al. (1962), some attention was devoted to discovering the characteristics of children who have difficulty in society. At the time of the study, River City, located in a county typical of the Midwest, was a town of about 44,000 residents. More than half the labor force was industrial. The city depended on river trade in the last century and still, according to the authors, had the characteristics of a river town. The largest percentage of people were in the lower socioeconomic class, with approximately 35 per cent in the middle and upper class.

The investigators defined the children's difficulties according to three types. One type was considered to be due to some "severe personality disturbance," consisting of either extremely aggressive behavior or of behavior indicating severe anxiety. Those with aggressive behavior were described by the authors as having little or no "inner moral control" and as having been brought up by parents who had neglected them and had failed both to "love and punish them with consistency." The second type of difficulty was associated with "adolescent development" and was seen as related to the conflicts of adolescence. The third type was related to problems within the social structure and was the most common type of difficulty. In this latter group of children and adolescents, there were those who were in conflict with society and alienated from it.

Havighurst and his coworkers reported that they encountered a "delinquent subculture" and that the children within this subculture came from families in which drunkenness and fighting were common, where sexual promiscuity was visible, and where stealing was openly condoned. Their study showed that most of the subjects were intellectually below average and were from the lower socioeconomic groups. In summary, these authors characterized members of the delinquent subculture as having low socioeconomic status, as being school dropouts, as having relatively low intelligence, and as coming from broken or inadequate homes. Much bitterness and resentment was encountered on the part of these children in the lower socioeconomic class against the middle- and upper-class children, and they did not participate in the social activities of the schools. Once having left school, they began to frequent places where there was less discrimination but which the middle-class people believed to be unsatisfactory places for children.

There were other children in the study who had similar problems and lack of opportunity and yet did not become delinquent. The explanation was made that those children who seek to achieve the prevailing standards of behavior in the community and who are supported by their parents and teachers will seek to live within the social code of behavior; but if they are unable to so achieve, they too are likely to become delinquent.

The authors concluded that an "affectionate family" can prevent delinquency even though a child fails in school or is born into the lower socioeconomic class. They also see delinquency as a failure of the process of growth and believe that effective ways of dealing with the problem must include the improvement of family life, efforts to help the adolescents to be successful in school, and provision of appropriate work experiences that will provide an alternative means of reaching adulthood for those who cannot be successful in school.

The view that an organized subculture exists has been modified by Short et al. (1963). These investigators concluded that while a subculture exists, it is to some extent indeterminant and thus does not provide sufficient models and learning opportunities. Sykes and Matza (1962) take the view that the concept of a subculture is not useful in that individuals in the areas are aware of the values of the larger culture and that other reasons for variability in behavior must be found. They point to two reasons for the inadequacy of the subcultural view: (1) Delinquent adolescents sometimes show guilt and realize that their behavior is not in accord with the expectations of society at large; and (2) in deteriorated sections of cities, there usually are parts that provide social roles and learning opportunities in accord with the society at large. Hence, if a delinquent is part of a subculture and he behaves in accord with the norms of this subculture, then he should exhibit no guilt upon being apprehended in activities against the mandates of the larger culture. But, sometimes an understanding clergyman will stand as an advocate of behavior outside of the normative values of the delinquent subculture and still be revered by the offenders. Thus, delinquent youth, although apparently believing in their own deviant system constituting their supposed subculture, still seem to revere the moral values of the larger culture.

It is for these reasons that Sykes and Matza do not believe that delinquents are completely immune to the socialization influences of the larger culture and, therefore, they reject the view that a delinquent subculture exists in which the individual is comfortable without qualification.

The Mirror Theory. A third theoretical approach maintains that the child's difficulties are only a mirror of the difficulties of the society at large. All societies have some individuals who have difficulty; consequently, any given society considered as "typical" or "normal" would be expected to have a certain number of individuals who do not conform (Durkheim, 1938; Merton, 1962). Since all societies have some difficulty, it may be assumed that social organizations will be characterized generally by ineffectual structural elements that cause difficulty for the individuals within the society and more difficulty for some individuals than others. Thus, a child who has difficulty growing up in a social system can be seen as a reflection of the difficulties characteristic of certain elements of the order; therefore, his behavior is a "mirror" of the society of which he is a part.

Bell (1962) believes that crime is something of a mirror to society and shows the morals and manners of society. In American history, according to Bell, a hero has always been important; he might be a frontiersman, a soldier, or even a gangster, but very often he has been a man with a gun. As the social structure has changed, so has the type of crime. While crime in America continues because of the desire for gain and money, organized city crime is changing with the absorption of ethnic groups into the American way of life and with the political changes bringing about an end to the local governmental conditions prevalent during the past half century.

Psychosocial Approaches

Social rules and normative behavior of the culture provide many qualifications, defenses, and flexibilities in social codes. One type of flexibility exists through a system of justification. The *justification theory* holds certain variants of behavior to be "techniques of neutralization." According to this approach, adolescents develop justification for their deviant behavior by a denial of responsibility and by viewing a particular behavior as resulting from forces beyond the control of the individual (Sykes and Matza, 1962). An adolescent, for example, may believe that he is forced into certain behavior by circumstances and in this way absolves himself from responsibility. Others justify their behavior by maintaining that it does not actually injure anyone. In a case of property destruction, for example, if the owner of the property can afford the loss, the youth justifies his behavior by asserting that no great harm can come from it. At times society seems to agree with this point of view and some vandalism is described as "pranks" or "playfulness."

Another type of justification is that the circumstances warrant the behavior. For example, action against other minority groups or against a teacher who is considered to be unfair is justifiable. Acts against such persons are looked upon as justified, although in reality the justification rests upon the upholding of the mandates of the general culture.

Further justification is found by those who, though not rejecting the beliefs of the general culture, choose between the codes of the larger culture and of their smaller group on the basis of expediency. When a youth must choose between friendship and social obligation to his group and the beliefs of the general culture, he tends to choose his own group. The norms, thus, of the larger group are not displaced because of the lack of concern for them but because of the more immediate importance of those values related to the smaller group.

Sykes and Matza (1962) believe that many youths have a confused set of values and will vacillate between those values of the general culture and the values of their own group. Such adolescents are not entirely influenced by a totally different value system or one unrelated to that of the larger social order; rather they are caught in an intermixture of values, a confusion too often unrecognized by adolescents themselves.

In searching for the causes of difficulties of children in society, evidence of causative environmental factors is sought—a discordance in the socialization process. An illustration of the meaning of the *discordance theory* is found in a study by Bennett (1960), who studied 50 "delinquent" children. He found that the delinquent children lacked "conditions essential for normal emotional development" in their families. A similar conclusion was reached by Andry (1960), who studied 80 delinquent and 80 nondelinquent boys. His subjects were matched on the basis of geographical location, age, IQ, socioeconomic status, and family background. Andry found that the delinquent boys tended to feel that their fathers had given them inadequate love.

On the other hand, discordance in the socialization process may also come from family dissolution (Monahan, 1960, 1962). If a child loses a parent by death, the deprivation is immediate, but because sympathy and interest are offered by the community, the results seem to be less deleterious than in divorce or desertion.

The recognition of the deleterious effect of family discord upon the development of children is not recent. Many years ago, Aichorn (1935) observed that all of the children at his institution came from families in which separation had occurred. The significance of family difficulty was also shown by Healy and Bronner (1936) in a study in which they found that nearly all of the delinquent children, as compared with only 13 per cent of the control subjects, gave evidence of having had discordant relationships with others in the family. In a much more recent investigation, Gregory (1965) studied 11,329 adolescents who had dropped out of school; he found delinquency to be higher among boys who had lost their father by separation or divorce.

Not all investigators agree on the importance of broken or father-absent homes as being a causative factor in difficulties in development. Lawton and Sechrest (1962) obtained family drawings from boys from father-present and father-absent homes. The investigators used such characteristics for a comparison as size of figures, amount of detail, and the like. Analysis of the characteristics of the drawings did not distinguish between father-present and father-absent groups. Similarly, Sterne (1964), as a result of his study of 1,050 delinquent boys, has expressed doubt that prevention of divorce or family breaks will necessarily avoid difficulty. Some support for such a view is that if divorce comes in adolescence, the families are no longer very important to adolescents. For example, reaction time of institutionalized juvenile delinquents to a word-association test was used as an indirect measure of conflict (Kass and Powell, 1964). Seven areas were studied: parent-child relationships, religion, vocational outlook, physical appearance, emotional tendencies, heterosexual relations, and social acceptability. The findings of this study indicated that heterosexual relationships and social acceptability were of greatest concern and parent-child relationships of least concern.

Since, theoretically, girls are also subjected to impairment by discordant factors in the family, it is not clear why boys have more difficulties than girls. Over the years, investigators have attributed sex differences in behavioral difficulties to the differences in training of girls and boys. Girls' difficulties are usually with the family and consist of behavior in which they run away or defy their parents with illicit sex relationships. Morris (1964) found in a study of delinquent girls that the girls came from broken homes or those with family tensions. The incidence of problems in their families was greater than in families of normal girls.

THE CHILD AND THE SOCIAL STRUCTURE

As children move away from the family, control of and influence on their behavior increasingly result from external forces—from rules and customs of the peer groups and from the social order's institutions. Peer groups, at least at first, do not function in conflict with cultural demands or legal restrictions, but at times and in certain areas as children enter adolescence, conflict with society begins. Difficulties in such instances become generally the problem of society, for the adolescents have usually left the family.

Microsocial Orders

Social or play groups in certain areas of large cities begin early to have a type of individuality. Although in many of them the loyalties of the members are transient and cannot be relied upon, in other, more permanent, groups loyalty is established and membership continues over long periods of time. These permanent groups may develop secret practices, passwords, ritualistic activities, and specific codes of behavior, with some groups turning directly to behavior against society. These latter groups may develop their own argot—a language sometimes related to adult criminal groups and sometimes related to the "hot" music characteristic of "joints" in the neighborhood. The group codes of behavior affect not only language, but also dress. In some of these groups, a lack of direction is the chief problem and provides, according to Neumeyer (1961), the beginning of a "demoralizing" process that ultimately affects each member. A boy with no strong identification with his family becomes a member of a peer group and sees activities taking place that he then accepts and follows. Sometimes, boys are drafted into the group and are made to understand that they *must* be a part of it. In such instances, fear holds members within the group, but at the same time association in the group provides protection and security as long as the members adhere to its code; only under certain circumstances can an individual go against the group or endanger its welfare.

The makeup of such children's or adolescents' groups cannot be characterized by one type of individual, but some characteristics are common: Adolescent members have few ties with parents or home; they have a poverty-stricken background; they have made little progress in school, have been truant, and have been rejected as troublemakers by their school; they often are illiterate and unable to read.

Groups established early in the adolescent period usually last until early adulthood; they are usually composed of boys, although girls may also be members. Some groups have a following of girls who incite the boys to fight by telling stories about alleged insults so that one group will turn against another. Most of the girls are sexually promiscuous, but they usually do not have an important role nor are they treated considerately. The experiences of Sallie Ann provide an example.

> Sallie Ann's life with a gang began and ended in her fifteenth year. In describing the events after being taken to a medical center by a welfare worker, she told about her first sexual contacts. One evening as she was walking home after dark, three boys whom she knew offered her a ride. She refused, but they drove to the end of the block, turned, and came back, This time they pulled her into the car. Sallie Ann was forced into the back seat with two of the boys. They pulled down her slacks, but because they too were very young and inexperienced, Sallie Ann managed to make them think they had been successful sexually. According to Sallie Ann, however, the third boy had had previous sexual experience and she attributed her pregnancy to him. After this initial episode Sallie Ann had continued her relationships with various boys of the gang until several months of her pregnancy had passed. She had given little thought to the consequences of her behavior and the boys also gave little thought to her welfare. Ultimately, it was the organizations of society that had to assume responsibility for her care and that of her child.

In a juvenile gang, status is gained by showing "heart." "Heart" is a disregard for one's own welfare and the consequences of rash behavior; it is shown when a member is willing to make a grab for a policeman's pistol as the policeman stands on a street corner or it is demonstrated by firing a gun into a group of high school students coming out of school. Some of the behavior called "heart" is an effort to gain status within the group, even though the status gain actually requires irrational behavior.

The search for status can cause not only an individual to approach suicidal behavior, but also at times the gang. Some gang fights result in many members' being incapacitated with serious wounds, yet leaders will deliberately provoke other fights. At times, the leaders of some gangs continue until knifings are fatal to many, with arrests being made and the group being destroyed. As time passes, certain members seeking further adventure and excitement, turn to disturbed leaders with homicidal tendencies; these leaders, in order to maintain a precarious hold on the group, lead the gang into vicious and sadistic types of behavior.

Gang warfare—the street fight, or "rumble"—may occur with little provocation or provocation based on fantasy. Short and Strodtbeck (1963) suggest that gang leaders tend to precipitate aggressive acts toward those outside the group when their own status is threatened. Rumbles can occur over real or imagined infringements of the "turf," the location of the gang's region of operations. The turf range is defended by members from invasion because it represents an area of known security containing the few possessions or associations open to the gang members. When a truce is established, it is referred to as a "cool"; sometimes during such a cooling-off period, or truce, rival gang members are permitted to cross the turf belonging to other gangs.

Fights are not necessarily fair, and several boys may attack an isolated member of another gang. Preparation for gang warfare includes secret conferences and examination of the gang's cache of weapons. Many of the weapons used in the fight are manufactured by gang members. For example, a "zip gun" is made with rubber bands, which force a firing pin against a 22-caliber cartridge in a barrel often made from the hollow section of a car radio antenna. Car radio antennas are particularly useful weapons as spears and whips, although usually the gangs have a wide variety of weapons, including dynamite caps, bottles of acid, steel chains, pieces of lead pipe, tire irons, broken bottles, pistols, hatchets, bottles of gasoline with rag for a wick, and switchblade knives. Gang members preparing for a rumble will often wear leather jackets, which provide some protection against knives, lashes of car aerials, and injury from "stomping" with nail-studded boots.

Ordinarily, a rumble is preceded by drinking and a retelling of insults and injuries. The members are worked into a frenzy through alcohol and through incitement from the leaders. Once sufficiently aroused, they attack almost anyone whom they encounter. Alcohol is seen as an important part of the crime of gangs, with most members beginning to drink at the ages of eleven or twelve and continuing to increase intake until alcohol excesses become the rule. Usually, the beverages obtained are of low quality and many are manufactured by criminal organizations. The criminal activities of the gang are associated with drunkenness and even their activities for "a good time" end with most of the boys or girls being drunk. Shannon (1963) found that liquor offenses are on the increase, basing his conclusions on his study of types of referrals to probation officers.

Even more serious for the gang members is the use of "dope" and various kinds of drugs. A dope salesman, "pusher," is usually near the gangs—gang members are not unwilling to try dope, thus they are good prospects for dope salesmen. Most adolescents who use narcotics do not work, trying instead through thievery and "rackets" to make "bread," or money, to get the drugs. Some satisfaction is obtained by engaging in behavior for which society at large has some aversion, and the "kick" from narcotics is an act generally disapproved by society. The addict tries to be as different as possible from the standards set by society and this desire is reflected in his disdain for the values of cleanliness and order, particularly in clothing. He frequently turns to a type of music generally accepted by other drug users but which makes little sense to individuals outside. In as many ways as possible, the addict tries to defy the standards of a society that he sees as an enemy.

Psychosocial Factors in the Child's Behavior in Society

Factors causing some social behavior lie in the personal characteristics of individuals. Psychosocial factors—a combination of psychological and social factors, including emotional response patterns in interaction with others such as anxiety, fear, hostility, courage, affection, and euphoria—are associated with social conditions and groups, as illustrated in the following story.

Bill Daniels was a boy who turned to the group for satisfaction and emotional support because he felt misunderstood and because he received little emotional support from his family. His father was in the armed forces and was away from home much of the time. In addition, his mother worked, so Bill was left to find his own satisfaction and entertainment. He became interested in motorcycles and collected a great deal of technical information about various models, their performance, and comparative merits. He compiled extensive information and pictures in a large looseleaf book. Much of the information was obtained from manufacturers and a national motorcycle organization. This book was a valuable possession and Bill spent many hours studying its contents.

In school Bill had made excellent grades and there was on file in the principal's office an intelligence test score that indicated that his performance was in the very superior range. But because of the lack of family ties and his preoccupation with motorcycles, Bill's grades dropped, and he incurred the displeasure of a number of his teachers. On one occasion, a teacher discovered that he was looking at his motorcycle book instead of studying his lessons. In anger, she took the book from Bill and while he watched in agony, she tore the pages until the whole book was destroyed. This episode was a turning point in Bill's rebellion against the school. He began to stay away from school without his mother's knowledge so that he could spend time around a motorcycle repair shop. Gradually, he became acquainted with older boys who were members of a motorcycle gang.

At this time his mother became concerned and Bill was sent to a child guidance clinic. There Bill found much satisfaction, for it was one place where he was allowed to talk about his consuming interest in motorcycles. As the result of the acceptance and interest received at the clinic, Bill began to give more attention to his studies and his grades improved as well as his school attendance. But again the problems at school became a turning point in his life. One day not long before the end of the term, Bill happily pointed out to his teacher that again his grades were excellent. The teacher, however, reminded Bill of his earlier poor grades and told him that despite his improvement he would still fail to advance to the next grade. On receiving this reaction from the teacher, Bill lost all interest in his studies and he began staying away from school for days at a time.

Although Bill did not have a motorcycle, he was able to go with the boys by riding behind on someone's machine. He was accepted in the gang because of his enthusiasm and willingness to work on their motorcycles and because of his great interest in the machines.

As he continued to fail in school and as his mother's concern mounted because of his time spent with the motorcycle gang, she decided to buy

Bill a motorcycle, hoping that the satisfaction derived from owning one would lessen his obsession. Because of Bill's knowledge about motorcycles, he was certain of the kind he wanted, so his mother allowed him to choose a model from a foreign country. His status in the gang was now assured and he was the center of attention because of his new machine. However, Bill's happiness was short-lived as he had the misfortune to carelessly damage his machine in a hill-climb contest by failing to provide proper machine maintenance. The motor was damaged from lack of oil. With the help of the other boys, he got his machine back to town and the next day was told at the repair shop that it would take several hundred dollars to repair it because the parts would have to be ordered from the foreign country where it was made. His mother, who had made some sacrifices to get Bill the machine, was distraught and upset. She was unwilling to pay for its repair. At this point, Bill and his mother were even further apart. Bill now quit school entirely and took a job in the motorcycle repair shop to try to earn enough money to repair his machine, but the work was intermittent and he could not earn enough. In a few months, Bill was old enough to volunteer for military service, and at the same time remove himself from conflict with his mother.

Bill's difficulties in society were related to three social organizations: the school, the guidance clinic, and the motorcycle gang. Eventually, he turned to a fourth agency, a military organization. Each had an influence on his life and his feelings about himself and society. Neither the school nor the clinic, however, which seemed to work in Bill's life in opposition, were able to help Bill cope with his difficulties. Thus, Bill himself determined his own destiny by turning first to a gang and then to military service. It should be noted that Bill's difficulties were associated with lack of family unity and factors in his relationships with social organizations.

SOCIAL CONTROL OF THE CHILD

Society has established organizations to insure that children conform. These organizations have legal authority on which agents can base their actions. For example, sometimes society finds it necessary to replace parents; it may set up a joint system of substitute parents, such as is found in institutions, or may authorize individuals to act as parents. To deal with children's problems, society has thus established a complex organizational system at various governmental levels. One of the important systems is part of the legal system, the juvenile court.

Social Power through the Legal System

A child's difficulty in society is often seen as growing out of his need for care, protection, and training. About the turn of the century and as a result of the work of Jane Addams and Julia Lathrop of Hull House in Chicago, efforts were made to obtain separate legal facilities for children. Early facilities consisted mainly of judges designated to hear juvenile cases in a separate court, the "juvenile court." Perhaps the most important effect of the separation of the court was the influence on public thought: A child was not to be regarded or held as a criminal; instead, he was to receive help as do other neglected children. As juvenile courts have multiplied across the nation and have become a part of the American legal system, facilities have also been extended to include appropriate place of detention, record keeping, and medical and psychological services. Thus, advances have been made, but Tappan and Nicolle (1962) as well as others have raised constitutional questions about proceedings in juvenile courts. For example, for many years a child was not entitled to counsel or a jury trial, and "due process" was not followed. Today, the child is provided with counsel, and attempts are being made to give him the legal rights of an adult.

The dual activity of juvenile courts was recognized long ago—that punishment and reformation, protection, and education should be mixed (Sutherland, 1939). The recognition of the juvenile courts' duality in function (that is, its responsibility to enforce the law and at the same time to show concern about the protection of children) continues today. Consequent to the double role, a misunderstanding about functioning exists. Although court officials in dealing with the children and their families become aware of the circumstances that bring a child into conflict with society and thus are moved to take action other than punishment, the fact that the court officials are the representatives of the law makes it hard for the young wrongdoers and their parents to see that rehabilitation and protection are the intent of the court officials (Alexander, 1963).

The court, in addition to dealing with infractions of the law and the deviant behavior of children, must deal with children who are improperly cared for by parents, and it must also help social agencies to reach decisions about neglected children's welfare. Frequently, legal action must be part of the action taken to offset the forces that are influencing deviant children in such a way that their behavior cannot be tolerated by the community or society. Through legal means, the courts can influence community agencies to take action on the behalf of children, and they can avoid the necessity for the child to commit some legal offense to obtain agency intervention.

Social Systems of Control through Institutions

Courts can take children away from their parents and place them in institutions or in foster homes, even though the parents may wish to keep the children. According to Robison (1960), several views justify such action. One view holds that children actually are wards of the public and that parents have them in trust, that parents represent the state in custody of the children and owe responsibility to the state to guard their welfare. Another view holds that parents' rights to the child are natural and the state should not interfere. Still another view maintains that since society and its legal system exist for the benefit of individuals and since the child is a member of society, the child is entitled to public concern for his welfare —group standards for welfare thus are to be placed above the individual standards of the parents.

Hence, institutions have been developed to help society carry out its parental role. Such institutions are the legal outgrowths of a social philosophy reflecting the beliefs and values of society. Institutions for deviant children serve three purposes, with the three usually being intermixed: (1) the purpose of punishment (2) the purpose of protection, and (3) the purpose of education and rehabilitation. A number of different types of institutions for children varying from community to community and state to state arc in existence today. In general, the various institutional types are usually classified according to the problems of the child: Children accused of crimes may be sent to detention or reformatory institutions (primarily punishment); those without homes are placed in orphanages (protection); and those with physical defects, such as blindness, deafness, mental deficiency, and mental disorders, are sent to specific institutions (education and rehabilitation with an admixture, in some cases, of protection).

In spite of recent efforts to select institutions in accordance with the needs of the children they serve, some children are nevertheless placed in institutions because no other place can be found for them. Too often children with various types of physical handicaps are placed in institutions with purposes at variance to the best interests of the children, in spite of the fact that these children need special attention and care. The difficulties of placing children in the proper institution come not alone from the limitations of the institutions themselves, but also from the multiplicity of factors causing the child's problems. For example, a child may be guilty of delinquent behavior, be homeless, and have epilepsy—Shall he be punished for the delinquent behavior, be given a home, or be sent to a hospital for treatment of the epilespy?

Some children eventually are placed in institutions because they have not successfully adapted to foster homes after the community, recognizing the difficulty and the adverse social conditions under which they lived, took them from their own homes. Some are put directly into institutions because of incorrigible behavior or because they are believed to be incapable of establishing emotional relationships in foster homes. The incapability may be realistic enough, but if a child is incapable of benefiting from a foster home, he is certainly unlikely to become capable within the institution. If he is placed in an institution under such an assumption, the placement may be tantamount to considering him hopeless and the institution's role considered to be only one of custody. Consequently, an important part of society's treatment of children in conflict should be directed toward the provision of relationships to supplant those missing in the family. Frank Jackson's behavior in adolescence illustrates the need for understanding by institutional personnel.

> Frank had grown into adolescence with very satisfactory conduct in an institution for the blind. He had learned to find his way about the institution's buildings and could walk from the classrooms to the gymnasium, to the cafeteria, and over the campus without difficulty. His entrance into adolescence and his interest in girls, however, had not been observed by institutional personnel and no opportunities for heterosexual activities had been provided for him.

> One day, on the way back to his dormitory room after lunch, he stopped at the corner of a building and waited for a girl whose walk and voice he knew. As she approached him, he threw his arms about her and, as is customary with the blind, began to feel her face and body. She too was blind and, frightened by the sudden seizure, she screamed. Institutional officials came hurriedly, and Frank was locked in his room pending referral to another institution for psychological study. During the subsequent study, Frank was quite remorseful about his behavior, while at the same time revealing his desire for companionship with girls. The institution had, in fact, a program for its adolescents with social dances, but Frank had not been included. Upon being provided specific opportunities for association with girls, Frank continued his good record and satisfactory behavior at the institution.

A POINT OF VIEW

In the interaction between the child and social organizations, certain complex considerations are apparent: Should society punish the individual for deviant behavior and at the same time seek to assist him to achieve both satisfying and satisfactory behavior? Should society seek to provide institutions according to types of difficulty? The first consideration, which relates to punishment and assistance is complex, because a social philosophy is involved as well as psychological realities of human perception. The perception of the social agencies that seek to punish and control as well as assist is likely to be confusing, particularly to the adolescent. The adolescent's recognition of assistance may even be overshadowed by the perception of punishment. Institutions set up to serve children on the basis of type of difficulty or medical diagnosis alone have difficulty in functioning realistically, since separation of biological and cultural factors in causation and even in predictions about outcomes is involved. Too often, decisions are based on expedience.

The whole institutional complex of society needs to be carefully reexamined. Instead of several types of institutions, perhaps one type that is differentiated only enough in its services and opportunities to meet specific needs might be more desirable. In any event, much more support by society must be given to institutions and agencies so that they can experiment and develop new approaches to help children find a place in society.

REFERENCES

Aichhorn, A., 1935. *Wayward Youth*. New York: Viking.
Alexander, T., 1963. *Psychotherapy in Our Society*. Englewood Cliffs, N.J.: Prentice-Hall.
Andry, R. G., 1960. *Delinquency and Parental Pathology*. Springfield, Ill.: Charles C Thomas.
Bell, D., 1962. "Crime as an American Way of Life," in *The Sociology of Crime and Delinquency,* edited by M. E. Wolfgang, L. Savitz, and N. Johnston, pp. 213–225. New York: Wiley.
Bennett, I., 1960. *Delinquent and Neurotic Children.* New York: Basic Books.
Cohen, A. K., 1955. *Delinquent Boys*. New York: Free Press.
Durkheim, E., 1938. *The Rules of Sociological Method,* 8th ed. New York: Free Press.
Gregory, I., 1965. "Anterospective Data Following Childhood Loss of a Parent," *Archives of General Psychiatry,* **13**, 99–109.
Havighurst, R. J., et al., 1962. *Growing Up in River City*. New York: Wiley.

Healy, W., and A. F. Bronner, 1936. *New Light on Delinquency and Its Treatment.* New Haven, Conn.: Yale.

Kass, N., and M. Powell, 1964. "Degree of Conflict in Institutionalized Juvenile Delinquents within Certain Areas of Psychological Adjustment," *Journal of Social Psychology,* **62**, 273–284.

Lawton, M. J., and L. Sechrest, 1962. "Figure Drawing by Young Boys from Father-present and Father-absent Homes," *Journal of Clinical Psychology,* **18**, 304–305.

Merton, R. K., 1962. "Social Structure and Anomie," in *The Sociology of Crime and Delinquency,* edited by M. E. Wolfgang, L. Savitz, and N. Johnston, pp. 236–243. New York: Wiley.

Monahan, T. P., 1960. "Broken Homes by Age of Delinquent Children," *Journal of Social Psychology,* **51**, 387–397.

Monahan, T. P., 1962. "Family Status and Delinquency," in *The Sociology of Crime and Delinquency,* edited by M. E. Wolfgang, L. Savitz and N. Johnston, pp. 321–330. New York: Wiley.

Morris, R. R., 1964. "Female Delinquency and Relational Problems," *Social Forces,* **43**, 82–89.

Neumeyer, M. H., 1961. *Juvenile Delinquency in Modern Society,* 3d ed. Princeton, N.J.: Van Nostrand.

Park, R. E., E. W. Burgess, and R. D. McKenzie, 1925. *The City.* Chicago: The University of Chicago Press.

Robison, S. M., 1960. *Juvenile Delinquency.* New York: Holt.

Shannon, L. W., 1963. "Types and Patterns of Delinquency Referral in a Middle-Sized City," *British Journal of Criminology,* pp. 24–36.

Shaw, C. R., 1929. *Delinquency Areas.* Chicago: The University of Chicago Press.

Short, J. F., and F. I. Nye, 1958. "Extent of Unrecorded Juvenile Delinquency: Tentative Conclusions," *Journal of Criminal Law, Criminology, and Police Science,* **49**, 296–302.

Short, J. F., and F. L. Strodtbeck, 1963. "The Response of Gang Leaders to Status Threats: An Observation on Group Process and Delinquent Behavior," *American Journal of Sociology,* **68**, 571–579.

Short, J. F., R. A. Tennyson, and K. I. Howard, 1963. "Behavior Dimension of Gang Delinquency," *American Sociological Review,* **28**, 411–428.

Sterne, R. S., 1964. *Delinquent Conduct and Broken Homes.* New Haven, Conn.: College & University Press.

Sutherland, E. H., 1939. *Principles of Criminology,* 3d ed. Philadelphia: Lippincott.

Sykes, G. M., and D. Matza, 1962. "Techniques of Neutralization: A Theory of Delinquency," in *The Sociology of Crime and Delinquency,* edited by M. E. Wolfgang, L. Savitz, and N. Johnston, pp. 249–254. New York: Wiley.

Tappan, P. W., and I. Nicolle, 1962. "Juvenile Delinquents and Their Treatment," *Annals of the American Academy of Political and Social Science,* **339**, 157–170.

Whyte, W. F., 1955. *Street Corner Society.* Chicago: The University of Chicago Press.

[*thirteen*]

Developmental Disorders

Theoretically, it is possible to say that normality consists of those characteristics that most people have and that abnormality consists of characteristics at the extremes away from the center where most individuals fall. Defining disorder with such a concept, however, has a number of disadvantages. First, a mixture of characteristics typifies an individual with a disorder—some are normal and some are not. The second part of the problem of a statistical definition is related to the concept of culture. Since cultures vary to such a great extent, an individual's disorder theoretically might conflict with one culture, yet might not with another. Conceptualization of a behavior disorder as culturally disapproved behavior means that such a disorder is culturally bound and relative. Kardiner's (1945) study of the people on the island of Alor and the study by Gladwin and Sarason (1953) of the natives on the island of Truk indicated that the people in these groups, although not considered deviant within their own culture, can generally be described as pathological according to our standards of effective behavior. Thus, such a determination of abnormality on the basis of cultural standards is relative.

Another approach to the problem of definition and determination of disorder is based on the effectiveness of individual behavior to fulfill constitutional needs. Because certain behavior patterns are necessary for a biological being to function, certain behavioral characteristics should be evident in every culture. Disorder, therefore, could be considered to exist when an individual engages in behavior that prevents the fulfillment of his basic organic needs. For example, the need for specific nutrients, such as protein, is a basic organic need of human beings in every culture; therefore, disordered behavior could be defined as behavior that does not meet this need. Such a definition would not always be satisfactory, since cannibalism could fulfill protein need, but in most societies such behavior evokes social and emotional restrictions.

Another problem in trying to understand behavior disorder in children is the determination of extent of the child's responsibility for his disapproved behavior. Some scientists hold that adults, at least, do have some responsibility for their behavior (Alexander, 1963; Mowrer, 1960; Szasz, 1960). The view that an individual has a responsibility for his disorder is controversial, however. There is rather wide emphasis on the view that mental disorder is a "disease" and contracted without individual responsibility. Advocates of this view believe that "mental illness" should have no social stigma attached to it (Ausubel, 1961) and individuals should not be held responsible for its development. It is likely that controversy will be lessened as knowledge about human development increases.

FUNCTIONAL BEHAVIOR DISORDERS

The functional behavior disorders are those disorders which seem to develop from the interaction of the individual with the environment. The significance of biological factors, however, cannot be wholly discarded and thus separation of "cultural" and "biological" influences is just as difficult in defining "disorder" as it is in other aspects of human behavior (see Chapters 5 and 7). The preponderant etiology of the functional behavior disorders, nevertheless, seems to be in the interaction of the individual with the environment.

Theoretical and Empirical Approaches

Historically, a number of theoretical approaches have been used in the definition of the term *behavior disorders*. Although Freud, a physician, usually is identified with a biological, or organic, approach, in reality he emphasized a functional point of view. His emphasis on unconscious motivation, distortions of reality in everyday life, and the significance of dreams as related to experience indicates a functional viewpoint. And his explanation of the struggle and interaction among the three parts of the "personality," the id (primitive urges), the ego (the experiencing and reality-oriented part of one's personality), and the superego (the part of the personality concerned with prohibitions as rules related to the idea of conscience), is further indication of his functional view.

In the past, anthropologists also have adopted a functional viewpoint. Boas (1911), Mead (1939), Benedict (1934), Frank (1953), and Whiting (1953) have emphasized the importance of learning within a society and the possibility of abnormality growing out of experiences. These writers have held that culture and society sometimes value an unfavorable or unstable type of behavior and actually bring about abnormality or ineffective behavior.

Karen Horney (1936, 1945) approached the problem differently, although still developing a functional view. She explained that disorders result from the confusion between what a person wishes to be and his opportunity or ability to achieve his goals. Hence, the discrepancy and discordance between what a person wants to be and the reaching of an ideal is a basis for conflict and abnormal behavior.

Current views about the causes of the behavior disorders can be placed in categories according to four types of conditions: (1) conflict conditions, which result because expected standards are not met; (2) socioeconomic conditions, which have an unfavorable effect on various aspects of development; (3) institutional conditions, which prevent normal acquisition of experience; and (4) traumatic conditions, which impair psychological development by causing continuing anxiety.

Conflict Conditions. Conflict conditions are those associated with *overcontrol* by the parents of the child's life and behavior and parental *rejection* of the child. Normally in early childhood the child begins a trend toward physiological autonomy and, as the helplessness of infancy gradually passes, he begins some management of his life processes with the establishment of a rhythm of food intake, sleep, and elimination. Ordinarily, the child enjoys this beginning of independence as he struggles with his parents for increased autonomy. Psychoanalytic theory, particularly, emphasizes the importance for the individual of the developmental changes in the relationship to the parent. Some parents, without insight, continue to try to control the child as they did when he was younger.

The opposite kind of relationship is one in which the parents avoid emotional involvement with the child. Rejection can take many subtle and obscure forms. Freud's concept of "unconscious motivation" is most clearly seen perhaps in the overprotective attitude of some mothers, who basically reject their child and yet seek to prove to themselves and to others that this is not so. (As noted elsewhere, however, overprotection is not always caused by rejection.) Some mothers, for example, find the physical demands of infant care so great that they reject their children; others are so emotionally unstable that dealing with the child's physical needs and his body processes upsets them and they too reject their children; or if a child is unwanted, the mother's revulsion of feeling toward the discovery of pregnancy, the actual physical difficulties of pregnancy, delivery, and the early care of the child all may cause resentment that is unrealistically directed toward the child. In some instances, economic hardship and interference with careers or social life are factors.

Socioeconomic Conditions. This second type of cause of behavior disorder stems from the circumstances in which the child lives. If the living conditions of the family are adverse, they can often impair psychological well-being as well as physical development.

When a child from a poor environment first goes to school, he may discover that he does not have the proper school equipment or clothing and he may not even have money to buy food in the cafeteria. Such children respond to this deprivation in different ways—some withdraw, while others frequently fight or disobey school regulations. When a child from the lower socioeconomic class reaches adolescence, deprivation has already left its mark, and he has formed a pattern of characteristic reactions, most of which are disapproved by middle-class society. Some children, however, submit to the restrictions growing out of the conditions that their homes impose on them and will deny the desire for possessions. Others identify with groups of "delinquent gangs" and lay a foundation for an antisocial type of existence in adult life.

Institutional Conditions. The third cause of behavior disorder involves the lack of emotional relationships. Institutions can, by the very nature of their organization and operation, bring about disorder. A number of writers in the past, particularly Bakwin (1942), Ribble (1943, 1965 rev. ed.), and Rheingold (1956), have pointed to the importance of caring for an infant's emotional needs. Some infants respond to an institutional lack of the ordinary stimulation obtained by most children in mother-child interaction by refusing to eat. Others may develop a lack of awareness or response to events about them, causing some clinicians to diagnose their behavior as "infantile autism," a serious mental disorder characterized by avoidance of external reality. Investigators have discovered that institutionalized children who are cared for by one person are greatly benefited through such relationships. The strength of the relationship is demonstrated by the fact that the child often acquires even the food preferences of the particular person assigned (Rheingold, 1956).

Some infants, however, although placed in institutions where little individual attention is given them, do not suffer and seem to progress reasonably well (Orlansky, 1949; Pinneau, 1950, 1955). Apparently, children best cope with emotional deprivation if they have not had a close attachment with their mothers. Those infants who are suddenly separated after having had a close relationship find separation traumatic. Some individuals who have grown up in children's homes continue the same detached emotional relationships with their own children. The problems of Bill Kirk illustrate the long-term effect of institutional life.

> Bill was a child referred to a child guidance clinic because of lack of satisfactory progress in school, although the school authorities were certain that he had the capacity to progress normally. It was observed that although Bill played with other children in a satisfactory manner, he did not develop close friends among them. His teacher too encountered a diffidence that kept him aloof from her offer of friendship. Her pleasure or displeasure with him seemed to make little difference. In the clinic it was found that Bill's parents had spent all their lives in the same orphanage. On reaching adulthood, they left the institution and married soon after; but when children came, the parents gave them little more affection than they themselves had found in institutional life. The long-term effects of deprivation of emotional interchange were thus continued in Bill's life through the behavior of his parents.

Traumatic Conditions. The fourth type of condition causing disorder is that of traumatic experiences. The following two cases are examples of traumatic experience: One boy was frequently awakened at night by his drunken father who beat him severely without provocation; and a young girl was greatly upset because her father, when drinking, would make her and the entire family stand against the wall while he shot a pistol at their feet. The fear and anxiety engendered by these experiences lasted into adulthood.

Traumatic experiences of children in wartime take varying tolls in later development. It was found during World War II that children separated from their families in order to escape exposure to bombing fared less well than children who stayed with their parents, even though they were exposed to attack. Investigators at that time suggested that children survive trauma better when they can be with their parents (Freud and Burlingham, 1943).

Types of Functional Behavior Disorders

In recent years increasing interest in the disorders of children has caused many investigators to develop nomenclatures and systems of categories.

Examples of these categories are helpful in indicating a trend over the years. Jenkins and Glickman (1946) and Jenkins (1954) used five categories: inhibition, unsocialized or aggressive behavior, delinquency, schizoid personality, and brain disorders. O'Kelly and Muckler (1955) also developed five categories: behavior mechanisms, psychoneuroses, psychoses, psychosomatic disorders, and behavioral reactions associated with disease. Hutt and Gibby (1957) used a classification containing four categories: transient (temporary) disorders, adaptive disorders (habit or conduct problems), persistent and non-adaptive disorders (psychoses), and constitutional disorders. Thus, over the years different groupings with considerable similarity have been used.

Other investigators have used a more statistical than clinical approach in the construction of groupings. For example, Peterson (1961) used factor analysis to study judgments of problem behavior of children in kindergarten and elementary school. In analysis of teacher ratings of 58 clinically frequent problems of 831 children he found two factors: conduct problems (tendencies to express impulses against society in such behavior as "disobedience" and "fighting"), and personality problems (tendencies such as "withdrawal" and "dysphonic mood"). In a similar study Fanshel et al. (1963) used a multitrait approach to identify ten clusters of traits: physical aggression, sexual activity, intellectual activity, compulsive cleanliness, lethargy, self-destructiveness, unsociability, self-recklessness, and anxiety-neurotic tendencies. In a study of boys between the ages of seven and twelve, Patterson (1964), by using observation and information about referral, identified five factors: hyperactivity, withdrawn behavior, immaturity, aggressiveness, and anxiety.

A classification based on clinical and empirical data is used in the following discussion: aggression, withdrawal, negativism, and asocial behavior (Alexander, 1963). This grouping of categories is similar to that of Jenkins (1954) and Ross (1959). It is, however, as Kessler (1966) maintains, a "phenotypic" categorization. Nevertheless, the descriptions of the categories are the tests of the value of the groupings, and some organization is necessary to deal with the information currently available.

Aggression. Aggressive behavior is observed early in childhood or even in infancy if one includes the act of reaching out for and taking food or objects in order to fulfill needs. If a rattle is held so that a very young child cannot quite reach it or freely manipulate it, the child will display outward signs of aggressive action as he struggles to obtain it. Or, if a very young child is being fed and food is delayed or withheld from him, he often will struggle violently to obtain it. Aggressive behavior, of course, is a part of life and is necessary for survival as an organism fulfills its need for food and protection. In one sense, an animal's taking the life of another for food is aggression, but it is also a part of the life cycle on earth. A child searches for fulfillment of needs and tries to overcome obstacles—unless he asserts himself and pushes toward achievement, he will be unable to fulfill his needs or meet the expectations of those about him. The searching for and overcoming of obstacles is necessary in any culture.

Parental teaching about proper and improper forms of aggression begins very early. If an infant, even in play, deliberately knocks the spoonful of food from the mother's hand to the floor, his mother will scold or show her disapproval. If a child reaches for forbidden objects in his home and endangers these objects, she also will likely scold or perhaps punish him. If he in anger strikes the mother or another member of the family, punishment probably will be his lot.

However, action that is disapproved aggression in one culture or society, may be approved in another. Many societies disapprove of internal aggressive behavior, but approve of aggression against those without because security for individuals rests upon collective protection. Thus, if aggression is used as a category in psychopathology, then it must be said to be abnormal only in certain cultures, in certain situations, and in certain individuals. Such qualification is necessary, because in some social roles aggression is acceptable, while in other social roles the same behavior is disapproved.

Not only are there variations in delineation of approved aggression in cultural and social roles, but variations are also found between social classes.

Lloyd Simmons, at the age of three, was taken to a nursery school by his middle-class mother. The mother was anxious that Lloyd make a good impression on the nursery school teachers. She wanted it to be clear to everyone that she had not encouraged dependence and that her son was quite able to manage on his own in this new situation. She then told Lloyd good-bye, turned her back, walked from the play yard to her car, and drove away. Lloyd sat on the edge of the sandpile watching two other children digging together. The other children had had previous nursery school experience and they dug in the sand with evident enjoyment in cooperative endeavor. They ignored Lloyd. Lloyd looked around him, but no teacher immediately came to him and no other children seemed to notice him. He sat for some time watching without receiving any response from others. A sand shovel with a long wooden handle lay nearby. In a moment of desperation, Lloyd picked up the shovel, raised it above his head, and brought it down with considerable force on the head of one of the children digging near him. As one might expect, he was immediately the center of attention; both the children pointed to him, crying, and with tears flowing, they blamed him for their unhappiness. Two teachers immediately ran to ascertain the cause of the outburst. Now no longer alone, he received longed for attention both from teachers and other children.

Middle-class parents generally disapprove of their sons' fighting, yet they also expect them to "take their part." In general, lower-class children are more often encouraged to take their part by fighting than are middle-class children; and a lower-class child often grows up in an environment where aggressive acts of verbal and bodily attack are sanctioned.

Harold Semler, a boy from the lower socioeconomic class, was continually in trouble at school. No sooner would he go out to the playground, than a fight ensued. The teacher would separate Harold from the other participant and take both boys to the principal's office. Harold many times was punished by spanking in the principal's office and threatened with expulsion. His parents had been called repeatedly to the school in regard to his fighting. At a child guidance clinic, it was observed that Harold usually began fights with boys with whom he was sure to win. He was large for his age, and the boys in his room were ones with whom he could successfully cope. Harold's parents revealed that they viewed his problem as one in which he was continually provoked. They saw him in the main as "only taking his part." At the clinic, it was discovered that there was much tension in the family and that Harold's parents fought frequently with physical blows.

Perhaps there are fewer opportunities for aggressive behavior in nursery school children, but as children grow older it is likely that more social interchange and opportunity for aggression occurs. Bildfell and Douglas (1965) found in a study of boys between six and twelve years of age that changes in aggression occurred. Often children in middle childhood are concerned with their own drives and needs and are relatively unconcerned about the needs of others. One study of aggression of subjects in late adolescence and early adulthood indicated that males showed more aggression against males than against females, but sex was not as important in aggressive behavior for females as it was for males. Sex differences were thus apparent both in the aggressor and the recipient of the aggression (Buss, 1963).

Models apparently influence sex differences in aggression. Bandura and Kupers (1964) in a study of children's behavior compared to models found that patterns of self-reinforcement closely matched their models and that adults seemed to provide more powerful modeling stimuli than did the children's peers. Hicks (1965) found that the male peer had the most immediate influence on aggressive behavior, but that the adult male had the most lasting effect.

The problem for the child in our society is to fulfill needs and to maintain his own personal integrity and safety within a framework of rules and expectations from the outside. As he grows older, he must learn to continue to fulfill his needs within a satisfactory concept about himself as a person with rights, having at the same time sympathy and concern for others.

Dealing with aggression by punishment is not always successful. Lefkowitz et al. (1963) found that the extent of physical punishment by parents tended to be associated with amounts of aggressive behavior. Acting on such findings, Redl and Wineman (1965), in their residential treatment program for aggressive children, sought to help their children to develop self-control so that frustration and failure would not produce unsocialized responses.

Withdrawal. Withdrawal is a frequent reaction to stress and difficulty in the environment and is the opposite of aggression. It is seen, of course, in infancy when a child removes his hand from a painful stimulus, such as a hot object. During development, certain situations bring about parental disapproval, and in the face of parental threat or scolding undue withdrawal may begin. In adolescence, withdrawal is sometimes a group affair that enables adolescents to get away from society with its demands and conflicts; thus, they turn to organizations, cliques, gangs, and informal gatherings which provide havens for those who share similar feelings.

The development of withdrawal behavior may be deliberately brought about by parents through the use of anxiety and fear in the child's training (Bandura and Walters, 1959), not only in our society, but also in primitive societies. Hopi Indian children, for example, are introduced in infancy to an education process, the main purpose of which is to instill fear. They are taught about Soyoko, a spirit who usually appears once a year to children who do not behave according to the parents' and family members' wishes (Eggan, 1953). The creation of such spirits frightens the Hopi children and enables the parents to force them into desired behavior. A parallel is found in our society when mothers try to frighten their children into conformity by using the "bogy man." The child is told that if he goes into a certain room or if he opens the lid of a box that this spirit will "get him" or will "hurt him." Through the teaching about frightening figures, the foundations are laid for the child's withdrawal from and avoidance of certain kinds of situations and behavior. Sometimes children learn too well and childish fears become phobias, causing in adulthood the fear of certain places, "germs," and the like.

As with aggression, it is not possible to condemn all withdrawal behavior, since aspects of it are taught and approved by society. For example, certain religious orders emphasize the importance and benefit of withdrawal from society. And the scholar may isolate himself from his fellows in order to try to understand the mysteries of some subject.

There are, of course, elements in everyone's life in which withdrawal and being alone is in evidence. Moustakas (1961) thinks that there is some value in withdrawal and isolation, since being alone may effect a clearer perception of the meaning of closeness to others. Moustakas sees some people as deliberately seeking isolation and withdrawal in order to find a meaning for their own existence. Admiral Byrd (1938), in his book *Alone,* gave such a reason for seeking isolation in Antarctica.

New meanings and perceptions are possibly obtained through isolation and withdrawal. However, withdrawal is the antithesis of human need fulfillment. Withdrawal by the disordered person is, in reality, an unhappy submitting to failure rather than an opportunity for introspection or of finding satisfaction. It often becomes a serious type of disorder, despite the fact that such behavior is less threatening to society than that of the aggressive and destructive person. Withdrawn behavior leads to depression, a sense of futility, and to emotional isolation. Warning signs of withdrawal should be recognized before the condition becomes severe, since an adolescent, for example, who withdraws and refuses to have interest in anything or anyone is very difficult to help.

Although withdrawal is an essential category in abnormal child behavior, it is encountered less frequently than aggressive behavior. More referrals to child guidance clinics are made because of aggressive behavior than withdrawn behavior (Gilbert, 1957). However, such findings that more aggressive children are referred for psychotherapy may be influenced by the fact that aggression, at least initially, is more disturbing to the parents than withdrawal.

Negativism. The child who acts in opposition to efforts to guide or direct him, is said to be negativistic; and although negativism is characteristic of most children, it can become extreme and continue into adult life. A person having difficulty in finding an acceptable social role may find satisfaction in thwarting the goals of other individuals or groups. Negativism, thus, is to some extent a mechanism to preserve integrity and to fulfill psychological needs for autonomy and social recognition. It is, however, not always adaptive. For example, in order to assert his rights, a child may refuse food or refuse to go to the toilet, although both refusals will likely bring discomfort.

While negativism may be most pronounced when the child reaches the age of four or five, it can occur throughout childhood in association with problems of food intake and bowel and bladder functioning. Some children who have certain diseases requiring continuing care may rebel against the strict regimen and actually endanger their lives by refusing to cooperate. If great care is not taken, the routine and rigid requirements developed in order to safeguard the child's well-being may become such a burden that the child feels he is forced to rebel even though it is dangerous. For example, negativistic behavior in diabetic children is a serious problem, because the disease allows little flexibility in its management.

> Nine-year-old Nicholas G. found it necessary to rebel against the regimen required for care of his diabetes. Early in his life when his mother gave him insulin injections, he participated in the management of the disease with every outward sign of cooperation. As he grew older, however, he began to protest the injections and complained to his mother that his brothers and sisters did not have to have them. A struggle ensued between Nicholas and his parents, and his father had to hold him tightly for each injection. This method solved the problem for only a little while, since Nicholas grew quite strong and the parents then could no longer enforce their demands. If Nicholas did not receive the injections, however, he was in danger of shock. The parents were greatly frightened by his refusal, but Nicholas adamantly refused to submit to the injections, although his mother patiently waited for long periods of time for his acquiescence. In addition to the conflict with Nicholas, the parents themselves became upset and angry at each other. Each parent blamed the other, and Nicholas blamed both of them. Trying to overcome the child's negativism by force only made matters worse. Solution for the problem was sought from a clinic, but the course of treatment was long and hazardous.

Negativism begins with the child's struggle for physiological autonomy and his opposition to the parents' effort to control his body processes. It develops when a child feels controlled to the point that he feels he must assert himself despite the consequences. To some extent negativism cannot be avoided—the child must give up certain rights in order to receive the benefits of being part of society. Relinquishing autonomy for other benefits is not an easy concept to acquire, and even with patient teaching some negativism inevitably develops.

Asocial Behavior. This category of functional behavior disorders is characterized by an individual's oppositon to the rules and standards of society. Such behavior could also be described appropriately as aggressive or negativistic, but the asocial categorization implies attack on society itself. It is behavior that is disapproved by the culture and directly threatens society's values. As with other types of behavior, it is difficult to draw a sharp line between behavior that is abnormal and that which is normal. Some people who have failed to conform to society's mandates have later been revered as people of vision and wisdom.

Asocial behavior more frequently occurs in families in the lower socio-economic class where the parents hold in low esteem the value system of the larger culture. For example, some lower-class parents view stealing as acceptable behavior as long as one is not caught. Parents who have this view for their children provide the beginning for asocial behavior, which later becomes much more in evidence. Individuals who find satisfaction in destroying property or life are considered abnormal, and such individuals are feared by other members of society since control of them can be maintained only by society's agents.

> Henry Brink was an asocial individual. A great deal of his behavior was not in keeping with society's customs (Alexander, 1963). He engaged in persistent thievery, showed little respect for the property of others, and at times engaged in destruction with no apparent purpose. In adolescence, he engaged in homosexual relationships with peers as well as with older men. Few aspects of Henry's life and behavior were in keeping with the expectations of middle-class people. Since his mother and father provided him with little or no affection, Henry saw little reason to conform to the wishes of them or others. He acted to a great extent on impulse and only turned from his own desires to avoid punishment. Thus, much of his behavior was *against* society.

Symptoms of Functional Behavior Disorders

In association with the fundamental behavioral problems just discussed (aggression, withdrawal, negativism, and asocial behavior), many symptoms occur; but, in general, they can be reduced to three primary categories of fear, language and speech difficulties, and somatic or body symptoms.

Symptoms within the categories occur in varying degrees of intensity and significance.

Fear. As a symptom of disorder, fear can be divided into two types: specific fear and generalized fear. If a child is frightened by a large dog rushing fiercely toward him, he must mobilize his strength in an effort to run away or defend himself. Emotion under these conditions is described as specific fear. In such an instance, certain physiological changes take place and his physical resources are at their best; but with the avoidance of the threat, the conditions return to normal and the physiological conditions previously occurring subside.

Fear of a generalized nature is usually called "anxiety," and this is distinguished from specific fear in that the individual having generalized fears is unable to explain the source of his fears. In generalized anxiety, a person may feel the necessity for taking some action, but because the cause of his anxiety is unclear, he is uncertain as to what type of action will be effective.

Anxiety represents a complex condition within an individual, since it is linked not only to external events but also to internal events in association with physiological changes which prepare the individual to fight or to flee. Anxiety can bring significant changes in heart rate, respiration, circulation, blood pressure, sensation, digestion, excretion, metabolism, and endocrine-gland secretion. Thus, severe anxiety can cause profound alterations in constitutional functioning; if it is prolonged, the results may be lethal.

Anxiety occurs early in development. Tennes and Lampl (1964) studied 19 infants between the ages of three and twenty-three months with observations of the infants and interviews with mothers. These investigators were particularly interested in fear of a stranger and anxiety about separation evoked by absence of the mother. They found that females had a higher level of stranger anxiety and males had a higher level of separation anxiety.

To some extent, anxiety can be adaptive in that a child concerned about an examination will make considerable effort at preparation in order to meet the threat successfully. Penny (1965) in a study of 178 children in the middle grades found that low anxiety was associated with a high degree of curiosity. In a study of academic progress of children in relation to intelligence and motivation, Hart (1964) thought that when most stress and anxiety was removed, little learning took place. He concluded that achievement of success, however, should be within the capability of children upon expenditure of reasonable effort.

Anxiety is an especially important symptom in all of the behavior disorders. Living requires a constant effort to obtain and maintain equilibrium by meeting physiological and psychological needs. Accordingly, if there is conflict, frustration and interference with the fulfillment of needs, or if inadequacies become apparent to the individual, fear and anxiety result. Although man has considerable potentiality for coping with fear and anxiety and possesses great capacity for overcoming obstacles to the procurement of food and shelter, he has also a wider opportunity for development of anxiety because his security rests on the meeting of complicated emotional and social needs—opportunities for affection, esteem, and achievement. Although anxiety is universal, it is nevertheless the path which leads to serious mental disorder.

Language and Speech Difficulties.   Difficulties in language and speech are related to the behavior disorders because language is the means through which an individual comes to understand his world. Disability in communication deprives the individual of needed experience and also blocks him in procuring things he wants. A child with a language or speech handicap has difficulty in asking for food, for help in solving a problem, or for affection and comfort. Furthermore, he has difficulty showing his ability and experience in play with others, and he is unable to demonstrate knowledge and competence in school.

Somatic, or Body Symptoms.   These symptoms of behavior disorder are numerous and widespread. Only a few of these will be discussed here. Training in regard to bowel and bladder control begins early in our culture, and this experience has varying degrees of significance according to the kind of training, attitudes, and emotions associated with it. Control is taught in a benign manner by some parents, while the training by others is traumatic. Many children learn control easily and without difficulty from siblings, and the learning is hardly noticed by child or parents. For other children, bowel and bladder training becomes a basis for a serious struggle between child and parents.

Some rejecting parents tie their child to a toilet chair and leave him for long periods; others punish their child severely for accidents or failure to achieve control. Some parents subtly reject their child because he does not attain satisfactory control. Because of the opportunity for difficulty, it is not surprising that problems with bowel and bladder control continue into later developmental periods. Some children learn to control the emptying of the bladder during the daytime but are unable to achieve control at night (nocturnal enuresis). Some clinicians believe that because parents cannot realistically blame the child for wetting the bed after he is asleep, the child uses this behavior to strike back at parents against whom he feels hostility. Similarly, difficulties in reference to bowel control are explained because the child, by refusing to go to the toilet, can upset his parents.

Psychophysiological Disorders

Psychophysiological disorders are those on the border between essentially physiological problems and those that stem primarily from interaction with the environment. Perceptual experience involving the frontal lobes of the brain, the cortex, the thalamus and the hypothalamus can, through connections with the autonomic nervous system, affect the functioning of organs in the viscera. For example, stimulation of specific areas of the frontal lobes will initiate secretion of gastric juice and gastrointestinal activity. Emotion involving response in the cortex affects the frontal areas of the cortex and then, through thalamic and hypothalamic activity, ultimately affects the viscera. This sequence, accordingly, can lead to significant body changes.

The autonomic nervous system supplies neural connections to the viscera, and the term *autonomic* means that the system has some independent function. When an individual perceives a situation as an emergency or as holding some threat, the heart rate increases, the adrenal glands are activated, and adrenalin and stored sugar are released into the bloodstream. Also, muscle tone increases, digestion slows or stops, and perspiration increases. All of these conditions prepare the individual for physical action. Hence, certain perceptions can continue "stirred-up" body states.

As stress increases, the organism becomes less efficient and at high levels of anxiety, organized and efficient behavior deteriorates. If the emotional state of tension is maintained at a high intensity for a considerable time, then the autonomic system will become disorganized as do the psychological processes. Selye's studies (1953) led him to believe that in extreme emotional states, certain hormones—ACTH and the corticoids—become more plentiful; as a result of these excessive secretions, pathological changes in the brain and other organs take place. Such changes cause edema, hemorrhages, a rise in intracranial pressure, epileptoid seizures, mental confusion, depression, and even unconsciousness. Many other conditions come about as a result of chronically excited states and physical ailments may stem directly from them.

Psychophysiological disorders can be related to allergic conditions, although the place of allergies in reference to psychological problems is not yet completely understood (Glaser, 1956). Such disorders also can involve the musculoskeletal portions of the body, causing cramps and various types of pain; they can involve the respiratory system, causing bronchitis, sinusitis, and asthma; they can involve cardiovascular reactions, including excessive heart rate, headaches, and elevated blood pressure; and even the blood and lymph systems may be involved.

A more frequent psychophysiological disorder is one involving the gastrointestinal tract and includes such conditions as ulcerative colitis, gastritis, constipation, and duodenal ulcers. Ulcerative colitis, a distressing and sometimes fatal disease, most often occurs in later childhood and adolescence (Gallagher, 1960). The genitourinary system may also be affected by stress and cause symptoms of painful urination and menstrual disturbance. Psychophysiological disorders may involve the endocrine gland system, particularly the thyroid gland with associated glandular and metabolic disorders. Even the nervous system may be affected with resulting fatigue, pains, or perhaps convulsive episodes. The sense organs, too, are susceptible with such conditions as inflammation of the eyes, impaired vision, hearing defect, and the like.

An outstanding characteristic of all of these disorders is exacerbation (the reappearance of the symptoms) and remission (disappearance of the symptoms) with particular periods of stress. Conditions may ultimately be incapacitating or fatal.

The dire effects of disordered parent-child relationships are sometimes well illustrated in the psychophysiological disorders. Such deleterious and slow-moving psychological and physiological processes often cover a span of years, and parents do not deal with the problem until serious illness is recognized. Sometimes, even the recognition of the severity of the problem is attained only with the aid of a physician. The child, of course, is unable to see the significance of his condition. Charles illustrates the devastating effects of severe parent-child discord.

> Charles' parents were rigid and strict, and they were quite concerned that their son learn early to meet their expectations. By the time Charles was 2½ years old, his parents demanded that he take care of both urination and bowel actions himself. At this age, however, Charles could not control urination at night, and his parents became annoyed. They began to scold and punish him physically. He became both fearful and hostile, but he could not express his hostility and anger openly at his parents. However, he did continue to wet the bed. By the time he was four, Charles extended his rebellion to a refusal to have bowel movements and would not go to the toilet at all. Whether his feelings were primarily hostility or primarily anxiety is unknown, of course,

but he did not go to the toilet for extended periods of time. As time passsed, he developed an intestinal impaction. The parents, not understanding the problem, punished him by spanking and scolding as they had done since his early life. As they dealt with the bowel problem, they were not aware of the dire condition of his urinary system. His bladder had become distended and it was losing its elasticity and power for muscular contraction. Urine had backed into the ureters and had caused them to enlarge. And, even more seriously, infection was present in the entire urinary system. The parents eventually became more concerned about his condition and took him to a physician who immediately understood the gravity of the child's condition.

With dismay the parents learned that Charles' life was indeed threatened. Both the functioning and anatomical condition of the urinary and intestinal systems were impaired to the point that serious surgery was necessary for both systems. Surgery at best will be palliative, and if Charles lives, he faces partial invalidism for the rest of his life. Thus, while Charles fought for autonomy, it may have cost him his life; and while the parents insisted on conformity, their efforts may cost them their son.

Why some persons have particular kinds of body difficulties as a result of stress is not entirely clear. Perhaps there is some genetically based predisposition in body structure, disease, or past trauma that has made one person's body more susceptible to the effects of stress. Of course, life represents a struggle to fulfill needs and to meet environmental demands. Psychophysiological disorders are those in which psychological stress has some unfavorable effect on the constitution of the individual, with the effects in some individuals becoming so severe that they are lethal.

The most serious psychological source of stress in children is the lack of basic security within themselves concerning their place in the parents' affection. Perhaps the most damaging kind of relationship occurs when the rejection is subtle and incompletely understood by the child and when there are protestations by the parents of affection without the existence of a close emotional bond.

CONSTITUTIONAL BEHAVIOR DISORDERS

An important approach to the understanding of developmental disorders is the investigation of the significance of constitutional factors. The term *constitution* is used to cover the summation of the physical characteristics of the individual. While developmental disorders, as has been emphasized, cannot be attributed to one type of factor alone, an individual's difficulty, nevertheless, can come primarily from organic defect or malfunction.

In the early part of the twentieth century, Emil Kraepelin (1907), a German psychiatrist, emphasized the relationship between organic conditions and behavior. His effort to classify mental disorders into a systematic pattern similar to other diseases provided the beginning for the organization of the rapidly growing knowledge about psychopathology.

The justification for viewing behavior disorders from an organic point of view is not without clinical and even experimental support. In certain studies, behavior of an individual has been observed to be disordered, bizarre, and distinctly abnormal; upon his death, examination of the brain confirmed that there was indeed abnormal structure. (The reverse, however, has also been found.) Organic approaches to psychopathology and the behavior disorders are currently bringing about much research in the area of virus diseases, bacteriology, biochemistry, anatomical aberrations of the central nervous system, and genetics.

Theoretical and Empirical Approaches

Theoretical approaches to the understanding of the role of constitutional factors in behavior disorders have been made by relating structural body characteristics, or type, to behavior and by relating certain genetic characteristics to behavior. Morphological, or structural, characteristics as related to behavior have been influenced by certain investigations of body type (Kretschmer, 1926; Sheldon, 1940, 1942). The role of heredity in bringing about psychopathology is still unclear. Some knowledge about genetic influences on behavior has been gained through studies of twins. Apparently, mental disorders occur more frequently in identical twins and there is, of course, evidence of the identical genetic factors. But even though there is similarity of inheritance, there still is also the possibility of a similarity of an unfavorable environment. Early studies of Galton (1914), Goddard (1914), and others, while of much interest, are presently viewed as being inconclusive, and even the later studies of twins by Newman et al. (1937) and Kallmann (1938, 1953) do not provide identification of specific genetic influences.

New knowledge about inherited defects of structure of the central nervous system is being acquired. Hereditary factors are certainly of consequence in behavior disorders, but current attention is directed primarily to inheritance of specific structural defects. For example, in the disease of phenylketonuria, the child inherits a metabolic defect that prevents the utilization of an amino acid. This defect may result in brain damage and ultimately in behavioral impairment. Hence, mental disorder is not directly inherited as a specific factor of mental dysfunction, but rather comes from a specific metabolic defect.

Since many causative factors exist that can alter development prenatally but subsequent to fertilization, it is not always known whether defects developed subsequent to the union of the germ cells or whether the defects actually were carried as genetic traits. Accordingly the view is changing from seeing mental disorder (for example schizophrenia) as an inherited disease to the view that a search should be made for the origin of a possible structural or physiological defect as factors of significance in etiology.

Types of Constitutional Behavior Disorders

Generally, constitutional stress, damage to the body, or alteration of the physiology and structure of the individual makes interaction with the environment more difficult. The well-integrated and stable individual who has grown up in a favorable environment can withstand constitutional stress, however, much better than one who has not had favorable experience. This fact is an important principle in dealing with problems of behavior, since, regardless of the particular stress, an individual can deal with it more effectively and with greater resistance to permanent alteration if he has had adequate and satisfactory experience during his developmental years.

Some bodily compensation may take place or the body may make a recovery so that under favorable conditions there is no longer impairment. But in some instances compensation or overcoming of the difficulty is limited. Regenerative powers of the brain, for example, are limited.

Some of the symptoms of neuropathology and aberrations of the brain are as follows: loss of memory; difficulties in comprehension; impaired judgment; lack of originality; difficulty in learning new responses in strange situations; irritability; inattentiveness; limited curiosity; emotional instability; an apparent lack of deep feeling; impaired language facility and speech defects; a tendency for repetitive arm, head, or body movements; and repetitive vocalization. More abstract qualities of impairment are exemplified by an insensitiveness to the concerns and desires of others, as well as a tendency toward what appears to be deliberate nonconformity. A variability in behavior may occur so that the child at one point can accomplish and understand required behavior and at another point the very same behavior that was apparently learned does not take place.

Probably all of these kinds of behavior can be observed in those with unimpaired brains, however. Thus, careful clinical investigations are necessary in order to determine etiology.

Acute traumatic conditions affecting the brain often are reversible and the individual may recover from their effects. For example, some conditions involving metabolic upset in the brain result from temporary nutritional inadequacies, such as deprivation of water, protein, and various salts. Upon adequate medical treatment and provision of the appropriate nutrients, the individual recovers, with lasting effects depending upon the actual destruction of nerve cells in significant numbers. *Chronic conditions* are those in which the damaging conditions last over long periods of time and involve destruction of nerve cells.

Some types of constitutional disorders begin before birth. Diseases of the brain may come about through hereditary transmission, through conditions occurring *in utero* (called "congenital factors") or through conditions at birth (referred to as "perinatal factors"), or through postnatal factors (causes occurring subsequent to birth).

Malformations and morphological aberrations of the brain may result from a number of hereditary causes, such as chromosomal variation. For example, research findings now indicate that an abnormal number of chromosomes are found in children with Down's disease, or mongolism. Such children have an extra chromosome, giving them 47, while normal children have 46 (Lejeune and Turpin, 1962). Some characteristics resulting from such abnormal inheritance are epicanthal folds, thickened tongue, stubby fingers, heart defects, impaired functioning of the brain, and susceptibility to infection of the upper respiratory tract.

Infections contracted by the mother may harm the embryo or fetus. A severe disease, such as poliomyelitis, would likely affect the developing infant, but even mild virus infections, such as Asian flu, can be harmful. The deleterious effect of the virus of rubella, or German measles, is particularly harmful at certain stages of prenatal development. This disease is difficult to diagnose and other factors may be operating so that attributing later defects to the disease is not always possible (Holt et al., 1961). Another infectious disease, which at times causes defect in the child *in utero,* is toxoplasmosis (Dekaban, 1959). In adults, this disease, caused by protozoa, is not usually severe, being characterized only by fever and enlargement of the lymph nodes; however, infection during pregnancy can lead to maldevelopment or death of the fetus. Spread of this disease is not completely understood, but it may be contracted from domestic and wild animals or through inadequately cooked meat, possibly pork.

Another source of difficulty is impairment resulting from serums, drugs, and toxic agents. Damage to the developing child's brain may be caused by the mother's intoxication from carbon monoxide, lead, arsenic, quinine, and the like. Blood incompatibility between mother and developing child can have a toxic effect on the developing embryo or fetus (Dekaban, 1959). If there is such blood-type incompatibility, the mother develops antibodies, which in some instances pass through the placenta into the body of the fetus, causing brain impairment. For example, the Rh factor in the blood sometimes is a basis for difficulty, the effect of this incompatibility resulting in severe jaundice and a yellow staining of brain tissue. Even blood-type differences of A, B, and O have had similar deleterious effects. Today, it is possible to obviate some of the difficulties of blood-type incompatibility by blood transfusions to the infant at birth, and new methods to prevent formation of antibodies are being developed. Now many factors in causing aberrations are incompletely understood and many influences are only suspected as causative factors in many of the central nervous system aberrations.

Some types of constitutional behavior disorders are caused *during or after birth*. Subsequent to embryonic and fetal development, complications of labor and delivery can result in damage to the brain. Lesions in the brain can result from tears of the meninges (membranes), ruptured blood vessels, and from destruction of brain tissue or nerve cells. Hemorrhage sometimes occurs at birth, and if considerable bleeding results more extreme effects are recognizable only later after neurological examination. The cells of the brain are particularly sensitive to oxygen deprivation, and the degree of impairment exists in proportion to deprivation (Dunphy and Pessin, 1962; Graham et al., 1957).

As in prenatal development, infections can also affect the child subsequent to birth. One such infection is encephalitis, an inflammation of the brain. Causes of encephalitis can include bacteria, fungus, syphilis, viruses, and vaccines (Dekaban, 1959). The symptoms of this disease are frequently poorly defined and the causes are often unaccountable. Permanent damage to the brain often results in impairment of the parts controlling the organ systems and body functions.

A number of physiological disorders associated with the metabolic processes (including both carbohydrate and protein metabolism) can affect the well-being of the brain. For example, there is phenylketonuria, a metabolic disorder, which develops subsequent to birth. At birth, the infant's physiology is normal, but his body is unable to utilize phenylalanine, an amino acid (Zellweger, 1961). Because of the lack of the body's capacity to deal with this protein constituent, interference occurs in all of the cell processes, particularly in the brain cells. If an early diagnosis of the disease is made, a diet low in phenylalanine may avoid damage to the brain; consequently, the age of diagnosis is gradually being pushed back so that the problem can be discovered in early infancy before extensive damage results. However, the condition presents serious problems to parents, as the disease is hereditary and more than one child in the family may be affected (Holt et al., 1961; Lowe and Auerbach, 1964).

Important symptoms of abnormal neurological conditions are found in the occurrence of convulsions. The convulsive disorders are really symptoms and manifestations of some brain pathology. Convulsive disorders, accordingly, do not constitute a diagnostic entity but are symptomatic of abnormal physiological or structural conditions in the brain (Ellingson, 1954). There are two general types of convulsive disorders: severe or "grand mal," seizures (mass muscular contractions usually of the entire body, often including some disorientation and partial or complete loss of consciousness) and, "petit mal" seizures of short duration, which affect only parts of the body, without unconsciousness. Some convulsive disorders, although frequently accompanying the occurrence of tumors, scars, abscesses, infections, or mechanical damage to the brain, occur with no known cause and these are called "idiopathic disorders."

The effect of convulsive disorders on general behavior is not entirely clear. Variability and abnormal behavior cannot be explained by the existence of the convulsive disorders, as external factors surrounding the child can cause varying degrees of anxiety stemming from the response of others to him or the precautions taken in his behalf.

Considerable success is now possible in the treatment of the convulsive disorders and a number of drugs control seizures to the extent that some children are completely relieved (Baird, 1964; Holt et al., 1961). Some children outgrow the difficulty and, after remaining on medication without symptoms for some time, the medication can be discontinued without recurrence of the seizures. With the rapid development of various types of drugs designed to influence the functioning of the central nervous system and brain, it is likely that new forms of drugs will be increasingly useful with the convulsive disorders.

Severe Mental Disorders

Much controversy has existed in the past about the etiology of the severe mental disorders, on the basis of conflict between the views that psychoses exist only in relationship to structural and physiological causes and that they are functional. Severe mental disorders in children seem to be more frequently associated with some physiological condition discovered often after careful investigation. Children seem to survive without extreme mental disorder despite considerable abuse if constitutions are relatively intact. But if adverse constitutional factors in the central nervous system occur as well, severe disorders are more likely to result.

It is rare that a severe disorder occurs without the coexistence of both a constitutional aberration and an environmental adversity. If parents and society reject a child with a constitutional defect, a vicious cycle ensues, with each type of difficulty augmenting the other. For a child's condition to be severe and to warrant the diagnosis of psychosis, the combined deleterious effect of physiological and environmental factors are usually found to be present. Kenneth Wilson's problems provide an example.

In early childhood, Kenneth had a number of severe convulsions, which stopped without a program of medication. He entered school and made progress along with the other children with only a few problems occurring. At times, though, his parents and teacher noticed that he had complaints about headache and nausea. Kenneth, too, occasionally had temper tantrums. As he progressed in school, he made better than average grades.

In middle childhood, at the age of ten, a crisis occurred in his family with the death of his father, and a year had scarcely passed when another serious adjustment was necessary. His mother married again, and Kenneth found that he had to learn to live with another person in the family. His stepfather had little patience with him and seemed to deliberately try to antagonize Kenneth. Several years passed with Kenneth's problems increasing. By the time he was fourteen, conflict between Kenneth and his stepfather increased to such a point that the mother sought help in dealing with the family's turmoil.

Kenneth's behavior had changed so much that his mother believed something must be causing his temper outbursts and moodiness. She took him to a medical center for study. An electroencephalogram showed abnormal electrical waves in the temporal area of Kenneth's brain as well as a pattern elsewhere typical of a convulsive disorder. A hypothesis seemed reasonable that Kenneth always had had some brain pathology, as was indicated by the fact that he had had earlier convulsions. He was able to manage with the slight constitutional impairment as long as stress was not great, but as stress increased with the conflict with his stepfather, adverse effects both psychological and physiological resulted. Kenneth was placed on an anticonvulsant drug and several months passed. The conflict with his stepfather, however, worsened and Kenneth became increasingly upset. Finally, in a fit of anger, Kenneth took a large knife and threatened to kill his stepfather. Tragedy was narrowly averted by the intervention of the police. In further clinical study it was found that Kenneth expressed feelings of great anger and resentment about his stepfather as well as hopelessness and complete lack of concern about what would happen to him. Kenneth's difficulty cannot be attributed to either the family conflict or to the brain abnormality discovered, but his severe disorder likely came from the combined factors.

It is possible that had Kenneth's home situation remained favorable and had his family life not been interrupted by unusual and traumatic events, he might not have developed the serious mental disorder that later occurred in adolescence. A combination of stressful forces of both a physiological and psychological nature is extremely serious and traumatic for any child and few can escape dire consequences.

Mental Retardation

Although it is possible for abnormal conditions to exist in the brain and still not interfere with comprehension and normal behavior, in some children constitutional problems do definitely cause varying degrees of deviant behavior (Garrison, 1963). That is, brain impairment may be of such a nature that despite favorable circumstances in the environment, the child still cannot develop and function as do other children.

Intelligence tests have been useful in determining concepts of impairment. A child scoring below the average range on intelligence tests will be described in many terms, such as mentally defective or mentally retarded. These terms developed from the theoretical bases associated with intelligence testing. The term *mental retardation* is widely used, even though its definition is unclear. The term does imply at least that the child's learning and mental capacity is less than that of a "normal" child. "Mental retardation" is used to categorize children who do not acquire basic skills, such as walking, dressing, and speaking, as early as do normal children. Subsequently, language and other skills may be acquired. At one time, *mental retardation,* or *mental deficiency,* was considered a diagnostic term, but now it is seen as a symptom of many problems.

Concepts of levels of intellectual defects are presently described in the following categorical terms: borderline, mild, moderate, severe, and profound (American Association on Mental Deficiency, 1961; Heber, 1959), with these terms replacing the old categorical terms of *moron, imbecile,* and *idiot.* As time has passed, a trend toward considering lower test scores as being within the normal range has developed. Part of this change is due to greater public interest in the difficulty of handicapped individuals and in those who cannot meet society's requirements, and part of the change is due to increased understanding of behavioral abnormality. The whole area of brain impairment and behavioral effectiveness has been neglected, and it is only in very recent years that substantial and significant investigations have been under way.

With increased knowledge, the terms *mental deficiency* and *retardation* are finding less and less usefulness and meaning as knowledge advances (Alexander, 1962). An example is found in the change in thinking about a frequently used term in the past. Some stigma has been attached to "familial mental deficiency," in part because of the low socioeconomic status and failure in cultural conformity characteristic of individuals believed to have the problem (Masland et al., 1958). Since few behavioral traits are now believed to be unitary, views have changed. Although anomalies of the brain can be inherited, with specific types of aberrations occurring more frequently in some families, most inadequacies apparently are due to a multiplicity of causes, with the identification of specific genes being presently either difficult or impossible. Consequently, such a concept as "familial mental deficiency" is quite vague.

Because of inadequate terminology and diagnostic procedures, the description of the incidence of brain impairment in the general population is inexact. The complex problem of diagnosis of conditions resulting in intellectual impairment with its multiple causative factors makes the problem of understanding difficult even in the best equipped medical and psychological centers.

The number of impaired children decreases rapidly as test scores become lower. As would be expected, children with severe difficulties are few in number as compared with those with milder types of impairment. This lower number probably results from a number of factors. Trauma causing great damage in the central nervous system is usually lethal, and many children with severely damaged brains do not survive; impaired constitutions arc less resistive to other types of disease; and the influence of lethal environmental factors may well be greater in more severely impaired individuals. Further, the statistical concept of the distribution of traits indicates fewer numbers at the extremes.

AMELIORATIVE METHODS

Society has approached amelioration of behavioral difficulties in a number of ways—through the establishment of "child guidance" and "mental health" clinics, health and welfare programs, and special programs within the schools. Two fundamental approaches are used to help troubled children and parents: One method is that of psychotherapy and the other is the use of psychoactive drugs.

Psychotherapy

Psychotherapy provides an experience in which the person learns to develop satisfying relationships with other people. The psychotherapist endeavors to bring about a channeling of the troubled individual's energy into effective problem-solving behavior, to help him realize his potentiality, and to help him feel that he can find a place in society where he is valued and where normal and satisfying human relationships are possible. In essence, psychotherapy has two main goals: (1) to increase the individual's capacity for emotional interchange with others, and (2) to lessen his anxiety and tension so that his energy and ability can be utilized effectively in problem-solving and need-fulfilling activity. Although psychotherapy is an experience involving emotional change, it also has the additional purpose of bringing about realistic and effective problem-solving behavior. A person after experiencing psychotherapy is more dependable, realistic, self-enhancing, socialized in his behavior, creative, and capable of changing and developing than previously (Rogers, 1963). Thus, through psychotherapy an individual is helped to continue his own development and to advance toward attainment of increasingly effective behavior.

Several systems of psychotherapy have developed since Freud expounded his system. McCary (1955) sees six different approaches as now being used, and Ford and Urban (1963) discuss ten. Differences have arisen in part because proponents of the several orientations have worked with patients with specific types of backgrounds or problems (Stein, 1961). Freud, for example, based his work largely on patients with hysteria and depression. Rogers based his "nondirective therapy" on the potentiality for change and growth within the individual, and he used the method with less severely disturbed individuals. Rogers' theoretical orientation has been characterized by constant change because he believes that theory is fallible and should be a stimulus for change (Ford and Urban, 1963).

The psychoanalytic (and oldest) technique, although including freedom for the individual to discuss whatever he wishes, relies upon interpretation, the uncovering and resolving of emotional problems in childhood experience, and upon a specific type of emotional relationship with the therapist. Modification of earlier psychoanalytic treatment has been undertaken by such people as Alexander and French (1946), as well as Heinz Hartman, David Rapaport, and Anna Freud. Despite differences in technique, all modern-day psychotherapists see psychotherapy as an experience in which the individual is helped to attain a change within himself.

Work with children closely aligned with the theoretical approach of Rogers is described by Allen (1942), Axline (1947, 1955), Hobbs (1951), and Moustakas (1959). Approaches based on psychoanalytic techniques developed for children are described by such writers as Bettelheim (1950), Blos (1961), Anna Freud (1928), Klein (1932), and Lippman (1939).

Since children cannot verbally express their feelings as well as adults, giving them an opportunity to "play out" feelings is common to all child techniques. Years ago, Levy (1939) emphasized the use of material in release of feelings. Other therapists have found puppets particularly useful in helping children to play out feelings that result from family conflict (Bender and Woltman, 1936; Machler, 1965). For example, Gordon and Cohn (1963) use a "doll-interview" technique with four- and five-year-old children in which a doll is asked questions, and the child answers for the doll. Moreno (1946, 1965) used psychodrama, or the taking of roles in spontaneous dramatization of conflict areas. Psychotherapeutic techniques with children are becoming increasingly similar in practice and depend upon "playing out" experiences for the child as well as offering parents counseling or psychotherapeutic programs (Phillips and Johnston, 1954; White, 1964). Siroka (1964) asserts that "sociodrama" is of benefit in working with Negro families who have had difficulties resulting from poverty, while Klapman and Rice (1965) hold that "family-group therapy" is of benefit even in cases of family disorder that many would consider to be untreatable.

Usually the room in which children are offered psychotherapy contains objects or material that will facilitate the child's expression of emotions. A playroom for psychotherapy with children contains a sandbox, a doll house, trucks, puppets, balls, playclothing, a punching bag or stuffed figures that can be struck, house utensils and furniture, paint, water, building blocks, crayons, and various kinds of paper.

Verbal explanations to the child about the experience are not nearly as important as the example of behavior provided by the therapist; however, the child may be told that he will be allowed to play in the room for an hour and that while there he can play with anything he likes, that he can use the material in any way he wants, and that he can say anything that he wishes. The therapist is attentive to and interested in whatever the child does but does not direct or interfere with him unless the child's safety is in question.

As the child plays out his feelings and the process of therapy advances, it comes to have similarities to adult therapy in which an adult explains feelings and thoughts. As in adult psychotherapy, children's play and expressions contain themes. A beginning theme of many children is their negative feelings—feelings of despair, anxiety, resentment, hostility, and perhaps hopelessness. A child who has never before been allowed to be destructive or disorderly in his behavior finds much satisfaction in expressing his resentment against the rules and regulations he has known outside. Sand, water, and paint are mixed in an array of broken toys and objects so that the general disorder of the room may express his repugnance at the order which has been forced upon him.

As a resentful child revels in the display of disorder and destructiveness, he is hardly aware of the therapist. As he finds it possible to express his resentment, he may attempt to use the therapist as an outlet for his feeling. As he throws objects about the room in a destructive frenzy, some may narrowly miss the therapist, but an experienced therapist realizes the child's intent and tells the child that he must not strike him and that even though he would like to hurt him, he cannot. He explains to the child that the destructive play, however, can be continued. Such remonstrance serves to keep the child close to some reality and at the same time helps him to become aware of the feelings of other people. Because of the freedom and opportunity for expression, most troubled children will respect the wishes of an experienced therapist and turn to other means of expression.

As the child returns week after week, cooperative and constructive play begins to emerge, and the child finds it less and less necessary to resort to frenzied and destructive behavior. As children play out in therapy many of the sources of conflict and unhappiness existing in their lives and in their families, their behavior becomes more acceptable. It is not always easy to demonstrate improvement in behavior; however, some investigators have reported demonstrable change. Seeman et al. (1964), for example, reported that children in individual play therapy showed less evidence of aggressive behavior according to teachers' ratings than did a control group. Moustakas (1964), in his work with a seven-year-old child who was extremely fearful of her school and her teacher, used a technique of discussion of fears. He reports that children respond favorably to a close relationship with a therapist and the opportunity to discuss their feelings.

The success of child psychotherapy rests on the child's unique relationship with the therapist. The therapist does not personally remove the child's difficulties, does not point out the ineffective and mistaken types of behavior, does not threaten with consequences of failure, does not give praise for reports of success, does not hold out unreal opportunities for a satisfying interpersonal relationship with the therapist, and does not even guarantee success in the venture of psychotherapy. The psychotherapist, however, can take advantage of a fundamental and powerful force within the individual—one basic to all human beings that compels them to seek to develop effective behavior and satisfying emotional interchanges with others. The therapist provides a stable relationship, so that when the child is depressed, the therapist, though sympathetic, is not unduly influenced; when the individual is elated and euphoric, the therapist is pleased and optimistic, but cautious. Thus, the psychotherapist, while showing sympathy, interest, and concern, allows the troubled individual to explore many directions in the effort to cope with his present difficulties.

In the case of children, psychotherapy is not an experience that they seek themselves. Usually a parent, welfare worker, school official, or juvenile court counselor brings the child for psychotherapy. The child may view the experience with suspicion or respond to it with antagonism and resentment. The parents' feelings about the process as well as their hopes influence the child; and if the parents become involved in the process and they too make an effort to change conditions within the family, psychotherapy for the child is much more likely to succeed (Graver, 1957; Moustakas, 1959). On the other hand, if the parents see little hope and feel that much of the problem lies with the child alone, important changes cannot reasonably be expected. The parents may complain about their child's misbehavior and the difficulties that they have with him; yet at the same time, they often see no relationship of the child's difficulties to their own problems.

The difficulties of some children are of such a nature that a number of professional people have previously believed that psychotherapy would be of no benefit, particularly for those children with evidence of central nervous system disorder or brain pathology. Because of these conditions, the child's behavior was seen as immutable and hope for change in psychotherapy unwarranted. Such an attitude has changed in recent years (Leland and Smith, 1965; Mehlman, 1953; Sternlicht, 1965; Wilcox and Guthrie, 1957). Parents too are being helped in their struggle to cope with the child's ineffective or inappropriate behavior. They often need help with their own feelings or their anxiety and concern about the child. Many children with constitutional defects or who are "mentally retarded" also have psychological problems that can be lessened if not "cured" through psychotherapy. Hence, arbitrary limitations based on intellectual level seem unnecessary.

Psychotherapy is indirectly influential in relation to conformity to social mores and customs. Although it may lessen an individual's conflicts about moral behavior, it cannot instill within a child a system of ethical or moral values. This limitation, of course, is related to the earlier discussion about the fact that psychotherapy cannot be imposed upon a person against his will. Change in a value system comes only through the desire of the individual. The therapist, however, probably has some influence on the person's values, even though awareness of the influence is not recognized (Buhler, 1962).

In any clinical facility, many more demands for psychotherapy are made than can be met. Consequently, clinicians have experimented with various methods to extend the experience. The extension of the experience to groups of people has been a practice for two decades (Slavson, 1947, 1965). In general, the principles of group therapy for children are similar to those of individual therapy. Slavson first devised a system of groups where children in middle childhood engaged in various projects involving handicrafts. The members of the groups were carefully selected on the basis of need for experience in association with others. Slavson called these groups "activity groups" and they were similar to present-day group psychotherapy sessions.

Ginott (1961), as a result of his experience with children in group psychotherapy in a child guidance clinic, sees such an experience as facilitating more rapid change in a child's behavior than would take place in individual therapy. By having other children in the experience, a disturbed child not only identifies with others who are fearful, but also can use the therapist as a parent surrogate. Also, a child may find it necessary to shift identification from therapist to another child and from child to child. Extremes of behavior may be modified by the identification with others. For example, a destructive child may become less destructive as a result of the presence of other children who are less inclined in this direction.

Because of the many variables influencing therapeutic change, group therapy with children cannot be unequivocally held to be more or less valuable than individual therapy. Individual variation in child and therapist makes generalizations unwise. Without doubt, both kinds of experiences can be demonstrated as successful or as failing. Group psychotherapy has a number of advantages aside from the one of extension to more people. Since group therapy takes place in a social setting and requires adjustment to and awareness of other individuals, it does provide a realistic experience. By participating in the struggle of others, some individuals can be more courageous in facing their own difficulties. They can find courage in the fact that others have fears and emotions similar to theirs. Interaction with others provides opportunities to try out new ways of behaving and new types of responses to others in the psychotherapeutic experience itself. Favorable reports in the use of the group approach in comparison with the individual process are made by Mullan and Rosenbaum (1962) and Novick (1965).

Some therapists have used short-term group therapy with a time limit imposed at the outset. Karson (1965) found such limitation to be of value in working with children and mothers in separate groups. He concludes that many of the disturbing characteristics of individuals in both groups were reduced.

In considering the usefulness of psychotherapy and its value to individuals and to communities, it is apparent that psychotherapy in itself cannot entirely meet family needs nor can it have much influence on broad social problems. The value of psychotherapy depends to a large extent upon conditions within society. Psychotherapy can only be a part of a broad concern for the welfare of children and family members. Society itself must provide opportunities for individuals to find satisfying social roles according to capacities. Psychotherapy is ameliorative, limited, and dependent upon the structure of society and its values (Alexander, 1963).

Psychoactive Drugs

Parents who are concerned about their children's restless activity often request their physician to give them some type of drug to lessen excessive activity and demanding behavior. Other parents, seeing their children's fearfulness and anxiety, seek some means of reducing these feelings. Some children trouble their parents with their listlessness and depression, and some children cause parental concern because of their ineffective and inadequate behavior resulting from impairment of the brain or central nervous system. These children are unable to meet their parents' hopes for achievement and success in school, and so the parents ask for some type of drug to improve general performance.

Only a short time ago, hope for drugs to do these things for children was quite remote, but now a number of drugs hold promise. The effectiveness of many drugs, however, has not been established and their value rests generally on clinical impressions. Two main problems exist in measuring the effect of drugs on behavior. The first problem lies in the suggestibility or hope of those seeking relief. Often, parents who are troubled because of their child's behavior and who desire to find some help, see an improvement in their child's behavior after the administration of a drug, although measurements indicate little or no behavioral change. Careful experiments should be carried on with psychoactive drugs to support the view that these drugs do bring significant alterations in children's behavior and particularly to insure that they do not have toxic effects (Shirkey and Barba, 1964). A second problem lies in the availability of appropriate techniques of measurement of human behavior. While it is possible to measure the performance of individuals on certain tasks (as has been done for many years), measurement of emotional change and general response is difficult (Irwin, 1962).

A large number of drugs are now available that are purported to be of value in many types of mental disorders. These drugs, according to Cole and Carr (1959), can be classified into tranquilizers, sedatives, and antidepressive agents. Some drug types are expected to prevent extremes of emotional behavior, some are expected to reduce activity and the expenditure of energy, and some are expected to stimulate the central nervous system so that it will function more effectively. The advance in the use of drugs is dramatic and will likely be much more so as research continues.

Illustrative of drug study in reference to behavior is an investigation made by Kugel and Alexander (1963) of the effect of a central nervous system stimulant. The design of the experiment included appropriate control subjects and the use of a placebo (an inert substance duplicating the drug in appearance). The drug was used with 42 subjects in the age range of six to thirteen. Thirty-five of the children had some form of central nervous system disorder and seven had a diagnosis of behavior disorder only. Measurement of behavior depended upon the Stanford-Binet Intelligence Scale, the Goodenough Intelligence Test, the Vineland School Maturity Scale, and an experimental test developed to study reasoning, use of stimuli, and emotional perceptions. Half of the 42 subjects were given the psychological tests, were then placed on the drug (100 milligrams daily) for three months, and were again tested. These subjects remained off medication for one month, next were placed on the placebo for three months, and then the final measurements were taken. The second half of the subjects received the placebo first and then the drug, with the same procedure of measurement as was used with the first group. The statistical treatment of the data was described in terms of a gain (or loss) in scores between appropriate appraisals, so that the analysis would reflect any change taking place between the initial appraisal and each of the subsequent appraisals. The investigators found that the drug did not bring significantly different scores. Thus, the findings of this study did not reveal any advantages of the drug or any measurable effect on the central nervous system.

The usefulness of drugs in treatment of mental disorders is still not established to everyone's satisfaction. Those using an "organic" orientation to mental disorder tend to rely on drugs, and some even take the view that drugs have a beneficial effect on the causal factors of the disorder. Others believe that the best treatment is with the psychotherapeutic interview and place little reliance on chemotherapy. Still others maintain that a combined therapeutic approach is necessary. Conners (1965) has asserted that various treatment programs have different effects and that variations must be demonstrated with various techniques. Hence, definite conclusions are not yet available, but the use of medication in the behavior disorders and in reference to behavioral change will undoubtedly be much accelerated in the ensuing years.

A POINT OF VIEW

It is important for those who study human development to know about developmental disorders: First, because knowledge about disorders can be of benefit in developing means of prevention; and, second, despite considerable effort by society some adverse conditions and some constitutional problems will occur so that there will likely always be some individuals who are disordered and who need specific kinds of assistance. Furthermore, by better understanding the origin of the disorders, it is possible to better understand the course of human development.

It may be, too, that by prevention of many of the disorders of development it will be possible to build a much better social order than we now have. It is difficult to say how many of the problems of society are related to adverse conditions during the developmental years, but a considerable number of society's difficulties brought about by irrational people or by people who are unable to meet the requirements of society are likely to have their beginning in the childhood years of these individuals.

REFERENCES

Alexander, F., and T. M. French, 1946. *Psychoanalytic Therapy*. New York: Ronald.
Alexander, T., 1962. "What Is Mental Retardation?" *Clinical Pediatrics*, **1**, 161–165.

Alexander, T., 1963. *Psychotherapy in Our Society*. Englewood Cliffs, N.J.: Prentice-Hall.

Allen, F. H., 1942. *Psychotherapy with Children*. New York: Norton.

Ausubel, D. P., 1961. "Personality Disorder Is Disease," *American Psychologist*, **16**, 69–74.

Axline, V. M., 1947. *Play Therapy*. Boston: Houghton Mifflin.

Axline, V. M., 1955. "Play Therapy Procedures and Results," *American Journal of Orthopsychiatry*, **25**, 618–626.

Baird, H. W., 1964. "Chronic or Recurrent Convulsions," in *Textbook of Pediatrics*, 8th ed., edited by W. E. Nelson, pp. 1220–1231. Philadelphia: Saunders.

Bakwin, H., 1942. "Loneliness in Infants," *American Journal of Diseases of Children*, **63**, 30–40.

Bandura, A., and C. J. Kupers, 1964. "Transmission of Patterns of Self-Reinforcement Through Modeling," *Journal of Abnormal and Social Psychology*, **69**, 1–9.

Bandura, A., and R. H. Walters, 1959. *Adolescent Aggression*. New York: Ronald.

Bender, L., and A. G. Woltmann, 1936. "The Use of Puppet Shows as a Psychotherapeutic Method for Behavior Problems in Children," *American Journal of Orthopsychiatry*, **6**, 341–354.

Benedict, R., 1934. *Patterns of Culture*. Boston: Houghton Mifflin.

Bettelheim, B., 1950. *Love Is Not Enough*. New York: Free Press.

Bildfell, G., and V. I. Douglas, 1965. "Children's Responses to Aggression: A Developmental Study," *Canadian Psychologist*, **6a**, 173–178.

Blos, P., 1961. "Delinquency," in *Adolescents: Psychoanalytic Approach to Problems and Therapy*, edited by S. Lorand and H. Schneer, pp. 132–151. New York: Hoeber-Harper.

Boas, F., 1911. *The Mind of Primitive Man*. New York: Macmillan.

Buhler, C., 1962. *Values in Psychotherapy*. New York: Free Press.

Buss, A. H., 1963. "Physical Aggression in Relation to Different Frustrations," *Journal of Abnormal and Social Psychology*, **67**, 1–7.

Byrd, R. E., 1938. *Alone*. New York: Putnam.

Cole, J. O., and C. J. Carr, 1959. "A Synoptic Review of Psychoactive Drugs," in *Child Research in Psychopharmacology*, edited by S. Fisher, pp. 3–19. Springfield, Ill.: Charles C Thomas.

Conners, C. K., 1965. "Effects of Brief Psychotherapy, Drugs, and Type of Disturbance on Holtzman Inkblot Scores in Children," *American Psychologist*, **20**, 201–202.

Dekaban, A., 1959. *Neurology of Infancy*. Baltimore, Md.: Williams & Wilkins.

Dunphy, D., and V. Pessin, 1962. "Correlation Between Cord Blood Oxygen Values and Psychological Test Scores," *Journal of the Iowa Medical Society*, **4**, 212–216.

Eggan, D., 1953. "The General Problem of Hopi Adjustment," in *Personality in Nature, Society, and Culture*, 2d ed., edited by C. Kluckhohn and H. A. Murray, pp. 276–291. New York: Knopf.

Ellingson, R. J., 1954. "The Incidence of EEG Abnormality among Patients with Mental Disorders of Apparently Nonorganic Origin: A Critical Review," *American Journal of Psychiatry,* **111**, 263–275.

Fanshel, D., L. Hylton, and E. F. Borgatta, 1963. "A Study of Behavior Disorders of Children in Residential Treatment Centers," *Journal of Psychological Studies,* **14**, 1–23.

Ford, D. H., and H. B. Urban, 1963. *Systems of Psychotherapy.* New York: Wiley.

Frank, L. K., 1953. "Cultural Control and Physiological Autonomy," in *Personality in Nature, Society, and Culture,* 2d ed., edited by C. Kluckhohn and H. A. Murray, pp. 119–122. New York: Knopf.

Freud, A., 1928. *Introduction to the Technic of Child Analysis.* New York: Nervous and Mental Disease.

Freud, A., and D. T. Burlingham, 1943. *War and Children.* New York: Medical War Books.

Gallagher, J. R., 1960. *Medical Care of the Adolescent.* New York: Appleton-Century-Crofts.

Galton, F., 1914. *Hereditary Genius: An Inquiry into Its Laws and Consequences.* London: Macmillan.

Garrison, M., 1963. "Attention and Activity Level," *Training School Bulletin,* **59**, 158–160.

Gilbert, G. M., 1957. "A Survey of 'Referral Problems' in Metropolitan Child Guidance Centers," *Journal of Clinical Psychology,* **13**, 37–42.

Ginott, H. B., 1961. *Group Psychotherapy with Children.* New York: McGraw-Hill.

Gladwin, T., and S. B. Sarason, 1953. *Truk: Man in Paradise.* New York: Wenner-Gren Foundation for Anthropological Research.

Glaser, J., 1956. *Allergy in Childhood.* Springfield, Ill.: Charles C Thomas.

Goddard, H. H., 1914. *Feeblemindedness: Its Causes and Consequences.* New York: Macmillan.

Gordon, J. E., and F. Cohn, 1963. "Effect of Fantasy Arousal of Affiliation Drive on Doll Play Aggression," *Journal of Abnormal and Social Psychology,* **66**, 301–307.

Graham, F. K., M. M. Pennoyer, B. M. Caldwell, M. Greenman, and A. F. Hartmann, 1957. "Relationship between Clinical Status and Behavior Test Performance in a Newborn Group with Histories Suggesting Anoxia," *Journal of Pediatrics,* **50**, 177–189.

Graver, P. A., 1957. "Facilitating the Results of Therapy," *Elementary School Journal,* **58**, 166–169.

Hallowell, A. I., 1953. "Aggression in Saulteaux Society," in *Personality in Nature, Society, and Culture,* 2d ed., edited by C. Kluckhohn and H. A. Murray, pp. 260–275. New York: Knopf.

Hart, N. W. M., 1964. "Academic Progress in Relation to Intelligence and Motivation in the Opportunity School," *Slow Learning Child,* **11**, 40–46.

Heber, R., 1959. *A Manual on Terminology and Classification in Mental Retardation.* A monograph supplement to the *American Journal of Mental Deficiency,* **64**, No. 2.

Hicks, D. J., 1965. "Imitation and Retention of Film-mediated Aggressive Peer and Adult Models," *Journal of Personality and Social Psychology,* **2,** 97–100.

Hobbs, N. 1951. "Group-Centered Psychotherapy," in *Client-Centered Therapy,* edited by C. R. Rogers, pp. 278–319. Boston: Houghton Mifflin.

Holt, L., R. McIntosh, and H. L. Barnett, 1961. *Pediatrics,* 13th ed. New York: Appleton-Century-Crofts.

Horney, K., 1936. "Culture and Neurosis," *American Sociological Review,* **1,** 221–235.

Horney, K., 1945. *Our Inner Conflicts: A Constructive Theory of Neurosis.* New York: Norton.

Hutt, M. L., and R. G. Gibby, 1957. *Patterns of Abnormal Behavior.* Boston: Allyn and Bacon.

Irwin, S., 1962. "Drug Screening and Evaluative Procedures," *Science,* **136,** 123–128.

Jenkins, R. L., 1954. *Breaking Patterns of Defeat* Philadelphia: Lippincott.

Jenkins, R. L., and S. Glickman, 1946. "Common Syndromes in Child Psychiatry. I. Deviant Behavior Traits," *American Journal of Orthopsychiatry,* **16,** 244–254.

Kallmann, F., 1938. *The Genetics of Schizophrenia.* Locust Valley, N. Y.: Augustin.

Kallmann, F., 1953. *Heredity in Health and Mental Disorder.* New York: Norton.

Kardiner, A., 1945. *The Psychological Frontiers of Society.* New York: Columbia.

Karson, S., 1965. "Group Psychotherapy with Latency Age Boys," *International Journal of Group Psychotherapy,* **15,** 81–89.

Kessler, J. W., 1966. *Psychopathology of Childhood.* Englewood Cliffs, N.J.: Prentice-Hall.

Klapman, H. J., and D. L. Rice, 1965. "An Experience with Combined Milieu and Family Group Therapy," *International Journal of Group Psychotherapy,* **15,** 198–206.

Klein, M., 1932. *The Psychoanalysis of Children,* translated by A. Strachey. London: Hogarth.

Kraepelin, E., 1907. *Clinical Psychiatry,* abstracted and adapted by A. R. Diefendorf from Kraepelin's *Lehrbuch der Psychiatrie.* New York: Macmillan.

Kretschmer, E., 1926. *Physique and Character.* New York: Harcourt, Brace & World.

Kugel, R. B., and T. Alexander, 1963. "The Effect of a Central Nervous System Stimulant (Deanol) on Behavior," *Pediatrics,* **31,** 651–655.

Lefkowitz, M., L. Walder, L. D. Eron, 1963. "Punishment, Identification, and Aggression," *Merrill-Palmer Quarterly,* **9,** 159–174.

Lejeune, J., and R. Turpin, 1962. "Somatic Chromosomes in Mongolism," in *Mental Retardation,* edited by L. C. Kolb, R. L. Masland, and R. E. Cooke, pp. 67–77. Baltimore, Md.: Williams & Wilkins.

Leland, H., and D. E. Smith, 1965. *Play Therapy with Mentally Subnormal Children.* New York: Grune & Stratton.

Levy, D. M., 1939. "Release Therapy," *American Journal of Orthopsychiatry,* **9**, 713–736.

Lippman, H. S., 1939. "Child Analysis," *American Journal of Orthopsychiatry,* **9**, 707–712.

Lowe, C. H., and V. H. Auerbach, 1964. "Inborn Errors of Metabolism," in *Textbook of Pediatrics,* 8th ed., edited by W. E. Nelson, pp. 280–329. Philadelphia: Saunders.

Machler, T. J., 1965. "Pinocchio in the Treatment of School Phobia," *Bulletin of the Menninger Clinic,* **29**, 212–219.

Masland, R. L., S. B. Sarason, and T. Gladwin, 1958. *Mental Subnormality.* New York: Basic Books.

McCary, J. L., 1955. "Introduction," in *Six Approaches to Psychotherapy,* edited by J. L. McCary and D. E. Sheer, pp. 1–7, New York: The Dryden Press.

Mead, M., 1939. *From the South Seas.* New York: Morrow.

Mehlman, B., 1953. "Group Play Therapy with Mentally Retarded Children," *Journal of Abnormal and Social Psychology,* **48**, 53–60.

Moreno, J. L., 1946. *Psychodrama.* Beacon, N. Y.: Beacon House.

Moreno, J. L., 1965. "Psychodrama in Action," *Group Psychotherapy,* **18**, 87–117.

Moustakas, C. E., 1959. *Psychotherapy with Children.* New York: Harper & Row.

Moustakas, C. E., 1961. *Loneliness.* Englewood Cliffs, N.J.: Prentice-Hall.

Moustakas, C. E., 1964. "The Burden of Sensitivity and Compassion in the Onset of a Brain Seizure," *Psychotherapy: Theory, Research, and Practice,* **1**, 67–74.

Mowrer, O. H., 1960. "Sin, the Lesser of Two Evils," *American Psychologist,* **15**, 301–304.

Mullan, H., and M. Rosenbaum, 1962. *Group Psychotherapy.* New York: Free Press.

Newman, H. H., F. N. Freeman, and K. J. Holzinger, 1937. *Twins: A Study of Heredity and Environment.* Chicago: The University of Chicago Press.

Novick, J. I., 1965. "Comparison Between Short-term Group and Individual Psychotherapy in Effecting Change in Nondesirable Behavior in Children," *International Journal of Group Psychotherapy,* **15**, 366–373.

O'Kelly, L. I., and F. A. Muckler, 1955. *Introduction to Psychopathology.* Englewood Cliffs, N.J.: Prentice-Hall.

Orlansky, H., 1949. "Infant Care and Personality," *Psychological Bulletin,* **46**, 1–48.

Patterson, G. R., 1964. "An Empirical Approach to the Classification of Disturbed Children," *Journal of Clinical Psychology,* **20**, 326–337.

Penny, R. K., 1965. "Reactive Curiosity and Manifest Anxiety in Children," *Child Development,* **36**, 697–702.

Peterson, D. R., 1961. "Behavior Problems of Middle Childhood," *Journal of Consulting Psychology,* **25**, 205–209.

Phillips, E. L., and M. S. Johnston, 1954. "Theoretical and Clinical Aspects of Short-term Parent-Child Psychotherapy," *Psychiatry,* **17**, 267–275.

Pinneau, S. R., 1950. "A Critique on the Articles by Margaret Ribble," *Child Development,* **21**, 203–228.

Pinneau, S. R., 1955. "The Infantile Disorders of Hospitalism and Anaclitic Depression," *Psychological Bulletin,* **52**, 429–452.

Redl, F., and D. Wineman, 1965. *Controls from Within: Techniques for the Treatment of the Aggressive Child.* New York: Macmillan.

Rheingold, H. L., 1956. *The Modification of Social Responsiveness in Institutional Babies.* Monographs of the Society for Research in Child Development, **21**, No. 2. Lafayette, Ind.: Child Development Publications, Purdue University.

Ribble, M. A., 1965. *The Rights of Infants.* New York: Columbia.

Rogers, C. R., 1963. "Concept of Fully Functioning Person," *Psychotherapy: Theory, Research, and Practice,* **1**, 17–26.

Ross, A. O., 1959. *The Practice of Clinical Child Psychology.* New York: Grune & Stratton.

Seeman, J., E. Barry, and C. Ellinwood, 1964. "Interpersonal Assessment of Play Therapy Outcome," *Psychotherapy: Theory, Research, and Practice,* **1**, 64–66.

Selye, H., 1953. "The General-Adaptation Syndrome in Its Relationships to Neurology, Psychology, and Psychopathology," in *Contributions Toward Medical Psychology,* Vol. 1, edited by A. Weider, pp. 234–274. New York: Ronald.

Sheldon, W. H., 1940. *The Varieties of Human Physique.* New York: Harper & Row.

Sheldon, W. H., 1942. *The Varieties of Temperament.* New York: Harper & Row.

Shirkey, H. C., and W. P. Barba, 1964. "Drug Therapy," in *Textbook of Pediatrics,* 8th ed., edited by W. E. Nelson, pp. 208–254. Philadelphia: Saunders.

Siroka, R., 1964. "Sociodrama and the Negro Family," *International Journal of Sociometry and Society,* **4**, 91–93.

Slavson, S. R., 1947. *The Practice of Group Therapy.* New York: International Universities Press.

Slavson, S. R., 1965, "Coordinated Family Therapy," *International Journal of Group Psychotherapy,* **15**, 177–186.

Stein, M. I., 1961. *Contemporary Psychotherapies.* New York: Free Press.

Sternlicht, M., 1965. "Psychotherapeutic Techniques Useful with the Mentally Retarded: A Review and Critique," *Psychiatric Quarterly,* **39**, 84–90.

Szasz, T. S., 1960. "The Myth of Mental Illness," *American Psychologist,* **15**, 113–118.

Tennes, K. H., and E. E. Lampl, 1964. "Stranger and Separation Anxiety in Infancy," *Journal of Nervous and Mental Disease,* **139**, 247–254.

White, R. W., 1964. *The Abnormal Personality.* New York: Ronald.

Whiting, J. W. M., 1953. "The Frustration Complex in Kwoma Society," in *Personality in Nature, Society, and Culture,* edited by C. Kluckhohn and H. A. Murray, pp. 137–145. New York: Knopf.

Wilcox, G. T., and G. M. Guthrie, 1957. "Changes in Adjustment of Institutionalized Female Defectives Following Group Psychotherapy," *Journal of Clinical Psychology,* **13,** 9–13.

Zellweger, H., 1961. "Aminoaciduria and Mental Retardation. Part II: Phenylpyruvic Oligophrenia, Phenylketonuria (PKU)," *Journal of the Iowa State Medical Society,* **51,** 536–540.

[*fourteen*]

Methods and Theories Contributing to Child and Adolescent Psychology

Present-day behavioral scientists believe that the understanding of a person's behavior must be based on information gathered objectively and according to scientific principles. The use of scientific methods to obtain understanding is in contradistinction to the use of intuition, unestablished information, and custom. Through understanding based on scientific methods, a child's life may ultimately bring more satisfaction to him, his parents, and society. Hopefully, through increased understanding of human development, a society can be created that will better meet the needs of its members for satisfaction in human relationships.

Knowledge about human behavior is constantly changing through the addition of new facts and reorganization of established information. No endpoint is in view in the process, and the search for knowledge shows that as understanding is gained about some phenomenon, more questions are raised than are answered. A scientist, accordingly, questions what is known and seeks to find ways to add to his experience and knowledge. Many scientists, wishing to make some use of their knowledge, will therefore often try to predict phenomena or events in the life of a child.

Facts about human behavior are patterned and related in some way, but these patterns are not always known to the scientist. Therefore, a great deal of his effort is devoted toward organizing facts into patterns. After determining the patterns, the scientist moves to uncover the principles that are necessary for the understanding of human development. The scientist must be ready to use any type of methodology that will bring about further knowledge. Usually a scientist begins by collecting natural facts, which become the basic information that he uses with subsequent research. The acquisition of knowledge and facts growing out of scientific endeavor becomes useful only if there is rational activity in reference to them. Such activity makes research findings the basis for new knowledge. In order to explain and to contribute to some theoretical system, the scientist tries to determine how the situation came into being and what conditions brought it about. And, ultimately, he sees his endeavor as only a small incident in the long search for knowledge. Hence, the scientist tries to plan his experiments so that they will systematically fit into some over-all design. Facts must be dealt with statistically or logically in such a way that their similarities and differences can be determined—this systematic treatment of data is part of the scientific method.

THE METHODS OF SCIENCE

According to Brown and Ghiselli (1955), the major methods of science are symbolization, description, explanation, and theorization.

Symbolization

Symbolization is necessary so that facts and the experience of the scientist can be adequately manipulated. Since an experiment and the gathering of facts are only momentary in the passage of time, the experience must in some way be perpetuated symbolically. Usually this perpetuation is done through language, although many other symbols are used to represent facts.

The vast complexity of present knowledge and scientific endeavor requires that scientists devote much effort to the development of a symbolic system that is both flexible and extensible. Despite the value of language as a symbolic system, it has a number of problems. For example, the same word is used at times for different meanings. In psychology, such a word is *personality,* a word that over the years has developed many different definitions. Obviously, much confusion can result. Sometimes it happens that language fails to reflect changes in the meaning of words as time passes. To add to the problem, one often finds a tendency to resist the development of new words or symbols, but scientists must seek to develop new symbolic systems as new discoveries are made.

Description

Through description, a second important method, facts or events can be ordered, manipulated, recorded, and kept. An anthropologist, for example, describes and records the kinship system in a primitive tribe by listing individuals in family groupings and their behavior in relationship to activities of the tribe. He may describe women's activities as harvesting various types of food and, at the same time, teaching young children about the spirits that influence the success of the harvest. By such descriptions, the anthropologist may then be able to develop theoretical principles about the significance of cultural teachings in human development.

Explanation

Explanation, a third method of science, contributes to the "why" of experience. This method involves complex abstraction and leads to the development of a theory. For example, the anthropologist in developing a theory of culture will explain primitive incantations during the planting of crops as a means of warding off evil spirits, which are believed to cause crop failure. The explanation brings an integrated pattern of meaning to make clear the significance of beliefs about the supernatural in influencing human behavior.

Theorization

Theorization, or the development of a theory, is characterized by the following steps: (1) assignment of labels to objects and events, as in the above example, the primitive vocalization while planting can be labeled "incantations to a spirit"; (2) classification, as in the above example, which is demonstrated by dividing the broad category of "incantations" into incantations related to "food gathering," "war activities," or others; and (3) categorical arrangements into a system; for example, in dealing with primitive supernatural beliefs, a number of beliefs can be categorically formed into a sacred system.

These three steps in the development of a theory lead to hypotheses, which can serve as means for substantiating covariation and other types of relationships. Much of the scientist's creative endeavor goes into the development and construction of a theory. In this sense, his work is similar to that of the artist who paints a picture without a specific goal. Out of the searching effort come organization, balance, and a valuable contribution.

As a scientist searches for new relationships and new ideas, his theorizing is enhanced by seeing relationships and by making predictions of a general nature. The theory he devises is a symbolic organization of that which he has been able to build from his direct observations. New facts are criteria for determining the value of the theory.

Theories should be constantly subjected to testing and change whenever some of the over-all plan fails to be substantiated. If failure occurs, other scientists can reinterpret the facts. Thus, out of a discarded theory, an entirely new one may be developed that will overcome the stumbling blocks of the earlier theory.

CURRENT RESEARCH APPROACHES

Principles constituting the body of knowledge about child and adolescent psychology are based on research findings. The methods through which the facts are obtained are important to the student reading about the behavior of children since he needs some basis for evaluation of the studies in order both to appreciate and to judge the value of the contributions of research workers.

Age, changes in physical growth, language, and behavior have been of particular interest to psychologists. Over the years, investigators have tried to establish more and more facts in the relationship of age to physical and behavioral change. Psychologists have also been interested in the importance of other variables that influence the behavior and development of the child. This search has led them to seek to understand pathological behavior and to learn of the significance of events deviating from those that ordinarily might be expected to come about in an individual's development.

Anderson (1954) described seven sources of material in the study of child and adolescent behavior: (1) present behavior through observations, measurements, and records in experimental situations; (2) products of the child's activities, including his drawings, letters, and compositions; (3) records of the child in the home, school, or in various agencies that gather data about children; (4) introspective reports of the child (although most investigators prefer spontaneous verbalization to this type of report); (5) memories of the child; (6) memories of others who have observed the child (a source avoided by most investigators); and (7) behavior of parents, siblings, or others. The latter type of study includes the various community studies related to delinquency or studies of socioeconomic factors. Most investigators today prefer to obtain data through the most direct and exacting methods possible.

The experimental method is the preferred method in the science of psychology at the present time. This preference results from the influence of other disciplines and the recognition of the value of the scientific method in establishing general principles. An experiment consists of objective observations made under carefully controlled conditions or situations.

The Classical Experimental Method

The classical experimental setup begins with a *description* of the problem, which must be stated in measurable form. Decision about the method of experimentation is possible only through careful analysis of a problem. An example of a problem is: Will the administration of a (specific) drug improve the performance of children on (specific) intelligence tests?

After the problem has been analyzed and defined, the *hypothesis* takes its place as the second step in research design. A hypothesis may be defined as an answer to the question raised in the problem. A hypothesis is characterized in several ways: (1) It must be related to the problem so that it provides one answer (an example related to the problem stated above would be: the specific drug will improve the subjects' performance on the specific test); (2) it must be the simplest answer possible, thus, in the example above, the hypothesis cannot be tested in terms of other drugs or tests not used in the experiment; (3) a hypothesis must be verifiable, hence, its testing must be within the capabilities of the experimenter; and (4) a hypothesis must be of such a nature that the experiment can either support it or refute it.

Other important elements of the experimental method are termed the *independent variable* and the *dependent variable*. The independent variable is the factor that is manipulated by the experimenter in order to determine its bearing on observed activity or change. A dependent variable is the factor that varies as the experimenter introduces the independent variable. These definitions of variables are in accord with the concept of *stimuli* and *responses*. Responses, or systems of responses, are characterized as the behavior of an individual; and the goal of the experimenter is to study the responses of the individual to specific stimuli. Accordingly, the independent variable is the stimulus and the dependent variable is the response. In the example mentioned above, the drug is the independent variable and the test performance is the dependent variable. In discovering the changes due to the independent variable, the experimenter will want to be sure that the response is actually due to the stimulus, in the above example, the drug. Consequently, a control group of subjects would be obtained and treated in the same manner with the exception that the subjects would receive an inert substance called a "placebo" instead of the drug. Other considerations in such studies are necessary and can be seen in the study done by Kugel and Alexander (1963) and described in Chapter 13.

It should be noted, however, in experimentation with children that other responses may be made by the child that are not necessarily due to or influenced by the independent variable. Despite the investigator's careful efforts, some factors cannot be prevented from influencing the dependent variable, or the action of the child. Conditions can be much better controlled in experiments in the physical sciences not involving life. In the behavioral sciences, however, and especially in the study of children, complete control of influences external to the experimental situation is impossible, and the investigator usually must be content with a "tendency." Consequently, the development of adequate controls is a very important effort, but despite arduous effort the behavioral sciences still lag behind the physical and biological sciences in the exactitude of experimentation.

A study of probability learning done by Stevenson and Zigler (1958) provides an example of the experimental method. Although the investigators used three experiments to complete the study, only the first will be used here as an illustration. They had noted that most of the probability learning studies had been done with adults; consequently, they sought to conduct similar studies with children in order to answer the questions: Do children show similar behavior in learning to that of adults? and What conditions influence that behavior? They had two hypotheses: that the responses of normal children are similar to those of adults and that certain conditions, such as pretraining or reinforcement, will influence the responses of normal children.

The subjects in the study were 45 nursery school children. The apparatus used in the study was a yellow, vertical panel with a row of three knobs, a red light, a hole from which marbles were delivered, and a plastic covered box to receive the marbles. (See Figure 14-1.) Installed behind the panel was a switch by which the investigator could turn on the light, the timer, and the mechanism, which was activated by the subject when he made the choice. When the subject pushed a knob, the light went off, the timer stopped, and the marble dropped (if the choice was correct). The subject was seated in front of the panel and told that he would play a game, that when the light came on he should push the knob that he thought would drop the marble into the box. After getting as many marbles as possible, the subject was told that he would be allowed to choose two toys as prizes. One experimenter operated the panel and the second one sat at some distance behind the subject and recorded the responses. A three-choice procedure was used in which responses to only one stimulus was reinforced. Two conditions were set up (for each subject one knob was correct). One-third of the children received 100 per cent reinforcement, and the marble was delivered 100 per cent of the time that the correct knob was pushed; another third received 66 per cent reinforcement; and the other third, 33 per cent reinforcement. Each subject had 80 choices before being given the prizes. The results of the experiment indicated that the responses of the children were similar to those of adults: There was a tendency for a rapid increase in frequencies of correct responses which occurred for a short period (see Figure 14-2) and the asymptotic values were similar to those of adults. It was also found that reinforcement would influence performance.

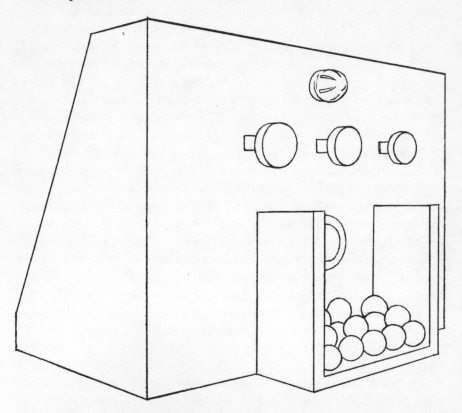

Figure 14.1. Apparatus for investigation of children's learning. Used by permission from H. W. Stevenson, "Probability Learning in Children," *Journal of Experimental Psychology*, vol. 56, 1958.

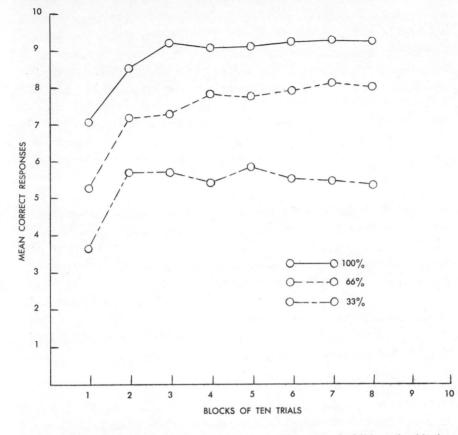

Figure 14.2. Mean number of correct responses by normal children for blocks of 10 trials. Adapted by permission from H. W. Stevenson, "Probability Learning in Children," *Journal of Experimental Psychology,* vol. 56, 1958, p. 187.

The Control Test Method

Another experimental method called the "control test" method is sometimes used. In this procedure, the performance is observed under "normal" conditions and then the condition is changed. This method is sometimes called the "method of differences." Such an approach can be used only where practice effect is not a factor.

The Equated Group Method

A frequently used technique in experiments with children and adolescents is that of observing two groups equated according to certain criteria and placed under similar experimental conditions. The presence or absence of one stimulus or element of the situation is the independent variable.

The dependent variable consists of a difference of performance between the two groups, with the results being a function of the independent variable. In such experimentation, difficulty often lies in the equating of the groups on the necessary criteria. Ideally, each group should be equated on all characteristics that might influence the experiment, but this ideal is usually impossible to achieve. In using a control group, the subjects are matched on the variables and criteria believed to be most likely to influence the results. Similarly, in the "matched pair" method, the control group is made up of subjects matched with the experimental group on as many factors as possible such as characteristics of age, sex, and so on.

Sometimes experimental psychologists are criticized because they do not study the behavior of the child outside the laboratory and under more natural conditions. But the reason that children are studied under laboratory conditions is that unless some control is exercised over the complexity of their behavior, one cannot attribute a change in behavior to one specific cause. The multiplicity of possible influences might lead an investigator to attribute behavior to a certain influence, yet in reality other influences might be the cause. Experimental information and data on being categorized by scientists can eventually provide a body of dependable knowledge (Underwood, 1957).

The Differential Method

The differential method involves the use of individual differences as variables. In such investigations, change of the independent variable is not used; instead, different subjects are chosen on the basis of various criteria. For example, a group of children may be chosen on the basis that they have the disease diabetes. They can be compared with another group that does not have the disease. Measurements of variables and of actions or performance of the children under similar conditions can be determined. The independent variable can be the disease of diabetes; however, it should be noted that the diabetes cannot be varied at will by the experimenters. Another type of investigation classified as a differential method is one that employs correlational techniques. An example of such a method is a study of a group of children by statistics to discover how close their performance on an intelligence test is to their performance on an arithmetic computation or vocabulary test.

The Cross-sectional Method

In this type of study, children at different ages are tested or measured. Two advantages accrue from this type of study: Some information can be gained on the growth process and norms can be established with which other children can be compared.

Much research in child psychology has been directed to obtaining information about motor, linguistic, and intellectual development. In seeking this type of information, the cross-sectional method has some advantages that have made it attractive to investigators; specifically, measurements can be taken in similar ways at each age level and can be compared with data at other levels. It is possible to obtain relatively uniform sampling at different levels and the data at successive age levels can be used to develop scales. A child's performance, accordingly, can be compared with the performance of other children, and a developmental position in terms of scores can be obtained. Such systematic compilation of norms has been a widespread practice during the first half of this century. In carrying out these types of investigations, influencing factors in sampling, such as parental occupation, geographical location, rural or urban homes, and the like, are taken into account.

Experimental methods can be used within a cross-sectional type of study. For example, the drug experiment described earlier could be carried out at different age levels to discover whether or not the drug might have an effect at varying age levels.

The Longitudinal Method

Since children develop along individual lines at different rates, developmental levels are reached at different times. Thus, to study individual differences another type of approach is often needed. For example, if one merely takes age level at the beginning of adolescence and selects the age thirteen, some adolescents will have reached puberty by this age and some will not; hence, factors influenced by this developmental event are not taken into account in a cross-sectional study that depends on age alone. However, the longitudinal method, which follows children over a period of time, provides an opportunity to study the developmental growth of each child and idiosyncratic characteristics can be brought to light. Growth increments can be established as well as relationships of growth to maturation and other factors influencing development (Bayley, 1965).

As with the cross-sectional method, the experimental method can be used in longitudinal research. For example, the experiment of Stevenson and Zigler could be performed at annual intervals in order to find out whether or not learning abilities, as measured on the tasks used in the study, change from year to year.

Some disadvantages of the longitudinal type of study are encountered, however, since inadequacies of the original sampling will, of course, continue to be a disadvantage for the duration of the study. In addition, inevitably some loss of subjects occurs. Also, in using the longitudinal approach, careful planning for the data to be collected is necessary, since once the study is under way, it is impossible to go back and make changes. A particular disadvantage of long-term longitudinal studies lies in the rapidly changing science of child psychology itself in which new ideas and techniques are constantly being developed. Once the longitudinal study is under way, changes in techniques usually are not feasible.

A common concern of the child psychologist is that of prediction. Isolated prediction about behavior, however, is difficult in the physical and natural sciences. In human behavior, prediction for individuals is usually defined statistically. It is customary to indicate the degree of confidence and the possible error in making generalized predictions when applied to individuals. The child psychologist is also interested in the control and influencing of individual events. Control, however, is in part based on prediction. Thus, as a result of his awareness of the limitations of his methods, the child psychologist is cautious about the prediction of individual events or prediction about individuals.

TECHNIQUES FOR RESEARCH

Since the turn of the century, a search has been under way to discover and develop new techniques for the study of children. Increasingly, attention has been given to the objectivity and scientific value of research methods. Many present-day techniques consist of refinements and changes in older ones.

The Psychometric Technique

The psychometric technique, testing intelligence and behavior, is used to obtain a brief sample of behavior. For example, a psychological test that measures the speed and accuracy with which a child solves a problem may provide information about a child's ability in comparison with that of other children. It also may provide information about the level at which the child under study customarily performs intellectual tasks and may make possible predictions about his ability to perform other similar tasks. An example of a test item involving both speed and precision would be one in which a child is required to arrange a series of pictures in the proper order within a given period of time. There are, however, many types of tasks as well as tests that are designed to measure intellectual performance and various types of behavior.

The Questionnaire Technique

Probably the first widely used research technique developed for the study of children was the questionnaire technique of G. Stanley Hall in his survey of the "contents of children's minds" (Baldwin, 1960). Although present-day psychologists do not use this method to a great extent, it was a beginning toward obtaining objective data about children.

The Anecdotal Technique

Another early technique used in the study of children is called the "anecdotal" technique. The data obtained with this technique are from observations with which generalizations about the child's behavior can be made. Prescott (1945) made use of the anecdotal record and improved the technique until the anecdotal record as he used it became a series of objective observations. Prescott and his staff had as their goal accurate descriptions of the child's action and language. They withheld evaluations and judgment about behavior until several descriptions of the child's behavior were obtained. According to Prescott, there are frequent misapplications of the anecdotal method: (1) evaluative statements before sufficient data are recorded; (2) explanations of the child's behavior on the basis of isolated facts are made; and (3) generalized rather than specific descriptions are given. The important goal in the anecdotal technique is that the investigator record exactly what the child said and that the situation in which the action took place be objectively described.

The Observational Technique

Observations made in systematic ways can be of much value in the study of child behavior. In some types of observations, the observer does not seek to control the child's environment nor does he in a predetermined way decide what type of behavior is to be recorded. It may be that the observer will seek to observe certain types of behavior or certain types of situations occurring between children; hence, he may have to wait until particular interaction takes place. The observer may decide to take small samples of behavior on succeeding occasions and record the behavior during the sampling periods.

It is possible, of course, that the observational situation can be controlled, as in an experiment. Usually, however, in experiments different types of measurements are used so that the records of the observer alone are not used. Many kinds of child behavior that do not naturally occur under laboratory situations may be of consequence to the child psychologist. Accordingly, some psychologists have devoted considerable effort to the use of observation. An example of the observational technique is found in an excerpt from an observational study of a seven-year-old boy done by Barker and Wright (1951). An observer went to the boy's home early in the morning before the child was awake. Part of the observer's record follows.

7:06   Raymond put on his blue jean pants as he stood by his bed. Honey, Raymond's fat, elderly fox terrier ambled into the room. Raymond greeted her in a sleepy, but friendly voice. "Hi, Honey."

   Honey put her front paws on Raymond's knees. He scratched her back and patted her as he finished buckling his belt.

7:07   Raymond turned to his dresser and rummaged around among the things on it until he obtained a candy Easter egg. He held up the candy and commanded, "Sit up, Honey, sit up!" The dog obeyed promptly and Raymond pushed the candy into her mouth.

   Just then his mother said from the hallway, "Are you dressed, son?" Seeing that he was, she said pleasantly, "Then go and wash up."

   Raymond immediately started for the bathroom.

   He went into the bathroom, left the door open, and washed briefly.

7:08   He came out of the bathroom carrying a bottle of hair oil. He shook a few drops of oil into the palm of his hand as he stood before his mirror.

   He set down the bottle and massaged his hair and scalp with both hands.

   His father, who had been reading the morning paper in the living room, came by in the hall on his way to breakfast. He turned into Raymond's room and greeted him in a friendly, jocular way, "Well, Clam, are you ready to eat?"

The foregoing observational record provides a descriptive sequence of behavior about part of a child's day. The observer tried, as objectively as possible, to record the actions and conversation of the people before him in order to obtain information about interpersonal exchanges and individual actions. In similar ways, child behavior can be observed in many other settings—the schoolroom, playground, and in social groups.

Some investigators have made records of child behavior by recording with sound equipment and camera. Gesell at Yale University used the motion-picture camera extensively in his study of children's developmental stages (Gesell and Ilg, 1949).

The Projective Technique

The imagination of children can be studied through "projective methods," or techniques (Alexander, 1955; Allen, 1958; Henry, 1956; Mussen, 1960; Rabin and Haworth, 1960; and Symonds and Jensen, 1958). These techniques now include a number of ways of discovering the child's perceptions, fantasies, reasoning processes, and feelings or emotions. The theoretical basis for this technique is that a person responds to test stimuli in ways similar to those that he uses in interaction with the environment. For example, a child on being shown a picture of a woman and a little boy is apt to describe the picture and what he thinks is taking place according to his own experience. It is likely, for example, that he will say that the woman is a "mother" and that she is in some conversation or emotional interchange with her "son." If the picture is ambiguous and the situation depicted in it is unclear as to whether this seems to be a happy interchange or an unhappy one, the child will probably reveal his own thoughts and experiences as he endows the figures in the picture with characteristics and feelings he has experienced in his own life. If the child is happy, the mother figure may be given benign characteristics and be seen as comforting her child or enjoying his company. On the other hand, if the child is unhappy and has been in much conflict with his mother, it is possible that he will see the picture as one in which the adult and child are in conflict with each other. Consequently, as Frank (1948) explains, the child in his response to the picture and in his telling of his thoughts about it, will disclose his views of the rights and duties of others, his beliefs, memories, and feelings. In telling a story about the picture, the child feels free to describe the characteristics of the individuals in the pictures because he does not see them as necessarily related to himself. It is likely that he will describe the stimulus situation, organize it, interpret it, account for it, and make predictions about it as he would in stimulus situations in his environment.

The Use of Ink Blots. One of the best-known projective techniques was developed by a Swiss psychiatrist, Rorschach (1942). The technique consists of ten cards with ink blots, some black and white and some multicolored. The subject is asked to tell what is seen in each blot. Scoring is an intricate process. The performance of an individual is scored according to the qualities of form, color, shading, movement, and part of the blot used. Significance is also attached to the individual's use of the whole blot or the fact that he confines himself to the use of details of it.

The Use of Pictures.   A second well-known projective technique is the Thematic Apperception Test, or TAT (Murray, 1943). The cards, consisting of 19 pictures and one blank card, are arranged in two series with ten cards each and usually are given to the subject in separate sessions. The subject is asked to tell a story about each of the pictures and, because the pictures are ambiguous, the individual must put much of himself into the stories. The ways of dealing with the problems presented by the ambiguous pictures are indicative of the ways the person generally deals with problems. Also, feelings that he attributes to the people depicted in the cards are feelings that he himself experiences or sees appropriate to the situation.

Symonds (1949) developed a set of pictures for adolescents that was standardized on boys and girls in junior and senior high school. He specifically sought to study such characteristics as aggression, anxiety, altruism, eroticism, and ambition. The themes appropriate to the pictures were those of family relationships, punishment, separation, illness, school, and so on. Norms were provided for the themes.

Bellak and Bellak (1952) developed a test consisting of ten animal pictures, as they believed that children could identify more easily with animals. The pictures reflect psychoanalytic issues of childhood activity and training.

Alexander (1955) developed a test for use in the study of interaction of adults and children. The Adult-Child Interaction Test consists of eight pictures of children and adults about which children are to tell stories. The stories are analyzed according to both form and content.

An example of the use of a projective test (The Adult-Child Interaction Test) in research is provided by a study by Tiller (1961) done at the Institute for Social Research in Norway. He studied the responses of 100 adolescents whose fathers spent long periods of time away from home on sailing and whaling trips. One group had fathers who were sailors who customarily were absent at sea for many months and sometimes years. Another group had fathers who were absent during the whaling season about six months each year. A control group with fathers who were absent for the usual working day also was used. Tiller believed that emotional and training situations differed in the three types of families. Among the findings in the study was the fact that boys from sailor families showed much hostility to the mother, while the girls did not. The boys from whaler families were particularly anxious and were concerned about feelings of ambivalence and conflict. Both of these groups differed from those who had fathers at home.

The Use of Play Material.   Other projective material has been used in play situations. Dolls have been particularly useful in studying children in two ways: (1) The feelings of children are revealed when they are attributed to a family of dolls; and (2) the theme that runs through doll play is indicative of important concerns. Children's play with puppets has been of interest as a technique to some investigators since children easily identify with puppet characters (Woltmann, 1960; Lovaas et al., 1965).

Future research with projective techniques should be directed toward the development of quantitative methods that will contribute to further theorizing. Much of the criticism of the use of projective techniques has been justified in that sufficient effort has not been made to relate the techniques to a theoretical orientation nor has sufficient effort been made to obtain objectivity or quantification of results.

The Case History Technique

The case history attempts to gather the important facts about a child and his environment. Information is obtained from a number of sources and people, so that the investigator can gain some perspective about the many influences affecting the child's behavior. Some investigators have reservations about the case history technique because of the nature of the sources of information and the difficulty in avoiding interpretation of isolated data.

VALIDITY AND RELIABILITY OF MEASUREMENTS

Two fundamental problems in relation to use of research techniques have concerned psychologists: *validity,* the extent to which an instrument measures what it is supposed to measure, and *reliability,* the consistency of the measurements. Validity, however, is not of great concern when investigations are composed of direct measures, as, for example, in the measurement of height. If, however, an arithmetic test is used as part of an intelligence test, the investigators are not interested particularly in the arithmetical characteristics of the test, but rather in the general functioning or intellectual level of the child. To this end, then, the purpose of the test determines whether or not it is a direct or indirect measure. In the use of indirect measures, validity is of much importance. A great deal of the important effort of the child psychologist has been, and continues to be, directed toward the development of new measures with validity.

Reliability, or the consistency of a measurement, is determined usually in three ways: (1) by repeating the measure at a different time with correlation made between these repeated measurements, (2) correlation between similar forms of the measurement, and (3) the division of the measurement into equivalent parts. The establishment of the reliability of a measure is particularly important if it is to be used for prediction or the determination of the performance of children, since children change rapidly and sometimes unevenly during the developmental years.

AUTOMATION IN RESEARCH

The important task and problem of psychology has been to plan and formulate questions that can be answered objectively. The use of data-processing machines now extends the investigator's capabilities and provides opportunities for experimentation that heretofore were impossible. Experimenters too are finding that in dealing with machines, problems must be very carefully formulated and therefore increased exactitude in experimental design is attained. The use of computers in the study of behavior not only is altering research methodology, but also is likely to alter subject matter (Borko, 1962a, 1962b; White, 1962).

Machines cannot substitute for the planning and thinking of an experimenter, but they can enable the experimenter to take a sequence of logical steps in a small fraction of time without an expenditure of energy (Mason and Bulgren, 1964). Nevertheless, a research worker must define his problem, state his hypotheses, make the appropriate observations, and plan the proper manipulations of the data—it is only then that machines can greatly facilitate his endeavor. Computers now can duplicate and simulate many important psychological functions. Simulation is particularly important in studying neurophysiological and social systems; machines, by creating analogs of remembering, differentiating, or simulating goal-directed behavior, can achieve control of experimentation heretofore impossible. Furthermore, as Lingoes (1962) has emphasized, computers in their processing of nonnumeric information (such as the alternations in the physiological condition of an organism, the simulation of a model of nerve function, or the simulation of physiological and chemical processes in the body) make possible a broader conceptualization of function than is subsumed under the usual terms of *data processing* or *computing*.

Language is an important source of data in the study of behavior particularly so in the normative and developmental studies of childhood. The use of computers may well revolutionize the analysis of certain types of data, particularly children's verbal output.

Alexander and Leaverton (1967) used the computer to study children's responses to pictures. Through preliminary studies with the computer, the investigators developed a lexicon of positive words referring to pleasure, satisfaction, and the like, and negative words referring to dissatisfaction and unhappiness. The lexicon was used to differentiate between normal children and those with behavior disorders. In addition to differentiations on the basis of the lexicon, the computer program made it possible to differentiate among the groups of children according to quantity of verbal output.

Computers and the automation now possible provide new horizons for the experimental approach in many of the areas of human behavior that have defied the application of exacting techniques of measurement or the study of large numbers of subjects. Moreover, easily accessible variations in experimental designs have not been possible nor have the creative variations of simulated behavior. Through the use of computers, not only are there many new avenues being opened to scientists but also many more opportunities not now seen may be possible through the use of techniques combining the scientist's creativity and the machine's versatility.

THEORETICAL APPROACHES TO DEVELOPMENTAL BEHAVIOR

A theory is both a tool and a goal for research workers. It is a tool when it directs empirical investigations and it is of value as a goal when it is used to integrate and order information (Marx, 1963). Although no single theory is considered adequate for a background of the understanding of human development nor for a way of integrating the body of facts accumulated through present-day research, a number of theoretical approaches are of use to investigators. Because these theories have grown out of particular disciplines, any unification of knowledge about development has been the problem of the individual scientist. Insufficient progress has been made toward the unification of knowledge and toward a unified theory of human behavior; yet partial theoretical approaches are becoming increasingly inadequate in modern scientific endeavor. Universality of scientific language and methods has outmoded individual systems of thought and now investigation requires an integration of language and symbolic representation. Such integration may be achieved through empirical testing of available individual systems and retaining only those approaches which are of value.

Psychoanalytic Theory

The theoretical system of Sigmund Freud stresses the developmental aspects of behavior. His ideas of child development grew out of his work with adults rather than from study of children themselves; many of his beliefs about children were gained from adults who in therapeutic interviews discussed their early experiences.

Freud saw difficulty in development coming not only from conflict, but also from the growth process itself. An important part of the child's learning to deal with frustrations and conflicts is by the reduction of tension through identifying with another person. According to Freud, the child seeks to be like a person who is successful in fulfilling needs. The child first identifies with parents, because they are an influence over him; later he turns to others outside the family. According to Freud, much of this identification takes place without the awareness of the child and it becomes a part of his "unconscious behavior." The child takes part of the behavior from one person that he wishes to emulate and other parts from other people.

Freud's thinking about the stages of human development has been of wide interest to many types of behavioral scientists. The first period of development consists of the first five years of life. The second period lasts for approximately five or six years, during which the characteristics remain similar; consequently, Freud designated this period as one of "latency." In adolescence, the third period, the "dynamics" of the earlier period again become present.

Although Freud's theory was developed from years of painstaking work, it still has had much criticism. Nevertheless, an important point is that he spent many hours a week over a period of years with one individual and thus had the opportunity to substantiate his ideas and views during this long period of time. Seldom are individuals in psychological research studied for the length of time that Freud spent with his patients. But primarily, Freudian theory itself has been attacked because its postulates cannot be established by experimental determination.

Critics have also been opposed to Freud's emphasis on "instinct"; some object to his lack of emphasis on the importance of environmental factors. Other workers have sought to offset these criticisms. Muuss (1962) calls attention to the modifications of psychoanalytic theory by Erikson (1950), Horney (1939), and Sullivan (1953), since they tend to avoid sole dependence on instinct and physiological determinants in the developmental process and attend more to consideration of the influence of social factors.

Although modern psychology and psychoanalytic theory have many areas of conflict, this theory has had a profound effect upon modern behavioral science. Freud is respected as a meticulous observer who had both courage and originality. He pointed the way to the importance of facing directly the many problems of man in modern society.

Field Theory

Field theory in psychology grew out of the thinking about the significance of field theory in physics and chemistry. Field theory in psychology developed first as the Gestalt, or "pattern," psychology described by Max Werthheimer, Wolfgang Köhler, and Kurt Koffka. The primary belief was that the perception of an object is determined by the context and that relationships among the parts of the field determine the perception. Kurt Lewin was the first to apply field theory to all branches of psychology by using a set of concepts to represent psychological reality. Essential elements of Lewin's field theory are: (1) behavior grows out of the field that exists at the time the behavior takes place; and (2) the field is the totality of interdependent facts in a situation or environment. He called this total psychological field "the life space."

Lewin in applying his theory to infant and child behavior directed research toward the study of behavior in natural settings particularly of children in group activities. He was not primarily concerned with the problems of development, seeing development instead as a continuous process. Thus, Lewin did not emphasize stages of development. He saw developmental changes taking place until about the age of three, but from that time on he maintained that the individual's makeup remained relatively constant until adolescence. He did not value age scales.

Lewin believed the perception of the environment depends upon the development and experience of the individual and that an unstable environment during adolescence will cause behavioral instability in the adult. Furthermore, Lewin maintained, to understand an individual one must see him in his environment and the environment must be seen as a collection of interdependent factors. Thus, Lewin attempted to combine biological, social, and environmental forces into one system (Baldwin, 1967; Hall and Lindzey, 1957).

Organismic Theory

This theory and viewpoint stems from a wide range of viewpoints brought together around the concept that the individual functions as a unified whole.

While a number of people in medicine have made notable contributions, particulary Kurt Goldstein (1939), in psychology the theory has been given impetus by Werner (1948), Murphy (1947), Rogers (1947, 1951), and Hilgard (1956). The principles of the organismic theory are (1) that organization is an essential state of the organism and the state is characterized by unity and consistency; (2) that parts cannot be isolated for study because the whole functions according to principles not isolated in parts [note the similarity to Gestalt and field theories]; (3) that the individual has one drive, which is self-actualization, meaning that the individual endeavors to develop his potentialities; (4) that emphasis should be on the organism's capacity for growth rather than on the influence of the environment; and (5) that investigators can learn more from one person than from studying the isolated functions of many. An important contribution of organismic theory is its fundamental rejection of the dualism of mind and body.

Ontogenetic Theory

A number of theories emphasize stages in human development and take the view that individuals move from one stage to another and that each stage has characteristics that set it apart from the previous stage. Arnold Gesell took such a view of behavior and had considerable influence on modern concepts of growth and development through his biologically oriented theory based on maturational changes (Gesell et al., 1956). Gesell rejected much of Freud's theory, specifically objecting to unconscious motivation and preferring to concentrate on observable behavior. He paid particular attention to the innate sequence of maturation and patterns of growth as characteristic of human species everywhere, taking the view that changes in growth and development follow biological determinants, as do ability and other aspects of behavior. In addition, he viewed much of behavior as instinctive.

Gesell characterized each year of development behaviorally and made considerable effort to contrast behavior from one age level to the next. His differentiation seemed to be closely associated with the year in which it is discussed and at the chronological age of the individual. Critics thus noting that the theory was in terms of the calendar rejected the idea of such fortunate coincidence. To differentiate so distinctly between the age levels from one yearly age level to another is not well supported by present-day knowledge—growth and development seem to be continuous and not necessarily bound to chronological age. Furthermore, some critics take issue with Gesell's ambiguous terminology; for example, when he said, that behavior "loosens up" or "goes to pieces."

Cognitive Developmental Theory

An important theoretical approach to understanding the intellectual development of children is that of Jean Piaget. He believes that intellectual capacity goes through a number of stages always with a similar order, but with the time of appearance varying with the individual and the environment. Piaget sees four factors contributing to cognitive development: (1) maturation of the nervous system, (2) experience, (3) social transmission, and (4) "auto-regulation" (Duckworth, 1964). The first three factors influence the individual while he is passive; that is, his physiological and anatomical systems mature without his effort and he is immersed in experience also without his effort. Piaget emphasizes the fourth factor, the individual's activity, as being of much importance, because the individual acts upon the world and transforms it. Training of children then must involve presenting them with situations with which they can experiment. They should be allowed to manipulate things and symbols, answer their own questions, and reconcile findings from one time to another. He believes children can learn better by doing things than being told how to do them and that "equilibration," or activity, is the most important element of learning and intellectual development.

Cultural Anthropological Theory

The theoretical approaches of cultural anthropology were emphasized by the work of Margaret Mead (1939). An important contribution of Mead, as a result of her study of primitive people, is related to the concept of "storm and stress" in adolescence. Mead found that in some primitive societies, "storm and stress" did not stand out as a particular characteristic of adolescence. From her point of view, adolescent difficulties come from conflict with the culture and society in which the individual develops.

Another important contribution was made by Benedict (1960) in her description of "continuities and discontinuities." She gave particular attention to the continuing pattern of the influence of the culture and its transfer from one generation to another through teaching and other influences external to the individual. An example of continuity in cultural teaching is provided by the practice of eating three meals a day. Very early in our culture, the child is taught to eat three meals a day and continues to do so throughout his life span. An example of discontinuity in Western culture is found in the repression of sexual interests and behavior during childhood, while during adulthood much value is placed upon sexual activity. The child is kept from facts about his sexual development; on the other hand, in adulthood, he must be able to deal with these facts in accordance with cultural expectations. However, major discontinuity in the life cycle, according to Benedict, is that a person at one point is a son and later a father. A son must obey and avoid assumption of adult responsibilities, but after becoming a father he must assert his authority and provide for the family. The individual, thus, must revise and change his behavior.

Benedict believes that the "storm and stress" encountered in our society comes from the discontinuous cultural institutions and not because of physiological change. Instead of helping a child to make necessary changes, adults tend to blame him, because he does not "spontaneously" change to the socially desired behavior at the proper time. By giving our attention to the physiological aspects of adolescence in our effort to account for the difficulties of the period, Benedict believes that we overlook the responsibility of society and the part that social institutions and expectations play in the difficulties encountered.

Stimulus-Response Theory

According to Hall and Lindzey (1957), this theory is best seen as a cluster of theories with similarities. An essential element is attention to the learning process and, thus, the theory is primarily concerned with the way the individual responds to internal and external stimuli. The theory began with the work of Ivan Pavlov, John B. Watson, and Edward L. Thorndike. Since learning is an essential part of this theory, the work of Edward C. Tolman, Edwin R. Guthrie, and Clark L. Hull are also of much importance. The theory has basic appeal because of its amplification through empirical investigation. Much of the research in support of this theory has come from animal experimentation, especially with the white rat. The theory has thus been called a "laboratory" theory.

Modification of the earlier stimulus-response position was made by Dollard and Miller (1950). These investigators concerned themselves with the formation and abolition of "habits." They took the view that a learning theory has as primary concern the circumstances with which a "response" and a "cue" (stimulus) are related. Learning, for Dollard and Miller, consisted of a process involving drive, cue, response, and reinforcement. As a result of learning, a response and a cue are associated in such a way that with the appearance of a cue, a certain response takes place. The connection between a cue and a response can be strengthened by a reward after response in association with a cue. The concept of habit is brought into their theory by conceiving of habit as the association between the stimulus and a response.

The main content of this theory is dependent upon the description of the conditions in which habits come to be formed or lost. Personality is seen as consisting mainly of habits growing out of the events that the individual has experienced. Change is brought about in habit by patterns of experience. In dealing with the theory, Dollard and Miller have not attempted to specify or categorize habits, but rather have been concerned with their formation and disappearance. An important concept in the stimulus-response theory is that of generalization. Generalization is of consequence because a stimulus varies from time to time and the individual is hardly likely to encounter an identical one. Thus, the tendency to respond similarly despite some stimulus variation indicates that the individual can and does generalize. Habits established in one situation, therefore, can be carried over to similar ones.

Sears (1951) espoused a view of "personality" similar to that of Dollard and Miller. He, however, added to the theory by placing an emphasis on action in social behavior. In using the term *dyadic* to refer to behavior, Sears related one individual's behavior to another's response. The dyadic situation was fitted into the basic characteristics of stimulus-response theory and, thus, helped to move a theory founded in the laboratory nearer to useful application than had been done earlier.

The recognition of the importance of the use of theory in research as a way of giving meaning to experimental results is fundamental for those people adhering to the stimulus-response view. They take the position that theoretical differences should be settled experimentally; hence, those who espouse the theory have come to stand for the "experimental" approach to the problems of human behavior. Some of the proponents have sought to go further and to emulate the methods of the physical sciences and to apply the methods of that area of knowledge to the study of human behavior.

Some critics hold that the stimulus-response theory is based primarily on studies of animals and that relevance for human behavior is yet to be achieved. Other critics have pointed out that for all the emphasis on objectivity and definition, the terms used in the stimulus-response theory are far from explicit. For example, an adequate definition of the terms *stimulus* or *response* is yet to be provided. A child's behavior is hardly the result of a "stimulus" but rather a host of stimuli, many of which cannot be observed or recorded. The same view can be taken in regard to response. Still other critics have taken the stand that the theory is merely a statement of observation of behavior which everyone makes. Criticism also stems from the fact that the research supporting the theory involves a small list of variables. Few critics, however, can fail to appreciate the insistence of the proponents of stimulus-response theory on objectivity and on the establishment of a body of knowledge through scientific methods.

A POINT OF VIEW

Present-day theories of child and adolescent behavior rely increasingly upon the support of systematic observation and experimental research. Advances in the physical and biological sciences have influenced research methodology in the study of human behavior and accordingly those studying human behavior have sought models of objectivity, careful experimental control, and systematic analysis of data similar to the methodology used in the physical sciences. The standards for rigorous scientific investigations set by physical scientists have left marks on those who now study human behavior. As a result of such standards, some theories and methods are finding less favor today and investigators are beginning to give their attention to aspects of human behavior which allow experiments to be carefully controlled. Many scientists argue that knowledge must be built bit by bit. Others maintain that the greatest progress made in the understanding of human behavior has come from Freud, who did not use experimental methods, but built his theory on clinical experience with psychopathology. A theoretical approach combining both experimental work and clinical observation may ultimately be devised.

REFERENCES

Alexander, T., 1955. *The Adult-Child Interaction Test: A Projective Test for Use in Research.* Monographs of the Society for Research in Child Development, **17**, No. 2. Lafayette, Ind.: Child Development Publications, Purdue University.

Alexander, T., and P. Leaverton, 1967. "Differentiation between Normal and Disordered Children by a Computer Analysis of Emotional and Verbal Behavior," *Journal of Psychology,* **67**, 141–146.

Allen, R. M., 1958. *Personality Assessment Procedures.* New York: Harper & Row.

Anderson, J. E., 1954. "Methods of Child Psychology," in *Manual of Child Psychology,* 2d ed., edited by L. Carmichael, pp. 1–59. New York: Wiley.

Baldwin, A. L., 1960. "The Study of Child Behavior and Development," in

Handbook of Research Methods in Child Development, edited by P. H. Mussen, pp. 3–35. New York: Wiley.

Baldwin, A. L., 1967. *Theories of Child Development.* New York: Wiley.

Barker, R. G., and H. F. Wright, 1951. *One Boy's Day.* New York: Harper & Row.

Bayley, Nancy, 1965. "Research in Child Development: A Longitudinal Perspective." *Merrill-Palmer Quarterly,* 11, 182–208.

Bellak, L., and S. S. Bellak, 1952. *Children's Apperception Test,* 2d ed., New York: C. P. S. Company.

Benedict, R., 1960. "Continuities and Discontinuities in Cultural Conditioning," in *The Adolescent,* 2d ed., edited by J. M. Seidman, pp. 305–315. New York: Holt.

Borko, H., ed., 1962a. *Computer Applications in the Behavioral Sciences.* Englewood Cliffs, N.J.: Prentice-Hall.

Borko, H., 1962b. "Computer Simulation of Neurophysiological and Social Systems," *Behaviorial Science,* 7, 407–412.

Brown, C. W., and E. E. Ghiselli, 1955. *Scientific Method in Psychology.* New York: McGraw-Hill.

Dollard, J., and N. E. Miller, 1950. *Personality and Psychotherapy.* New York: McGraw-Hill.

Duckworth, E., 1964. "Piaget Rediscovered," in *Piaget Rediscovered,* edited by R. E. Ripple and V. N. Rockcastle, pp. 1–5. Ithaca, N. Y.: Cornell.

Erikson, E. H., 1950. *Childhood and Society.* New York: Norton.

Frank, L. K., 1948. *Projective Methods.* Springfield, Ill.: Charles C Thomas.

Gesell, A., and F. L. Ilg, 1949. *Child Development.* New York: Harper & Row.

Gesell, A., F. L. Ilg, and L. B. Ames, 1956. *Youth: The Years from Ten to Sixteen.* New York: Harper & Row.

Goldstein, K., 1939. *The Organism.* New York: American Book.

Hall, C. S., and G. Lindzey, 1957. *Theories of Personality.* New York: Wiley.

Henry, W. E., 1956. *The Analysis of Fantasy.* New York: Wiley.

Hilgard, E. R., 1956. *Theories of Learning,* 2d ed. New York: Appleton-Century-Crofts.

Horney, K., 1939. *New Ways in Psychoanalysis.* New York: Norton.

Kugel, R. B., and T. Alexander, 1963. "The Effect of a Central Nervous System Stimulant (Deanol) on Behavior," *Pediatrics,* 31, 651–655.

Lingoes, J. C., 1962. "Information Processing in Psychological Research," *Behavioral Science,* 7, 412–417.

Lovaas, O. I., D. M. Baer, and S. W. Bijou, 1965. "Experimental Procedures for Analyzing the Interaction of Symbolic Social Stimuli and Children's Behavior," *Child Development,* 36, 237–247.

Marx, M. H., 1963. "The General Nature of Theory Construction," in *Theories in Contemporary Psychology,* edited by M. H. Marx, pp. 4–46. New York: Macmillan.

Mason, E. E., and W. G. Bulgren, 1964. *Computer Applications in Medicine.* Springfield, Ill.: Charles C Thomas.

Mead, M., 1939. *From the South Seas.* New York: Morrow.

Murphy, G., 1947. *Personality.* New York: Harper & Row.

Murray, H. A., 1943. *Thematic Apperception Test*. Cambridge, Mass.: Harvard.

Mussen, P. H., ed., 1960. *Handbook of Research Methods in Child Development*. New York: Wiley.

Muuss, R. E., 1962. *Theories of Adolescence*. New York: Random House.

Prescott, D. A., 1945. *Helping Teachers Understand Children*. Washington, D.C.: American Council on Education.

Rabin, A. I., and M. R. Haworth, eds. 1960. *Projective Techniques with Children*. New York: Grune & Stratton.

Rogers, C. R., 1947. "Some Observations," *American Psychologist*, **2**, 358–368.

Rogers, C. R., 1951. *Client-Centered Therapy*. Boston: Houghton Mifflin.

Rorschach, H., 1921. *Psychodiagnostik*. Bern: Huber.

Sears, R. R., 1951. "A Theoretical Framework for Personality and Social Behavior," *American Psychologist*, **6**, 476–482.

Stevenson, H. W., and E. F. Zigler, 1958. "Probability Learning in Children," *Journal of Experimental Psychology*, **56**, 185–192.

Sullivan, H. S., 1953. *The Interpersonal Theory of Psychiatry*. New York: Norton.

Symonds, P. M., 1949. *Adolescent Fantasy*. New York: Columbia.

Symonds, P. M., and A. R. Jensen, 1958. "Psychoanalytic Concepts and Principles Discernible in Projective Personality Tests. VI. The Predictive Significance of Fantasy," *American Journal of Orthopsychiatry*, **28**, 73–84.

Tiller, P. O., 1961. "Father-Separation and Adolescence: A Study of Attitudes and Personality of Adolescent Sailor and Whaler Children." Oslo: Institute for Social Research.

Underwood, B. J., 1957. *Psychological Research*. New York: Appleton-Century-Crofts.

Werner, H., 1948. *Comparative Psychology of Mental Development*, rev. ed. Chicago: Follett.

White, B. W., 1962. "Computer Applications to Psychological Research: Studies in Perception," *Behavioral Science*, **7**, 396–401.

Woltmann, A. G., 1960. "Spontaneous Puppetry by Children as a Projective Method," in *Projective Techniques with Children*, edited by A. I. Rabin and M. R. Haworth, pp. 305–312. New York: Grune & Stratton.

Name Index

Subject Index